W9-CFF-208

GFWC
Centennial Cookbook

★ ★ ★ ★ ★ ★ ★ ★

A selection of favorite family recipes submitted
by Clubwomen from throughout the Federation.

GFWC CENTENNIAL COOKBOOK

Recipes submitted by clubwomen from throughout the Federation.

GFWC history and material furnished by GFWC Headquarters.

Editor:	Karen S. McClung
Art Director:	Tony Raffa
Designer:	Julie A. Beaty
Editing & Proofreading:	Mary Jane Caldwell Kathy Woods Kay Tucker Lynn Frame Norma Bowers Patsy Amick
Food Photographer:	Fred Hansen
Food Stylist:	Joe DeCosmo
Styling Assistant:	Helen Marshall
Recipe Judging:	Dr. Nadine Tope Dr. Carolyn Lackey Dr. Jacquelyn W. McClelland Rachel Kirby Kinlaw Shirley H. Usry

Manufactured in the United States of America.

Recipes from Cover—Pages 103 & 117
Back Cover—Pages 339 & 352

TABLE OF CONTENTS

	Page
Appetizers	9
Beverages	39
Soups	47
Salads, Salad Dressings, Fruit Casseroles	59
Breads, Yeast & Quick	95
Meats & Meat Sauces	121
Fish & Seafood	171
Poultry	191
Vegetables	215
Pasta	237
Rice & Other Grains	247
Eggs & Cheese	255
Cakes	265
Candy	293
Cookies	307
Pies	335
Other Desserts	357
Index	380

"A PAST TO REMEMBER, A FUTURE TO MOLD"

The General Federation of Women's Clubs (GFWC)—the world's largest and oldest nonpartisan, nondenominational volunteer service organization of women—is celebrating its Centennial in 1990, marking a century of volunteer service in large and small communities all over the United States and the world.

The General Federation traces its roots back to Jane Cunningham Croly, an accomplished New York newspaperwoman, who wrote under the pen name of Jennie June. Indignant that she and other women were denied admittance to a banquet honoring Charles Dickens in 1868 at the all-male New York Press Club simply because they were women, she determined to organize a club for women only.

The name chosen for this club was Sorosis, a Greek word meaning "an aggregation; a sweet flavor of many fruits." Although its founders originally supposed they were starting a new movement, they became aware over the years of the existence of other women's clubs that had formed independently to meet the needs of women in the new and growing country.

As Sorosis approached its 21st year, Mrs. Croly proposed a conference in New York of women's clubs, and a call went out. Delegates from 61 clubs attended that first organizational meeting. On the last day of the conference, the women took action for forming a permanent organization. A committee to draft a constitution and plan of organization to be ratified the following year was chosen, with Sorosis President Ella Dietz Clymer as chairman. The constitution was adopted in 1890, and the General Federation of Women's Clubs was born. The Federation was chartered by Congress in 1901.

Ella Dietz Clymer gained a particular place of honor in Federation history as the author of the motto, "Unity in Diversity." Speaking to the delegates at the first conference, she said, "We look for unity, but unity in diversity. We hope that you will enrich us by your varied experiences . . ."

The aptness of the motto is evident in the diverse interests and methods of GFWC members have for implementing a broad range of programs and projects tailored to meet the needs of their communities. It set the tone for the flexibility that has allowed GFWC to grow and adapt to the changing and diverse lifestyles and concerns of women throughout a century of volunteer work. The organization now numbers 400,000 members in 10,000 clubs across the United States, with additional millions of members in 46 countries.

In 1922, the General Federation purchased a five-story brick and stone mansion in Washington, D.C., which became its headquarters. Located at 1734 N Street, NW, the building has an interesting history of its own. It was built in 1875 by Rear Admiral William Radford upon his retirement from the U.S. Navy. By 1895, the neighborhood was well developed and ready to welcome the colorful character of the next owner, General Nelson A. Miles, of Spanish and Indian Wars fame, and later Commanding General of the U.S. Army. Popular subscription raised funds for the purchase of the house as a gift to the distinguished soldier who made it his home until 1903.

GFWC Headquarters
General Federation of Women's Club Headquarters
1734 N Street, N W
Washington, D.C. 20036

Later owners of the Nelson A. Miles Mansion, as it was known, were Mr. and Mr. John Jay White. Mr. White was a great traveler and big-game hunter who frequently accompanied former President Theodore Roosevelt on expeditions. It was during White's residency that the impressive murals that adorn the walls of the drawing room were painted by renowned muralist Alfred Herter, father of the late Secretary of State Christian Herter.

During eighteen months following World War I, the house was used as the Czechoslovakian Legation. Today the building provides office space for the professional staff that administers programs and services for the large organization, and also is the residence of the International President during her two-year term. The building retains much of its original character and elegance, and is toured each year by clubwomen from throughout the country and world. The beautiful drawing room and dining room are the setting for formal and informal receptions each year.

In 1984, the GFWC Women's History and Resource Center was opened in the adjacent townhouse for the purpose of cataloging club histories and volunteer efforts and providing research facilities.

As GFWC moves into its 100th year and beyond, it honors its distinguished past and lays the groundwork for a future of volunteer work for the common good.

SELECTION PROCESS OF RECIPES
GFWC CENTENNIAL COOKBOOK

Bringing the GFWC Centennial Cookbook to life was a task of great magnitude! The call for recipes went out to clubs nationwide in June of 1987. The response was overwhelming. Over 12,000 recipes were submitted for consideration. The recipes were boxed and delivered to North Carolina State University where the selection process began.

A panel of five judges was chosen to evaluate the recipes. All five women are tenured faculty members in the University's School of Agriculture and Life Sciences, Foods and Nutrition Department. They are currently working as Extension Professors and Foods and Nutrition Specialists with the North Carolina Agricultural Extension Service in Raleigh. Three of the women hold doctorates in the field of nutrition. Based on their collective experience, they were well qualified to handle the monumental task before them!

Once the recipes reached the University, the first step in the judging process was to sort them into sixteen predetermined categories based on main ingredients (appetizers, beverages, breads, cakes, etc.). Then, the recipes in each individual category were divided into groups based on type (Example Cakes were further separated into yellow and white, poundcakes, fruitcakes, chocolate, fruit and nut, tortes and cheesecakes) Work Study students at the University assisted in this phase of the process.

To balance the finished cookbook, it was determined that a fairly even number of recipes should represent each category Guidelines were set as to how many recipes were needed for each category. Criteria were established for selection. For instance, since this would be a commemorative cookbook one objective was to include both old-fashioned and modern recipes in each category if possible.

Once the initial sorting process was completed, the judges' work really began They tested and evaluated recipes to determine the most pleasing variety for each category. They selected approximately 1000 of the best recipes to be included in the finished cookbook.

Over 12,000 recipes entered. Boxed and delivered to North Carolina State University for judging.

Recipes being individually sorted and categorized.

Panel of judges and selection of recipe winners.

Photography: Herman Langford, Dept. of Agricultural Communications, N.C. State University

GFWC
GENERAL FEDERATION OF WOMEN'S CLUBS

CENTENNIAL CELEBRATION
1890-1990

"A PAST
TO REMEMBER-
A FUTURE
TO MOLD"

Appetizers

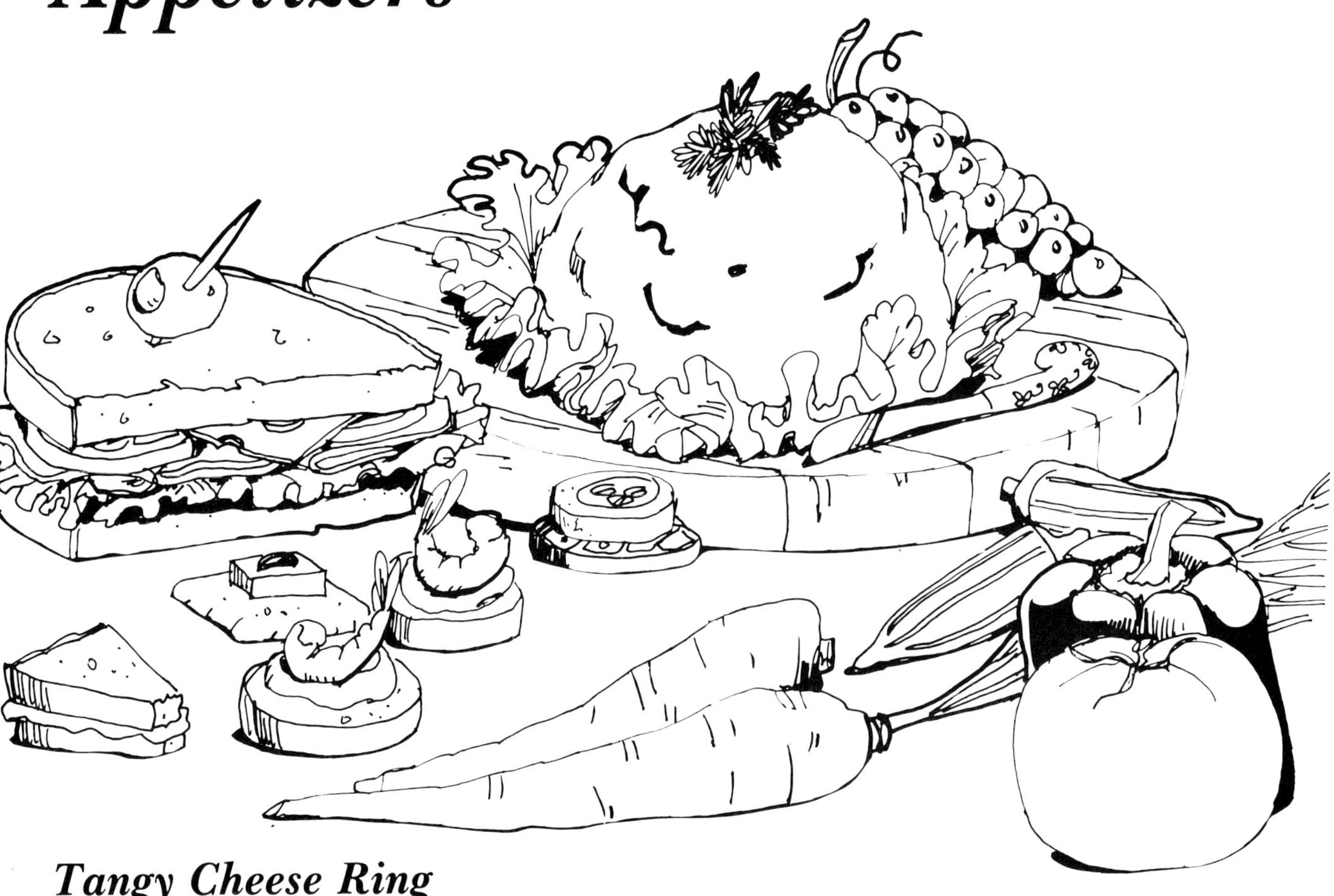

Tangy Cheese Ring

- 1 8 ounce package sharp cheddar cheese
- 1 8 ounce package cream cheese
- 1 8 ounce package Velveeta cheese
- 1 8 ounce package Monterey Jack cheese with jalapeno pepper or 2–3 drops hot sauce
- 3 tablespoons Worcestershire sauce
- 1 teaspoon garlic, minced
- 1 medium onion, grated
- 1 cup mayonnaise
- 1 cup chopped pecans
- 1 18 ounce jar peach preserves or any kind

Combine all ingredients except pecans and preserves. Sprinkle about ¼ cup pecans in an oiled, 7-cup ring mold and press cheese mixture into mold. Chill until firm. Unmold on platter and put remaining pecans onto cheese ring. Place crackers around cheese ring with preserves in center of cheese ring. Garnish with parsley. Serve on crackers with preserves on top (if desired).

Jane Puttick
GFWC—Brundidge 3-Arts Club
Brundidge, Alabama

Photo features: Susan's Fruit Dip—Page 24
Tangy Cheese Ring—Page 9

Pineapple Cheese Ball

- 2 8 ounce packages cream cheese
- 1 8½ ounce can crushed pineapple, drained well Put on paper towel to remove excess juice.
- 2 cups chopped pecans (divided 1¼ cup and ¾ cup)
- ¼ cup finely chopped green pepper
- 2 tablespoons finely chopped onion
- 1 tablespoon seasoned salt

In medium bowl, beat cream cheese until smooth. Gradually add pineapple. Set aside 1¼ cup pecans to roll ball in. Add remaining ¾ cup pecans, pepper, onion and salt; mix well. Shape into ball. Roll in pecans, wrap in foil and refrigerate overnight. Serve with snack crackers of your choice.

Freda Akers
GFWC—Fayetteville Woman's Club
Fayetteville, West Virginia

Curry Almond Spread

- 1 pound cream cheese, softened
- ½ cup chopped chutney
- 2 tablespoons curry powder
- ½ teaspoon dry mustard
- ½ cup chopped almonds, toasted

Soften cream cheese in bowl. Add other ingredients and mix well by hand. Shape into ball. Chill. Take out 15–20 minutes before serving. Serve with crackers. Makes 2 cups.

"This is a favorite spread served by the USNA Class of 1953 at the Naval Academy home game tailgate parties."

Nancy Ritchie
GFWC—Woman's Club of Springfield, Inc.
Springfield, Virginia

Minnesota Wild Rice Appetizer

- 1 cup cooked wild rice
- 1 3 ounce package cream cheese
- 2 small green onions, chopped
- 1 teaspoon curry powder
- 2 teaspoons lemon juice
- Dash of cayenne pepper
- ⅓ cup chutney, well drained
- Chopped pecans or walnuts
- Chopped parsley
- Toasted sesame seeds

Blend wild rice into the cream cheese with a fork, along with the onion, curry powder, lemon juice, and cayenne pepper. When a smooth mixture, add the chutney. (May omit chutney). Shape into balls the size of small walnuts. Roll each ball in chopped pecans, walnuts, chopped parsley or toasted sesame seeds. Chill until firm. May also be used as a dip. Serve with crackers.

Lorraine Schlauderaff
GFWC—Woman's Study Club of Litchfield
Litchfield, Minnesota

Almond Cheese Ball

- 8 ounces cream cheese, softened
- 1 cup crushed pineapple, drained
- 1/4 cup white or dark raisins, chopped
- 1/4 cup Angel Flake coconut
- 1 teaspoon almond extract
- 2 cups almond delight, crushed

Save 1/4 cup of almond delight to roll ball in. Mix remaining ingredients together. Form ball. Roll in 1/4 cup almond delight saved back. Refrigerate till chilled.

Jane Pickering
GFWC—Sorosis Club
Springfield, Missouri

Mushroom Cheese Ball

- 1 8 ounce package shredded cheddar cheese
- 1 8 ounce package cream cheese, softened
- 3 tablespoons milk
- 1 teaspoon horseradish
- 1 2 1/2 ounce jar sliced mushrooms (drain and reserve 1 tablespoon of liquid)
- 1/2 cup chopped pecans

Coarsely chop mushrooms. In small bowl, combine cheeses, milk, horseradish and reserved mushroom liquid; beat until smooth. Stir in chopped mushrooms. Chill about 2 hours. Shape into ball (on plastic wrap) and roll in pecans. Chill again until serving.

"An old family favorite . . . variation of a cheese ball recipe found in a cookbook dated back to 1940."

Rosemarie Cavanaugh
GFWC—East Brunswick Woman's Club
East Brunswick, New Jersey

Joan's Cheese Ball

- 1/2 pound grated cheddar or colby cheese
- 1–2 hard-boiled eggs, chopped fine
- 2 tablespoons diced pickle relish
- 2 tablespoons minced onion
- 3 tablespoons chopped green pepper, optional
- 3 stuffed olives, diced, optional
- 1/2 cup crushed soda crackers
- 1/4 cup mayonnaise

Combine all. Stir till well blended. Press cheese mix into plastic wrap-lined rounded bowl. Cover and refrigerate at least one day. Unmold on plate. Surround with assorted crackers. Place with a couple of butter knives so can spread on crackers. May roll in nuts, parsley or paprika.

Jean L. Mumm
GFWC—Durant Federated Woman's Club
Durant, Iowa

Macadamia Nut Cheese Ball

- **2 packages cream cheese, softened**
- **1½ cups grated cheddar cheese**
- **2 teaspoons minced onion**
- **½ cup sweet pickles, chopped**
- **1 teaspoon salt**
- **½ cup macadamia nuts**

In a small bowl, combine cream cheese, cheddar cheese, onion, sweet pickles and salt; mix well. Shape into a ball; roll ball in chopped nuts. Cover and refrigerate several hours or until well chilled. Serve with crackers.

"This is great for holidays or any special occasion. It may be kept in the refrigerator for about 2 weeks."

Doris Wahlert
GFWC—Entre' Nous
Hillrose, Colorado

Braunschweiger Ball

- **1 pound braunschweiger**
- **½ cup chili sauce**
- **2 tablespoons horseradish**
- **5 or 6 dashes of tabasco**
- **8 ounces cream cheese**
- **2 tablespoons mayonnaise**

Blend softened cream cheese and mayonnaise. Set aside. Blend remaining ingredients and beat until well mixed. Refrigerate, covered, until mixture firms up. Mold mixture into a ball and frost with cream cheese. Decorate with sliced stuffed olives and finely chopped parsley.

Grace M. Frame
GFWC—Woman's Club of Woodbury
Woodbury, New Jersey

Walnut Stuffed Mushrooms

- **12 large, fresh mushrooms**
- **1 3 ounce package cream cheese with chives**
- **¼ cup finely chopped walnuts**
- **1 teaspoon lemon juice**
- **1 dash of bottled hot pepper sauce**

Wash and dry mushrooms. Remove stems and finely chop. In a small micro-safe bowl, micro cook cream cheese, uncovered at medium-low for 1½ minutes or until softened. Stir in mushroom stems, walnuts, lemon juice and hot pepper sauce. Fill each mushroom with one tablespoon cream mixture; arrange in a circle on a 9 inch micro-safe pie plate. Cook on 100% power (high) 3–4 minutes turning plate once after 2 minutes.

Stuff mushrooms with cream cheese and nuts for an elegant appetizer for the holidays or for anytime.

Barbara Trimble
GFWC—Woman's Club of Westview Park
Catonsville, Maryland

Mushrooms Stuffed with Walnuts and Cheese

- **12 medium sized mushroom caps**
- **1 tablespoon olive oil**
- **1 tablespoon butter**
- **½ cup chopped onion**
- **2 tablespoons chopped walnuts**
- **1 clove garlic, minced**
- **1 teaspoon dill weed**
- **5 ounces frozen chopped spinach, squeezed dry**
- **1 ounce Feta cheese, crumbled**
- **1 ounce Swiss cheese, crumbled (prefer to use Gruyere cheese)**
- **Salt and pepper to taste**

Wipe mushroom caps with damp paper towel and set aside. Saute onion in butter until tender. Add walnuts and garlic to saute another minute or so. Sprinkle with dill weed and add spinach. Cook another 5 minutes, stirring. Remove from heat and cool slightly. Add cheeses, season to taste. Preheat oven to 400 degrees. Fill mushroom caps with mixture and set in baking dish. Bake in upper third of oven for 8 to 10 minutes. Serve immediately.

Joan Krafka Meany
GFWC—Cedar Falls Woman's Club, Junior Department
Cedar Falls, Iowa

Cauliflower Patties

- **1 small head of cauliflower**
- **4 eggs**
- **1 tablespoon flour**
- **1 teaspoon baking powder**
- **¼ teaspoon salt**
- **⅛ teaspoon pepper**
- **1 tablespoon grated cheese**
- **1 tablespoon parsley**

Remove leaves of cauliflower. Break cauliflower into flowerets. Cook, covered in a small amount of boiling salted water 10 minutes or until soft. Drain, set aside. In a large bowl, beat 4 eggs, add salt, pepper, cheese and parsley, mix. Add to mixture, 1 tablespoon flour and 1 teaspoon baking powder—mix well. Add cauliflower to mixture—mix slightly. Drop by full tablespoon into one inch hot oil (375 degrees). Cook until golden brown, turn once. Drain on paper towels.

Catherine Sasso
GFWC—Woman's Club of Arlington, New Jersey
Kearny, New Jersey

Artichoke Nibbles

- **2 jars marinated artichoke hearts**
- **¼ cup bread crumbs**
- **2 tablespoons parsley**
- **Salt, pepper, and oregano to taste**
- **1 small onion, chopped**
- **4 eggs**
- **½ pound sharp cheddar cheese, shredded**

Drain liquid from one jar of artichokes into pan. Chop artichokes and set aside. Add onion to liquid in pan and saute. (Add a little garlic salt). Beat eggs, add bread crumbs and seasonings. Stir in cheese, parsley, artichokes and onion. Put in greased 9 × 9 pan. Bake at 325 degrees for 30 minutes. Cut into one inch squares and serve hot or cold.

Kathy Turner
GFWC—Valdosta Junior Woman's Club
Valdosta, Georgia

Chili Rellano Won Tons Appetizers

- **1 package Won Ton skins—around 50 per package**
- **8 ounces extra sharp cheddar cheese, grated**
- **1 small can diced green chilies**
- **4 green onions, diced**
- **1 3 ounce package of softened cream cheese**

Mix all of the above ingredients except Won Ton skins together and blend well. Fill Won Ton skins with ½ teaspoon of mixture. (Place mixture in center of skin, moisten edges and seal). Filled skins are then dropped into 6 inches of oil that has been heated for deep frying. They take around 30–45 seconds in oil to become crispy and golden. Remove with slotted spoon to paper towels and cool. To freeze place on foil lined cookie sheet and freeze until hard. Store in box or plastic bag. Preheat oven 325 degrees and reheat until hot.

Bette Jameson
GFWC—Walnut Valley Woman's Club
Walnut, California

Mexican Pinwheels

- **1 8 ounce package cream cheese**
- **3 flour tortillas, 12″ round**
- **1 green onion, chopped**
- **1½ tablespoons green chilies, chopped**
- **1 heaping tablespoon pimiento, chopped**
- **1 4 ounce can chopped, black olives, drained**

Soften cream cheese. Spread on tortillas. Arrange garnishes on top. Roll up tightly. Store in plastic wrap in refrigerator until ready to serve. Cut into ¾ inch slices. Place cut side down on serving tray.

Marylou McDaniel
GFWC—Prospectus Study Club
Stratford, Texas

Mushroom Roll-Ups

- **2 bunches green onions, sliced**
- **2 pounds fresh mushrooms, diced**
- **½ cup margarine**
- **1 teaspoon each of basil, rosemary, marjoram, thyme**
- **Salt to taste**
- **2 loaves fresh white bread**
- **2 cloves garlic, diced**
- **4 tablespoons lemon juice**
- **½ cup flour**

Mince garlic, onion, mushrooms in food processor. Melt margarine in skillet, saute minced mix about 10 minutes, stirring constantly. Add lemon juice, flour and seasoning and chill thoroughly. Remove crusts from 2 loaves of fresh bread. Roll slices flat as possible with rolling pin. Spread with 1 teaspoon mushroom mixture per slice, spreading evenly to edges of bread. Roll up tightly, place seam side down on lightly oiled cookie sheet, and brush with melted butter. (Can be frozen at this point). Preheat oven to 400 degrees. Cut rolls crosswise into 2 or 3 pieces. Bake for 10–15 minutes, or until lightly browned. Makes about 60 roll-ups.

Tammy Guensler
GFWC—North Sacramento Woman's Club
Sacramento, California

Poor Man's Caviar

- **1 eggplant, about 2 pounds**
- **6 tablespoons olive oil**
- **½ teaspoon sugar**
- **1½ teaspoons salt**
- **1 teaspoon finely chopped garlic**
- **1 cup finely chopped onions**
- **½ cup finely chopped green pepper**
- **¼ cup tomato paste or puree**
- **2–3 tablespoons lemon juice**
- **½ teaspoon pepper**
- **Dark rye bread or sesame seed crackers**

Preheat oven to 425 degrees. Bake eggplant on rack in center of oven for 1 hour. Turn it over once or twice until it is soft and its skin is charred and blistered. Meanwhile, cook onions in 4 tablespoons oil over moderate heat for 6–8 minutes until soft but not brown. Stir in green pepper and garlic and cook, stirring occasionally, for 5 minutes longer. Remove from heat. When eggplant is cool enough to handle, remove skin and finely chop. Add to frying pan with onion and pepper. Add tomato paste, sugar, salt, and pepper. Add 2 more tablespoons oil, replace pan over heat, thoroughly combining ingredients by stirring while they cook. Cook until mixture is very thick about 20 minutes, stirring often, watching it doesn't burn. Stir in lemon juice. Chill. Can be made up to a week in advance. Serve with bread or crackers. Makes 3 cups.

Helen M. Hill
GFWC—Shepherdstown Woman's Club
Shepherdstown, West Virginia

Mushroom Logs

- **2 8 ounce cans refrigerated crescent dinner rolls**
- **1 8 ounce package cream cheese, softened**
- **1 4 ounce can mushroom stems and pieces, drained and chopped**
- **1 teaspoon seasoned salt**
- **1 egg, beaten**
- **1–2 tablespoons poppy seeds**

Separate crescent rolls into 8 rectangles. Press perforations to seal. Combine cream cheese, mushrooms, and salt, mixing well. Spread mushroom mixture in equal portions over each rectangle of dough. Starting at long sides, roll up each rectangle—jellyroll fashion. Pinch seams to seal. Slice logs into 1-inch pieces. Place seam side down on ungreased baking sheet. Brush each log with beaten egg and sprinkle with poppy seeds. Bake at 375 degrees for 10–12 minutes. Makes 40 logs.

Lynda Swetz
GFWC—Arlington Junior Woman's Club
Jacksonville, Florida

Stroganoff Mushrooms

- **1 tablespoon margarine**
- **1 tablespoon olive oil**
- **1½ pounds sliced, fresh mushrooms**
- **1 bunch scallions, chopped**
- **1 clove garlic, minced**
- **½ can tomato paste**
- **¼ cup sweet vermouth**
- **1 teaspoon salt**
- **2 tablespoons fresh parsley**
- **1 cup sour cream**
- **3 tablespoons parmesan cheese**
- **Bread squares or crackers**

Saute mushrooms, scallions and garlic in 1 tablespoon margarine and olive oil, for 5 minutes—drain off liquid. Add tomato paste, vermouth, salt, parsley and sour cream. Heat through but do not boil. Place in chafing dish and sprinkle with parmesan cheese. Serve hot with bread squares or crackers.

"An original recipe, adapted from a favorite soup recipe."

Patricia S. Williams
GFWC—Allentown Woman's Club
Allentown, Pennsylvania

Olive and Curry Hors D'Oeuvres

- **1 cup black olives, chopped**
- **½ cup green onions**
- **1½ cups cheddar cheese, shredded**
- **½ cup mayonnaise**
- **2 teaspoons curry powder**
- **Sliced cocktail rye bread**

Mix and spread on bread. Place on cookie sheet and freeze. When ready to serve, heat at 250 to 300 degrees on cookie sheet until bubbly.

Lucille Dolan
GFWC—Brookside Woman's Club
Brookside, New Jersey

Shrimp Spread

- 1½ cups celery, finely chopped
- ¾ cup onion, finely chopped
- ¾ cup green pepper, finely chopped
- 1 pound small curd cottage cheese, blended smooth
- 1 cup salad dressing
- ½ teaspoon salt
- 2 envelopes plain gelatin
- ⅓ cup cold water
- 1 can undiluted tomato soup, heated thoroughly
- 1 can shrimp, drained

Mix 2 envelopes plain gelatin in ⅓ cup cold water. Let stand to gel (1–2 minutes). Add the very warm tomato soup to the gelatin and stir till dissolved (3–4 minutes). Add chopped celery, onion, green pepper, salt and cottage cheese. Mix and then add 1 can shrimp. Mix until blended. Pour into a 6-cup mold and refrigerate overnight. Unmold before serving on bed of lettuce. Serve with crackers.

Diane Duffett
GFWC—Hudson Junior Woman's Club
Hudson, New Hampshire

Olive Nut Sandwich Spread

- 6 ounces cream cheese
- ½ cup mayonnaise
- ½ cup chopped pecans
- 1 cup olives, chopped

Let cheese stand at room temperature until soft. Mash with a fork and add ½ cup of mayonnaise. Chop 1 cup olives and add to cheese, along with 2 tablespoons of olive juice and a dash of pepper. Add ½ cup pecans. Stir well. This will be mushy. Put in jar and refrigerate for 24 to 48 hours. It will then be thick. Serve on very thin toast or bread. Cut sandwiches into small finger size.

Theresa Vail
GFWC—Monmouth Woman's Club
Monmouth, Illinois

Water Chestnut Wraps

- 2 cans whole water chestnuts
- Bacon

Sauce

- ⅔ cup brown sugar
- 2 tablespoons catsup
- 1 teaspoon mustard
- 1 teaspoon soy sauce
- 1 teaspoon Worcestershire sauce
- 1 teaspoon butter

Wrap each water chestnut with half slice of bacon and stick a toothpick through center to hold bacon. Bake on cookie sheet at 350 degrees for 15–20 minutes, until bacon is brown. While baking, stir all sauce ingredients together in saucepan and cook over medium heat until smooth and sugar dissolves. Serve hot and either serve the wraps in the sauce or dip each wrap as served.

Jeanette Holbert
GFWC—We Moderns Club
Lewistown, Missouri

Liptauer Spread

- **1 8 ounce package cream cheese**
- **1 tablespoon caraway seed**
- **1 tablespoon minced onion**
- **1 tablespoon capers**
- **¼ teaspoon salt**
- **A shake of MSG**
- **⅛ teaspoon pepper**
- **⅛ teaspoon garlic powder**
- **3 tablespoons light cream or milk**

Soften cream cheese and mix with the cream. (Extra cream may be used if you want the dip to be thinner). Add the rest of the ingredients and stir. Let set at room temperature for an hour before serving. Serve as a dip with crackers.

Marcia Eliot
GFWC—Lyndon Woman's Club
Lyndonville, Vermont

Crab Meat Canape Spread

- **1 8 ounce package cream cheese**
- **1 small onion, grated**
- **½ can mushroom soup, undiluted**
- **1 envelope gelatin, dissolved in ⅛ cup water**
- **½ cup mayonnaise**
- **½ cup celery, finely chopped**
- **1½ cups crab meat**
- **Touch of salt**

Heat soup; stir in dissolved gelatin and cheese. Add remaining ingredients. Put in butter-greased mold. Chill in refrigerator 12–24 hours. Serve with crackers. Can freeze 1–2 months.

Linda Grainer
GFWC—Nelly Custis Junior Woman's Club
Quinton, Virginia

Sweet/Hot Cracker Spread

- **1 18 ounce jar pineapple preserves**
- **1 small can dry mustard, about ¼ cup**
- **1 18 ounce jar apple jelly**
- **1 small jar horseradish, about 8 ounces**
- **1 tablespoon cracked pepper**

Blend all ingredients together. Keeps well stored in refrigerator. Spoon over softened cream cheese, spread on favorite snack crackers. Recipe may be reduced for smaller amount.

Ann Koelsch
GFWC—Gun Lake Area
Shelbyville, Michigan

Cucumber Cream Cheese Spread

2 3 ounce packages cream cheese
2 cucumbers
1 onion
Salt to taste
1/8 teaspoon hot pepper sauce
Mayonnaise

Mash cream cheese with a fork. Grate cucumber and onion; press out juice of cucumber. Combine cucumber, onion and cream cheese. Add salt and hot pepper sauce. Add mayonnaise until spreading consistency. Serve as sandwiches.

Christine Jordan
GFWC—Westhampton Junior
Richmond, Virginia

Missouri Pate

4 tablespoons unsalted butter
1/2 pound fresh mushrooms, chopped
1 onion, minced
2 tablespoons bourbon
1 tablespoon cognac
8 ounces liverwurst
2 8 ounce packages cream cheese, softened
1 teaspoon chopped fresh dill
1 teaspoon chopped parsley
2 teaspoons mustard
Salt and freshly ground pepper to taste

Melt butter in skillet. Saute mushrooms and onion until soft. Stir in bourbon and cognac; cool. Place mushroom mixture and remaining ingredients in a food processor or blender; process until very smooth. Transfer to serving bowl. Refrigerate for at least 24 hours before serving.

Wilda C. Stacey
GFWC—Independence Study Club
Independence, Missouri

Country Ham Butter

8 tablespoons or 1 stick unsalted butter
1 cup minced, baked country ham, firmly packed and free of fat

Combine the butter and ham in the bowl of a food processor and process until perfectly smooth. Chill and serve with hot biscuits, buttered toast, or crackers.

Bessie B. Johnson
GFWC—The Woman's League of Eden
Eden, North Carolina

So-o-o Good Cream Cheese

- **1 8 ounce package cream cheese, softened**
- **2/3 cup celery, finely chopped**
- **3 tablespoons mild onion, finely chopped**
- **1/2 cup walnuts, finely chopped**
- **1/2 cup mayonnaise**

Beat cream cheese; add mayonnaise. Mix together all other ingredients until well blended. Refrigerate. Serve with your favorite crackers or pumpernickel bread triangles.
Note: Celery, walnuts and onions can be put in a food processor and chopped together.

Mae Carlson
GFWC—Masury Brookfield Woman's Club
Brookfield, Ohio

Boursin Cheese

- **16 ounces cream cheese, softened**
- **1/2 pound butter, softened**
- **1 teaspoon oregano**
- **1/4 teaspoon thyme**
- **1/4 teaspoon dill weed**
- **1/4 teaspoon marjoram**
- **1/4 teaspoon pepper**
- **1/4 teaspoon basil**
- **2 small or 1 large garlic, minced**

Mix well and pack into jars. Refrigerate. Serve on crackers.

Barbara M. Knechtel
GFWC—Orange Woman's Club
Orange, Massachusetts

Chickpea Spread

- **1 3/4 cups cooked chickpeas or garbanzo beans, drained, reserve liquid**
- **2 tablespoons lemon juice**
- **1 tablespoon mayonnaise**
- **1/4 teaspoon garlic powder**

Mash and blend chickpeas. Add 1 tablespoon chickpea liquid, lemon juice, mayonnaise and garlic powder. Mix until smooth. If too thick, add more reserved liquid. Spread on bread or crackers.

Charlotte Yodow
GFWC—Pen Chat
Burnet, Texas

Cheddar Curry Spread

- **1 cup shredded cheddar cheese**
- **6 ounces cream cheese**
- **¼ cup chutney**
- **Dash tabasco**
- **1 tablespoon chopped green onion**
- **2 tablespoons sherry**
- **½ teaspoon curry**
- **Pinch of salt**

Blend all ingredients in blender or food processor for a few minutes. Serve with crackers or bagel crisps. Makes about 2 cups.

Nona Maher
GFWC—The Woman's Club of Upper Saddle River
Upper Saddle River, New Jersey

Green Pepper Dip

- **3 egg yolks**
- **3 tablespoons sugar**
- **3 tablespoons vinegar**
- **8 ounces cream cheese**
- **½ green pepper, chopped**
- **1 chopped pimiento or ½ red pepper, chopped**
- **1 teaspoon grated onion**

Cook egg yolks, sugar and vinegar until thick. Remove from heat and add remaining ingredients.

This dip is delicious served with raw vegetables.

Ruth W. Warmkessel
GFWC—The GFWC Woman's Club of Macungie
Macungie, Pennsylvania

Pink Shrimp Dip

- **6 ounces cream cheese, softened**
- **½ teaspoon minced, dehydrated onion**
- **⅓ cup mayonnaise**
- **3 tablespoons chili sauce**
- **2 teaspoons lemon juice**
- **¼ teaspoon Worcestershire sauce**
- **1 cup cooked fresh shrimp, chopped**

Mix cream cheese thoroughly until there are no lumps. Add onion, mayonnaise, chili sauce, lemon juice and Worcestershire sauce. Stir until completely mixed. Add chopped shrimp and mix lightly. Serve with crackers or chips.

Nina C. Foley
GFWC—The Woman's Club of Little Falls
Little Falls, New Jersey

Jessie's Dip

- 2 cans minced clams and juice
- 1 cup bread crumbs
- 1 cup grated swiss cheese
- 1 small chopped onion
- ½ stick melted butter
- 1 teaspoon oregano
- 1 teaspoon lemon juice
- ¼ teaspoon garlic powder

Mix ingredients in bowl. Transfer to greased baking dish. Bake at 350 degrees for ½ hour. Serve with crackers.

Catherine Tuohy
GFWC—The Woman's Club of Lyndhurst
Lyndhurst, New Jersey

Vegetable Dip

- 1 cup mayonnaise
- ¼ cup chili sauce
- ¼ cup catsup
- 1 medium onion, grated
- 2 cloves garlic, minced
- 1½ teaspoons dry mustard
- 1 teaspoon pepper
- Dash paprika
- Dash hot sauce

Combine all ingredients. Chill 3 to 4 hours. Serve with assorted raw vegetables or cold boiled shrimp.

This recipe can also be used as a salad dressing. Add ¼ cup salad oil.

Sheila Rice
GFWC—England Heritage Club
England, Arkansas

Polynesian Ginger Dip

- 1 cup mayonnaise
- 1 cup sour cream
- 2 tablespoons soy sauce
- ¼ cup finely chopped onion
- Dash salt, no more
- ¼ cup chopped parsley
- ½ cup chopped water chestnuts
- 2 tablespoons crystalized ginger
- 2 cloves minced garlic

Combine mayonnaise, sour cream and soy sauce in medium mixing bowl with wire whip. Beat one minute. Add all remaining ingredients and beat one minute. Cover; refrigerate several hours before serving. To add color and spice, sprinkle additional ginger on top of dip before serving. Makes 2 cups. Use sesame melba toast or sesame crackers for dippers.

Vivian R. Lee
GFWC—Victory Study Club
San Angelo, Texas

Hot Broccoli Dip

½ cup chopped onion
½ cup chopped celery
½ cup chopped mushrooms
3½ tablespoons butter or margarine
1 package frozen broccoli, cooked and drained
1 6 ounce package garlic cheese
1 10¾ ounce can cream of mushroom soup, undiluted
¼ teaspoon lemon juice

Saute onion, celery and mushrooms in the butter. Add to the broccoli. Blend in undiluted mushroom soup and cheese. Cook over low heat until cheese is melted. Add lemon juice. Serve in chafing dish with corn chips.

Substitution: If garlic cheese is not available, use grated cheddar cheese and add garlic powder.

Alberta Shelby
GFWC—Iowa Falls Woman's Club
Iowa Falls, Iowa

Low Fat–Low Cholesterol Cheese Dip

½ cup skim milk yogurt
2 teaspoons seasoning salt
2 cups skimmed milk cottage cheese or baker's cheese
2 teaspoons chopped parsley
1 tablespoon Worcestershire sauce

Press through a fine sieve or blend in an electric mixer for smoother dip the skim milk cottage cheese. Add skim milk yogurt, seasoning salt, chopped parsley and Worcestershire sauce. Refrigerate for an hour or more to blend flavors. Serve in a bowl surrounded by chilled, crisped raw vegetables. Also suitable for melba toast or snack crackers. Makes 2½ cups. Serves 20 generously.

"In this day of heart attacks, high blood pressure and awareness of cholesterol levels, people appreciate snacks at a gathering that will taste fat but keep them skinny."

Charlotte Chastain
GFWC—Cupertino Federated Woman's Club
Cupertino, California

Dill Dip

⅔ cup mayonnaise
⅔ cup plain yogurt
1 tablespoon dried parsley flakes
1 teaspoon dill weed
½ teaspoon salt
⅛ teaspoon garlic powder
⅛ teaspoon onion powder
⅛ teaspoon celery seed

Mix all ingredients. Cover and chill several hours to blend flavors. Serve with raw vegetables or with chips, etc.

Bettye Nimmer
GFWC—Mequon-Thiensville Junior Woman's Club
Mequon-Thiensville, Wisconsin

Avocado Dip

- 4 large avocados, really ripe
- 8 ounces sour cream
- 1 bunch of green onions, finely diced
- 1 large tomato, finely diced
- 1 tablespoon lemon juice
- 1 teaspoon Worcestershire sauce
- Picanto sauce to taste
- 1 teaspoon garlic salt
- ½ teaspoon onion salt
- ½ teaspoon salt
- 1 teaspoon pepper

Mash avocados and add ¼–½ carton sour cream. Stir in chopped onions, tomato and remaining ingredients to taste. If not serving immediately, place in bowl and cover. Place avocado seed in the middle and refrigerate. The seed will help keep the dip from turning dark.

Becky K. Mathews
GFWC—Estudie Club
Kiswa, Kansas

Susan's Fruit Dip

- 1 8 ounce can unsweetened crushed pineapple, drained
- 1 8 ounce package cream cheese, softened
- 1 medium carrot, grated
- 1 small apple, grated
- ¼ cup finely chopped pecans
- 2 tablespoons sugar
- ½ teaspoon vanilla

Place pineapple on paper towels and press out excess juice. In a medium bowl, beat cream cheese until smooth. Add pineapple, carrot, apple and pecans. Stir until well mixed. Fold in sugar and vanilla. Use as spread on apple slices, muffins or crackers. Makes about 2 cups

Susan Gaule
GFWC—Rochester Woman's Club
Rochester, Illinois

Curry Vegetable Dip

- 1½ cups mayonnaise
- 3 tablespoons curry powder; add more if curry is not very strong
- 1 teaspoon lemon juice
- ½ teaspoon mustard
- 4 tablespoons chutney

Add everything into a blender. Blend. Taste; curry powder and chutney might need to be added because of varieties and different tastes! Serve with raw vegetables.

Mary Alice Lesko
GFWC—Costa Rica Woman's Club
San Jose, Latin America

Elegant Fruit Dip

- **1 egg, well beaten**
- **½ cup sugar**
- **1 tablespoon grated orange peel**
- **2 tablespoons grated lemon peel**
- **2 tablespoons lemon juice**
- **1 cup whipping cream**

Combine above ingredients in saucepan. Stir over low heat until thick. Cool completely. Fold in 1 cup whipping cream. Serve well chilled in a pretty dish surrounded by selection of colorful and fresh fruit of season. Makes 1 cup.

Gail Birket
GFWC—Gainesville Woman's Club
Gainesville, Florida

Cream Cheese Vegetable Dip

- **1 8 ounce package cream cheese**
- **1 egg, slightly beaten**
- **1 tablespoon sugar**
- **1 tablespoon cider vinegar**
- **2 tablespoons minced green pepper**
- **1 tablespoon minced onion**

Soften cheese; combine egg, sugar, vinegar in top of double boiler. Cook, stirring constantly over simmering water until thick. Remove from heat at once. Add to cream cheese and stir until smooth. Stir in green peppers and onions. Chill. Remove one hour before serving and whip with a spoon. Serve with fresh vegetables cut into bite-sized pieces. Makes 1½ cups.

"I usually make a double batch as it disappears so rapidly."

Edna Viets
GFWC—What Not
Lyndon, Kansas

Artichoke Chili Dip

- **1 can artichoke hearts, (not pickled ones) cut up**
- **1 small can green chilies, diced**
- **1 cup mayonnaise**
- **1 cup parmesan cheese**

Mix all ingredients together. Put in serving/baking dish and bake at 350 degrees for 30–45 minutes, or until nicely brown on top. Serve with crackers or chips.

Pauline S. McMahon
GFWC—San Buenaventura Woman's Club
Ventura, California

Georgia Pecan Dip

- **1 12 ounce package cream cheese**
- **3 tablespoons salad dressing**
- **1 clove fresh garlic, chopped fine**
- **2 tablespoons Worcestershire sauce**
- **¾ cup finely chopped pecans**
- **¼ cup milk**
- **Tabasco or hot sauce to taste**

Mix all ingredients until fluffy and serve with king size corn chips. Note: This recipe can be doubled; use less milk so the cheese is firmer, then shape in tree shape or wreath. Decorate with stuffed sliced olives and pimiento.

"The above is truly my own concoction inspired by the North American Ladies Society, Central America, when they asked me for a real southern recipe of my very own."

Martha Adams
GFWC—Norcross Woman's Club
Norcross, Georgia

Shrimp 'N' Cheese Sunday Nighters

- **1 can small shrimp, cleaned**
- **½ medium onion, chopped fine**
- **½ cup celery, chopped small**
- **⅓ cup mayonnaise**
- **Dash of pepper**
- **4 hot dog buns, halved and buttered**
- **2–3 bacon slices, raw, cut into small pieces**
- **½ cup cheddar cheese, grated**
- **Paprika**

Place buttered and halved hot dog buns on baking sheet. Mix together the cleaned and broken-up shrimp, chopped onion, chopped celery, mayonnaise and pepper. (May add more mayonnaise to moisten to a shrimp salad consistency.) Spread shrimp salad mixture on buttered bun halves. Over all, sprinkle grated cheddar cheese. Top this with raw bacon pieces. Sprinkle each bun half with paprika. Broil until bacon appears crisp and cheese melts, about 3–4 minutes. Sandwich halves may be made early in the day, covered with waxed paper or plastic wrap and refrigerated.

"I received this broiled sandwich recipe from my mother 35 years ago."

Dorothy Bruer
GFWC—West Suburban Woman's Club
Hopkins, Minnesota

Western Style Sandwich

- **1 pound ground beef (lean chuck)**
- **1 medium size onion, diced**
- **½ green pepper, chopped (optional)**
- **1 teaspoon prepared mustard**
- **2 tablespoons pickle relish**
- **¼ cup ketchup (generous)**
- **½ teaspoon salt**
- **Pepper**
- **1 egg**
- **Milk**

Mix all but beef together. Beat 1 egg; add milk to make ½ cup. Add to onion and ketchup mixture. Mix all into ground beef so that it will spread easily. Toast 1 side of bread under broiler. Spread beef mixture onto untoasted side of bread. Put under broiler until meat is done. Sprinkle top with grated cheese. Serve open faced; garnish with pickles, potato chips or salad.

"This is an old Binghamton, NY recipe from about 1934."

Isabelle C. Bosman
GFWC—Mountainside Woman's Club, Inc.
Mountainside, New Jersey

"Small Army Stromboli"

- **1 loaf frozen bread dough**
- **6–7 ounces sandwich pepperoni, sliced thin**
- **6–7 ounces mozzarella cheese, shredded**
- **6–7 ounces jalapeno cheese, shredded**
- **¼–⅓ cups raw vegetables (mixture of onions, green peppers, mushrooms), chopped and sauteed in 2 teaspoons vegetable oil**
- **Italian seasoning**

Defrost bread dough in greased pans 3–4 hours at room temperature. Saute vegetables in oil; set aside. Shred cheeses; keep separate. Set oven temperature at 375 degrees. Cut dough in half; roll out on lightly floured board or marble slab to 10 × 8 or 9 × 6 rectangle, whichever is easier. Sprinkle dough with ½ teaspoon Italian seasoning. Sprinkle with mozzarella cheese to cover dough. Place 3–4 slices of pepperoni along small end of rectangle, starting ½″ from edge of dough. Repeat layers until ½″ from opposite end of dough. Sprinkle with jalapeno pepper cheese. Sprinkle with sauteed vegetables. Roll up jelly-roll fashion from end where you started with pepperoni, tucking in ends of dough. Place seam side down on greased cookie sheet that has been dusted with cornmeal. Brush top of dough with oil. Bake at 375 degrees for 25–30 minutes.

Loretta McCullough
GFWC—Intermediate Woman's Club of Allegheny Valley
Natrona Heights, Pennsylvania

Super Duper Taco Burger

- **2 pounds hamburger**
- **1 package taco seasoning mix**
- **1 17½ ounce can spicy refried beans**
- **1 8 ounce bottle taco sauce**
- **1 small onion, diced**
- **1 small hot pepper, diced**
- **1½ cups shredded lettuce**
- **1 diced tomato**
- **1 cup shredded cheddar cheese**

Mix hamburger, taco seasoning mix and ½ bottle taco sauce. Divide in half and press each half into a hamburger pattie. Spread ½ can refried beans on 1 pattie; top with diced hot pepper and ½ diced onion. Place other pattie on top and pinch edges together. Place on preheated grill (med) 15 minutes per side. When done, remove from grill; place on serving platter. Top with remaining taco sauce, onion, lettuce, tomato and cheese. Serve with heated refried beans and taco chips.

Carol Cooper
GFWC—Centennial Belles
Osborne, Kansas

Fabulous Garlic Loaf

- **1 1 pound loaf sweet French bread**
- **½ cup butter**
- **6 cloves fresh garlic, crushed**
- **2 tablespoons sesame seeds**
- **1½ cups sour cream**
- **2 cups cubed Monterey Jack cheese**
- **¼ cup grated parmesan cheese**
- **2 tablespoons dried parsley flakes**
- **2 teaspoons lemon pepper seasoning**
- **1 14 ounce can artichoke hearts, drained**
- **1 cup shredded cheddar cheese**
- **1 6 ounce can pitted ripe olives**
- **Tomato slices and parsley sprigs for garnish**

Cut French bread in halves lengthwise. Place halves on aluminum foil-covered sheet. Tear out soft inner portion of bread in large chunks, leaving crusts intact. Melt butter in a large skillet and stir in garlic and sesame seeds. Add bread chunks and fry until bread is golden and butter is absorbed. Remove from heat. Combine sour cream, jack cheese, parmesan cheese, parsley flakes and lemon pepper seasoning. Stir in drained artichoke hearts and toasted bread mixture. Mix well. Spoon into bread crust shells and sprinkle with cheddar cheese. Bake at 350 degrees for 30 minutes. Meanwhile, drain olives. Remove bread from oven and arrange olives around edges of bread and tomato slices and parsley sprigs down center. Makes 8 servings.

Irene Forsyth
GFWC—North Long Beach Woman's Club
Long Beach, California

Lentil Oatburgers

- **1 cup lentils**
- **2½ cups water**
- **¼ cup catsup**
- **¼ teaspoon garlic powder**
- **1 small onion, or ¼ teaspoon onion powder**
- **1 cup quick cooking oats**
- **1 egg**
- **Whole wheat flour, if necessary**

Cook lentils in water about 45 minutes or until water is absorbed. Mix all ingredients together. Form into patties. If they do not keep their shape, add enough whole wheat flour to help. Can be broiled or fried in oil. Serve as hamburgers on a bun with lettuce, tomato, catsup, etc. Patties are high in protein and can be used other ways as hamburgers.

Honorine Highsmith
GFWC—Thomasville Woman's Club
Thomasville, Georgia

Ham and Cheese Sandwich

- **2 sticks soft margarine**
- **3 tablespoons mustard**
- **1 tablespoon Worcestershire sauce**
- **3 tablespoons poppy seeds**
- **1 small onion, grated**
- **½ pound sliced ham**
- **½ pound sliced Swiss cheese**
- **2 dozen dinner rolls**

Mix the first five ingredients. Spread on opened dinner rolls. Add ham and cheese and top with dinner roll. Cover with foil and heat in a 350 degrees oven until cheese melts, about 20–25 minutes.

Frances Godwin
GFWC—Rockingham Intermediate Woman's Club
Rockingham, North Carolina

Appetizer

- **1 or 2 heads iceberg lettuce**
- **2 finely chopped onions**
- **1 finely chopped green pepper**
- **6 tablespoons butter or margarine**
- **1 4 ounce can peeled green chilies**
- **1 small, fresh hot pepper, seeded and chopped**
- **3 cups finely diced cooked chicken (3 breasts and 4 thighs)**
- **1½ cups cooked rice**
- **1½ teaspoons dried basil**
- **1 teaspoon salt**
- **1 teaspoon fresh ground pepper**
- **⅓ cup cognac**
- **Chicken broth, as needed**
- **¼ cup chopped parsley**
- **¾ cup toasted shaved almonds**

Wash and separate lettuce. Arrange whole leaves in a bowl and chill. Saute onion and green pepper in butter in large skillet until wilted. Add canned, chopped chilies, the fresh hot pepper (be sure to use plastic gloves when working with this!), the chicken and rice. Mix well; cover and simmer for 5 minutes. Add basil, salt, pepper, cognac and enough broth so that mixture is moist but not sloppy. Heat through. Arrange in a low dish and garnish with parsley and almonds. Place lettuce leaves next to mixture. Each guest spoons some of the chicken mixture onto a lettuce leaf, rolls it up, and it is eaten with the fingers. Really finger licking good! Can be made the day before and heated just before serving.

Mrs. Donald C. Phillips
GFWC—Woman's Club of Butler
Butler, Pennsylvania

Little Smokies Appetizers

- **2 packages "Little Smokies" sausage**
- **1 bottle chili sauce**
- **1 can cranberry sauce**
- **1 heaping tablespoon honey**
- **1 tablespoon lemon juice (bottled)**

Boil everything together for at least 1 hour—uncovered.
If you can't find "Little Smokies", use cocktail franks.

Vivian Woebcke
GFWC—Colony Club of Cranford
Cranford, New Jersey

Taco Tarts

1 cup oleo
2 3 ounce packages cream cheese
2 cups flour
2 packages (1¼ to 1½ ounces each) taco seasoning mix (divided)
1 pound ground chuck
¾ pound Monterey Jack cheese

In bowl, combine oleo, cream cheese, flour and 2 teaspoons of the taco seasoning mix. (Reserve remainder of seasoning to add to meat or for other uses). Mix with fingers until well blended. Cover and refrigerate at least ½ hour or until dough is firm. Meanwhile, season ground chuck with remaining whole package taco seasoning mix. (If spicier flavor is desired, add remainder of reserved seasoning package.) Cook meat according to package directions. Remove dough from refrigerator. Using balls of dough about size of a pecan, flatten with hands and press into miniature tart or muffin pans. There should be about 48 pastry crusts. Fill crusts with about 1 rounded teaspoon meat mixture. Bake at 350 degrees for 10 minutes. Meanwhile, cut cheese into ⅛-inch slices. Cut slices into 1-inch squares. Remove pans from oven and top each tart with cheese slice. Return to oven and bake 2 minutes longer. Serve hot or warm.

Bonnie L. Pottinger
GFWC—Glendale Woman's Club
Glendale, Wisconsin

Baked Clams

2 4 ounce cans minced clams
¼ cup Italian seasoned bread crumbs
1 tablespoon minced onions
1 teaspoon parsley flakes
⅛ teaspoon oregano
⅛ teaspoon garlic powder
2 tablespoons butter
2 tablespoons cooking sherry
1 tablespoon milk

Separate clams from liquid and save liquid. Mix clams with bread crumbs and seasonings; brown in frying pan with butter. Add sherry, milk and ½ clam liquid. It will be very soupy; cook till it thickens, but do not let it go dry. Put in clam shells; sprinkle with paprika. Bake at 350 degrees till lightly brown, about 10–15 minutes. Mixture may be made the night before and refrigerated, then spooned into shells when ready to heat. Great appetizer or as an hors d'oeuvres.

Sylvia Lewis
GFWC—Floral Park Junior Woman's Club, Inc.
Floral Park, New York

Pickled Party Shrimp

- **1 pound cooked and cleaned shrimp**
- **1 pint sliced onions**
- **7–8 bay leaves**
- **1¼ cup salad oil**
- **¾ cup white vinegar**
- **2 teaspoons salt**
- **2½ teaspoons celery seed**
- **2½ tablespoons capers and juice**
- **Dash tabasco sauce**
- **1 teaspoon liquid smoke**

Mix the shrimp and onions together in a bowl. Combine the rest of the ingredients together and pour over the shrimp. Refrigerate for several days or up to a week.

Ruth Dorney
GFWC—Colonial Heights Federated Woman's Club
Colonial Heights, Virginia

Swedish Meatballs

- **1 cup bread crumbs**
- **1 cup milk**
- **2 pounds ground meat**
- **1 cup chopped onions**
- **2 beaten eggs**
- **1½ teaspoons salt**
- **¼ teaspoon pepper**
- **1 teaspoon nutmeg**
- **½ cup butter**
- **¼ cup flour**
- **3 beef bouillon cubes**
- **3 cups hot water**
- **1 can cream of mushroom soup**

Soften bread crumbs in milk. Add beef, onion, eggs and seasoning. Mix together. Shape into 1″ balls (about 96). Heat butter or margarine in large fry pan; add meatballs few at a time and brown. Dissolve beef cubes in water. Shake flour with a little water and add to cubes. Add soup. Cook and stir 3 minutes. Add meatballs and simmer 15 minutes. If gravy is too thick, add milk.

Ruth T. Walsh
GFWC—Woman's Club of Wyckoff, Evening Membership Department
Wyckoff, New Jersey

Seafood Paté

8 ounces cream cheese
1 cup mayonnaise
3/4 pound chopped, cooked shrimp
1/4 pound chopped, cooked scallops
1/4 pound shredded crabmeat
2 tablespoons grated onion
1 tablespoon Worcestershire sauce
1 dash cayenne pepper
1 small jar pimientos, chopped
Salt to taste
1 1/2 envelopes unflavored gelatin
1/2 cup water

Cream first two ingredients with mixer until creamy. Add seafood, onion, Worcestershire sauce, pepper and salt. Mix gelatin and water together; heat in saucepan until mixed together. Pour into seafood mixture; stir. Pour into greased mold and refrigerate (for at least 4 hours). Optional: chop spring onion for color. Great dish for Christmas gatherings. Serve with crackers or hard bread slices.

Cheryl Murray Crumbley
GFWC—Milledgeville Junior Woman's Club
Milledgeville, Georgia

Zesty Meatball Appetizers

1 pound lean ground beef
2 eggs, slightly beaten
1/2 teaspoon garlic salt
1/4 teaspoon pepper
1 small onion, minced
1/2 cup crushed seasoned croutons

Mix above ingredients and roll into small balls. Roll in flour and brown carefully in well-oiled fry pan. Serve with sauce in fondue pot.

Sauce

1/4 cup soy sauce
1/4 teaspoon powdered ginger
1/2 cup catsup
1/4 cup brown sugar
1/4 cup pineapple juice

Heat ingredients for sauce and add meatballs to sauce. Simmer a few minutes. May keep warm in fondue pot or on a toothpick. Place small pieces of pineapple atop each meatball and serve on a heated platter.

Hilda Van Valkenburg
GFWC—North Park Woman's Club
Walden, Colorado

Tuna Paté

- 1 8 ounce package cream cheese, softened
- 2 tablespoons chili sauce
- 2 tablespoons snipped parsley
- 1 teaspoon instant minced onion
- ½ teaspoon bottled hot pepper sauce
- 1 6½ ounce can tuna, drained

Blend all ingredients with a fork (do not use an electric mixer) until smooth. Pack in a 2–4 cup mold or small bowl; chill thoroughly. Unmold on serving plate. Decorate with sliced green olives and serve with assorted crackers.

Gladys K. Cordts
GFWC—Woman's Club of Nutley, Inc.
Nutley, New Jersey

Tuna Chiffon Mold

- 1 can chicken broth
- ¼ cup cold water
- 2 envelopes unflavored gelatin
- ¾ cup chopped onion
- 1 13 ounce can tuna, drained
- ¼ cup parsley
- ½ cup chopped walnuts
- 1 tablespoon lemon juice
- 1 teaspoon salt
- 1 cup mayonnaise

Combine broth and water in a pan. Sprinkle gelatin over. Let stand 5 minutes. Heat mixture over low heat until dissolved and becomes clear. Cool. Saute onion and celery. Flake tuna in large bowl. Add parsley, nuts, lemon juice, salt, mayonnaise, gelatin mixture, onion and celery. Pour in 5-cup mold. Serve with crackers.

Lillie Reutlinger
GFWC—Cupertino Federated Woman's Club
Cupertino, California

Beef Rolls

- 18–20 thin slices roasted beef tip
- 2 3 ounce packages cream cheese
- ½ grated cucumber
- 3 tablespoons grated radishes
- 2 teaspoons onion salt

Cream or beat cream cheese to soften; add cucumber, radishes and onion salt, mixing to combine. Spread on slices of cold roast beef, allowing about 2 teaspoons for each slice. Roll up slices; wrap and chill. To serve, cut rolls in halves or thirds. Secure each piece with a small wooden pick. Makes 3–4 dozen rolls. Garnish platter with sprigs of parsley and cherry tomatoes.

"This recipe makes a hearty, tasty addition to any buffet. It may be made ahead the day before, so flavors may blend."

Hilda Van Valkenburg
GFWC—North Park Woman's Club
Walden, Colorado

Scotch Eggs

- **4 eggs, hard-boiled and shelled**
- **2 teaspoons seasoned flour**
- **Worcestershire sauce**
- **½ pound sausage meat or skinless sausages**
- **1 egg, beaten**
- **Fat for deep frying**

Dust eggs with seasoned flour. Add a few drops of Worcestershire sauce to the sausage meat and divide into 4 portions. Form each ¼ into a flat cake and work it around an egg, making it as even as possible. Brush with beaten egg and toss in bread crumbs. Heat fat until it will brown a cube of bread in 40–50 seconds. Fry eggs for about 7–8 minutes. When they are golden brown on the outside, remove from fat and drain on paper towel. Cut eggs in half lengthwise. Serve hot with tomato sauce or cold with a green salad.

Jackie Lester
GFWC—North Coast Junior Woman's Club
Carlsbad, California

7 Layer Spread

- **8 ounces cream cheese**
- **1 can shrimp, drained**
- **½ bottle chili sauce**
- **1 green pepper, chopped**
- **1 onion, chopped**
- **Shredded cheese**
- **Ripe olives, sliced**

Spread cream cheese on flat plate. Sprinkle shrimp on top. Spread chili sauce on top of shrimp. Sprinkle green pepper and onion on top of sauce. Shred mozzarella or sharp cheese on top and then decorate with sliced ripe olives.

Larene Castor
GFWC—West Side Evening Woman's Club
Forty Fort, Pennsylvania

Roasted Pecans

- **2 cups pecans**
- **3 tablespoons butter**
- **3 tablespoons soy sauce**
- **Dashes of tabasco**
- **Little red pepper to taste**
- **1 teaspoon salt**

Melt butter in saucepan; add soy sauce, tabasco, red pepper and salt. Stir in pecans to coat them completely and then spread pecans on large sheet pan (9 × 13). Roast for 30 minutes at 300 degrees, stirring often.

Dolores Loupe
GFWC—The Woman's Club of Lockport, Inc.
Lockport, Louisiana

Spinach Bread

3 cups sifted flour
2 teaspoons baking powder
½ cup vegetable oil
Milk, if needed
2 eggs
½ teaspoon salt
¼ teaspoon pepper

Filling

2 pounds spinach
2 tablespoons grated cheese
1 clove garlic, chopped
1 pound Italian sausage, out of casing and browned
½ cup vegetable oil
Salt and pepper to taste
½ cup chopped black olives or anchovies

Mix all ingredients for crust. Knead for 20 minutes. Cover with towel and let rise for one hour.

Cook spinach, drain and squeeze. Mix with rest of filling. Divide crust in half and roll out in rectangle. Fill with half of filling and roll up like a jelly roll. Bake at 375 degrees for 35–40 minutes, until brown. Makes 2 rolls.

Alma Lacourciere
GFWC—North Branford Woman's Club
North Branford, Connecticut

Omaha Crackers

Unsalted top saltine crackers
Butter or margarine
Seasoned salt
Garlic powder

Soften margarine and spread on both sides of crackers. Sprinkle both sides of crackers with seasoned salt. Sprinkle one side of crackers with garlic powder. Soak in ice water for eight minutes. Place on cookie sheet and bake in a 450 degree oven for 10 minutes. Then lower the heat to 375 degrees and bake until dark brown and dry, about 25–30 minutes. Do not underbake.

Betty Jean Pelt
GFWC—Cosmopolitan Woman's Club of Mobile
Mobile, Alabama

Orange Wheat Crackers

- **1 cup flour**
- **1 cup whole wheat or rye flour**
- **¼ cup brown sugar**
- **2 teaspoons baking powder**
- **1 teaspoon orange zest**
- **⅛ teaspoon salt**
- **½ cup margarine**
- **⅔ cup orange juice**

In a medium mixing bowl, stir together flours, sugar, baking powder, zest and salt. Using a pastry blender, cut in margarine until mix resembles coarse crumbs. Stir in orange juice; form into ball. On well-floured surface, roll dough half at a time to 1/16 inch thickness. Use fluted, round cookie cutter to cut crackers. Prick each several times. Place on unbuttered cookie sheet. Bake in a 350 degree oven 12 to 15 minutes. Makes 72 crackers.

Lucy Mitchell
GFWC—Bethel Woman's Club
Bethel, Connecticut

Aunt Carmella's Freselles

- **3½ cups all-purpose flour**
- **¾ teaspoon salt**
- **2 teaspoons baking powder**
- **¾ teaspoon coarse ground pepper**
- **¾ cup cooking oil**
- **1 cup cold water**

Mix all dry ingredients together and then add oil and water. Stir all ingredients together. Dough will be stiff. Divide dough and roll on board to resemble long bread sticks. Slice off pieces about ½ inch long. Bake on ungreased cookie sheet for 15 to 20 minutes at 400 degrees, not browned—barely golden like pie crust.

Jean M. Fadus
GFWC—Newtown Woman's Club
Newtown, Connecticut

Chinese Chips

- **24 Wonton skins, 1 package**
- **¼ cup melted butter**
- **½ cup parmesan cheese**
- **1 teaspoon crushed basil**
- **¾ teaspoon chopped garlic**
- **¾ teaspoon chopped onion**

Brush a 15 × 10 × 1 inch jelly roll pan with butter. Place skins on pan. Melt butter, cheese, basil, garlic and onion; brush onto skins. Cut into triangles. Bake at 400 degrees for 5–6 minutes, until crisp but not brown. Makes 48. Great served alone or with a dip.

Barbara R. Kelley
GFWC—Orangewood Woman's Club
Orange, Connecticut

Beverages

Coffee Eggnog

- **2 cups double strength coffee**
- **1 stick cinnamon**
- **6 whole cloves**
- **1 pint milk**
- **1 quart vanilla ice cream**
- **6 ginger berries**
- **2 quarts eggnog mix or prepared eggnog**

Simmer the coffee with the spices and after cooking, add the milk, eggnog mix and ice cream.

"This recipe comes from the Woman's Club of Abilene, Texas file and is about 50 years old or older."

Mrs. Charles D. Leonard
GFWC—Progressive Study Club
Normangee, Texas

Photo features: Non-Alcoholic Punch—Page 42
Coffee of Vienna's Empire—Page 45

Christmas Fruit Punch

- **1 6 ounce can frozen orange juice**
- **2 6 ounce cans frozen limeade**
- **1 6 ounce can frozen lemonade**
- **1 large can pineapple juice**
- **1 pint cranberry juice cocktail**
- **2 to 4 cups cold water**
- **2 quarts chilled ginger ale**
- **1 quart plain chilled soda water**
- **1 quart frozen strawberries**
- **Fruit**
- **Mint Garnish**

Empty frozen juices, pineapple and cranberry juice and water in a large container. Let stand until frozen juice is thawed; stir well. Add frozen strawberries. Pour mixture into punch bowl. Add ice cubes. Just before serving, gently pour in ginger ale and soda water. Top with fruit ice ring and sprigs of mint.

Fruit Ice Ring:
Use any combination of lime, lemon or orange slices. Arrange in pattern in ring mold; add water to cover fruit and freeze.

Marian J. Westling
GFWC—Ladies' Tourist Club
Henderson, Minnesota

Frozen Fruit Punch

- **4 cups sugar**
- **6 cups water**
- **2 5½ ounce cans apricot juice**
- **1 46 ounce can unsweetened pineapple juice**
- **3 cups unsweetened, frozen orange juice**
- **¾ cup lemon juice**

Bring to boil sugar and water; let cool. Add the juices. Blend together. Freeze in appropriate size containers, according to the number you will serve at one time. To use: partially thaw. To 2 parts juice add 1 part ginger ale.

Lula Nickason
GFWC—The Woman's Club of Oakwood
Hannibal, Missouri

Coffee Wedding Punch

- **⅓ cup instant coffee**
- **1 cup sugar**
- **1 cup water**
- **5 cups evaporated milk, chilled (may use half and half cream)**
- **1 quart vanilla ice cream**
- **1 quart carbonated water**

Combine coffee, sugar and water. Beat and stir well until blended. Chill. Stir in milk. To serve, pour into punch bowl. Spoon in ice cream. Stir until partially melted. Pour in carbonated water. Makes 24 ½-cup servings.

Carolyn Glascoe Woodall
GFWC—Roxboro Woman's Club
Roxboro, North Carolina

Holiday Tea

- **½ gallon cranberry juice**
- **1 3 ounce can frozen orange juice**
- **¼ cup lemon juice**
- **1½ cups water**
- **¼ cup sugar**
- **1 stick cinnamon**
- **1 teaspoon cloves**

Mix juices. Mix together water and sugar. Put cloves in a cloth bag and simmer with cinnamon in sugar water for 1½ hours. Add juices.

Diana Storm
GFWC—Patrician Club
Kansas City, Missouri

Rhubarb Punch

- **8 quarts rhubarb, chopped but not peeled**
- **8 quarts water**
- **1 bottle 7-Up**
- **1 6 ounce can lemonade**
- **1 3 ounce package cherry gelatin**
- **1 46 ounce can pineapple juice**
- **5½ cups sugar**

Cook rhubarb and water until mush. Press through a sieve. To rhubarb juice add gelatin, pineapple juice and sugar. Bring to a boil; pack in sterilized freezer jars and freeze. When ready to serve, add 7-Up and lemonade mixture.

Delores Joens
GFWC—Dunkerton Federated Woman's Club
Dunkerton, Iowa

Strawberry Iced Tea

- **4 cups water**
- **1 cup orange juice**
- **½ cup sugar**
- **⅓ cup instant tea**
- **1 10 ounce package frozen strawberries, thawed**

Combine all ingredients, except water, in blender. Blend until frothy. Add water and blend briefly. Pour over ice and serve.

Joy Harding
GFWC—White Mountain Woman's Club
Show Low, Arizona

May Magic

- **1 quart rhubarb, cut into ¼ inch pieces**
- **¾ cup sugar**
- **1 quart water**

Put rhubarb, sugar and water in stainless steel kettle. Bring to a gentle boil for 3 minutes, stirring gently several times. Remove from stove and let drain through sieve. Do not press through sieve! Cool and serve. This will be clear and a very pretty pink if strawberry rhubarb is used.

Josephine D. Burroughs
GFWC—Woman's Club of Somersworth
Somersworth, New Hampshire

Cocoa Banana Special Drink

1 small banana
3 tablespoons cocoa
3 tablespoons granulated sugar
1¾ cups milk

Slice banana into blender. Add cocoa and sugar, blending until smooth. Add ½ cup of milk and blend until foamy. Add remaining milk; blend well. Serve immediately or store in the refrigerator, stirring before serving.

Kathy Adamczyk
GFWC—Woman's Club of Garfield
Garfield, New Jersey

Wedding Punch

5 cups sugar
2⅔ cups water
5 handfuls fresh mint or 1½ ounces dried mint
5 quarts lime ice sherbert
8 quarts ginger ale
20 lemons or 1 can lemon concentrate

Boil the water and sugar. Pour over mint and let stand overnight. Strain and add lemon juice. Fold in ice sherbert and slowly add ginger ale.

"This punch was served at the Sigma Kappa House at K.U. in the early 1950's. I served it at my wedding in 1951."

Mary A. McElroy
GFWC—Goddard Woman's Club
Goddard, Kansas

Wedding Punch

2 quarts apple cider
1 25.4 ounce bottle sparkling grape juice
1 bottle ginger ale

Mix just before serving. Serve with a decorated ice ring, using seasonal foliage and fruits.

Margaret Anne Smith
GFWC—Sesame Club
Hillsboro, Texas

Non-Alcoholic Punch

2 cans frozen orange juice
2 cans frozen lemonade
8 cans water
2 cups grenadine
Juice of 3 lemons
3 quarts chilled ginger ale
Orange slices
Cherries

Mix all ingredients well. Float orange slices on top. Add cherries.

Geraldine Lee
GFWC—North Long Beach Woman's Club
Long Beach, California

Abigail Adams' Champagne Punch

1½ cups sugar
1 cup strong black tea
1½ cups orange juice
Rind of 2 lemons, thinly sliced
½ cup lemon juice
1 cup light or dark rum
1 fifth chilled champagne (26 ounces)
Fresh orange slices and mint sprigs (optional)

Dissolve sugar in tea. Add orange juice, lemon rind and juice and rum. Chill. Just before serving, pour rum mixture and champagne over ice in a punch bowl. Garnish with fresh orange slices and mint sprigs, if desired. Makes 2 quarts or 16 4 ounce servings.

"This refreshing punch was popular for women's gatherings in the 1700's."

Anita C. Jackson
GFWC—Old Colony Union Woman's Club of Bourne
Bourne, Massachusetts

Spiced Wine Punch

4 4-inch sticks cinnamon, broken
3 cardamon pods, opened
2 whole cloves
⅔ cup grape juice
2 tablespoons sugar
2½ cups dry, red wine

Tie broken cinnamon, cardamon pods and cloves in a cheesecloth bag. In a 4-cup microwave measure, combine grape juice, sugar and the spice bag. Micro cook, uncovered, on 100% power 3 minutes. Stir in wine. Micro cook on high 2–3 minutes or until hot. Discard spice bag. Pour wine mixture into mugs and serve warm.

Barbara Trimble
GFWC—Woman's Club of Westview Park
Catonsville, Maryland

Christmas Punch

1 cup sugar
4 cinnamon sticks
5 lemon slices
2 cups pineapple juice
2 cups orange juice
6 cups dry, white wine
½ cup lemon juice
1 cup apricot brandy
2 lemon slices for punch, extra for garnish

Boil the sugar, lemon slices and cinnamon sticks in ½ cup of water for 5 minutes. Strain and combine the resulting syrup with the remaining ingredients. Chill and serve over ice; garnish with lemon slices.

Janice Baskin
GFWC—Junior Woman's Club of Falls Church
Falls Church, Virginia

Yolie's Old Fashioneds

- **1 fifth 100 proof bourbon**
- **3 tablespoons sugar**
- **1 teaspoon angostura bitters**
- **2 teaspoons peychaud bitters**
- **1 teaspoon absinthe**
- **2 lemons**

Dissolve sugar in 2 tablespoons of hot water. Add to bourbon. Add bitters and absinthe. Mix well. Cut thin skins from the lemons; add to bourbon mixture. Let stand for 5 days. Remove peel. Serve over ice. Garnish with orange slice and cherry.

Frances T. Pere
GFWC—Woman's Club of Abbeville
Abbeville, Louisiana

Boerenjongen's Cocktail

- **2 cups raisins, use half light and half dark for color**
- **3½ cups water**
- **2 cups sugar**
- **2 cups whiskey**

In large saucepan, combine raisins and water. Bring to boiling. Reduce heat; simmer 2 minutes. Add sugar. Stir until sugar is dissolved. Remove from heat. Stir in whiskey. Fill 4 pint jars with raisin-whiskey mixture, seal and let stand at least 1 month. Serve in tiny cordial glasses; garnish with a slice of lemon.

"This is a traditional Christmas drink in our family for over 100 years. Originated in the Netherlands."

Mildred Pierce
GFWC—Gun Lake
Shelbyville, Michigan

Amaretto Punch

- **1 cup sugar**
- **4½ cups water**
- **6 ounces orange juice, thawed and undiluted**
- **6 ounces lemonade, thawed and undiluted**
- **1 cup amaretto**
- **1 liter bottle Diet 7-Up**

Combine sugar and water in a small pan. Stir well and boil until sugar dissolves. Reduce heat and simmer 15 minutes. Combine with other ingredients except 7-Up. Stir well. Freeze overnight. When ready to serve, thaw until mushy and add 7-Up.

Charlotte Williams
GFWC—St. Simons Woman's Club
St. Simons Island, Georgia

Coffee of Vienna's Empire

5 cups strong brewed coffee
1 cup brandy
½ gallon real vanilla ice cream
½ cup shaved bittersweet chocolate
1 pint whipped cream
6 tall glasses

Brew coffee and let cool slightly. Fill glasses with 2 scoops of ice cream. Stir brandy into coffee and slowly pour into glasses. Top with scoops of whipped cream and sprinkle with chocolate. Serve with straws and spoons!

Rita F. Koval
GFWC—Fountain Valley Junior Woman's Club
Fountain Valley, California

Big Sky Slush

1 6 ounce can frozen orange juice
1 6 ounce can pink lemonade
1 large can pineapple juice
1 large can apricot nectar
1 cup apricot brandy
1 cup vodka
Ginger ale

Mix and freeze. When serving, fill glass ½ full and add ginger ale.

Marge Uhlrich
GFWC—Lewistown Woman's Club
Lewistown, Montana

Soups

Creamy Old Fashioned Bean Soup

- **1 pound pea beans, dried**
- **1 quart boiling water**
- **2 pounds smoked ham hocks or meaty ham bone**
- **2 teaspoons salt—may not need as much—depends upon saltiness of meat**
- **¼ teaspoon pepper**
- **3 tablespoons oleo**
- **1½ cups chopped onion**
- **1 pound carrots, finely grated, optional**
- **1 quart tomatoes, with juice**
- **2 cups milk or skim milk**
- **1½ cups chopped celery**

Wash and clean beans; cover with cold water and soak overnight. Drain and place in saucepan with boiling water, ham, salt and pepper. Heat to boiling; reduce heat, cover and simmer 2½ hours. Remove from heat. In small saucepan, melt oleo; add onion and saute until tender. Remove meat from broth and cut off from bones; add to broth along with sauteed onion and tomatoes, celery and carrots. Mix well; cover and simmer 1 hour longer. Stir in milk; heat and serve.

"Published in the Milwaukee Journal food section about 30 years ago."

Sarni Dornoff
GFWC—Woman's Club of Greenfield
Greenfield, Wisconsin

Photo features: Swedish Fruit Soup—Page 55

Simple and Easy Chili

- **2 pounds lean ground beef**
- **2 32 ounce cans of stewed tomatoes**
- **1 32 ounce can tomato sauce**
- **2 diced green peppers**
- **2 16 ounce cans kidney beans, drained**
- **Salt to taste**
- **Pepper to taste**
- **Chili powder to taste**

In large dutch oven, brown and crumble ground beef; add green pepper once meat is browned. Add stewed tomatoes and tomato sauce; heat thoroughly. Add kidney beans just before serving. Season to taste. Can be frozen.

Sandi Frieling
GFWC—Fox River Woman's Club
Mukwonago, Wisconsin

Quick And Easy Microwave Chili

- **1 pound ground chuck**
- **1 large onion, sliced**
- **½ cup chopped green pepper**
- **1 16 ounce can tomatoes**
- **1 6 ounce can tomato paste**
- **1 15½ ounce can dark kidney beans, undrained**
- **1 bay leaf**
- **1 teaspoon salt**
- **2 tablespoons chili powder**
- **¼ teaspoon garlic powder**
- **⅛ teaspoon paprika**
- **⅛ teaspoon cayenne pepper**
- **½ cup water**

In a covered 2-quart casserole, microwave ground chuck, onion and green pepper until meat is cooked, about 5 minutes on high. Drain and add remaining ingredients, mix well. Recover and microwave for 8 minutes on roast. Stir and turn casserole. Microwave 8 more minutes on roast. Let stand covered 5 minutes. Sprinkle cheddar cheese, shredded over bowls of chili and serve with oyster crackers. Remove bay leaf before serving.

Diane P. Luebke
GFWC—Brandywine Woman's Club
Old Hickory, Tennessee

Italian Chicken Stew (Diet)

2 cups cooked, cubed chicken
1 32 ounce can tomato juice
1 cup shredded cabbage
1 cup sliced carrots
1 cup sliced zucchini
½ cup chopped peppers
½ cup chopped onions
1 teaspoon basil
1 teaspoon dried parsley
½ teaspoon oregano
½ teaspoon salt
Dash of pepper

Combine all ingredients in a 2-quart casserole. Cover with a tight-fitting lid or plastic wrap. Microwave on high 100% for 8–10 minutes or until boiling. Stir occasionally. Microwave on medium 50% for 70–75 minutes or until vegetables are soft.

Jean Joyal
GFWC—Winchendon Woman's Club
Winchendon, Massachusetts

Sausage Bean Chowder

1 pound mild pork sausage
1 can red kidney beans
1 16 ounce can tomatoes
2 cups water
1 medium onion, diced
2 medium potatoes, chopped
1 bay leaf
½ teaspoon salt
¼ teaspoon garlic salt
¼ teaspoon thyme
⅛ teaspoon pepper
¼ cup chopped green pepper

Brown sausage in skillet. Pour off fat. In large saucepan, combine kidney beans, water, tomatoes, onions, bay leaf, salt, garlic salt, thyme and pepper. Add sausage, potatoes and green pepper. Simmer, covered for 1 hour.

Linda Brown
GFWC—Beverly Shelton Girls Town Club
Independence, Missouri

Mast-O-Khiar (Cold Yogurt Soup)

16 ounces plain yogurt
¼ cup raisins
¼ cup chopped walnuts
¼ cup small, chopped onion
¼ cup shredded cucumber
Garlic powder to taste

Mix all the above together. Chill to allow the flavors to mix. Pour into bowl and garnish with dill and parsley. Serve with rice dishes.

Colleen Sadollah
GFWC—Westwood Junior Woman's Club
Richmond, Virginia

Beaufort Cream of Crab Soup

1 onion, finely chopped
1 tablespoon butter
1 cup chicken stock
1 quart half and half
1 tablespoon finely chopped parsley
½ teaspoon mace
1 pound crabmeat
2 tablespoons flour
¼ cup dry sherry
Salt to taste
Pepper to taste

In a skillet, saute onion in butter until transparent. Add chicken stock and slowly pour in half and half. Stir well. Add seasonings and crabmeat, stirring until mixed. Simmer 15 minutes. Make a thin paste of flour and a little water. Stir into soup to thicken slightly; just before serving, add sherry. Stir once and serve immediately.

"Taken from Savannah sampler cookbook, 'A Collection of the Best Low Country Cookery,' a favorite of President George Washington. Served during a South Carolina visit in 1791."

Mary Jane Davis
GFWC—Young Woman's Industrial of Upland
Upland, Indiana

Benson Bean Broth

¼ cup of 10 different beans, peas, etc.
1 large onion
1 large can tomatoes
1 clove garlic
1 teaspoon chili powder
1 ham bone

Wash beans and soak overnight. Simmer for 2 hours until beans begin to soften. Add seasonings, vegetables and ham bone. Cook for approximately 1 hour. Good served with corn bread and a salad.

Buy 1 pound of each bean. Put ¼ cup of each in jar. Looks nice when layered. Add recipe with a tag. Makes 10 jars to be used as hostess gifts or as a bazaar item.

Joan Thelander
GFWC—Benson Woman's Club
Benson, Arizona

Avocado-Cucumber Soup

2 cucumbers
1 small onion
1 large clove garlic
1 avocado
2 teaspoons lemon juice
½ teaspoon hot sauce
1 teaspoon salt
2 teaspoons dill weed
1 pint sour cream or low-fat plain yogurt

Peel and seed cucumbers. Place in food processor with onion and garlic. Puree. Add lemon juice, seasonings and avocado. Blend again. Add sour cream with "pulse" on blender just until mixed. Chill well before serving. Makes about 4 cups.

Shirley Lawrenson
GFWC—Newtown Woman's Club
Newtown, Connecticut

Quick Bean Soup

2 tablespoons olive oil
1 teaspoon minced garlic
1 onion, minced
2 stalks celery, minced
½ pound sausage, crumbled
1 carrot, grated
1 teaspoon oregano
1 teaspoon dried parsley
1 teaspoon salt
¼ teaspoon pepper
1 teaspoon chicken bouillon
1 28 ounce can tomatoes
1 16 ounce can refried beans
3 cups water

Brown garlic, onion, celery and sausage in oil. Puree tomatoes in blender. Add all remaining ingredients. Cook 20 minutes to blend flavors.

Philippa Benson
GFWC—Coquille Woman's Club
Coquille, Oregon

Low-Fat Bean Soup

2 teaspoons margarine
1 cup carrot slices
1 cup sliced celery
½ cup chopped onion
1½ cups canned tomatoes
1 can tomato bisque soup
1 can of water
1 16 ounce can pork and beans
1 16 ounce can kidney beans
1 16 ounce can white beans
1 teaspoon lemon juice
1 teaspoon marjoram leaves, crushed (optional)

Cook carrots, celery and onion over medium heat in the margarine until tender. Gradually stir in other ingredients. Heat to boiling; reduce heat to low and simmer 20 minutes.

Frances M. Wilkinson
GFWC—Cobb Woman's Club
Cobb, Wisconsin

Presidential Peanut Soup

- **¼ cup butter**
- **1 cup thinly sliced celery**
- **1 medium onion, chopped fine**
- **2 tablespoons flour**
- **2 quarts chicken broth**
- **1 cup creamy peanut butter**
- **1 cup light cream**

Melt butter in large saucepan over low heat. Add celery and onion; cook until tender, not browned. Add flour and stir until mixture is smooth. Gradually add chicken broth, bringing to boil. Blend in peanut butter and simmer 15 minutes. Stir in cream just before serving.

Mary Jane Davis
GFWC—Young Woman's Industrial of Upland
Upland, Indiana

Cauliflower Cream Soup

- **1 small head cauliflower**
- **2 tablespoons water**
- **1 medium onion, chopped**
- **⅓ cup butter or margarine**
- **⅓ cup flour**
- **1 teaspoon salt**
- **4 cups light cream or milk**
- **4 ounces American cheese (about 1 cup, cubed)**
- **2 teaspoons mustard, dijon-style**

Cut cauliflower into small pieces. Combine with water, onion and butter in 2-quart casserole with cover. Microwave covered 5–6 minutes or until tender. Combine flour, salt and cream, mixing well. Stir into vegetables. Cover. Microwave 8–9 minutes until mixture boils and thickens, stirring 2–3 times. Stir in cheese and mustard. Microwave, uncovered, 2–3 minutes or until cheese is melted.

Sandra Langdon
GFWC—Toulon Woman's Club
Toulon, Illinois

Easy But Great Brunswick Stew

- **1 pound ground lean beef**
- **1 pound ground lean pork**
- **2 1 pound cans chopped tomatoes, peeled**
- **2 1 pound cans creamed corn**
- **4 medium-sized onions, chopped**
- **3 tablespoons Worcestershire sauce**
- **Salt to taste**
- **Smoked barbecue sauce to taste**

Brown beef and pork mixed together in frying pan; drain. In a 5-quart boiler, add tomatoes and onions to meat. Cook about 1 hour until well done. Add creamed corn, Worcestershire sauce, smoked barbecue sauce and salt to taste. Cook until thick, uncovered.

"Handed down—about 75 years old."

Frances Seaborn Reed
GFWC—Nacoochee Woman's Club
Sautee-Nacoochee, Georgia

Clam and Vegetable Chowder

2 large potatoes, peeled and diced
1 8 ounce bottle clam juice
3 slices bacon, diced
2 cloves garlic, minced
1 one pound can tomatoes
2 8 ounce cans minced clams
1 cup boiling water
½ cup grated mild cheese
3 medium onions, chopped
1 medium green pepper, chopped
2 teaspoons chili powder
Salt and pepper to taste

In 5-quart kettle, cook 1 diced potato in boiling water and clam juice until very tender. Put in blender and blend till smooth. Stir in cheese and set aside. Rinse and dry kettle; add bacon, fry until crisp. Add onion, garlic and green pepper; cook till onion is translucent, about 5 minutes. Stir in tomatoes, chili powder and clams, including liquid. Stir in remaining diced potatoes and mashed potato. Cover and simmer 20–30 minutes until diced potato is tender, stirring occasionally. Season to taste with salt and pepper.

Debbie Inman
GFWC—Walnut Valley Woman's Club
Walnut, California

Mom's Old Fashioned Turkey-Vegetable Soup

12 ounces zucchini, sliced
½ pound fresh mushrooms, sliced
2 cubed potatoes
1 pound package ground turkey
2 cups chopped carrots
1 tablespoon oil
1 tablespoon cumin
1 tablespoon salt
1 teaspoon pepper
1½ cups fresh, diced string beans
1 16 ounce can stewed tomatoes
1 large onion, chopped
1 clove garlic, minced
5 cups chicken broth stock

Saute onion in 1 tablespoon oil; add garlic and turkey and simmer slowly. Add spices, broth and tomatoes. Bring to boil, adding carrots, string beans and potatoes. Add zucchini and mushrooms when carrots are soft, so as not to overcook. Cook over medium heat until done, about 1 hour.

Rosemarie Cavanaugh
GFWC—East Brunswick Woman's Club
East Brunswick, New Jersey

Cheese and Meatball Soup

Soup

2 cups water
1 cup whole kernel corn
1 cup chopped potato
1 cup chopped celery
½ cup carrot slices
½ cup chopped onion
2 beef bouillon cubes
½ teaspoon hot sauce
1 16 ounce jar processed cheese spread

Combine all ingredients together except cheese spread in a saucepan; add meatballs, stirring gently and bring mixture to a boil. Cover and simmer on low heat until vegetables are tender, about 2 hours. Right before serving add cheese spread, stirring gently until melted and blended.

Meatballs

1 pound very lean ground beef
¼ cup bread crumbs
1 egg
½ teaspoon salt
½ teaspoon hot sauce

Make meatballs first. Combine all ingredients. Brown meatballs well.

Marcia Pera
GFWC—Federated Women for the Arts
Rushford, Minnesota

Egg Lemon Soup

4 10½ ounce cans condensed chicken broth
4 eggs
1 lemon for juice
1½ cups cooked white rice
Salt and pepper to taste
1 lemon for garnish

Heat broth with seasoning in large saucepan for 10 minutes. Beat eggs until very fluffy. Slowly stir in lemon juice and beat 2 minutes. Remove ½ cup of hot broth and stir in egg mixture, a little at a time. Still stirring, add to remaining broth. Cautiously heat until all is evenly combined. Add cooked rice slowly, stirring carefully. Serve immediately. Garnish with lemon slice.

"This recipe is a favorite Greek family cooking delicacy."

Helen N. Braams
GFWC—Franklin Federated Woman's Club
Franklin, Nebraska

Diet Consomme

- **2 cups beef consomme**
- **2 cups tomato juice**
- **1 teaspoon lemon juice**
- **½ teaspoon sugar**
- **1 onion, sliced**
- **Celery tops**
- **4 cloves**
- **1 teaspoon celery salt**

Combine ingredients and simmer 20 minutes in covered pan. Strain and serve.

Laurel T. Bessesen
GFWC—Bona Venture
Minneapolis, Minnesota

Swedish Fruit Soup (Fruktsoppa)

- **2 cups mixed dried fruits (apricots, peaches, pears and pitted prunes)**
- **½ cup seedless raisins**
- **2 quarts water**
- **1 cup sugar**
- **3 inch-piece stick cinnamon**
- **3 tablespoons tapioca**
- **2 teaspoons aromatic bitters**
- **Few drops of red food coloring**
- **Whipped or sour cream**

Place dried fruits in large kettle with tight-fitting cover. Pour cold water over fruits and let soak for one hour. Add sugar and cinnamon; cook slowly, covered, for one hour. Soften tapioca in ½ cup cold water for 5 minutes. Add aromatic bitters and pour into soup. Cook until soup clears, about 10 minutes. Remove from heat and add food coloring. Cool. Then chill thoroughly in refrigerator. Serve in soup bowls with a dab of sweet whipped or sour cream.

Eleanore Radloff
GFWC—Higginsville Woman's Club
Higginsville, Missouri

Schnit Suppe-German Fruit Soup

- **1 12 ounce package mixed dried fruit**
- **1 cup raisins**
- **10 cups water**
- **1 cinnamon stick**
- **½ cup sugar**
- **1 tablespoon flour**
- **1 cup sweet cream**

Boil fruit and water until fruit is tender, but not overly done. Mix sugar and flour then add slowly sweet cream to that. Add this to the hot soup and cook till thickened a little. Serve hot or cold.

Midge Trupp
GFWC—Nogales Woman's Club
Nogales, Arizona

Lentil Sausage Main-Dish Soup

2 hot and 4 sweet Italian link pork sausages (about 1 pound)
1/4 cup water
2 large onions, chopped medium fine (about 2 cups)
1 clove garlic, minced
4 medium carrots, sliced 1/8 inch thick (about 2 1/2 cups)
1 large celery rib, coarsely chopped (about 3/4 cups)
1/4 cup parsley sprigs, minced
2 cups lentils, rinsed
1 17 ounce can peeled plum tomatoes, quartered and undrained
2 1/2 quarts water
1 1/2 tablespoons salt
1/4 teaspoon ground pepper
1 tablespoon dried basil

In a covered saucepot (about 8 quarts), over low heat, cook sausage in the 1/4 cup water until water evaporates. Brown sausage, uncovered, and drain on brown paper or paper towels. Slice 1/2 inch thick and reserve. Pour off all but 1/4 cup of the drippings or if necessary, add enough oil to make that amount; add onion and garlic and cook gently until onion is wilted. Stir in carrots, celery, parsley, lentils, tomatoes, the 2 1/2 quarts water, salt, pepper and basil. Bring to boil, over medium-low heat; simmer, covered, for about 30 minutes. Stir in the sausage and simmer until lentils are tender and flavors are blended, about 20 minutes longer. Makes about 4 quarts.

Lorraine Dabney
GFWC—Lutz/Land O'Lakes Woman's Club
Lutz/Land O'Lakes, Florida

Tuna Chowder

3 cans evaporated milk
2 cans Mexican-style corn
2 cans cream of asparagus soup
2 large cans of white tuna in water
1 cup shredded cheese of your choice
1 tablespoon margarine
1 onion, sauteed
1/2 gallon milk

Cook in double boiler all the ingredients after you have sauteed the onion in 1 tablespoon margarine. Do not overcook. It will curdle if cooked over high heat. Use medium flame.

Gaby Burse
GFWC—Woman's Club of Salem
Salem, New Jersey

Ilse's Potato Soup

½ pound bacon, diced
14 medium potatoes, diced
1 carrot, diced
4 cups water, or just enough to cover potatoes
1½ tablespoons salt
1 teaspoon black pepper
½ teaspoon garlic powder
1 10 ounce package frozen small peas
1 quart half and half cream
1 bunch green onions, thinly sliced

Brown bacon in large soup pot. Remove and drain bacon on paper towel. Add diced potatoes, carrots, water, salt, pepper and garlic powder to the bacon fat. Cook at medium temperature until potatoes are tender. Stir occasionally as potatoes will make the mixture thicker as they cook. Turn off heat. Mash the potatoes slightly. Add the peas and let set for 5 minutes. Stir in half and half cream, chopped green onion and bacon. Stir. Turn on heat and continue cooking on medium heat for about 10 minutes, stirring often. Do not boil. Adjust seasonings to taste. Serve while hot.

"Recipe is about 110 years old. It came from my Alsatian great-grandmother who came to America in 1880."

Helen Wagenhoffer
GFWC—Woman's Club of Dublin
Dublin, California

Old Virginia Pumpkin Soup

3 tablespoons butter
2 cups chicken stock
2 cups whole milk
⅓ teaspoon fresh grated nutmeg
1 small chopped onion
2 tablespoons flour
1 teaspoon sage
7–8 tablespoons thyme
1 tablespoon chopped parsley
Dash paprika
Dash allspice
2 cups pumpkin puree

Melt butter in saucepan; add onion and saute until soft. Add flour and salt, stirring well. Add chicken stock, pumpkin, milk, thyme, nutmeg, sage, paprika, allspice and parsley. Stir until thickened. If using bought canned pumpkin, be sure to use unsweetened. Sugar will affect the flavor.

"Old family recipe. Used by my great-grandmother during the Civil War."

Lucy W. Harris
GFWC—Lynchburg Suburban Woman's Club
Lynchburg, Virginia

Salads, Salad Dressings and Fruit Casseroles

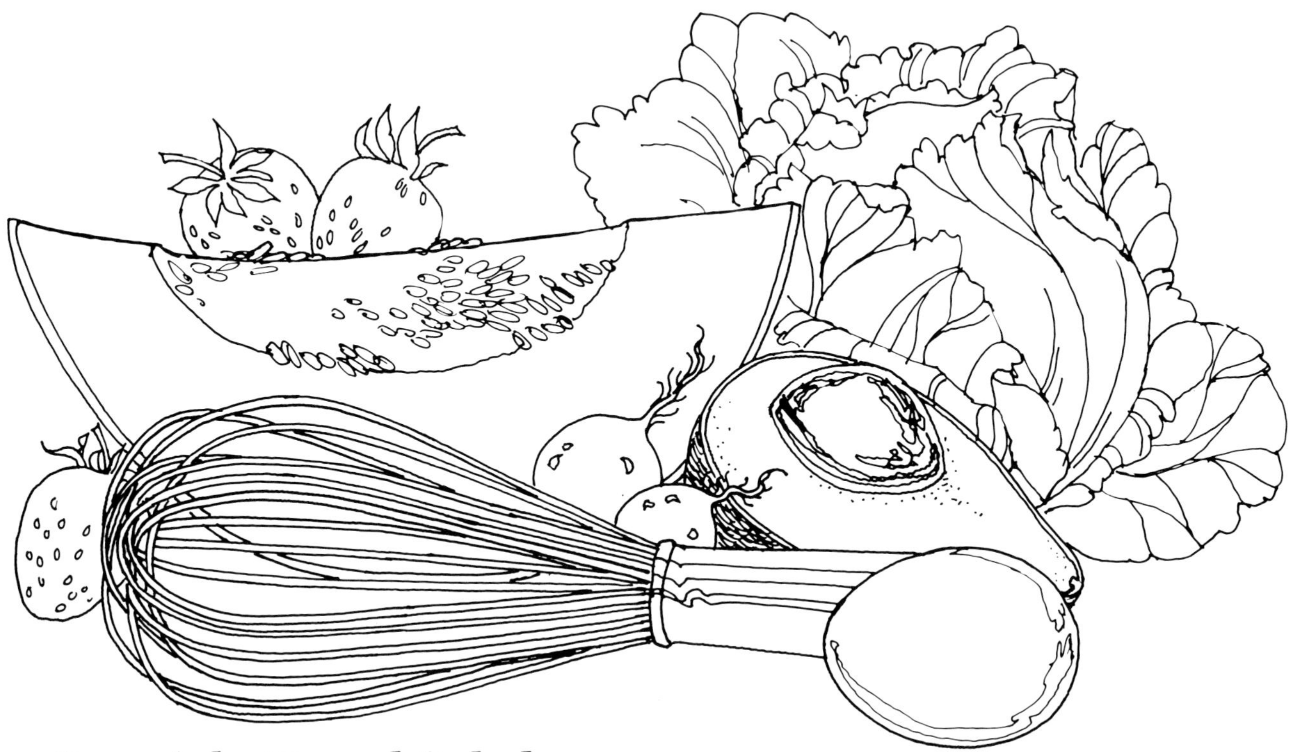

Overnight Tossed Salad

1 medium head lettuce
1 medium onion, chopped fine
½ cup celery, chopped
1 10 ounce package frozen peas
1 cup mayonnaise
2 tablespoons sugar
4 ounces grated cheese
12 ounces bacon, fried and crumbled

Use bowl with tight-fitting lid. Break lettuce into bite-size pieces. Cover with layer of onions and celery. Sprinkle with frozen peas. Cover peas with mayonnaise. Sprinkle sugar on mayonnaise. Next, cover with grated cheese, then bacon. Cover and chill overnight. Do not toss salad until ready to serve.

Helen Shanks
GFWC—Bathgate Study Club
Bathgate, North Dakota

Photo features: Spinach Mold—Page 71
Spinach, Bacon & Apple Salad—Page 60

Spinach, Bacon, Apple Salad

¼ cup salad oil
3 tablespoons red wine vinegar
1 teaspoon sugar
½ teaspoon prepared mustard
Salt and freshly ground pepper
5 slices bacon
1 cup slivered almonds
1 pound fresh spinach, torn into bite-size pieces
2 unpeeled red apples, cored and coarsely chopped

Combine oil, vinegar, sugar, mustard, salt and pepper in jar with tight lid; shake well and refrigerate. Cook bacon, drain well and crumble. Discard all but 1 tablespoon fat. Toast almonds in remaining fat. Combine spinach, bacon, apple and almonds. Just before serving, pour dressing over and toss.

Bernettie E. Swift
GFWC—Artesia Woman's Club
Artesia, New Mexico

Cauliflower Salad

½ head lettuce, broken into pieces
1 medium head cauliflower, broken into very small pieces
8 slices bacon, cooked
1 medium onion, optional
1 cup mayonnaise
¾ cup parmesan cheese

Layer lettuce, cauliflower, onion and crumbled bacon. Top with mayonnaise. Sprinkle with cheese. Let set overnight or several hours. Toss when ready to serve.

Alice Driscoll
GFWC—Lutz/Land O'Lakes Woman's Club
Lutz, Florida

Zesty Spinach Salad with Buttermilk Dressing

- **16 ounces fresh spinach**
- **6 slices bacon, cut into pieces**
- **2 hard-boiled eggs**

Wash spinach; tear into bite-size pieces and drain well. Cook bacon, reserving drippings. Sieve the eggs. Place all in salad bowl.

Dressing

- **¾ cup mayonnaise**
- **1 teaspoon dill weed**
- **¼ teaspoon pepper**
- **½ teaspoon salt**
- **¼ cup sliced green onions**
- **2 tablespoons bacon drippings**
- **1 cup buttermilk**

Dressing: Mix mayonnaise, dill, pepper, salt and onions in a bowl. Add bacon drippings alternately with buttermilk, beating well. Pour dressing over spinach and toss well.

Ruth Dorney
GFWC—Colonial Heights Federated Woman's Club
Colonial Heights, Virginia

Frozen Fruit Salad

- **1 16 ounce can apricots and syrup**
- **1 20 ounce can crushed pineapple and syrup**
- **½ cup water**
- **2 tablespoons lemon juice**
- **1 10 ounce package frozen strawberries, thawed**
- **3 small bananas**
- **½ cup sugar**
- **1 6 ounce can frozen orange juice**

Blend apricots and pineapple with syrup. Add orange juice, water and lemon juice; mix. After blended, add strawberries. Break up slightly. Slice bananas into a 9 × 13 inch pan. Pour mixture on top. Freeze at least 24 hours. Before serving, let set at room temperature about 10 minutes. Cut and serve on lettuce leaf.

Dolores Gioia
GFWC—Art and Literature Club
Parkville, Missouri

Frosted Fruit Salad

- **1 3 ounce package lemon gelatin**
- **1 3 ounce package orange gelatin**
- **2 cups hot water**
- **1½ cups cold water**
- **Juice of one lemon**
- **1 1 pound 4 ounce can crushed pineapple, drained and save juice**
- **2 bananas, diced**
- **1 cup miniature marshmallows or 10 marshmallows, diced**

Dissolve gelatin in hot water, add cold water and lemon juice. Chill until partially set. Fold in pineapple, bananas, and marshmallows. Pour into a 9 × 13 inch pan. Chill until firm.

Topping

- **2 tablespoons flour**
- **½ cup sugar**
- **1 egg, slightly beaten**
- **1 cup pineapple juice**
- **½ cup grated cheese**
- **1 cup cream, whipped**

Mix and cook until thick, stirring constantly. Add 2 tablespoons butter or margarine, stir until dissolved, then cool. When cold, fold in 1 cup whipped cream. Spread on gelatin and sprinkle with ½ cup grated cheese. Refrigerate for several hours until well set. Cut into squares or serve on lettuce. Best when made in morning and served in the evening.

Gudrun Harstad
GFWC—Goose River Pioneer Daughters
Mayville, North Dakota

Fruity-Lemon Freeze

- **2 3 ounce packages cream cheese, softened**
- **½ cup mayonnaise**
- **2 teaspoons lemon juice**
- **1 teaspoon lemon extract**
- **1 8 ounce can crushed pineapple, drained**
- **½ cup diced maraschino cherries**
- **½ cup chopped pecans**
- **2 cups sliced bananas**
- **1 cup whipping cream**
- **½ cup sugar**

Beat cream cheese until smooth. Add mayonnaise, lemon juice and extract; mix well. Stir in pineapple, cherries and pecans. Add bananas, toss gently. Beat whipping cream until foamy; gradually add sugar, beating until soft peaks form. Fold into fruit mixture. Spoon into any mold or type of container you wish; and freeze until firm. (I prefer using foil cup cake paper in a muffin tin.) Serve on lettuce and garnish with a pineapple slice topped with a cherry. Let stand 20 minutes at room temperature before serving.

Mrs. Viney Veum
GFWC—Hoople Monday Nite Study Club
Hoople, North Dakota

Frozen Salad

- **1 3 ounce package cream cheese**
- **½ of 8 ounce carton whipped topping**
- **1 16 ounce can crushed pineapple**
- **12 maraschino cherries, chopped**
- **½ cup mayonnaise**
- **Pinch of salt**

Beat cream cheese with mixer until fluffy. Stir in the whipped topping. Add pineapple, with juice, and chopped cherries. Then add mayonnaise and salt. Stir until well blended. Pour into 6 × 10 inch container. Freeze for at least 6 hours. Remove from freezer 15 minutes before serving.

"I received this recipe from my mother. It has been in our family for more than 50 years."

Mary C. Neff
GFWC—Crestline Woman's Club
Crestline, Ohio

Frozen Mint Salad

- **2 13¼ ounce cans crushed pineapple**
- **1 small package lime gelatin dissolved with 2 cups boiling water**
- **1 10½ ounce package miniature marshmallows stirred into hot gelatin**
- **1 package butter mints, crushed**
- **1 pint whipping cream**
- **¼ teaspoon mint extract**

Mix first three ingredients and set in the refrigerator overnight. Crush butter mints in blender, whip cream and add mint extract. Add crushed butter mints to the gelatin mixture and fold in the whipped cream. Pour into 9 × 13 inch pan. Keep in freezer.

Natalie Orme
GFWC—Ladies Literary League
Nephi, Utah

Mary Ann's Champagne Salad

- **1 8 ounce package cream cheese**
- **¾ cup sugar**
- **1 large can crushed pineapple, drained**
- **1 10 ounce package strawberries, frozen**
- **2 sliced bananas**
- **½ cup chopped nuts**
- **1 large container whipped topping**

Soften and blend cheese with sugar. Blend in whipped topping. Mix in another bowl, drained pineapple, strawberries with juice, bananas and nuts. Blend all together, freeze in a 9 × 13 inch pan. To serve set out 20 minutes. Cut in squares. Can be refrozen.

Caroline Lapeyre
GFWC—Ponderosa Woman's Club
Riverton, Wyoming

Frozen Cranberry Salad

- **1 16 ounce can whole cranberry sauce**
- **2 tablespoons lemon juice**
- **½ pint whipping cream, whipped**
- **¼ cup powdered sugar**
- **1 teaspoon vanilla**
- **¾ cup chopped nuts**

Put cranberry sauce into a 9 × 9 inch glass dish. Add lemon juice and mix. Combine whipped cream, sugar, nuts and vanilla. Spoon over top of cranberry layer and freeze. Remove from freezer half hour before serving. Cut into squares and put on crisp lettuce. Serves 6. I triple this and freeze in 9 × 13 inch glass dish for 16 servings.

Jean Nunnelley
GFWC—Beechmont
Louisville, Kentucky

Apricot Salad

- **4 cups apricot nectar, 2 cups heated for gelatin**
- **2 3 ounce packages lemon gelatin**
- **2½ cups drained, crushed pineapple**
- **8 ounces cream cheese**
- **½ cup mayonnaise**
- **1 cup chopped celery**
- **½ cup chopped walnuts**

Chill the first three ingredients in a 9 × 13 pan. Soften cream cheese, adding the mayonnaise, celery, walnuts and ½ of the gelatin mixture before it sets completely. Pour over the set gelatin and top with crushed walnuts.

Doris Eriksen
GFWC—Woman's Club of St. John
St. John, Washington

Crunchy Fresh Grape Salad

- **3 cups red, seedless grapes, firm and refrigerated**
- **3 cups seedless, green grapes, firm and refrigerated**
- **6 tablespoons dark brown sugar**
- **8 ounces sour cream**
- **1 cup pecan halves**

Rinse grapes in colander. Remove from stems. Make sure they are well-drained. Layer grapes in glass bowl. Smooth sour cream over grapes, as if frosting a cake. Sprinkle dark brown sugar over sour cream. Last, sprinkle the pecan halves over the brown sugar. Do not combine until it is ready to be served.

Judy Stringer
GFWC—Owensboro Junior Woman's Club
Owensboro, Kentucky

Blueberry Salad

- **1 small package pineapple gelatin**
- **3/4 cup boiling water**
- **1/2 pint sour cream**
- **1 small package cherry gelatin**
- **3/4 cup boiling water**
- **1 can blueberry pie filling**

Dissolve pineapple gelatin in water. Cool. With electric hand beater, beat in sour cream. Pour into lightly oiled 9-inch square mold. Chill until almost set. Dissolve cherry gelatin in water. Cool, then stir in pie filling. Pour gently over first layer. Chill until firm.

Ellen N. Penterman
GFWC—Woman's Club of Beaver, Inc.
Beaver, Pennsylvania

Orange-Cream Fruit Salad

- **1 20 ounce can pineapple tidbits**
- **1 10 ounce can mandarin orange slices**
- **1 16 ounce can peach slices**
- **1 3 3/4 ounce package instant vanilla pudding mix**
- **1 cup milk**
- **1/2 cup (1/3 cup) frozen orange juice**
- **2 medium yellow apples, chopped**
- **3 medium bananas, sliced**

Drain canned fruit and put in a large bowl. Beat with rotary beater the instant vanilla pudding mix, milk and frozen orange juice (thawed for 2 minutes). Fold into fruit mixture. Cover and chill. Before serving, add apples and bananas. Serve in lettuce cups. Garnish with mandarin orange sections.

Donna E. Beck
GFWC—Endicott Woman's Club, Inc.
Endicott, New York

Molded Citrus Salad

- **1 1 pound can grapefruit sections**
- **Water**
- **1 3 ounce package lemon gelatin**
- **1 cup buttermilk**
- **1/2 cup minced celery**
- **1/4 cup diced walnuts**
- **1 11 ounce can mandarin orange segments, well drained**
- **Dairy sour cream**
- **Grated citrus peel for garnish**

Drain grapefruit; reserve syrup and add water to make 1 cup. Heat syrup. Add gelatin, stirring until dissolved. Cool to room temperature. Blend buttermilk into cooled gelatin and chill to consistency of unbeaten egg white. Fold celery, nuts, drained grapefruit and orange segments into thickened gelatin. Spoon into 1 quart mold and chill until set. Unmold and serve with sour cream and grated citrus peel for garnish. The buttermilk imparts the tang to the crunchy salad.

Annie Laurie P. Clark
GFWC—Bradenton Woman's Club
Bradenton, Florida

Mandarin Orange Mold

- **1 large package orange gelatin**
- **2 cups boiling water**
- **1 large can undiluted, frozen orange juice**
- **2 cans mandarin oranges, drained**

Dissolve gelatin in boiling water. Add orange juice, stir until completely blended. Add mandarin oranges and chill at least 5 hours. Unmold on large platter. Garnish with fresh mint leaves and fresh orange slices.

"Have had this recipe over 20 years, great color for Thanksgiving."

Shirley A. Drumheller
GFWC—Country Club of Washington Township
Fremont, California

Pineapple-Cheese Salad

- **1 cup crushed pineapple, partially drained**
- **Juice of one lemon**
- **½ cup cold water**
- **½ cup grated American cheese**
- **½ cup chopped walnuts, optional**
- **¾ cup sugar**
- **1 tablespoon unflavored gelatin**
- **½ pint cream, whipped or 1 pint whipped topping**

Boil 5 minutes: pineapple, sugar and lemon juice. Dissolve gelatin in cold water. Add to pineapple mixture and cool until it begins to thicken. Fold in remaining ingredients. Pour into mold. Let set until firm in refrigerator.

Margaret Fitzgerald
GFWC—Gemini
Camas and Washougal, Washington

Rhubarb Salad

- **2 cups rhubarb, cut up**
- **½ cup sugar**
- **¼ cup water**
- **1 small package strawberry gelatin**
- **1 cup hot water**
- **2 tablespoons pineapple, crushed**
- **2 small apples, chopped**
- **¼ cup black walnut meats**

Combine rhubarb, sugar and the ¼ cup water. Bring to a rolling boil, reduce heat and simmer about 5 minutes. Remove from heat and let stand, covered, until partially cooled. Dissolve gelatin in the 1 cup water. Stir and blend in warm rhubarb mixture. Chill until thickened. Fold in pineapple, apple and nuts. Chill until set; can be frozen.

Iris Meseke
GFWC—Ladies Reading Circle
Alma, Kansas

Fruity Ginger Ale Mold

- **1 3 ounce package lemon gelatin**
- **1 cup boiling water**
- **1 cup ginger ale, chilled**
- **1 medium apple, cut in wedges**
- **1 8¼ ounce can pineapple tidbits**
- **1 small apple, chopped**
- **½ cup halved, seedless, green grapes**

Dissolve gelatin in boiling water. Cool to room temperature. Slowly add ginger ale. Arrange apple wedges in 4½ cup mold. Pour in ¾ cup of the gelatin mixture. Chill until almost firm. Chill remaining gelatin until partially set. Fold in pineapple, chopped apple, and halved grapes. Pour over first layer. Chill until firm. Unmold on lettuce lined platter.

Martha Hauser
GFWC—Child Welfare
Winterset, Iowa

Salmon Mousse

- **1 pound can salmon**
- **2 envelopes unflavored gelatin, 2 teaspoons**
- **1 can undiluted tomato soup**
- **½ cup cold water**
- **⅓ cup green pepper, chopped**
- **1 cup margarine**
- **4 tablespoons onion, minced**
- **½ lemon squeezed**
- **⅓ cup grated carrots**
- **1 8 ounce package cream cheese**

Drain and flake salmon. Heat soup. Dissolve gelatin in cold water. Add gelatin and all other ingredients to hot soup. (Cream cheese first). Stir with whisk until smooth mixture. Rinse mold with cold water—line with mayonnaise. Fill. Allow to set in refrigerator for several hours. Unmold—decorate if you wish.

Ethel Lange
GFWC—Woman's Club of South Milwaukee
South Milwaukee, Wisconsin

Cherry-Cola Salad

- **2 packages black cherry gelatin**
- **6 ounces cream cheese, frozen**
- **1 large can crushed pineapple**
- **1 can bing cherries, pitted**
- **1 16 ounce bottle cola**
- **1 cup chopped pecans**

Drain pineapple and cherries. Stir juices in gelatin and heat. Cool and stir in cola. Add cherries, pineapple and pecans. Pour into rectangular glass dish. Freeze cream cheese, then grate and sprinkle on top of salad

Bobbie Sue Finch
GFWC—Twentieth Century Club
Iuka, Mississippi

Jellied Beet Salad

- **1 3 ounce package lemon gelatin**
- **1 cup boiling water**
- **¾ cup beet juice**
- **3 tablespoons cider vinegar**
- **1 cup chopped beets, cooked or canned**
- **½ teaspoon salt**
- **2 tablespoons grated onion**
- **1 tablespoon horseradish or 1 teaspoon instant horseradish in 2 teaspoons water**
- **¾ cup chopped celery**

Dissolve gelatin in boiling water, add beet juice and let thicken. Then add remaining ingredients and pour into mold. Unmold and serve with mayonnaise or favorite dressing.

Arlene E. Dadley
GFWC—Revere Woman's Club
Revere, Massachusetts

Christmas Salad

- **3 small packages strawberry gelatin**
- **1 cup boiling water**
- **1 10 ounce package frozen strawberries**
- **1 16 ounce can crushed pineapple, undrained**
- **1 16 ounce can whole cranberry sauce**
- **1 cup dairy sour cream**

Dissolve gelatin in boiling water. Add frozen strawberries, whole cranberry sauce and undrained, crushed pineapple. Pour half of the mixture into a 9 × 13 inch glass dish or mold. Place in refrigerator until almost firm. Stir sour cream and spread evenly over almost firm gelatin. Spoon remaining gelatin on top of sour cream and refrigerate until set.

Dee Totah
GFWC—Decora Study Club
Victoria, Texas

Deluxe Pineapple/Cranberry Salad

- **1 large package raspberry gelatin**
- **2 cups boiling water**
- **1 20 ounce can crushed pineapple**
- **1 cup chopped walnuts**
- **1 cup celery, finely cut**
- **1 16 ounce can cranberry sauce**
- **1 4 ounce package soft cream cheese**
- **1 pint sour cream**

Mix first six ingredients and place in a 9 × 13 inch pan. Put last two ingredients on top after gelatin is set. Sprinkle more nuts on top.

Marion Koester
GFWC—Colton Woman's Club
Colton, California

Red, White and Blue Salad

2 3 ounce boxes red raspberry gelatin
3 cups hot water
1 envelope unflavored gelatin
½ cup cold water
1 cup milk
1 cup sugar
1 teaspoon vanilla
1 8 ounce package cream cheese, softened
1 cup walnuts, finely chopped
1 16 ounce can blueberries in syrup

First layer:
Dissolve 1 box raspberry gelatin in 2 cups hot water. Pour into 9 × 13 inch pan and allow to set before making the next layer.

Second layer:
Dissolve unflavored gelatin in ½ cup cold water. Combine milk and sugar, heat to scalding point. Stir into gelatin. Add vanilla and cream cheese. Blend thoroughly using a blender or a mixer on high speed. Cool slightly; stir in nuts. Pour over first layer and allow to set before making the next layer.

Third layer:
Dissolve the second box of raspberry gelatin in 1 cup hot water. Add blueberries with their liquid. Pour over second layer and allow to set before serving. Serves 8 to 10.

Helen M. Gibbs
GFWC—Las Noches Woman's Club
Tempe, Arizona

Strawberry Pretzel Salad

2 cups crushed pretzels (Put pretzels in plastic bag. Use a rolling pin to crush but not too fine.)
3 tablespoons sugar
3 cups melted margarine
1 8 ounce package softened cream cheese
½ cup sugar
1 4 ounce package whipped topping, prepared
1 6 ounce package strawberry or raspberry gelatin
2 cups boiling water
2 10 ounce packages strawberries, frozen
1 small can crushed pineapple

Melt margarine, add sugar and mix with pretzels, press into 13 × 9 inch pan or dish. Bake at 400 degrees for 7 minutes. Cool. Cream cheese with sugar; fold into whipped topping. (I use a portable mixer). Spread over pretzel crust to seal. Make gelatin. Add partially thawed strawberries and pineapples. Spread over second layer, refrigerate.

Helen R. Kroesser
GFWC—Ocean City Civic Club
Ocean City, New Jersey

Deviled Egg Salad

1 envelope gelatin
½ cup cold water
1 teaspoon salt
2 teaspoons lemon juice
¼ teaspoon Worcestershire sauce
¾ cup mayonnaise
1½ teaspoons grated onion
½ cup finely diced green pepper
¼ cup diced pimiento, optional
½ cup finely diced celery
Several dashes ground cayenne pepper
1¼ cups or 4 hard-boiled eggs, chopped

Soak gelatin in cold water for 5 minutes. Place over boiling water and stir until gelatin is dissolved. Remove from heat and add the salt, lemon juice and Worcestershire sauce. Cool 10 minutes. Stir in mayonnaise, grated onion, celery, green pepper, pimiento, cayenne pepper and eggs. Turn into a mold, or individual ones, and chill until firm—several hours. Turn out on salad greens and garnish as desired. Ripe olives are good for this. Protein variations: instead of eggs, chopped ham, diced, cooked chicken, tuna, boiled shrimp or crabmeat may be used, but adjust seasoning to taste.

"This was in a magazine ad for gelatin, and I have used it for over 35 years."

Zelma W. Smalling
GFWC—College Community Club
Emory, Virginia

Super Slender Salad

1 3 ounce package sugarless orange gelatin
1¼ cups cottage cheese
½ cup diet mayonnaise
2 tablespoons lemon juice
1 small onion, grated
1 cup grated carrots
1 cup chopped celery
Optional: Chopped cabbage, green pepper, other veggies

Dissolve gelatin in 1 cup boiling water. Cool. Blend cottage cheese until creamy. Add mayonnaise, lemon juice, cooled gelatin; blend thoroughly. Fold in vegetables and mold.

Ruth Ketcham
GFWC—Spencer Federated Woman's Club
Spencer, Iowa

Spinach Mold

- 2 3 ounce packages lemon gelatin
- 1¾ cups hot water to dissolve
- 3 drops tabasco, optional
- 3 tablespoons vinegar
- 1 cup mayonnaise, beat in
- 1 package chopped, frozen spinach, uncooked
- ⅔ cup diced celery
- 2 tablespoons chopped onion
- Salt and pepper to taste
- 1½ cups small curd, cottage cheese, folded in.

Assemble ingredients in order listed—spinach should be partly thawed. Pour into 6-cup mold.

Dot Southerington
GFWC—Park Ridge Woman's Club
Park Ridge, Illinois

Popeye Salad

- 1 package frozen, chopped spinach, thawed and all water squeezed out
- 1 package lemon gelatin
- 1 cup boiling water
- ½ cup cold water
- 1½ tablespoons vinegar
- ½ cup chopped onion
- ¾ cup cottage cheese
- 1 cup mayonnaise
- ⅔ cup chopped celery
- ¼ teaspoon salt
- 4 ounce jar red pimiento

Dissolve lemon gelatin in boiling water. Add cold water, vinegar and salt. Combine remaining ingredients. When gelatin is partially set, add the remaining ingredients. Refrigerate. Pan can be a mold or 9 inch square pan.

Eleanor M. Baird
GFWC—Mediapolis Study Club
Mediapolis, Iowa

Five Minute Tomato Aspic

- 1 can tomato sauce
- 1 package orange or lemon flavored gelatin
- 1¼ cups hot water
- 1½ tablespoons vinegar
- ½ teaspoon salt
- Dash pepper

Dissolve gelatin in hot water. Add tomato sauce and other ingredients. Blend together. Pour into molds and chill. Makes 4–6 servings. For extra spice add any of the following before chilling: celery salt, grated onion, horseradish or Worcestershire sauce.

Virginia S. Davis
GFWC—Chesmond Woman's Club
Richmond, Virginia

Shrimp Spread Mold

- **1 can tomato soup**
- **3 3 ounce packages cream cheese**
- **1 tablespoon unflavored gelatin**
- **2 4½ ounce cans, very small, deveined shrimp**
- **1 cup mayonnaise**
- **¾ cup finely chopped celery**
- **½ cup finely chopped onion**
- **Salt and pepper to taste**

Soak gelatin in a little less than ¼ cup water. Heat cheese in soup. Add gelatin and cool. Mix celery, onion, salt, pepper and mayonnaise. Add to soup mix. Pour layer of mix into gelatin mold, then a layer of shrimp. Continue alternating, ending with a layer of mix. Chill at least 1 hour before serving.

Jackie Lester
GFWC—North Coast Junior Woman's Club
Carlsbad, California

Marinated Pork Salads

- **1 pound pork cutlets**
- **2 tablespoons mayonnaise**
- **2 teaspoons Worcestershire sauce**
- **½ cup croutons**
- **4 cups lettuce, washed and torn**
- **⅓ bottle Italian dressing**
- **1 tablespoon lemon juice**
- **4 drops hot pepper sauce**
- **2 tablespoons shredded cheese**
- **Pepper**

Cut cutlets in small strips. Marinate in the Italian dressing for 2 hours, turning occasionally. Combine mayonnaise, lemon juice, Worcestershire sauce and hot pepper sauce. Cover pork with this sauce and broil 3 minutes on each side. Toss pork, lettuce and croutons. Then add cheese and pepper; mix together. Serve topped with mayonnaise and cheese.

Mildred Rohrer
GFWC—Cary Circle
Wellington, Kansas

Emerald Salad

- **1 can fruit cocktail**
- **1 package lime gelatin**
- **¾ cup evaporated milk**
- **¼ teaspoon salt**
- **½ cup nuts**

Drain juice from fruit cocktail. Add enough water to juice to make 1½ cups. Heat juice and stir in gelatin. Chill thoroughly. Stir in milk and salt. Chill until slightly thicker than unbeaten egg whites. Beat mixture until foamy. Fold in fruit and nuts. Pour into greased mold. Chill thoroughly before serving.

"I have had this recipe for 38–40 years."

Louise M. Woodall
GFWC—Panarama
Birmingham, Alabama

Baked Seafood Salad

- **1 medium green pepper, chopped**
- **1 medium onion, chopped**
- **1 cup diced celery**
- **1 6½ ounce can crabmeat, flaked**
- **1 5¾ ounce can smallest shrimp**
- **1½ cups cooked rice**
- **½ teaspoon salt**
- **⅛ teaspoon pepper**
- **1 teaspoon Worcestershire sauce**
- **1 cup mayonnaise**
- **1 cup bread crumbs, buttered**

Combine all ingredients except bread crumbs. Place in baking dish and crumble bread crumbs on top. Bake at 350 degrees for 30 minutes.

Barbara S. Stone
GFWC—Junior Woman's Club
Stuttgart, Arkansas

All-You-Want-For-Lunch Salad

- **1 cup carrots, grated**
- **1 cup celery, chopped**
- **2 7 ounce cans light tuna**
- **1 cup lite mayonnaise**
- **1 small onion, chopped**
- **Dash of salt**
- **2 hard-boiled eggs**
- **1 can shoestring potatoes**

Combine and chill the first 5 ingredients with salt. Before serving, add shoestring potatoes and garnish with parsley and fresh tomatoes, if in season. Eggs may be used as garnish or added with the first five ingredients.

Virginia Sachau
GFWC—Cedar Heights Woman's Club
Cedar Falls, Iowa

Colonial Salad

- **2 3 ounce packages orange gelatin**
- **1 cup salad dressing**
- **1 13½ ounce can drained, crushed pineapple**
- **½ cup chopped celery**
- **2 cups boiling water**
- **1½ cups grated carrots**
- **½ cup chopped raisins, optional**

Prepare orange gelatin in boiling water. Let cool. Add salad dressing and remaining ingredients. Chill.

Mildred Piontek
GFWC—Gemini
Camas and Washougal, Washington

A Dieter's Dream Shrimp Salad

1 4½ ounce can shrimp
1 1 pound can cut green beans
1 garlic clove, thinly sliced
1 tablespoon salad oil
¼ teaspoon dry mustard
½ teaspoon sugar
¼ cup vinegar
2 chicken bouillon cubes
⅔ cup uncooked rice
1 cup sliced celery
½ cup sliced scallions
2 cups shredded crisp lettuce
Soy sauce, optional

Drain shrimp and beans, reserving the bean liquid. Crush garlic in a large salad bowl. Add oil, mustard, sugar, vinegar, shrimp and beans. Toss well; refrigerate. Heat bean liquid; add bouillon cubes and stir until dissolved. Add enough water to make two cups. Add rice and cook rapidly, uncovered, about 8 minutes or until rice stands above water line. Reduce heat; cover and steam 12 or 14 minutes. Spread rice in shallow pan to cool. Refrigerate 10 minutes or until needed. At serving time, add rice to shrimp and bean mixture; toss together with celery, onion and lettuce. Serve with soy sauce.

Helen Wellman
GFWC—Westmoreland Woman's Club
Huntington, West Virginia

Shrimp Ring

1 bunch green onions, chopped
1 cup celery
1 can mushroom soup
8 ounces cream cheese
¾ cup mayonnaise
1¼ envelopes gelatin
3 tablespoons cold water
½ pound shrimp
½ teaspoon dill weed

Warm soup; add gelatin that has been softened in water. Mix in soft cream cheese and mayonnaise. Add hot soup, heat until smooth. Add remaining ingredients. Fill one-quart ring mold. Rinse mold in cold water before filling. Chill and let congeal.

Emma Belle Armistead
GFWC—The Worthwhile Club
Thomasville, Alabama

Bombay Salad

- 2 7 ounce cans shrimp or tuna
- 1½ cups cold cooked rice
- 1 cup chopped celery
- Dash lemon juice
- ½ to 1 teaspoon curry powder
- ½ teaspoon salt
- ⅛ teaspoon pepper
- ½ cup mayonnaise
- 4 tablespoons chopped green pepper
- 1 cup raisins
- 1 cup Spanish peanuts

Drain tuna or shrimp. Mix all ingredients, except green pepper, raisins and peanuts. Chill. Add remaining ingredients just before serving.

Marge Griffin
GFWC—Orangevale Woman's Club
Orangevale, California

Tomato Soup Salad

- 1 package lemon gelatin
- 1 cup mayonnaise
- 1 large carton cottage cheese
- ½ cup diced green pepper
- 1 can tomato soup
- 1 can small shrimp
- ½ cup diced onion
- ½ cup celery

Heat soup to boiling and add gelatin; cool. Mix cottage cheese and mayonnaise. Add to soup mixture and then add other ingredients. Chill. Serve on a bed of lettuce. Add slices of avocado for special touch.

"Recipe file dated 1969 from a friend."

Lois C. Mills
GFWC—Norwalk Woman's Club
Norwalk, California

Shrimp Macaroni Salad

- 2½ cups shell macaroni
- 1½ pounds small, cooked shrimp
- ⅔ cup chopped celery
- 1 medium onion, chopped
- 1 cup salad dressing
- ¼ cup catsup
- ½ cup sweet pepper relish
- Juice of 1 lemon
- 2 dashes hot sauce
- ½ teaspoon salt
- ¼ teaspoon pepper

Cook macaroni according to package directions; drain; rinse with cold water; drain. Combine macaroni, shrimp, celery and onion; mixing well. Stir together remaining ingredients. Pour salad dressing mixture over macaroni mixture; stir well. Chill.

Louise Farley
GFWC—Woman's Club of South Charleston
South Charleston, West Virginia

Informal Salmon Salad Loaf

- **1 cup ripe olives, pitted**
- **2 cups or 1 large can flaked, canned salmon**
- **2 cups shredded raw carrot**
- **1 cup finely cut celery**
- **½ cup pickle relish**
- **1 pint cottage cheese**
- **1 cup mayonnaise**
- **2 tablespoons lemon juice**
- **2 teaspoons salt**
- **Few drops tabasco sauce**
- **1½ tablespoons plain gelatin, ½ teaspoon more in hot weather**
- **¼ cup cold water**

Combine olives, salmon, carrot, celery, pickle relish, lemon juice, salt and tabasco sauce. Soften gelatin in cold water and dissolve thoroughly. Blend the cottage cheese with mayonnaise; add dissolved gelatin and mix well. Combine with olive-vegetable mixture and blend thoroughly. Pour into loaf pan or fish mold and chill. Unmold onto platter garnished with salad greens; use sliced olive for eye if fish mold is used. Served with hot rolls, this makes a filling luncheon or Sunday night supper.

Dorothy S. Sudrabin
GFWC—Past Presidents' Club Sixth District
Berkeley Heights, New Jersey

Beef Spinach Salad

- **3 cups cooked roast beef, sliced in thin strips**
- **3 cups cooked long grain and wild rice**
- **1 cup Italian dressing**
- **1 tablespoon soy sauce**
- **6 sliced mushrooms**
- **½ teaspoon sugar**
- **¾ cup celery, sliced thin**
- **2 cups firmly-packed fresh spinach, torn in pieces**
- **1 medium zucchini, thinly sliced and halved**
- **½ cup dry roasted sunflower seeds**

Combine ½ cup of the Italian dressing, soy sauce and sugar with the cooked rice, blend well. Add the roast beef and remaining ½ cup dressing. Cover and place in refrigerator to chill. Add remaining ingredients and toss just before serving. Garnish with cherry tomatoes.

Hilda Van Valkenburg
GFWC—North Park Woman's Club
Walden, Colorado

Mandarin Chicken Salad

- **3 cups cooked chicken, cut-up**
- **1 tablespoon minced onion**
- **1 teaspoon salt**
- **2 tablespoons fresh lemon juice**
- **1 cup thinly sliced celery**
- **1 cup seedless grapes**
- **⅓ cup salad dressing**
- **1 11 ounce can mandarin orange segments, drained**
- **½ cup toasted, slivered almonds**
- **6 lettuce cups**
- **6 pitted ripe olives**

In bowl, combine chicken, onion, salt, lemon juice, celery. Refrigerate several hours or until well chilled. At serving time, toss chicken mixture lightly with grapes, mayonnaise and all but a few orange segments and almonds. Line salad bowl with lettuce cups. Arrange chicken mixture on top; garnish with reserved orange segments, almonds and ripe olives. Makes 6 servings.

Dot Dellinger
GFWC—Grundy Woman's Club
Grundy, Virginia

Fruit, Cheese and Tuna Salad

- **½ cup mayonnaise**
- **1 cup dairy sour cream**
- **1 tablespoon fresh lemon juice**
- **¼ teaspoon curry powder**
- **⅛ teaspoon dried thyme**
- **1 7 ounce can tuna in spring water, drained and flaked**
- **2 cups Danish cheese, diced**
- **1 cup seedless grapes, halved**
- **1 cup fresh apple, diced, not peeled**
- **2 cups cooked, small macaroni**

Blend together mayonnaise, sour cream, lemon juice and spices. Fold in remaining ingredients. Serve on lettuce leaves; decorate with small bunch of grapes and several slices of unpeeled apple.

Helen C. Pikul Walker
GFWC—East Brunswick Woman's Club
East Brunswick, New Jersey

Rice and Shrimp Salad

1 package chicken Rice-A-Roni, cooked as per package directions
½ pound cooked fresh shrimp, or crab
1 can water chestnuts, chopped, or turnip
1 jar marinated artichoke hearts, drained and chopped
½ cup green onions, chopped
½ cup green pepper, chopped
1 cup mayonnaise, more or less to moisten, as desired

Mix well and season with curry, salt and pepper, as desired. Chill well and serve.

Mildred Stebbins
GFWC—Monday Alpha Club
Sacramento, California

Dairyland Summer Salad

½ cup sour cream
½ cup mayonnaise
½ cup shell macaroni
½ pound ground beef
Salt and pepper to taste
3 cups torn fresh spinach
½ cup radish, sliced
½ cup celery, sliced
2 green onions, chopped
½ cup cucumber, sliced
1½ cups cheddar cheese, shredded

Mix the sour cream and mayonnaise. Set aside. Cook the macaroni until almost done; drain, rinse and cool. Brown the beef, add salt and pepper. Drain. In bowl, combine the macaroni, browned beef, spinach, radish, celery, onion, cucumber and shredded cheese. Add the sour cream and mayonnaise. Toss well.

Topping

1 cup cottage cheese
1 cup plain yogurt
Salt and pepper to taste
6 slices bacon
Parsley flakes

In blender, mix the cottage cheese, yogurt, salt and pepper. Spread over salad. Cover and chill 1 hour. Cook and crumble the bacon. Top with bacon before serving. Sprinkle with parsley flakes. Serve with buttered toast.

Ethel Mueller
GFWC—Chilton Woman's Club
Chilton, Wisconsin

My Emergency Pasta Salad

- 1 16 ounce package of your favorite pasta
- 1 16 ounce package frozen vegetables—broccoli, cauliflower, carrots
- 1 bottle zesty Italian dressing
- Green onions
- Parmesan cheese to taste
- Optional ingredients:
- Fresh or canned mushrooms
- Red or green peppers
- Red onions
- Celery
- Canned peas
- Ham
- Zucchini
- Pimientos
- Cucumbers
- Olives
- Tomatoes
- Pepperoni
- Smoked sausage
- Favorite cheese

Cook pasta as directed, cool, add frozen vegetables, green onions and dressing. Add parmesan to taste. You may then add any of the optional ingredients. Refrigerate.

Lois Jones
GFWC—TFWC Contemporary Woman's Society of Kingsport
Kingsport, Tennessee

Nadine's Pasta Salad

- 1 box of rotini pasta (orange, green, white spirals)
- 1 box small shell pasta
- 1 chopped green pepper
- 1 large jar pimientos
- Salt and pepper to taste
- 2 carrots, chopped
- ¼ cup minced onion
- 2 stalks chopped celery
- 1 large bottle Italian dressing

Cook pasta according to directions on box. Drain well. Add other ingredients in order given. Add salt and pepper to taste. Add entire bottle of dressing. Mix well. Refrigerate overnight.

Nadine Phillips
GFWC—Woman's Club of Fort Mill
Fort Mill, South Carolina

Spaghetti Salad

- **2 tomatoes, cut in small pieces**
- **2 cucumbers, cut in small pieces**
- **2 green peppers, cut in small pieces**
- **6 green onions, tops and all, cut in small pieces**
- **1 16 ounce bottle of Italian dressing**
- **½ cup parmesan cheese**
- **½ bottle of salad supreme**
- **1 pound thin spaghetti, cooked and drained**

Mix together Italian dressing, parmesan cheese and salad supreme. Cook and rinse spaghetti with cold water and drain well. Add cut up vegetables, pour dressing over, and mix well. Make one or two days ahead.

Mrs. Arthur G. Kern
GFWC—Dwight Woman's Club
Dwight, Illinois

Oriental Pea Pod and Chicken Salad

- **1 cup spiral macaroni**
- **2 cups fresh pea pods, blanched**
- **2 cups cubed cooked chicken**
- **½ cup sliced green onions**
- **½ cup sliced water chestnuts**
- **Lettuce leaves**
- **½ cup mayonnaise**
- **1 tablespoon soy sauce**
- **¼ teaspoon pepper**
- **½ teaspoon ginger**
- **1 tablespoon sherry, optional**
- **¼ cup toasted slivered almonds**

Cook macaroni, drain and rinse. In large bowl, combine macaroni, pea pods, chicken, onions and water chestnuts. In small bowl blend mayonnaise, soy sauce, pepper, ginger and sherry. Pour over pea pod mixture. Mix well. Cover and refrigerate at least 3 hours. Line serving bowl with lettuce leaves and garnish with almonds.

Melba L. Mielke
GFWC—Streamwood Junior Woman's Club
Streamwood, Illinois

Garden Pasta Salad

1 12 ounce package pasta twists
3/4 cup onion, chopped
3/4 cup fresh green peppers, chopped
3/4 cup fresh carrots, chopped
3/4 cup celery, chopped
3/4 cup frozen peas, thawed
2 large eggs
16 ounces ricotta cheese
1/2 teaspoon crushed mint
1/2 teaspoon salt

Cook pasta and drain. Mix eggs, ricotta, mint and salt in separate bowl. Add ricotta mixture to pasta. Add chopped vegetables and peas. Mix thoroughly. Chill and serve. To turn this into a main dish, simply add cooked, chopped chicken, shrimp or crab.

Patricia Briguglio
GFWC—The Woman's City Club of Norwich
Norwich, Connecticut

Spaghetti And Pea Salad

7 or 8 ounces very thin spaghetti
1/4 cup mayonnaise
16 ounce can small sweet peas, drained
2 ounce jar chopped pimientoes, drained
2 tablespoons grated onion
2 tablespoons celery seeds

Cook, wash, drain and cool spaghetti. Mix with other ingredients and let stand in refrigerator overnight.

"This was my mother's recipe long before pasta salads. I have modernized it with accurate measurements."

Martha Melton Roberson
GFWC—Tifton 20th Century Library Club
Tifton, Georgia

Sweet and Sour Macaroni Salad

3/4 cup sugar
3/4 cup oil
3/4 cup vinegar (wine vinegar is good)
1 can tomato soup
1 teaspoon salt
1 pound small shell macaroni
1 large onion, chopped
2 green peppers, chopped
3 cucumbers, sliced and quartered
1 jar pimientos, drained

Put first 5 ingredients in blender and blend well. Cook macaroni and rinse well. Mix all ingredients and marinate for 24 hours before serving, stirring occasionally.

Janet W. Stephenson
GFWC—Woman's Club of Ripley
Ripley, West Virginia

Pea Salad

1 16 ounce package frozen peas, do not cook
1 cup sweet relish
1 cup Spanish peanuts
Salad dressing to taste
Sugar to taste

Mix all ingredients. Serve in a salad dish.

Helen M. Gibbs
GFWC—Las Noches Woman's Club
Tempe, Arizona

Cornbread Salad

2 packages cornbread mix
½ cup celery, diced
½ cup green pepper, diced
½ cup green onion, diced
2 firm, ripe tomatoes, coarsely chopped
1 can whole corn, drained
3 boiled eggs, grated
1 cup or more mayonnaise
Salt and pepper to taste

Prepare cornbread as directed on package. Cool. Crumble and mix with other ingredients. Garnish with green pepper rings.

Annette White
GFWC—Lyda Wright Club
Gurdon, Arkansas

Broccoli Salad Deluxe

2 bunches broccoli
1 small head cauliflower
1 shredded carrot
1 onion, grated
10 strips bacon, fried crisp
½ cup unsalted peanuts
⅔ cup raisins
1½ cups mayonnaise
⅓ cup sugar
4–6 tablespoons vinegar

Wash and prepare vegetables. Break off flowering buds from broccoli and cauliflower. Mix with shredded carrot, grated onion, crumbled bacon, nuts and raisins. Mix mayonnaise, sugar and vinegar (to taste) together. Pour mixture over vegetables and toss until well coated.

Olive H. Milgate
GFWC—Woman's Club of Ocean City
Ocean City, Maryland

Broccoli Salad Supreme

- **4 cups chopped raw broccoli**
- **1 cup chopped celery**
- **1/4 cup chopped green onion**
- **1/2 pound bacon, fried crisp and crumbled**
- **2/3 cup slivered almonds, toasted**
- **1 cup seedless green grapes**
- **1 cup seedless red grapes**
- **1/3 cup sugar**
- **1 cup mayonnaise**
- **1 tablespoon vinegar**

Toss together the vegetables, bacon, nuts and grapes. Mix the sugar, mayonnaise and vinegar to make a dressing. Pour dressing over mixture and stir gently to allow dressing to coat evenly. Refrigerate overnight before serving if time allows for flavors to mix.

Joan Krafka Meany
GFWC—Cedar Falls Junior Woman's Club
Cedar Falls, Iowa

Parmesan Potato Salad

- **2 pounds red potatoes**
- **1 9 ounce package frozen French style green beans**
- **1 cup creamy cucumber dressing**
- **1/3 cup chopped parsley**
- **1/4 cup grated parmesan cheese**
- **1 13 3/4 ounce jar marinated artichoke hearts, drained and quartered.**

Cook potatoes 25–30 minutes uncovered in boiling, salted water. Drain and chill one hour. Slice. Cook beans according to package directions. Drain. In small bowl, combine dressing, cheese and parsley. Mix well. In large bowl, combine potatoes, green beans and artichoke hearts. Toss gently with dressing mixture. Cover and chill at least one hour before serving.

Rika Simmons
GFWC—Mequon-Thiensville Junior Woman's Club
Mequon, Wisconsin

Pea Salad

- **3 cans green peas, drained**
- **1 medium onion, chopped**
- **3/4 cup celery, diced**
- **2 hard-cooked eggs, chopped**
- **1/2 green pepper, chopped—optional**
- **2/3 cup cheese, diced**
- **1 cup cooked macaroni**
- **Salt and pepper to taste**
- **Mayonnaise to taste**

Mix all ingredients and chill.

"A recipe of my late, great aunt. This was a family favorite and was always on the table at family dinners."

Carolynn Hickey Greenwood
GFWC—Madisonville Woman's Club
Madisonville, Tennessee

Cucumber Salad

3 large cucumbers
1 green pepper, sliced
1 onion, sliced if desired
4 stalks celery, sliced or chopped
1 cup tomato, cut into bite-sized pieces
1 pint sour cream
Salt to preferred taste
¼–½ cup vinegar
Sprinkle of pepper

Pare and slice cucumbers. Sprinkle with salt and let stand for 30 minutes. Drain off water that has accumulated. Mix sour cream and vinegar well; coat cucumbers with sour cream and vinegar. Add onion, celery and peppers. Sprinkle with pepper. Add tomatoes before serving. If crisp cucumbers are preferred, omit the 30 minutes waiting time, otherwise, cucumbers will be slightly wilted. May be fixed ahead of time. Better chilled.

"Handed down from my Czech mother who came to the U.S. in 1907 at age nine. Usually made from garden fresh vegetables."

Marguerite Gauntt
GFWC—Woman's Literary Club
Rochester, Texas

Spinach Salad

1 large bunch spinach
1 small onion, sliced
8 ounces mushrooms, sliced
1 hard boiled egg
⅓ cup parmesan cheese
⅓ cup safflower oil
¼ cup sugar
2 tablespoons vinegar (cider)
½ teaspoon dry mustard

Thoroughly wash spinach but do not soak. Remove stems and gently tear large leaves into bite-size pieces. Pat dry before tearing or spin in vegetable spinner. In large bowl put spinach, mushrooms, chopped egg, parmesan cheese and onion. Toss gently. Blend oil, sugar, vinegar and dry mustard. Beat with egg beater until mixture becomes thick and milky color. Pour dressing over salad and toss. Serve immediately.

Amy Rearick
GFWC—Junior Woman's Club of Milton
Milton, Pennsylvania

Egg White Salad

2 extra large, hard-boiled eggs, use only whites in salad
1 tablespoon minced onions
1 tablespoon chopped celery
4 sprigs parsley, chopped
1 tablespoon "lite" mayonnaise or salad dressing

Mix all ingredients together and serve on lettuce, crumbling a bit of yolk on top of your salad.

Adalaide Horneff
GFWC—Woman's Club of Cherry Hill
Cherry Hill, New Jersey

Wild Rice Spinach Salad

2 cups cooked rice
½ pound fresh spinach
1 small onion, minced
4 hard-cooked eggs, chopped
½ cup frozen peas
¼ cup diced celery
6 medium fresh mushrooms
½ cup pimiento, chopped
½ cup walnuts, broken
Mushrooms

Dressing

6 slices bacon, save grease
1 cup olive oil
1 teaspoon lemon juice
¼ cup wine vinegar
1 crushed fresh clove garlic
Salt and pepper

Cook wild rice, rinse, drain and chill. Wash and trim spinach; save some leaves for garnishing side of bowl. Tear remainder into large bowl. Cook bacon strips, drain, cool and crumble. In a small bowl, mix olive oil, ¼ cup more or less of bacon grease, lemon juice, vinegar, garlic, salt and pepper. Add rice to spinach; then add onion, celery, mushrooms, pimiento, nuts and eggs. Sprinkle with crumbled bacon. Pour half the dressing on and toss lightly. Add remaining dressing and toss again. Garnish with spinach leaves around edge.

Phyllis Anderson
GFWC—Tomah Woman's Club
Tomah, Wisconsin

One Can Salad

1 16 ounce can cut green beans
1 16 ounce can sweet peas
1 15 ounce can kidney beans
1 12 ounce can Mexicorn
1 4 ounce can green chilies
1 4 ounce can waterpacked mushrooms
2 chopped bell peppers
¼ cup vinegar
3–4 tablespoons sugar
1 4 ounce jar Italian salad dressing
Salt and pepper to taste

Open all canned goods. Drain, rinse and put in large bowl. Add bell peppers and mix. Add vinegar, sugar, salad dressing, salt and pepper. Cover and marinate in refrigerator overnight.

Johnnie Taylor
GFWC—Unique Club
Opelousas, Louisiana

Lake Arrowhead Chinese Slaw

Salad

2 tablespoons oil
¼ cup sliced almonds
¼ cup sesame seeds
10 green onions, finely sliced
½ head green cabbage, finely chopped
½ head red cabbage, finely chopped
2 3 ounce packages ramen noodles, broken

In a heated skillet with oil, toast sesame seeds and almonds until lightly browned. Combine with onions, cabbage, noodles and dressing. Cover and chill several hours. Do not cook noodles; do not use flavor packet.

Dressing

¼ cup sugar
1 teaspoon black pepper
½ teaspoon salt
1 cup oil
6 tablespoons rice vinegar
1 teaspoon M.S.G.

Combine and mix well.

Lois Hurwicz
GFWC—Woman's Club of Lake Arrowhead
Lake Arrowhead, California

Tortellini Vegetable Salad

1 16 ounce bag frozen broccoli, carrots and cauliflower combination
1 10 ounce package frozen broccoli flowerets
1 7 ounce package cheese-filled tortellini
1 8 ounce bottle Italian dressing
2 tablespoons mustard, dijon style

Cook broccoli, carrots, cauliflower and broccoli flowerets in boiling water for 3 minutes. Put immediately into ice water. When cool drain well. Cool tortellini according to package directions. Drain well. Combine vegetables and tortellini. Mix mustard and dressing, pour over and toss. Chill.

Ruth Best
GFWC—Burlington Woman's Club
Burlington, North Carolina

Cajun Red Bean Salad

2 16 ounce cans red beans, drained and rinsed
3 medium potatoes, cooked, peeled and cubed
2 Polish sausages, sliced (about ½ pound)
1 small onion, chopped
2 teaspoons horseradish mustard
3 tablespoons vinegar
2 tablespoons salad oil
4 tablespoons mayonnaise
½ teaspoon herb seasoning

Combine beans, potatoes, Polish sausage and onion. Combine remaining ingredients well. Toss all together. Chill. Rich in fiber.

Dorothy Milburn
GFWC—Richfield Study and Social Club
Richfield, Kansas

White Peg Corn Salad

1 can white peg corn
½ cup sliced green onions, including tops
1 green pepper
1 can diced pimientos
1 cup celery
1 package frozen peas
⅓ cup vinegar
¼ cup vegetable oil
⅓ cup sugar
Salt to taste

Mix together and refrigerate overnight.

Mildred Stebbins
GFWC—North Sacramento Woman's Club
Sacramento, California

Shoe Peg Salad

¾ cup sugar
½ cup oil
¾ cup vinegar
1 teaspoon salt
1 teaspoon pepper
1 17 ounce can tiny peas
1 17 ounce can French cut beans
1 can shoe peg corn, white
1 small jar cut pimiento
½ cup chopped celery

Mix sugar, oil, vinegar, salt and pepper. Boil and let cool. Drain peas, beans, corn and pimiento. Chop celery and onion fine. Mix drained vegetables; add pimiento, celery and onion. Cover with cooled dressing. Mix salad, let stand overnight.

Edith L. Fouts
GFWC—Terrace Heights Federated Woman's Club
Yakima, Washington

Tomato/Onion Mint Salad

- **1 ripe fresh tomato, sliced**
- **2–3 green onions, chopped or ¼ cup chopped sweet onion**
- **1 tablespoon chopped fresh mint**
- **Salt to taste**

About 30 minutes before serving, sprinkle tomato slices with onion and mint. Salt lightly. Refrigerate. For added servings, simply make layers of tomato/onion/mint. Be sure to salt each layer.

Anna W. Peterson
GFWC—Woman's Club of Buckingham County
Buckingham, Virginia

Hot Fruit Casserole

- **1 No. 2 can peach halves**
- **1 No. 2 can pear halves**
- **1 No. 2 can apricot halves**
- **1 No. 2 can pineapple chunks**
- **1 bottle red maraschino cherries**
- **1 dozen macaroon cookies**
- **2 ounce slivered almonds**
- **4 tablespoons butter**
- **½ cup brown sugar**

Drain all fruit and save juices. Layer fruit in a clear glass casserole. Bring to a boil ½ cup of juice, butter and brown sugar. Pour this over the fruit. Top with almonds and crushed macaroons. Bake covered at 350 degrees for 20 minutes. Uncover. Bake additional 10 minutes.

Myrna Johnson
GFWC—Northwood Literary Club
Northwood, North Dakota

Pineapple Souffle

- **1 large can crushed pineapple, drained**
- **1 cup pineapple juice, if necessary add water to make 1 cup**
- **1 cup sugar**
- **3 tablespoons flour**
- **1 stick oleo**
- **4 slices bread, cubed or crumbled**

Combine juice, flour and sugar; cook until thick. Add stick of oleo. Set aside to cool slightly. Combine bread crumbs and pineapple. Pour in casserole and pour liquid mixture over bread and pineapple. Gently work this together to blend well. Bake at 350 degrees for 30 minutes or until golden brown.

Lorain Middleton
GFWC—Jacksonville Woman's Club
Jacksonville, Illinois

Buttery Cinnamon Skillet Apples

1/3 cup margarine or butter
1/2 cup sugar
2 tablespoons cornstarch
1 1/2 cup water
1/2 teaspoon cinnamon
6 medium cooking apples, cored, peeled and cut in half

In skillet melt butter over medium heat. Stir in sugar and cornstarch; mix well. Add remaining ingredients. Cover; cook over medium heat, spooning sauce over apples occasionally until apples are fork tender and sauce is thickened (12–15 minutes). To serve, place 2 apple halves in dish; spoon sauce on top. Can be served with main dish or used as a dessert.

Judy D. Burner
GFWC—Abingdon Junior Woman's Club
Gloucester, Virginia

Spiced Apple Rings

2 cups water
1 cup white sugar
1/4 teaspoon cinnamon
Red food coloring
8–10 cooking apples

Bring above ingredients, except apples, to a boil. Drop peeled apples, cut into rings, into mixture and cook until tender.

Marilyn V. Knoop
GFWC—Fort Mill Woman's Club
Fort Mill, South Carolina

Carrot and Apple Casserole

1 bunch or can cooked carrots
1 can pineapple or apple pie filling
1/2 cup sugar
Butter

Mix first three ingredients. Dot with butter and bake about 45 minutes at 350 degrees.

Mrs. Gordon P. Hogan
GFWC—Pierian
Ruston, Louisiana

Hot Pineapple Casserole

2 cans chunk pineapple
1/2 stick butter or oleo
5 tablespoons plain flour
3/4 cup sugar
1 1/2 cups grated cheddar cheese
3/4 cup crushed buttered crackers

Drain pineapple and put in large casserole dish. Mix flour and sugar and pour over pineapple. Add cheese as next layer. Sprinkle crackers on top. Melt butter and pour over all. Bake at 350 degrees for 30 minutes.

Emma Frank Bowers
GFWC—The Woman's Study Club
Clanton, Alabama

Zero Dressing

2 cups tomato juice
½ envelope unflavored gelatin
Juice of 2 lemons
½ teaspoon dry mustard
1 cup finely chopped celery
¼ cup chopped onion
½ cup chopped green pepper
Parsley, if desired
Salt, pepper and artificial sweetener to taste

Soften gelatin in juice, heat to dissolve. Add lemon juice and mustard. Cool. Add remaining ingredients. Refrigerate. Use as dressing on lettuce or vegetable salads.

"This is considered a 'no calorie' salad dressing for dieters."

Anita Hamm
GFWC—Nemaha Federated Woman's Club
Nemaha, Iowa

Honey Fruit Dressing

½ cup sugar
½ teaspoon celery seed or ¼ teaspoon celery salt
1 teaspoon dry mustard
¼ teaspoon onion salt
½ cup honey
⅓ cup lime juice
1 cup cooking oil

In small bowl, combine sugar, celery seed, dry mustard and onion salt; mix well. Beat in honey and lime juice at low speed of electric mixer. Gradually pour oil in a thin stream while beating at high speed. Serve over cantaloupe wedges, honeydew melon wedges, fresh grapes and fresh strawberries made up on a lettuce bed.

Verona Schlueter
GFWC—Beemer Beta Club
Beemer, Nebraska

Poppy Seed Dressing

¾ cup honey
¼ cup vinegar (white preferred)
½ teaspoon salt
1 teaspoon dry mustard
1 small onion, grated
1 tablespoon poppy seed
¾ cup salad oil

Grate onion in blender, add honey, vinegar, salt and dry mustard. Beat to form an emulsion and slowly add salad oil and poppy seed. Excellent for fruit salads including waldorfs.

Freda Reitz
GFWC—Sigorneyan
Caney, Kansas

Salt-Free Herbed Buttermilk Dressing

- **1 cup buttermilk**
- **1 cup mayonnaise**
- **1½ teaspoons fresh lemon juice**
- **2 teaspoons parsley flakes**
- **4 teaspoons dried basil**
- **4 teaspoons instant minced onions**
- **2 teaspoons dry mustard**
- **1 teaspoon garlic powder**
- **1 teaspoon herb seasoning**
- **1 teaspoon dried chives**
- **½ teaspoon each tarragon, oregano, marjoram, savory, thyme**
- **Freshly ground pepper to taste**

Whisk all in small bowl. Pour into jar. Cover and refrigerate at least 1 hour before using. Crumbled blue cheese can be added if desired. Amounts of dried herbs can be varied according to preference.

Lorelei Anderson
GFWC—El Dorado Woman's Club
Long Beach, California

Low-Sodium Seasoning

- **1 tablespoon garlic powder**
- **1 tablespoon dry mustard**
- **1 tablespoon paprika**
- **1½ teaspoon pepper**
- **1 teaspoon basil**
- **½ teaspoon thyme**

Thoroughly mix and store in airtight container. Sprinkle over vegetables and meat. Less than 1 calorie per teaspoon.

Lois Phillips
GFWC—Elk Valley Community Woman's Club
Pinch, West Virginia

Baked Potato Dressing

- **1 pound margarine**
- **½ cup grated onion**
- **1 8 ounce carton cottage cheese**

Have margarine and cottage cheese at room temperature. Beat with mixer until light and fluffy. Stir in onions and refrigerate. This can be frozen.

"This has less calories than butter and sour cream."

Frances Godwin
GFWC—Rockingham Intermediate Woman's Club
Rockingham, North Carolina

Grandmother Clarke's Boiled Potato Salad Dressing

1 cup vinegar
1 cup water
2 eggs
3 tablespoons sugar
1 teaspoon salt
1 teaspoon dry mustard
1 tablespoon cornstarch
¼ cup butter
1 cup milk

Put vinegar and ¾ cup water in small cast iron skillet and place on slow-heat spot on wood stove. Beat eggs; add sugar, salt, and mustard. With wooden spoon, stir into vinegar/water. Dissolve cornstarch in ¼ cup of water and add to cooking mixture. Add butter and cook gently for a few seconds. Add milk, and when thoroughly blended, move to back part of stove so that it can barely simmer for ½ hour, stirring occasionally. Serve warm or cold. Pour over a bowl of diced white cooked potatoes to which has been added ¼ cup of diced onions. Top with celery seed just before serving.

"This recipe dates back to the mid-nineteenth century and no one could quite get the elegant taste that Grandmother Clarke could. Grandmother died in 1936 at age 81, and this recipe came from her mother."

Annette H. Rowe
GFWC—The Woman's Club of Mt. Washington
Baltimore, Maryland

Fruit Salad Dressing

½ cup light corn syrup
1 tablespoon enriched flour
½ cup vinegar
1 teaspoon salt
2 teaspoons paprika
1 tablespoon grated onion
2 teaspoons celery seed
¾ cup salad oil

Blend corn syrup with flour; gradually add vinegar. Cook over low heat, stirring constantly, until smooth and thick. Add remaining ingredients except oil; mix thoroughly. Pour oil into mixture very slowly while beating constantly. This dressing is good on greens, not just for fruit salads.

Jean E. Bueter
GFWC—Freeport Woman's Club
Freeport, Maine

Fruit French Dressing

1 cup salad oil
¼ cup orange juice
3 tablespoons lemon juice
1 tablespoon vinegar
⅓ cup sugar
1 teaspoon salt
1 teaspoon paprika
1 teaspoon grated onion

Mix all ingredients in a jar. Cover and shake vigorously. Chill. Shake before serving. Serve this over a salad of romaine lettuce, cut up oranges, walnuts and a few red onion rings.

Isabelle C. Bosman
GFWC—The Mountainside Woman's Club, Inc.
Mountainside, New Jersey

Pennsylvania Dutch Hot Dressing

4 strips bacon, cut small
1 tablespoon flour
2 tablespoons sugar
Few grains salt and pepper
1 egg, beaten
3 tablespoons vinegar
½ cup milk
½ cup water

In heavy fry pan, fry cut up bacon pieces over medium heat. When brown, stir in flour, sugar, salt and pepper. In a bowl, beat egg. Add vinegar, milk and water. Stir into bacon mixture, stirring to blend. Cook over medium heat until thickened. Use over chopped dandelion in spring, or cut endive or other greens. Serve while still hot for best results. Paprika may be added for color. Sometimes chopped onion can be added to chopped greens. This can be adapted to cabbage by sauteing shredded cabbage in the bacon fat before adding dry ingredients and milk liquids.

Marion R. Hull
GFWC—Woman's Club of Shillington
Shillington, Pennsylvania

Creamy French Dressing

2 cups salad oil (not olive)
2 tablespoons brown sugar
½ cup vinegar
3 tablespoons catsup
1 teaspoon salt
1 teaspoon paprika
⅛ teaspoon dry mustard
2 teaspoons grated onion, or juice
½ egg white, unbeaten
2 cloves garlic

Mix thoroughly all ingredients except garlic. Cut the garlic in half and add last (this may be impaled on a toothpick). Chill thoroughly for several days. Remove garlic before using dressing. This will keep in refrigerator, closed tightly, for a long time.

"This was accepted by the River Road's Cookbook, Baton Rouge Junior League, Baton Rouge, La. Their comment: 'Excellent. Delicious on tossed green salad.' "

Zelma Smalling
GFWC—College Community Club
Emory, Virginia

Breads, Yeast & Quick

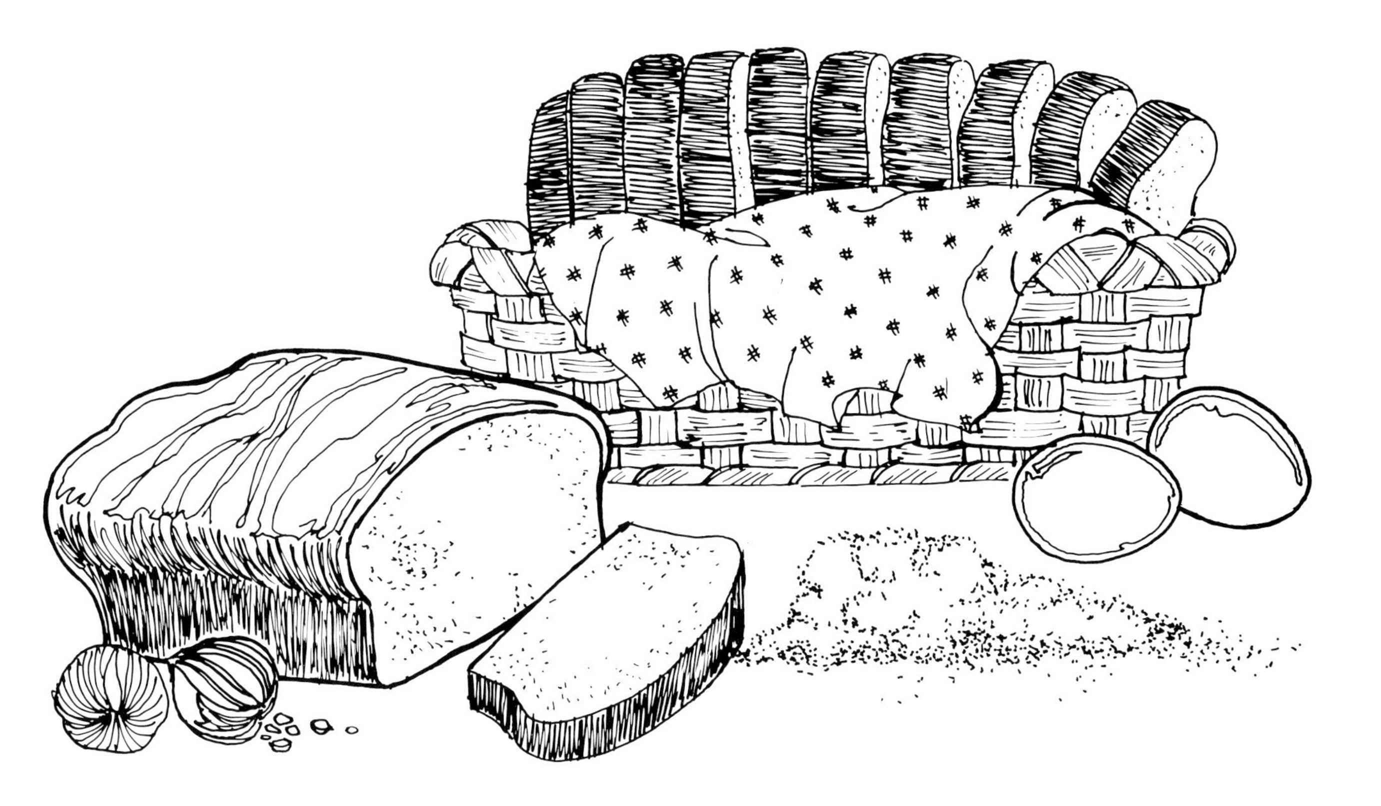

Athenaeum Rolls

2 cups milk, scalded
½ cup shortening
2 cakes yeast
¼ cup warm water
1 egg, slightly beaten
2 teaspoons salt
½ cup sugar
5 cups flour
Melted butter
Sugar
Cinnamon
Raisins
Pecans
Powdered sugar icing

Add shortening to scalded milk. Dissolve yeast in water and add to milk mixture. Add egg, salt, flour and sugar. Mix well. Allow to rise until double; about 2 hours. Roll dough out to ½ inch thick. Brush with melted butter. Sprinkle with sugar, cinnamon, raisins and pecans. Roll up and cut into 1 inch slices. Lay pieces on greased baking pan. Dot with butter and let rise until doubled—about 1 hour. Bake 10–15 minutes in a 400 degree oven. Brush with powdered sugar icing while hot. Makes 4 dozen.

Helen Hughes
GFWC—Kansas City Athenaeum
Kansas City, Missouri

Photo features: German Christmas Bread—Page 103
Zucchini Herb Cornbread—Page 117

Prune Coffee Cake

½ cup lukewarm water
1 package yeast
1 cup milk
½ cup sugar
⅓ cup shortening
1 teaspoon salt
2 eggs, well beaten
3 cups flour

Prune Filling

1 quart prunes
1–2 eggs
Butter
Sugar to taste
Flour to thicken
Pinch of salt

Dissolve yeast in lukewarm water; let stand 10 minutes. Scald the milk, sugar, shortening and salt. Cool. Add the yeast and eggs. Stir in about 3 cups flour, or enough to handle lightly. Let rise 1½ to 2 hours, then knead lightly. Let rise 10 minutes and roll out like heavy pie crust. Put on the prune filling and another crust on top. Butter top and sprinkle with sugar and cinnamon. Bake in a 9 × 13 inch pan at 375 degrees for 25 minutes or until light brown. (May beat 1 egg and brush on top then sprinkle with sugar and cinnamon.)

Cook and mash prunes. Add eggs and sugar to taste. Add a little salt and just enough flour to make it slightly thick. Add butter the size of an egg.

"The coffee cake recipe was brought from Blasheim, Germany by my great-grandparents Anton and Louise Spilker who came to Baltimore, Maryland, U.S.A., September 18, 1883. This recipe has been in our family over 100 years. My mother, Anna Marie, baked it every Christmas. We have continued the tradition."

Erna Pohlmann Martens
GFWC—Deshler Woman's Club
Deshler, Nebraska

Quick Apple Strudel

2 cups sifted flour
3 teaspoons baking powder
½ teaspoon salt
2 tablespoons sugar
4 tablespoons shortening
⅔ to ¾ cup milk
3 cups chopped apples
½ cup sugar
1 teaspoon cinnamon

Sift flour, baking powder, salt and sugar. Cut in shortening and add enough milk to make a soft dough. Turn out on floured board. Knead gently. Roll ¼ inch thick. Brush with melted butter. Cover with chopped apples. Sprinkle with cinnamon and sugar. Roll jellyroll fashion and form into crescent shape on a greased baking sheet. Bake 400 degrees for 20–25 minutes. While warm, frost with a powdered sugar glaze.

Theodora Skubic
GFWC—Virginia Study Club
Virginia, Minnesota

Bubble Wreath

- **1 package dry yeast**
- **3½–3¾ cups sifted flour**
- **1¼ cups milk**
- **¼ cup sugar**
- **¼ cup shortening**
- **1 teaspoon salt**
- **1 egg**
- ***Sugar Fruit Topping***
- **1 tablespoon butter or margarine**
- **2 tablespoons light corn syrup**
- **½ cup packed, brown sugar**

In a large bowl, combine yeast and 2 cups of flour. In saucepan, heat together milk, sugar, shortening and salt just until warm, stirring constantly to melt shortening. Add to flour mixture in bowl; mix well. Stir in egg. Beat on low speed of electric mixer for ½ minute, scraping sides of bowl constantly. Beat 3 minutes at high speed. By hand, stir in enough of remaining flour to make a soft dough. Turn out onto lightly floured surface; knead until smooth. Place dough in greased bowl, turning once to grease surface. Cover and let rise until doubled in volume, about 2 hours. Grease a 10 inch tube pan. Melt butter, add corn syrup and brown sugar to make topping. Spread bottom with sugar fruit topping. Place 16 halved candied cherries, cut side up, and a few blanched, slivered almonds or walnuts on sugar mixture. Shape dough into 48 small balls; roll in melted butter, and then in a mixture of half cup sugar and 1 teaspoon cinnamon. Place in layers in pan. Let rise until double. Bake in 400 degree oven for 35 minutes or until done. Loosen coffee cake from tube pan; turn out quickly onto serving plate.

Marlene R. Mincher
GFWC—Pennington Woman's Club
Pennington, New Jersey

Amish Dilly Bread

- **1 package dry yeast**
- **1 cup creamy cottage cheese**
- **2 tablespoons sugar**
- **1 tablespoon minced onion**
- **¼ teaspoon baking soda**
- **¼ cup warm water**
- **1 tablespoon butter**
- **1 egg**
- **2¼ to 2½ cups flour**
- **2 teaspoons dill seed**
- **¾ teaspoon salt**

Mix yeast and warm water. Set aside. Whisk egg in this lightly. Heat cottage cheese to lukewarm, add butter. Transfer to large bowl and add yeast mixture. Add soda, salt, sugar, minced onion and dill seed. Gradually add flour. Mix well. Let rise until double, punch down and put in well-greased bread pan. Let rise again. Bake at 350 degrees for 45 minutes. Brush with melted butter.

Viola Ross
GFWC—Lantana Woman's Club
Lantana, Florida

German Coffeebread (Kuga)

- **1 cup scalded milk**
- **2 teaspoons salt**
- **1 package yeast dissolved in ¼ cup lukewarm water**
- **2 beaten eggs**
- **½ cup sugar**
- **¼ cup shortening**
- **5 cups flour**

Custard Topping

- **1 beaten egg**
- **¾ cup sugar**
- **2 heaping tablespoons flour**
- **Pinch of salt**
- **1 teaspoon vanilla**
- **1 cup cream (soured)**
- **3 12 ounce cartons cottage cheese, small curd**

Rivel

- **2 cups flour**
- **1 cup melted butter or margarine**
- **¾ cup sugar**
- **½ cup oil**

Sweet dough: Mix the first four ingredients, allow them to cool down before blending in the eggs. Add 2½ cups flour, beat until smooth. Add remaining flour and let rise. Punch down. Let rise again. Roll out like pizza dough and put into greased pans. Immediately top with custard topping and rivel. Custard topping: Beat eggs. Add remaining ingredients and beat until smooth. Rivel: Mix all ingredients until crumbly and sprinkle over custard. Bake at 350 degrees for 30 minutes.

Shari Damrow
GFWC—Douglas Civic Club
Douglas, Wyoming

Cheese Strudel

- **1 pound pot or farmer cheese**
- **½ cup sugar**
- **2 egg yolks**
- **½ cup raisins (rinsed and drained)**
- **Grated rind of 1 lemon**
- **2 egg whites, beaten stiff**
- **1 package defrosted phyllo dough**

Mix egg yolks with sugar until foamy. Make cheese mixture by putting it through a ricer, adding raisins, lemon rind and egg yolks with sugar. Fold egg whites into mixture. Place 1 sheet of phyllo dough on damp cloth, brush with melted butter, sprinkle with plain bread crumbs and top with another sheet. Repeat procedure until you have 4 sheets of phyllo dough. Spread filling lengthwise on dough and using damp cloth, roll up dough and place roll on an ungreased cookie sheet, like a jelly roll. Makes at least 4 strudels. Brush tops with melted butter. Bake 50–55 minutes at 350 degrees until golden brown. Cool 30 minutes, sprinkle with confectioners' sugar.

Sylvia Lewis
GFWC—Formers Second District
Long Island, New York

Hot Rolls (Food Processor Method)

- **½ cup warm water**
- **1 teaspoon sugar**
- **1 package fast rising yeast**
- **1¾ cups warm water**
- **1 teaspoon salt**
- **½ cup shortening**
- **1 egg**
- **¾ cup sugar**
- **6–8 cups flour**

Dissolve yeast and sugar in ½ cup warm water. Stir to dissolve. Place 3 cups flour in processor bowl. Add salt, shortening, sugar and process to blend. Add the remaining water and egg; process to blend. Add yeast mixture and process, adding flour ½ cup at a time until the dough is moist but not sticky. Put in warm bowl and let rise until double. Make into rolls and let rise until at least double. Bake at 375 degrees for 15–20 minutes. As soon as they come from the oven, put a light coating of butter on the tops to make shiny.

Helen Quinn
GFWC—Walnut Valley Woman's Club
Walnut, California

Cheese Puffs

- **3 cups flour**
- **1 tablespoon sugar**
- **1 teaspoon salt**
- **¼ teaspoon celery seed**
- **2 tablespoons fresh chopped onion (optional)**
- **2 tablespoons shortening**
- **1¼ cups warm water**
- **1 package active dry yeast**
- **1 egg**
- **1 cup shredded cheddar cheese**
- **Olives (optional)**

Blend the first six ingredients. Dissolve yeast in warm water. Blend in egg. Add ⅔ flour mixture and cheese to yeast mixture. Beat until smooth; no kneading necessary. Let rise until double. Grease muffin tins well. Beat batter hard—spoon into cups, about half full. You may press an olive in center of each. Let rise until batter reaches tops of cups. Bake at 425 degrees for 10–15 minutes.

Mary M. Dardis
GFWC—Emmetsburg, Iowa
Emmetsburg, Iowa

Cinnamon Raisin English Muffins

- **1 cup milk**
- **1/4 cup water**
- **1/4 cup margarine**
- **4–4 1/2 cups flour**
- **1/4 cup packed brown sugar**
- **1 tablespoon cinnamon**
- **1 teaspoon salt**
- **1 package dry yeast**
- **2 eggs**
- **1 cup raisins**
- **1/4 cup corn meal**

In a small saucepan, heat milk, water, and butter until warm (120–130 degrees). Lightly spoon flour into cup. Level off. In large bowl, combine warm liquid, 2 cups flour, brown sugar, cinnamon, yeast, salt and eggs. Beat 2 minutes at medium speed. By hand, stir in remaining flour and raisins. Cover and let rise in warm place until doubled in size—about 30–45 minutes. On floured surface, knead until smooth and elastic—about 2 minutes. Cover and let rest 10 minutes. Roll out dough to 3/8 inch thickness. Cut into 3 inch rounds. Lightly press each side in cornmeal. Place on ungreased cookie sheets. Cover, and let rise until doubled in size—about 30–45 minutes. Bake at 375 degrees for 7–8 minutes; turn with spatula and bake 7–8 minutes more. To serve, split and toast. Butter and spread with cream cheese or jelly if desired.

Ruth A. Frazee
GFWC—Junior Achievers
Appleton City, Missouri

Easy Potato Buns

- **1 tablespoon yeast**
- **1 cup warm water (105–115 degrees)**
- **1 cup mashed potatoes**
- **3/4 cup granulated sugar**
- **1/4 cup cooking oil**
- **5–6 cups unsifted flour**

Cook potatoes in boiling water. Drain, mash and measure out 1 cup, firmly packed. Meanwhile, dissolve yeast in warm water. Add potatoes, sugar, oil and 5 cups flour. Mix and add last cup of flour, if needed, as you knead mixture for about 10 minutes. Put in greased bowl. Let rise 4 hours. Roll to 3/4 inch thickness. Cut into 16 squares. Place on greased cookie sheets. Let rise 2 hours. Bake at 350 degrees for 15–20 minutes.

Edna J. Haas
GFWC—Woman's Club of Boyertown
Boyertown, Pennsylvania

Bran Rolls

1 package yeast
1/4 cup lukewarm water
1/3 cup molasses
1 1/2 cups boiling water
1/3 cup butter
1 egg, beaten
1 tablespoon (scant) salt
1 cup bran flour (flaked)
1 1/2 cups whole wheat flour
1 1/2 cups white flour
3/4 cup raisins

Dissolve yeast in lukewarm water with molasses. Boil water and melt butter in it. When lukewarm, add egg and salt. Combine with yeast. Mix all the flour with raisins. Stir in yeast mixture. Beat hard three minutes. Set to rise in warm place, covered with tea towel. When doubled in bulk, stir down. Shape in cloverleafs in cupcake tins. Let rise again. Bake at 375 degrees about 25 minutes. If baking too fast, reduce heat to 325 degrees.

Bea Phillips
GFWC—Newport Woman's Club
Newport, Vermont

My Favorite White Bread

2 cups warm water
1 cup dry milk
3 tablespoons sugar
2 1/2 teaspoons salt
6 tablespoons shortening
2 tablespoons dry active yeast
5 cups sifted enriched flour

In mixing bowl of electric mixer, mix water, milk, sugar, salt, yeast and shortening, plus about 3 cups of the flour; mix well. Put on dough hooks and add rest of the flour and mix about 5 or more minutes. Pour out on floured board and knead until smooth and elastic. Not much kneading will be necessary if left in the mixer long enough. Place in greased bowl and let rise until doubled in bulk. Turn out on board and divide in half. Let rise 15 minutes or so. Shape in loaves and place in loaf pans. Let rise in warm place for about 1 hour or about doubled in bulk. Bake at 350 degrees for 40 minutes or until nice and brown.

Nadine Price
GFWC—Duncan Woman's Club
Duncan, Arizona

French Bread

- **2½ cups warm tap water (110–115 degrees)**
- **1 package dry yeast**
- **2 to 4 tablespoons sugar**
- **2 teaspoons salt**
- **5 to 6 cups flour**
- **1 to 2 tablespoons margarine or shortening, softened**
- **¾ cup nonfat dry milk**
- **Cornmeal**
- **1 egg white, lightly beaten**
- **Sesame or poppy seeds (optional)**

Dissolve sugar and salt in water; add yeast. Add two cups flour. Beat well. Add margarine and dry milk. Add remaining flour to make a soft dough. Knead well until smooth and elastic. Place in greased bowl. Cover with plastic wrap and allow to double in bulk. Punch down. Divide in half, knead and shape into 2 long loaves. Place loaves on greased cookie sheet, sprinkled with cornmeal. Cut diagonal slits 1 to 2 inches deep in top of loaf. Brush loaves with warm water to help make a hard crisp crust. Let rise until almost double in bulk. Bake at 375 degrees for 30 minutes. Remove and brush lightly with beaten egg whites to give a shiny golden crust. Sprinkle with seeds. Bake 10 minutes more. For a harder crust, place pie pan of hot water in bottom of oven during baking. This can be used for crust for pizza.

Florence M. Grams
GFWC—Canby Woman's Club
Canby, Minnesota

Italian Bread

- **2 cups warm water**
- **1 package yeast**
- **1 tablespoon sugar**
- **2 teaspoons salt**
- **2 pinches Italian seasonings**
- **4½ cups flour**
- **½ cup chopped chives or onion tops**

Egg Wash

- **1 egg beaten with 1 teaspoon water**
- **Sesame or poppy seeds for garnish**

Dissolve yeast in warm water, add sugar and salt. In work bowl of food processor, mix the flour, seasonings and chives. With processor running, pour the yeast water through the feed tube and continue mixing until dough forms a ball and cleans the sides of the work bowl. Allow processor to knead dough about 1 minute longer. Turn out into greased bowl, cover and set aside to rise until doubled in size—about 2 hours. Punch down, divide in half and pat out each half to flatten and remove air bubbles. Roll up into long, narrow loaf and place in well-oiled baguette pan or onto cookie sheet. Dough can also be divided into thirds and braided into one very large loaf. Cover, allow to rise about 45 minutes. Egg wash the top of loaves and sprinkle with sesame or poppy seeds. Bake at 400 degrees for about 1 hour.

Joan Krafka Meany
GFWC—Cedar Falls Junior Woman's Club
Cedar Falls, Iowa

German Christmas Bread

7 cups of flour
1 ounce yeast
½ cup sugar
¼ pound butter
3½ cups of prune and pear juice (approximately, saved from cooking prunes and pears. This will make a dark dough. Milk can be used if a lighter color bread is preferred.)
½ tablespoon salt
1 pound prunes and pears (dried, cooked and chopped)
5 ounces figs
6 ounces raisins
½ tablespoon ground cinnamon
½ tablespoon cloves
3½ ounces chopped nuts
Mixed glazed fruits to taste

Mix flour, butter, yeast, salt, sugar and juice. Let stand about 15 minutes in a warm place. Mix in rest of ingredients. Let rise (preferably overnight or at least until it has doubled in size). Knead lightly and form into 2–4 loaves depending on size of pans. Bake in a 300 degree oven for an hour or hour and fifteen minutes, depending on size of loaves. Tester should have no dough clinging to it. Leave in turned off oven a few minutes and remove.

"This recipe came from my grandmother who brought it from the Black Forest area of Germany near Switzerland. She called it 'Schnitzbrot'."

Verna M. Johnson
GFWC—The Woman's Club of Bloomfield
Bloomfield, New Jersey

Potato Yeast Bread

6 potatoes
1 quart boiling water
1 quart flour
1 cup sugar
3 cakes yeast
1 quart milk
1 cup yeast mix
Enough flour to make dough

Potato yeast: Boil six potatoes and mash very fine. Pour 1 quart boiling water over 1 quart flour; mix well. Add potatoes and one cup sugar. When cool, add 3 cakes yeast softened in one cup warm water. Mix thoroughly and set in warm place for several hours. Covered and refrigerated, this will keep for at least 3 weeks. Potato yeast bread: Combine one quart warm milk and one cup potato yeast mix. Stir in enough flour to make a soft batter and set in warm place to rise. When very light, add enough flour to make a stiff dough; knead thoroughly. Let rise again until very light. In 4 greased bread pans, bake at 350 degrees for 45 minutes to 1 hour.

Suzanne M. Meredith
GFWC—Endwell League of Community Action
Endwell, New York

Oatmeal Bread

- **2 cups boiling water**
- **1 cup rolled oats (quick cooking)**
- **2 tablespoons shortening**
- **½ cup molasses (light)**
- **2 teaspoons salt**
- **2 packages yeast (dry)**
- **½ cup warm water**
- **½ cup powdered milk**
- **5–6 cups flour (white)**

Pour boiling water over oats and shortening. Cool. Add molasses and salt. Dissolve yeast in warm water and add to above. Add powdered milk and flour. Knead until smooth. Put in greased bowl and let rise to double. Divide in 3 parts and make loaves. Put in 3 pans. Let rise to double. Bake 40–45 minutes at 350 degrees.

Mae Moore
GFWC—Centuria Woman's Club
Centuria, Wisconsin

Spinach Cheese Bread

- **3 cups biscuit mix**
- **1 can condensed cheddar cheese soup (undiluted)**
- **3 large eggs**
- **¼ cup vegetable oil**
- **1 box (10 ounces) frozen chopped spinach (thaw, squeeze dry)**
- **1 tablespoon caraway seed**

Heat oven to 350 degrees. Grease 9 × 5 × 3 loaf pan. Mix all ingredients, except spinach, until well blended. Beat 1 minute; stir in spinach until well blended. Pour into pan. Bake at 350 degrees for 55–60 minutes or until toothpick inserted in center comes out clean. Cool 20 minutes; remove from pan.

Margaret Triplett
GFWC—Gibbon Federated Woman's Club
Gibbon, Nebraska

Cheese Bread

- **12 ounces aged (sharp) cheddar cheese**
- **1 cup milk**
- **½ cup (1 stick) butter**
- **2 eggs, beaten**
- **1 envelope dry yeast**
- **1½ teaspoons salt**
- **1 teaspoon sugar**
- **½ teaspoon dry mustard**
- **Approximately 5 cups unbleached flour**

Shred cheese into large bowl. Mix 1½ cups of the flour, salt, sugar and mustard with the yeast. Toss well with the cheese. Heat milk and butter until melted. Cool to quite warm. Add beaten eggs. Add liquid to cheese mixture all at once. Blend well, but do not beat. Let stand 5 minutes. Add balance of flour gradually until dough is firm but not stiff. Let rise one hour (dough will not double in bulk). Divide into four parts and place in well-greased, small loaf pans. Let rise in warm place until dough has rounded over tops of pans. Bake in preheated 350 degree oven for 40 minutes. Cool on rack; store in bags in refrigerator. Slice when cold. Toast and butter lightly. Cut diagonally and serve for elegant snacks or appetizer.

Kathryn G. Lapp
GFWC—Plymouth Woman's Club
Plymouth, Wisconsin

Onion-Cheese Supper Bread

- ¾ cup fresh or frozen chopped onion
- 2 beaten eggs
- 3 tablespoons parsley
- 2¼ cups biscuit mix
- 1½ tablespoons butter
- 1½ cups shredded cheddar cheese
- ¾ cup milk

Preheat oven to 400 degrees. Cook onions in butter until tender, not brown. Combine beaten eggs and milk; add to biscuit mix. Stir only until biscuit mix is moistened. Add butter and onions, half the cheese and parsley. Spread dough in greased 9 to 10-inch round baking pan. Sprinkle dough with rest of cheese and parsley. Bake at 400 degrees until wooden toothpick comes out clean, about 20 to 25 minutes.

Voni Lindgren
GFWC—Rochester Woman's Club
Rochester, Illinois

Easy Food Processor Pizza Dough

- 1 package active dry yeast
- 1 teaspoon sugar
- ⅞ cup warm water, 110 degrees
- 1 tablespoon olive oil
- 2⅓ cups flour
- ½ teaspoon salt (optional)
- 1 tablespoon Italian herbs or seasonings

Stir the yeast, sugar and warm water together and let stand until foamy—about 10 minutes. Fit food processor work bowl with steel blade; add flour, salt and Italian herbs. Turn machine on for 5 seconds to combine ingredients. With machine running, add wet ingredients. Process until dough forms a ball at the side of the bowl. Add olive oil and process 15–20 seconds more. If dough does not ball up, add warm water in small doses through the feed tube until it does. If the dough seems excessively sticky and wet, add a bit more flour. Dough should be soft and slightly sticky if done properly. There is very little dough left on the sides and bottom of the work bowl. Place dough on counter and knead it by hand for several minutes, until it is smooth. Dust with flour if it sticks to your hand at all. Dough is now ready for use, it should be smooth and satiny. Roll out on lightly floured surface. Lightly grease pizza pan with a little oil and sprinkle with cornmeal. Place dough only on pizza pan and trim edges. Bake at 425 degrees for 10 minutes. Remove from oven, lightly brush crust with more oil. Top with sauce and toppings. Bake 15–20 minutes on bottom of oven.

Loretta McCullough
GFWC—Intermediate Woman's Club of Allegheny Valley
Natrona Heights, Pennsylvania

Pizza Crust—Whole Wheat

2 cups whole wheat flour
¼ cup wheat germ
1 envelope yeast
¾ teaspoon salt
1 tablespoon oil
1 tablespoon honey
1 cup water

Mix together first four ingredients. Add next three. Let it rest 10 minutes. Then spread dough on a greased cookie sheet. Add your favorite toppings. Bake at 350 degrees for 15–20 minutes.

Eleanor Oliver
GFWC—Junior Woman's Club of Raleigh
Raleigh, North Carolina

Pita (Pocket Bread)

1 package yeast
1 teaspoon sugar
2 cups warm water
2 teaspoons salt
6 cups flour (may use 3 cups white flour and 3 cups whole wheat flour)

Dissolve yeast and sugar in water; let soak 10 minutes. Combine all ingredients, work into a medium-stiff ball. Knead until smooth and elastic. Cover; let rise in warm place until double in bulk (2 hours). Form dough into 16 smooth balls. Cover and let rise on cloth for 30 minutes. Roll into ¼ inch thick circles. Cover and let rise 30 minutes. Heat oven at 475 degrees. Place circles of dough directly on oven rack, which has been moved to lowest position in oven. Watch closely. As soon as dough puffs, 2–4 minutes, remove from oven and place under broiler for few seconds, until lightly browned. Cool and store or freeze. When ready to use, slice across the circle and fill the pocket with a sandwich filling of your choice.

Jan Anderson
GFWC—Literary Club
Carrington, North Dakota

Scones

1 cup all purpose flour
2 teaspoons baking powder
½ teaspoon salt
1¼ cups graham flour
⅓ cup granulated sugar
½ cup shortening
1 egg
Water

Stir together first 5 ingredients. With pastry blender, cut in shortening until crumbly. Break egg into measuring cup and beat with a fork. Pour off about 1 tablespoon of egg into saucer. Fill measuring cup to ⅔ mark with water. With a fork, stir this liquid into flour mixture to make a soft, slightly sticky dough. Turn dough out on a lightly floured surface and knead gently 8–10 times. Roll out or pat into ½ inch thick circle. Cut into wedges. Brush tops with reserved egg. Bake on ungreased sheet in 425 degree oven for 12–15 minutes, until light golden brown.

Jeannette Pauplis
GFWC—Hudson Woman's Club
Hudson, Massachusetts

Italian Bread Sticks

- **1 cup flour**
- **½ teaspoon oregano**
- **½ teaspoon salt**
- **¼ cup butter or margarine, softened**
- **1 cup shredded mozzarella cheese**
- **¼ cup water**

Heat oven to 400 degrees. Combine flour and seasonings. Cut in butter and cheese. Stir in water. Shape dough into a ball. Knead until dough holds together. Shape tablespoonfuls of dough into sticks, about ½ inch thick and 6 inches long. Place on cookie sheet. Bake 20 minutes. Remove from pan immediately.

Dorothy Richards
GFWC—Illinois Valley Woman's Club
Cave Junction, Oregon

Baked Apple Doughnuts

- **1½ cups sifted flour**
- **1¾ teaspoons baking powder**
- **½ teaspoon salt**
- **½ teaspoon nutmeg**
- **½ cup sugar**
- **⅓ cup shortening**
- **1 egg, beaten**
- **¼ cup milk**
- **½ cup grated raw apple**
- **½ cup melted butter**
- **⅓ cup sugar**
- **½ teaspoon cinnamon**

Sift together dry ingredients. Cut in shortening. Add egg and mix. Add milk and apple—mix well. Pour into greased muffin pan and bake at 350 degrees for 20–25 minutes. Remove from pan and immediately roll doughnuts in melted butter and then in sugar and cinnamon mixture. Serve warm.

Lenora Kenney
GFWC—Belleville Woman's Club
Belleville, New Jersey

Cinnamon Popovers

- **3 eggs**
- **1 cup milk**
- **1 cup all-purpose flour**
- **3 tablespoons melted margarine**
- **1 teaspoon ground cinnamon**
- **¼ teaspoon salt**

In electric blender, combine all ingredients and blend 30 seconds. Grease 12 muffin cups and preheat in hot oven. Fill half full and bake at 400 degrees for 40 minutes.

Joyce Miller
GFWC—Coalesce Club
Cape Girardeau, Missouri

Cranberry Doughnuts

- **1 cup sugar**
- **2 tablespoons cooking oil**
- **2 eggs**
- **¾ cup milk**
- **1 tablespoon vinegar**
- **3½ cups flour, sifted (all purpose)**
- **2 teaspoons baking powder**
- **1 teaspoon baking soda**
- **½ teaspoon salt**
- **½ teaspoon ground cinnamon**
- **1 cup of sliced fresh cranberries**
- **Vegetable oil for deep frying**
- **Confectioners' sugar**

Combine sugar, oil and eggs; beat until smooth. Stir in milk and vinegar. Sift together flour, baking powder, soda, salt and cinnamon. Beat into creamed mixture. Stir in cranberries. Turn out onto floured board and knead in enough flour (about ¼ cup) so dough is not sticky. Wrap and chill one hour. Roll dough on well-floured board to ⅓ inch thickness. Cut with floured 2½-inch doughnut cutter. Fry in deep vegetable oil at 375 degrees until golden brown—about 1 minute on each side, turning once. Drain. Shake in bag containing confectioners' sugar. Yields 2 dozen.

Nellie Mae Shideler
GFWC—Federated Woman's Club of Morongo Valley
Morongo Valley, California

Grammy Hooper's Sour Milk Doughnuts

- **1 can condensed milk**
- **1 egg, beaten lightly**
- **1 teaspoon ginger**
- **1 teaspoon nutmeg**
- **1 tablespoon melted shortening**
- **¾ cup sour milk (3 teaspoons vinegar added to sour the milk)**
- **1½ teaspoons soda**
- **½ teaspoon salt**
- **3½ cups flour**

Put ⅓ of mixture on floured board, knead slightly, pat and roll out ¼ inch thick. Shape with doughnut cutter, fry in deep fat, take up on skewer, and drain on brown paper. Add trimmings to ½ remaining mixture. Roll, shape, and fry as before; repeat. Doughnuts should come quickly to top of fat, browned on one side, then be turned to brown on other. The fat must be kept at a uniform temperature (370 degrees). If too cold, doughnuts will absorb fat. If too hot, doughnuts will brown before sufficiently risen.

Beverly A. Goodrich
GFWC—Wolfeboro Woman's Club
Wolfeboro, New Hampshire

Harvest Bread

- 1½ cups finely chopped dried apples
- ½ cup butter or margarine, softened
- ⅔ cup sugar
- 2 eggs, beaten
- 2 cups all-purpose flour
- 1 teaspoon soda
- ½ teaspoon salt
- ¾ cup shredded cheddar cheese
- ½ cup chopped walnuts

Cook apples according to package directions; drain well and set aside. Cream butter and sugar until light and fluffy; add eggs, beating well. Combine flour, soda and salt; add to creamed mixture. Stir in apples, cheese, and nuts. Pour into a greased 9-inch loaf pan. Bake at 350 degrees for 50–55 minutes. Cool 10 minutes in pan. Remove from pan and cool on rack.

May B. Windle
GFWC—The Wednesday Club
Galveston, Texas

Grandmother's Famous Cranberry Bread

- 2 cups sifted flour
- 1 cup sugar
- 1–1½ teaspoons baking powder
- 1 teaspoon salt
- ½ teaspoon soda
- ½ cup margarine
- 1 egg, slightly beaten
- 1 teaspoon grated orange peel
- ¾ cup orange juice
- 1½ cups light raisins
- 1½ cups fresh cranberries, chopped

Sift together flour, sugar, baking powder, salt and soda in a large bowl. Cut in butter until mixture is crumbly. Add egg, orange peel and orange juice all at once. Stir just until mixture is evenly moist. Fold in raisins and cranberries. Spoon into 9 × 5 × 3 inch loaf pan. Bake at 350 degrees for 1 hour and 10 minutes, or until a toothpick inserted in center comes out clean. Remove from pan and cool on wire rack.

Helen L. Covey
GFWC—Elmira Travel Club
Elmira, New York

Orange Date and Nut Bread

- 1 cup cut-up dates
- 1 cup hot water
- 1 teaspoon butter
- 1 beaten egg
- ⅔ cup brown sugar
- 2 cups flour
- 1 teaspoon baking soda
- ¼ teaspoon salt
- ½ cup broken nuts
- ½ cup orange marmalade

Combine dates, water and butter. Cool. Add egg and brown sugar. Sift together flour, baking soda and salt. Stir into date mixture. Add nuts and marmalade. Combine well. Place in a greased 8-inch loaf pan. Bake at 300 degrees for 1 hour. Test for doneness before removing from oven. Turn out on rack to cool.

Doris R. Siegel
GFWC—Bridgewater Woman's Club
Bridgewater, New Jersey

Soft Molasses Gingerbread

- ½ cup sugar
- ½ cup butter and lard, mixed
- 1 cup molasses
- 2½ cups sifted all-purpose flour
- 1 egg, beaten
- 1 cup hot water
- 1 teaspoon cinnamon
- 1 teaspoon ginger
- ½ teaspoon cloves
- ½ teaspoon salt
- 1½ teaspoons soda

Cream shortening and sugar. Add beaten egg and molasses; mix well. Stir in sifted dry ingredients. Add hot water last and beat until smooth. Bake in greased, shallow pan in moderate oven at 350 degrees for 35 to 40 minutes, or until done.

Louise Spinney
GFWC—Pittsfield Tuesday Club
Pittsfield, Maine

Poppy Seed Bread

- 3 cups flour
- 2¼ cups sugar
- 1½ teaspoons baking powder
- 1½ tablespoons salt
- 3 eggs
- 1½ cups milk
- 1⅛ cups oil
- 1½ tablespoons poppy seeds
- 1½ tablespoons vanilla
- 1½ tablespoons almond extract
- 1½ tablespoons butter flavoring

Glaze

- ¾ cup sugar
- ½ tablespoon vanilla
- ½ tablespoon butter flavoring
- ¼ cup orange juice
- ½ tablespoon almond extract

Mix all except glaze ingredients together; beat 2 minutes. Bake in two large greased loaf pans for 1 hour at 350 degrees. Glaze: Mix glaze ingredients together and pour over hot bread. Let cool before removing from pan.

Deborah P. Henry
GFWC—Darterette Junior Woman's Club
Loudon, Tennessee

Blueberry Pecan Bread

- **1 medium orange**
- **2 cups flour**
- **½ cup sugar**
- **½ cup light brown sugar**
- **1½ teaspoons baking powder**
- **½ teaspoon soda**
- **½ teaspoon salt**
- **½ cup butter, melted**
- **Boiling water**
- **1 egg, slightly beaten**
- **1 cup blueberries**
- **1 cup pecans, chopped**

Grease a 9 × 5 loaf pan. Grate rind and squeeze juice from orange; add water to make ½ cup. Set aside. In large bowl combine 1¾ cups flour, sugar, light brown sugar, baking powder, baking soda and salt. In measuring cup stir together butter, orange rind, juice and enough boiling water to make ¾ cup. Add liquid ingredients and egg. Stir just until blended. Dredge blueberries with ¼ cup flour and mix. Pour into loaf pan and bake at 350 degrees for 60–65 minutes.

Doris H. Grandone
GFWC—Webster Woman's Club
Webster, Massachusetts

"Blue Ribbon" Pumpkin Bread

- **3 cups sugar**
- **4 eggs, beaten**
- **3½ cups flour**
- **3½ teaspoons pumpkin pie spice**
- **2 teaspoons baking soda**
- **⅔ cup water**
- **1 cup oil**
- **1 pound can pumpkin**
- **1 teaspoon baking powder**
- **2 teaspoons salt**

Combine sugar, oil, eggs and pumpkin. Set aside. Sift all dry ingredients together. Add to pumpkin mixture. Pour in water and mix until smooth. Pour into loaf pans and bake at 350 degrees for 50–60 minutes.

Deborah Halpin
GFWC—Michiana Junior Woman's Club
South Bend, Indiana

Low Cholesterol Banana Bread

- **1½ cups all purpose flour**
- **2 teaspoons baking powder**
- **½ teaspoon baking soda**
- **⅛ teaspoon salt**
- **½ cup wheat germ**
- **2 tablespoons egg substitute**
- **⅓ cup firmly packed brown sugar**
- **½ teaspoon cinnamon**
- **¼ cup lowfat buttermilk**
- **¼ cup vegetable oil**
- **1 cup mashed, ripe banana**

Use vegetable cooking spray in baking pan. Combine dry ingredients; set aside. Combine egg substitute, buttermilk and oil in a large bowl; stir well. Stir in bananas and add flour mixture. Stir just until moistened. Pour batter into 8½ × 4½ × 3 inch loaf pan, coated with cooking spray. Bake at 350 degrees for 45 minutes or until pick comes out clean. Cool on rack for 10 minutes. Remove from pan and cool completely on wire rack.

Hannah E. Long
GFWC—Selbyville Community Club
Selbyville, Delaware

Pineapple Nut Bread

- 1½ cups firmly packed brown sugar
- ¾ cup shortening
- 2 eggs
- 4 cups sifted flour
- ¾ teaspoon salt
- 2 teaspoons baking soda
- 1 6 ounce can frozen orange juice, thawed
- 1 15½ ounce can crushed pineapple (do not drain)
- 1 cup chopped walnuts

Cream sugar and shortening until fluffy. Add eggs, beating well. Sift together flour, baking soda and salt. Alternately add dry ingredients and orange concentrate to creamed mixture. Mix well after each addition. Stir in pineapple and nuts. Turn into 2 greased and floured loaf pans—8½ × 4½ inches. Bake at 350 degrees for 50–60 minutes. Check with toothpick for doneness.

Ethel I. Bonham
GFWC—Wednesday Research Club
Jasonville, Indiana

Apricot Bread

- 1 cup dried apricots
- 1 cup warm water
- 1 cup sugar
- 2 tablespoons butter, melted
- ¼ cup apricot nectar or juice
- 2 cups flour
- 2 teaspoons baking powder
- ¼ teaspoon soda
- ½ cup orange juice concentrate
- 1 cup chopped nuts

Chop apricots; soak 30 minutes in water; drain excess water and reserve (may be used as substitute for nectar). Stir in sugar, butter, reserved water or nectar and orange juice. Sift flour, baking powder and soda together. Add nuts and coat with flour mixture. Combine all ingredients; stir only enough to mix well. Let stand 20 minutes before baking. Grease and flour a loaf pan; bake for 1 hour and 15 minutes at 325 degrees.

Michelle McIntyre
GFWC—Lemon Grove Woman's Club
Lemon Grove, California

Cranberry Orange Muffins

- **1 cup fresh or frozen cranberries**
- **¾ cup sugar**
- **2 teaspoons grated orange peel**
- **2 cups unsifted all-purpose flour**
- **2 teaspoons baking powder**
- **½ teaspoon salt**
- **½ cup salad oil**
- **½ cup orange juice**
- **2 large eggs**
- **½ cup chopped pecans or walnuts**

Preheat oven to 375 degrees. Grease muffin pan. Combine cranberries, ¼ cup sugar and orange peel. Set aside. In large bowl, combine flour, remaining ½ cup sugar, baking powder and salt. Combine oil, orange juice and eggs. Pour all at once into dry ingredients and stir until moistened. Blend in cranberry mixture and nuts. Spoon batter into muffin pan. Bake at 375 degrees for 25 minutes.

Deloris Pravettoni
GFWC—Starlight Woman's Club
Glendale, Arizona

Whole Grain Muffins

- **2 cups milk**
- **2 eggs**
- **½ cup oil**
- **1½ cups bran**
- **2 cups rolled oats**
- **1½ cups whole wheat flour**
- **2 tablespoons baking powder**
- **¼ cup brown sugar**
- **1 cup raisins dredged in 1 tablespoon whole wheat flour**
- **½ cup sunflower seeds**

Combine first 5 ingredients in large bowl. Let stand. Mix flour, baking powder and brown sugar. Stir together. Add to milk mixture, raisins and sunflower seeds. Dip ¼ cup batter into each greased muffin pan. Put in preheated oven. Bake at 350 degrees for 30 minutes.

Anna L. Channel
GFWC—Centralia Reading Circle
Centralia, Kansas

Beer and Cheddar Muffins

- **2 tablespoons unsalted butter**
- **1¼ cups cornmeal**
- **¾ cup flour**
- **2 tablespoons sugar**
- **1 tablespoon baking powder**
- **½ teaspoon cayenne pepper**
- **1 small onion, minced**
- **1 egg**
- **1 cup beer**
- **1½ cups grated cheddar cheese**
- **1 4 ounce can green chilies**

Melt butter and set aside. In a large mixing bowl, add flour, cornmeal, sugar, baking powder, cayenne pepper, onion. Set aside. Add beer and egg to melted butter. Mix. Make a well in center of dry ingredients and pour in beer mixture. Stir briskly to combine, being careful not to overstir. (Batter should be lumpy.) Stir in cheese and peppers. Grease a 12-cup muffin tin with vegetable cooking spray. Fill muffin cups ⅔ full. Bake at 400 degrees for 20–25 minutes. Remove from cups immediately and set on a wire rack to cool.

Judy Stringer
GFWC—Owensboro Junior Woman's Club
Owensboro, Kentucky

Zucchini Oatmeal Muffins

- **2½ cups all-purpose flour**
- **1¼ cups sugar**
- **1 cup pecans, chopped**
- **½ cup quick-cooking oats, uncooked**
- **1 tablespoon double-acting baking powder**
- **¼ teaspoon salt**
- **1 teaspoon ground cinnamon**
- **1 cup golden raisins**
- **4 eggs**
- **¾ cup salad oil**
- **1 medium zucchini (10 ounces), finely shredded**

Grease twelve 3-inch muffin pan cups. Into large bowl, measure all dry ingredients. In medium bowl, with fork, beat eggs slightly; stir in zucchini and oil. Stir mixture all at once into flour mixture just until flour is moistened. (Batter will be lumpy.) Spoon batter into muffin pan cups. Bake at 400 degrees for 25 minutes or until toothpick inserted in center of muffin comes out clean. Remove muffins from pan. Serve muffins warm or cool on wire rack to serve later.

Enid Bernabe
GFWC—Woman's Club of Parsippany-Troy Hills
Parsippany, New Jersey

Apple Muffins

- **4 tablespoons softened butter**
- **¼ cup brown sugar**
- **½ cup granulated sugar**
- **1 egg**
- **1 cup buttermilk**
- **1¾ cups flour (plain)**
- **4½ teaspoons cinnamon**
- **1 teaspoon baking soda**
- **¼ teaspoon salt**
- **1 large red delicious apple (or other eating apple), peeled and cut into ½-inch chunks**
- **⅓ cup brown sugar**

Grease a 12-cup, full-size muffin tin, including area between the cavities. Cream butter and sugars until fluffy. Mix in egg. Quickly fold in buttermilk; do not overmix or batter will curdle. In separate bowl, mix flour, cinnamon, baking soda and salt. Add gradually to sugar-egg mixture, making sure there are no lumps, but mixing no more than necessary. Fold in apple chunks. Fill each cavity in muffin tin nearly to the top. Sprinkle extra brown sugar on top. Bake at 400 degrees for 15 minutes.

Mrs. James R. Durall
GFWC—Valamont Woman's Club
Chattanooga, Tennessee

Sugar Plum Muffins

- **1 cup sugar**
- **½ cup oil**
- **2 beaten eggs**
- **2 jars plum strained baby food**
- **1 cup self-rising flour**
- **¼ teaspoon cinnamon**
- **¼ teaspoon cloves**
- **½ teaspoon vanilla**

Combine sugar and oil. Mix by hand, using a whisk. Add 2 beaten eggs and the 2 jars of strained baby food plums, self-rising flour, cinnamon, cloves and vanilla. Spray muffin pans or use liners. Makes 12 large and 12 small. Bake for 15–18 minutes at 400 degrees.

Verna C. Spradlin
GFWC—Lenoir Woman's Club
Lenoir, North Carolina

Easy Bran Muffins

- **4 large eggs**
- **1 quart buttermilk**
- **1 teaspoon salt**
- **5 teaspoons baking soda**
- **3 cups sugar**
- **1 cup vegetable oil**
- **1 15 ounce box of All-Bran (not flakes) cereal**
- **5 cups all purpose flour**

Beat eggs, milk and oil together. Stir flour, baking soda, salt and sugar together. Stir box of bran into dry ingredients. Add dry ingredients to wet ones; stir and let stand 2 days in refrigerator. Pour into greased muffin tin as needed. Bake at 375 degrees for 15–20 minutes. Batter may be left in refrigerator for 5–7 days.

Jean M. Fadus
GFWC—Newtown Woman's Club
Newtown, Connecticut

Oatmeal Dill Spoon Bread

- **2 cups whole wheat flour**
- **2 tablespoons dry active yeast**
- **¼ cup hot water**
- **3 tablespoons butter or margarine**
- **2 teaspoons salt**
- **2 cups cream style cottage cheese**
- **¼ cup sugar**
- **2 eggs**
- **1 cup quick oatmeal**
- **2 tablespoons dill seeds**
- **2 tablespoons minced onions**
- **1½ cups unbleached flour**

In large bowl of electric mixer, place whole wheat flour and yeast. In blender, combine onion, water, cottage cheese, butter, salt, sugar and eggs. Blend until smooth; add to dry ingredients and beat 2 minutes. Stir in oats, dill seeds and white flour. Turn in buttered bowl, cover and let rise in warm place until double in bulk, about 1 hour. Stir down; put into well-buttered 1½ quart casserole. Let rise, uncovered until almost double in bulk, about 45 minutes. Bake at 350 degrees for 35 minutes or until loaf sounds hollow.

Mildred C. Enninga
GFWC—Fulda Federated Reading Club
Fulda, Minnesota

E-Z Spoon Bread

- **1 cup corn meal**
- **2 tablespoons butter**
- **4 cups milk**
- **1¾ teaspoons salt**
- **4 eggs, well beaten**

Preheat oven to 400 degrees. Mix milk and corn meal. Scald; stir to make smooth, then cook in top of double boiler until consistency of mush. Remove from heat; add butter and salt. Fold in well-beaten eggs slowly. Pour into greased 1½ quart casserole dish. Bake for approximately one hour at 400 degrees.

Hazel Braxton
GFWC—Woman's Club of Clayton
Clayton, North Carolina

Corn Fritters

- **1 pint fresh or frozen grated corn**
- **½ cup flour**
- **1 teaspoon baking powder**
- **¼ teaspoon salt**
- **2 beaten eggs**
- **½ cup milk**
- **¼ teaspoon pepper**

Make a batter of flour, baking powder and milk. Add eggs, corn and seasoning. Drop by tablespoon or small dipper into a very hot oiled pan. Serve hot with pancake syrup. These should be fried to a golden brown on each side and drained on a paper towel.

Kay Graybill
GFWC—Strasburg Area Woman's Club
Strasburg, Pennsylvania

Zucchini Herb Cornbread

- 6 cups grated zucchini
- 2 teaspoons salt
- 2 cups cornmeal
- 1 cup unbleached flour
- 3 tablespoons sugar
- 1 tablespoon baking powder
- 3 eggs, beaten
- 1½ cups milk
- 2 tablespoons fresh basil or 2 teaspoons dried basil

Place zucchini in a colander and sprinkle with 1 teaspoon of the salt. Toss to coat. Weight with heavy plate and drain for 30 minutes. Sift together the cornmeal, flour, sugar, baking powder, and remaining salt. Mix the eggs, milk and basil. Combine dry and wet ingredients and stir to mix. Rinse the zucchini and squeeze out the liquid. You should have 3 cups of zucchini. Stir the zucchini into the batter. Grease a 9-inch springform pan and pour in the batter. Bake for 40 minutes at 350 degrees. Cool for 10 minutes before serving. Cut into wedges to serve. Square pans may be used.

Nell J. Bastin
GFWC—Homemakers' Club of Hickman Mills
Kansas City, Missouri

Corn Bread

- ½ cup sugar
- ½ cup flour
- ½ cup cornmeal
- 1 egg
- 1 cup sour cream
- 1 teaspoon soda
- 1 teaspoon salt

Mix all ingredients together and stir well with a spoon. Pour into greased and floured 8-inch pan. Bake at 350 degrees approximately 20 minutes. Serve piping hot with butter and split-pea soup or ham/beans, etc.

"This recipe came to me from my paternal grandmother and was originally my great-grandmother's."

Honey Hudson Kuhn
GFWC—Mentone Reading Club
Mentone, Indiana

Zucchini Fritters

- 2 medium zucchini, sliced paper thin or grated
- 1 cup flour
- 2 eggs, beaten
- Salt, pepper, oregano to taste
- 1 clove garlic, minced
- ¼ cup water
- ¼ cup grated parmesan cheese
- 1 cup oil

In mixing bowl, combine all ingredients except oil. Mix thoroughly by hand. Heat oil in skillet. When hot, drop batter by tablespoons into oil and fry until golden brown. Drain on paper towels.

Diane P. H. Williams
GFWC—Melbourne Area Junior Woman's Club
Melbourne, Florida

Whole Wheat Angel Biscuits

1 package yeast dissolved in ¼ cup warm water
5 cups flour (½ white, ½ whole wheat)
5 tablespoons sugar
1 teaspoon baking powder
1 teaspoon salt
1 teaspoon soda
1 cup shortening
2 cups buttermilk

Sift dry ingredients. Work in shortening. Add yeast and mix slightly, then add buttermilk, a small amount at a time, stirring well. Refrigerate for at least one hour. Cut and bake 10–12 minutes in oven at 400 degrees. Dough may be kept several days or cut into biscuits and frozen.

Louise H. Wilson
GFWC—Eden Woman's Club
Eden, North Carolina

Sour Dough Biscuits

1 package dry yeast
1 cup warm water
2 cups buttermilk
½ cup oil
¼ cup sugar
1 teaspoon salt
4 teaspoons baking powder
¼ teaspoon soda
6 cups flour

Dissolve yeast in warm water. Add buttermilk (either cultured or powdered mixed with water as directed on package.) Add oil, sugar, salt, baking powder, soda and flour. Stir with spoon. Store in refrigerator in tight container. Do not use unless dough has been refrigerated overnight or 6 hours. Roll out and cut with floured biscuit cutter. Let rise 10 to 15 minutes after cutting. Place in pan. Bake at 350 degrees for 20 to 30 minutes.

Nancy Sue McPheeters
GFWC—Tuesday Study Club
Braymer, Missouri

Freezer Biscuits

4 cups flour (sifted)
8 teaspoons baking powder
4 tablespoons sugar
1 teaspoon cream of tartar
1 teaspoon salt
1⅓ cups milk
1 cup shortening

Mix dry ingredients and cut in 1 cup shortening; add 1⅓ cups milk; mix. Pat or roll out and cut out biscuits. Place on cookie sheet for 10 minutes to freeze, then put in a bag. When ready to bake, either thaw or bake frozen at 450 degrees for 10 minutes. Makes about 2 dozen biscuits.

Audrey Ann McGinness
GFWC—Wakeeney Locust Club
Wakeeney, Kansas

German Apple Pancake

3 large eggs
3/4 cup milk
3/4 cup flour
1/2 teaspoon salt
1 1/2 tablespoons butter

Filling

1 pound tart fresh apples
1/4 cup melted butter
1/4 cup sugar
Cinnamon and nutmeg to taste

Pre-heat oven to 450 degrees. Beat eggs, milk, flour and salt. In a heavy 12-inch skillet, melt 1 1/2 tablespoons butter. Pour batter into skillet and place in oven. Bake 15 minutes; reduce temperature to 350 degrees and bake for an additional 10 minutes.

During baking of pancake, peel, core and slice apples and place in a microwave dish. Add sugar, butter, nutmeg and cinnamon. Microwave on full power for 3 minutes. Stir and test for tenderness. Pour apple mixture over baked pancake and serve.

Linda Johnson
GFWC—Newton Junior Woman's Club
Newton, New Jersey

Oatmeal Pancakes

1/2 cup whole wheat flour
1 1/2 cups oatmeal
1 tablespoon baking powder
1 teaspoon salt
1 tablespoon vegetable oil
1 tablespoon honey
1 1/2 cups milk
1 egg

Cinnamon Syrup

1 1/2 cups sugar
1 cup milk
1 tablespoon oleo
1/2 teaspoon cinnamon

Stir dry ingredients together in mixing bowl. Add beaten egg, oil, honey and milk. Stir together gently. Fry on hot griddle. Serve with hot cinnamon syrup. Syrup: Mix ingredients. Cook in heavy pan on low heat until slightly thickened.

Donna Brock
GFWC—Adelpha Club
Oregon, Missouri

Pancakes

1 cup yogurt
3/4 cup flour
1 teaspoon salt
1 teaspoon soda
1 stick butter or margarine, melted
2 eggs, beaten

Mix all ingredients together. Pour on hot griddle. When top bubbles, flip pancakes.

Eleanor Oliver
GFWC—Junior Woman's Club of Raleigh
Raleigh, North Carolina

Meats & Meat Sauces

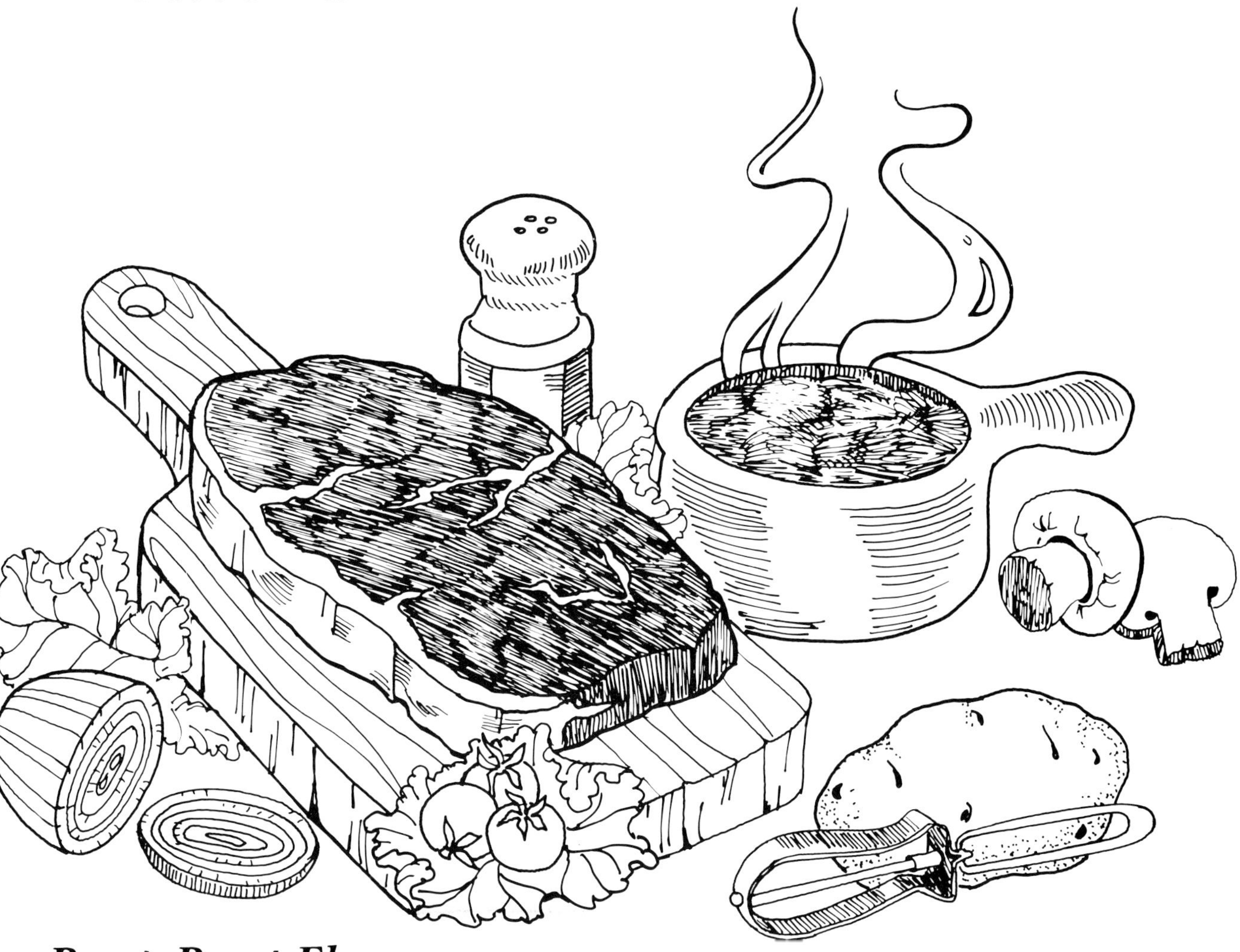

Rump Roast Elegance

- **1 large rump roast**
- **2 teaspoons garlic salt**
- **¼ teaspoon pepper**
- **1 clove garlic**
- **1 tablespoon vegetable oil**
- **6 carrots**
- **⅓ cup dry red wine or vermouth**
- **½ cup water**
- **1 6 ounce can tomato juice**
- **½ teaspoon sweet basil**
- **1 medium onion, finely chopped**

Season meat with garlic salt and pepper. Stick garlic in fat on roast. Heat oil in heavy pan. Brown meat on all sides. Add remaining ingredients, except carrots. Bake 3–4 hours at 325 degrees. Add carrots 1½ hours before done. Thicken meat juice with flour to make gravy. Small, whole potatoes may also be added with the carrots to make a complete Yankee-type pot roast dinner.

Joan Krafka Meany
GFWC—Cedar Falls Woman's Club, Junior Department
Cedar Falls, Iowa

Photo features: Beer Braised Loin of Pork—Page 141

Sauerbraten

- 3 pounds beef (round or shoulder)
- ½ cup vinegar
- 1 cup water
- 1 small onion, thinly sliced
- 2 bay leaves
- 3 whole cloves
- 2 teaspoons salt
- Dash of pepper
- 4 tablespoons fat
- 1 cup water

Place meat in glass or non-porous bowl. Combine vinegar, water, onion, bay leaves, cloves, salt, pepper and blend. Pour over meat. Let stand, refrigerated, for 18–24 hours, turning twice. Melt fat in dutch oven. Brown meat thoroughly on both sides. Add water to liquid in which meat was seared; pour over meat. Cover, simmer over low heat 3 hours or until meat is tender. Remove meat, make gravy from juices in pan and serve with noodles or spatzles (little dumplings).

Patti Unger
GFWC—Canton Junior Guild
Canton, Ohio

Myra Williard
GFWC—Suburban Woman's Club of Beaver Falls
Beaver Falls, Pennsylvania

Fruited Brisket

- 5 pounds beef brisket
- 1 envelope onion soup
- 2 tablespoons brown sugar
- 1 teaspoon cinnamon
- 1 teaspoon pepper
- ¾ teaspoon ground ginger
- 1 tablespoon grated lemon rind
- ¼ cup honey
- 2 tablespoons orange marmalade
- 1 tablespoon brandy
- ½ teaspoon Worcestershire sauce
- 1 small package dried apricots, chopped to make 1⅓ cups
- 1 cup pitted prunes, chopped
- 1 can beer

Prepare onion soup according to directions. Pour over brisket, cover and bake for 3 hours at 350 degrees. Cool completely and slice thin. Mix remaining ingredients; cover meat with mixture. Cover and bake 1 hour at 325 degrees or longer if frozen or cold.

Carolyn Street
GFWC—Intermediate League of Butler
Butler, Pennsylvania

Italian Beef

- 1 6 pound sirloin tip roast
- 2 packages brown gravy mix
- 2 onions, sliced
- 1 16 ounce bottle low-cal Italian dressing
- 8 ounces red wine
- 1 cup water
- Garlic, oregano, rosemary and black pepper to taste

Rub roast with rosemary and cook at 325 degrees until meat thermometer reads 140 degrees. Refrigerate overnight. Slice into thin slices.

Gravy: Saute onions in butter or microcook until soft. Prepare gravy according to package directions. Add onions and remaining ingredients to gravy.

Heat beef in gravy and serve on hard rolls.

Jean Lipinski
GFWC—Burlington Junior Woman's Club
Burlington, Iowa

Tenderloin Deluxe

- 2 pounds whole beef tenderloin
- ¼ cup chopped green onion
- 2 tablespoons soy sauce
- Dash pepper
- 2 tablespoons softened butter
- 2 tablespoons butter
- 1 teaspoon dijon mustard
- ¾ cup dry sherry

Spread tenderloin with first 2 tablespoons butter. Place on rack in shallow baking pan. Bake, uncovered, in hot oven (400 degrees) for 20 minutes. In small saucepan, cook onions in remaining butter until tender. Add soy sauce, mustard and pepper. Stir in sherry. Heat to boiling and pour over tenderloin. Bake at 400 degrees for 20–25 minutes longer. Baste frequently with the sauce and serve sauce with meat.

Ellyn Dahnke
GFWC—Oconomowoc Junior Woman's Club
Oconomowoc, Wisconsin

Rib Eye Roast

- 1 medium clove of garlic
- ½ cup prepared mustard
- 2 tablespoons soy sauce
- 2 tablespoons olive or salad oil
- ½ teaspoon coarsely ground black pepper
- ¼ teaspoon ground ginger
- 1 4 pound beef rib eye roast
- Parsley for garnish

Press garlic into small bowl. Stir in mustard, soy sauce, oil, pepper and ginger. Place roast on rack in open roasting pan. With pastry brush, brush half of mustard mixture over top of roast. Insert meat thermometer into center of thickest part of roast. Roast at 350 degrees until thermometer reaches 140 degrees for rare (about 20 minutes per pound). About 10 minutes before roast is done, baste with remaining mustard mixture. To serve, evenly press parsley on mustard mixture on roast. Place on warm platter.

Nona Maher
GFWC—The Woman's Club of Upper Saddle River
Upper Saddle River, New Jersey

Perusky

- **1 loaf Italian bread, top sliced off and scooped out**
- **1 pound chopped meat or ground beef or turkey**
- **1 3 ounce can mushrooms**
- **2 hard-boiled eggs, chopped**
- **1 small, chopped onion**
- **1 tablespoon parsley flakes**
- **1 teaspoon marjoram**
- **½ teaspoon tarragon**
- **Pepper**
- **Salt**
- **1 stick margarine**
- **3 tablespoons white wine or brandy**

Saute onion in ½ stick margarine. Brown meat. Add parsley, tarragon, marjoram, mushrooms and wine. Simmer covered for 10 to 15 minutes. Add chopped eggs and scooped out bread. Mix together. Salt and pepper to taste and add a little more wine if desired. Put mixture into bread shell. Thickly spread one side of loaf of bread with remaining margarine. Wrap in foil. Bake in 350 degree oven until heated through. Open foil and brown bread.

"Americanized version of the Russian meat-filled pastries. Especially good way to use leftover meat."

Rebecca Oberkirch
GFWC—Poultney Woman's Club
Poultney, Vermont

Beef and Noodle Casserole

- **1 8 ounce package thin noodles**
- **3 small onions, chopped**
- **1 tablespoon butter**
- **1½ to 2 pounds ground beef**
- **¾ cup olives, sliced once**
- **1 can mushroom soup**
- **1 soup can milk**
- **½ pound cheddar cheese, grated**
- **1 tablespoon lemon thyme**
- **1 tablespoon chives**
- **¼ pound slivered almonds**
- **1 cup chow mein noodles**

Cook noodles and drain. Set aside. Saute onions in butter; set aside. Brown beef and drain fat. Add onions, olives, soup, milk and herbs. Place a layer of noodles on the bottom of a greased casserole dish; a layer of meat sauce. Sprinkle with grated cheese. Continue to alternate layers until casserole is full. Bake covered for ½ hour at 350 degrees. Remove cover and sprinkle with mixture of almonds and chow mein noodles. Bake 30 minutes more.

Marguerite Thompson
GFWC—Hightstown Woman's Club
Hightstown, New Jersey

Gourmet Encore

Meatballs

- 2 pounds ground chuck
- ½ cup soft bread crumbs
- ¾ cup milk
- 2 teaspoons salt
- 1 teaspoon dry mustard
- 1 teaspoon Worcestershire sauce

Sauce

- 1 cup celery
- 1 cup green pepper
- 1 cup onion
- ½ pound fresh mushrooms, sliced
- 1 can cream of mushroom soup
- 1 soup can water
- ¼ cup white wine
- 1 cup pitted ripe olives
- 2 small jars chopped pimiento
- 1¼ cups wild rice

Make meatballs and brown in 3 tablespoons oil in heavy dutch oven. Remove meatballs from pan. For sauce add the celery, green pepper, onion and brown. Add remaining ingredients. Cover and bake in 350 degree oven for 50 minutes. Remove cover, add meat balls and sprinkle with 1 cup grated cheese. Cover and bake for 45 minutes longer or until rice is tender.

Evie Gloistein
GFWC—Monticola Club
Susanville, California

German Skillet Supper

- 1 tablespoon butter
- 1 14 ounce can sauerkraut, drained
- ⅔ cup uncooked rice
- 1 medium onion, chopped
- 1 pound ground chuck beef, uncooked
- 1¼ teaspoons salt
- ¼ teaspoon pepper
- 1 8 ounce can tomato sauce

In large skillet, heat butter. Spread sauerkraut over butter, sprinkle with rice, then onion. Top with ground chuck, salt, pepper, and tomato sauce. Cook covered over low heat for 25 to 30 minutes. May rinse sauerkraut a bit if you wish—I don't.

Marion VanNorman
GFWC—Woman's Club of Hellertown
Hellertown, Pennsylvania

Hamburger Casserole

- **2 pounds lean ground beef**
- **1½ pounds white potatoes, washed, peeled and sliced thin**
- **2 large yellow onions, sliced thin**
- **2 large green peppers, sliced thin**
- **1 large can of crushed tomatoes with juice**
- **1 cup Carolina rice, uncooked**
- **1 pound mozzarella cheese**

Butter bottom of a 13 × 9 inch pan; place rice in bottom evenly. Add in green peppers, onions in a layer and potatoes. Top with ground beef patted to make an even layer to cover the length of the pan. Pour on the crushed tomatoes to form an even layer. Add enough water to cover potatoes. Bake at 375 degrees for approximately 1½ hours or until potatoes are done. Top with thin slices of the mozzarella cheese and place under the broiler until lightly brown.

Carolyn Stang
GFWC—Junior Woman's Club of Newton
Newton, New Jersey

Texas Hash

- **1 medium onion, chopped**
- **1 green pepper, chopped**
- **1 pound ground lean beef**
- **2 cups (approximately) canned tomatoes**
- **2 teaspoons chili powder**
- **1 teaspoon salt**
- **½ cup raw rice**

Mix all ingredients in baking dish, breaking up tomatoes well. Cover and bake one hour at 325 degrees. It is important to cover the dish.

"This recipe has been a basic in my family for years."

H. R. Brantley
GFWC—The 1933 Study Club
Jefferson, Texas

Potato Mogsaka

- **1½ pounds ground beef**
- **3 onions, chopped**
- **¼ cup celery, chopped fine**
- **6 potatoes, peeled and sliced**
- **2 tablespoons butter**
- **Salt and pepper to taste**
- **4 tablespoons tomato paste or ketchup**
- **½ cup water**
- **Oil**
- **1 teaspoon oregano**
- **3 eggs**
- **2 cups milk**

Saute onions and celery. Add meat, oregano, salt and pepper. Saute all until meat is lightly browned. Stir in water and tomato paste and simmer for 10 minutes. Fry sliced potatoes in oil and butter; set aside. In 9 × 13 baking dish alternate layers of meat and potatoes. Beat eggs and add milk (reserve 1 cup). Pour over casserole. Bake at 350 degrees for 15 minutes. Remove from oven. Pour remainder of eggs and milk over top. Bake 30 minutes.

"Has been in our family at least 80 years."

Daisy M. Hamilton
GFWC—Upton Woman's Club
Upton, Massachusetts

Potato Hamburger Pinwheels

1 pound hamburger
2 tablespoons minced onion
1 tablespoon chopped parsley
1 egg
1 teaspoon salt
4 cups seasoned mashed potatoes

Mix hamburger, onion, parsley, egg and salt together. Place mashed potatoes between 2 pieces of waxed paper and roll to oblong 3/8-inch thickness. Remove top waxed paper. Spread meat mixture on top of mashed potatoes and roll as a jelly roll. Chill. Cut in 1-inch slices and place in broiler pan 3 inches from heat. Broil 7 minutes on each side or until browned.

Mary Kosak
GFWC—Woman's Club of Cape May
Cape May, New Jersey

Serendipity Beef

7 tablespoons soy sauce
1½ tablespoons cornstarch
6 tablespoons cooking oil
4 tablespoons sherry or other dry wine
Pinch of salt
1½ pounds top of round beef steak
2 packages frozen string beans (julienne cut)

Cut beef in quarter-inch strips and marinate (room temperature) for 1 hour in soy sauce, cornstarch, salt and sherry. Cook frozen string beans as directed (slightly crisp). Drain beans. Heat oil in wok or skillet. Add beef and cook for about 1 minute, turning frequently with fork. Add string beans and stir-fry until meat is done (about 2 to 3 minutes). Serve over rice or fried noodles.

"This is from a Chinese family residing in Hawaii."

Dorothy S. Hamilton
GFWC—Plymouth Valley Woman's Club
Norristown, Pennsylvania

Curried Beef 'n Broccoli

1 pound flank steak
2 cups broccoli flowerets
1 medium onion
1 cup beef broth
2 tablespoons all purpose flour
2 tablespoons curry powder
¾ teaspoon salt
3 tablespoons cooking oil

Slice steak in 2-inch strips. Cut up broccoli and cut onion in wedges. Set meat and vegetables aside. Blend broth, flour, curry powder and salt, and set aside. Heat 2 tablespoons oil and stir-fry broccoli and onion for 3 minutes. Remove vegetables. Heat remaining oil and stir-fry steak 2 minutes. Stir in flour-broth mixture and cook until bubbly. Return vegetables to pan; heat 1 minute more. Serve over rice.

Barb Bialy
GFWC—Rancho Viejo Junior Woman's Club
Lake Forest/El Toro, California

Cheesy Beef-Stuffed Peppers

- **3 large green peppers cut in half lengthwise**
- **1 pound ground beef**
- **1 cup creamed cottage cheese**
- **1 8 ounce can tomato sauce**
- **1 small onion, finely chopped**
- **1 egg**
- **⅓ cup bread crumbs**
- **1 tablespoon Worcestershire sauce**
- **2 teaspoons salt**
- **1 cup shredded processed American cheese**

Place peppers in 2 quart (12 × 7) glass baking dish; set aside. Combine remaining ingredients, except shredded cheese, in medium mixing bowl; mix well. Spoon meat mixture into green pepper halves. Cover with waxed paper. Covering holds moisture, which helps tenderize. Microwave for 24 to 26 minutes on roast, 70 percent, or until meat is well done (about 140 degrees). Top with shredded cheese and continue cooking on roast until cheese is melted.

Belinda Mills Crouch
GFWC—Chatom Junior Woman's Club
Chatom, Alabama

Stuffed Cabbage (Austrian Style)

- **1 large cabbage**
- **2 pounds ground steak**
- **1 cup rice**
- **1 large minced onion**
- **Salt to taste**
- **Pepper to taste**
- **Garlic powder to taste**
- **1 large can tomatoes**
- **2 small cans tomato paste**
- **3 tablespoons vinegar**
- **2 tablespoons brown sugar**
- **2 tablespoons honey**
- **4 gingersnaps**

Cook cabbage, head down, a few minutes in boiling water until leaves can be peeled off and are pliable. Mix meat, rice, onion, salt, pepper, garlic powder and 3 tablespoons tomato paste. Fill each cabbage leaf with meat mixture and fold like an envelope. Lay in casserole, opening down, using very small cabbage leaves at bottom to line casserole. Cover mixture with tomatoes, paste and 3 paste cans of water and rest of ingredients. Cover casserole and cook over medium heat or in 350 degree oven for 3 hours. Stir occasionally. You can adjust the sweet or sour taste to suit the cook.

Aileen Moss
GFWC—Woman's Club of Tenafly
Tenafly, New Jersey

Popover Casserole

1 pound ground beef, browned and drained
1 teaspoon seasoned salt
½ teaspoon pepper
½ teaspoon garlic powder
1 teaspoon parsley flakes
2 teaspoons instant beef bouillon dissolved in ¼ cup hot water
1 4 ounce can green chilies, diced (optional)
1 4 ounce can mushrooms (optional)
4 cups shredded cabbage
¾ cup cottage cheese
1 tablespoon cornstarch
½ cup sour cream

Popover Batter
2 eggs
1 cup milk
1 tablespoon butter or oil
1 cup flour
1 teaspoon salt
Optional: Sprinkle ¼ cup poppy seeds on top

Mix dry ingredients with hamburger; add bouillon. Spoon cabbage over meat mixture and simmer 5 minutes. Mix together: cottage cheese, sour cream, and cornstarch. Stir into meat and cabbage until thickens. Pour into 13 × 9 greased pan. Spread popover batter over. Bake in preheated 400 degree oven for 35 minutes.

Lillian Esala
GFWC—Virginia Study Club
Virginia, Minnesota

Sweet and Sour Meatloaf

1½ pounds ground round
1 medium onion, chopped fine
1 cup bread crumbs
¼ teaspoon pepper
1½ teaspoons salt
½ cup tomato sauce
1 beaten egg
½ cup tomato sauce
1 cup water
2 tablespoons vinegar
2 tablespoons prepared mustard
2 tablespoons brown sugar

Mix first seven ingredients, adding more bread crumbs if necessary to shape into a loaf. Place loaf on a greased baking pan. Combine remaining ingredients and pour over meatloaf. Baste 3 or 4 times while baking in 350 degree oven for 1½ hours.

C. Edna Rios Sissman
GFWC—Latham Woman's Club
Latham, New York

Beef Risotto Pie

1½ pounds ground beef
1 egg
½ cup bread crumbs
¼ cup milk
¼ cup chopped onion

Filling

2 cups cooked rice
¼ cup chopped green pepper
1 beef bouillon cube
1 16 ounce can Italian stewed tomatoes (crushed)
1 cup cheddar cheese, grated
1 teaspoon sugar
Salt and pepper to taste

Combine beef, egg, onions and bread crumbs. Salt and pepper to taste. Combine and mix well. Press into the bottom and up sides of 10-inch round casserole dish to make meat shell. Meantime prepare filling.

Saute green pepper in a little butter until soft. Add bouillon cube to ½ cup hot water to dissolve; add to tomatoes and pour all into rice. Mix well and simmer for 15 minutes. Pour rice mixture into meat shell. Top with cheese. Bake at 350 degrees for 25 minutes.

Catherine M. Denman
GFWC—Federated Woman's Club of Morongo Valley
Morongo Valley, California

Wow Meatloaf

1 pound ground beef
6 ounces cottage cheese
1½ slices whole wheat bread
1½ teaspoons Worcestershire sauce
1 teaspoon finely chopped fresh oregano
1 teaspoon finely chopped fresh marjoram
1 teaspoon finely chopped fresh rosemary
1 teaspoon finely chopped fresh thyme
¼ teaspoon curry powder
2 teaspoons chopped green onions with tops
½ teaspoon salt

In food processor, process bread crumbs. Add cottage cheese and process a few seconds. In bowl combine ground beef, cottage cheese-crumb mixture and all seasonings. Mix well and pat into small loaf pan. Bake in 350 degree oven for 45 minutes to 1 hour. Pour off drippings during baking as juices accumulate.

"This recipe is an original I created for a herbfest."

Ginnie Mulkey
GFWC—Tercera
Poseyville, Indiana

Meatloaf Roll

1 package chopped broccoli
2 pounds hamburger
2 eggs
¾ cup soft bread crumbs
¼ cup catsup
3 slices mild cheese, cut in halves
¼ cup milk
½ teaspoon salt
¼ teaspoon pepper
¼ teaspoon dried oregano leaves
1 teaspoon salt
1 8 ounce package ham, sliced

Rinse broccoli under running cold water to separate; drain. Mix hamburger, egg, bread, catsup, milk, salt, pepper and oregano. Pat hamburger mixture into rectangle, 12 × 10 inches, on a piece of aluminum foil 12 × 15. Arrange broccoli on hamburger mixture; arrange ham on broccoli. Roll up rectangle carefully, beginning at 10 inch side and using foil to lift. Press edges and ends of roll and seal. Place in baking dish, uncovered in 350 degree oven for 1¼ hours. Overlap cheese on top and cook just long enough to melt the cheese. (Center of meat loaf may be slightly pink due to ham).

Shari Damrow
GFWC—Douglas Civic Club
Douglas, Wyoming

Chafing Dish Meatballs

2 pounds round beef, ground twice
1 pound pork tenderloin, ground
6 eggs, beaten
2 teaspoons salt
¼ teaspoon pepper
¼ cup enriched all-purpose flour
3 tablespoons flour
½ cup salad oil
2 cans condensed beef consomme
1 tablespoon bottled sauce for gravy
¾ to 1 cup sherry

Gently mix together first 6 ingredients until blended. Shape with teaspoon into balls about ¾ inch in diameter. Brown a few at a time in hot salad oil. When meatballs are browned, put in chafing dish. Stir 3 tablespoons flour into fat left in skillet. Stir until smooth. Add consomme and gravy sauce; cook, stirring until thickened. Add sherry, pour over meatballs. Serve with buttered wide noodles topped with chopped chives.

Margaret Desris
GFWC—Twentieth Century Club
Rib Lake, Wisconsin

Meatball Medley

Meatballs

1 pound hamburger
1 medium onion, chopped
1 tablespoon parsley flakes
¾ cup quick oats
2 eggs
Dash salt
Dash pepper

Combine ingredients and shape into 1½-inch meatballs. Place in 9 × 13 inch pan. Bake 450 degrees for 25 minutes or until meatballs are browned. Drain fat. Set aside meatballs in the pan.

Sauce

4 ounces egg noodles, cooked and drained
2 small zucchini, thinly sliced
2 tomatoes, diced
1 10 ounce can cheddar cheese soup
1¼ cups water
1 teaspoon celery seed
½ cup grated cheddar cheese

Set aside grated cheese. Dilute soup with water. Combine remaining ingredients with soup. Pour soup and vegetable mixture over meatballs. Sprinkle with grated cheddar cheese. Cover with foil and bake at 350 degrees for 45 minutes. Uncover and bake 15 minutes longer.

Marlene Wright
GFWC—Sahuaro Juniors
Tucson, Arizona

Beef Burgundy

1 pound stew beef cut into 2-inch cubes
1 10 ounce can consomme, undiluted
¾ cup burgundy wine
1 medium onion, sliced
¼ cup bread crumbs
¼ cup flour
¾ teaspoon salt
¼ teaspoon pepper
1 can mushroom pieces, optional

Combine beef, wine, consomme, salt, pepper and onion in dutch oven pan. Mix flour with bread crumbs. Stir into meat mixture. Cover and bake at 300 degrees about 3 hours. Stir occasionally. Mushrooms can be added before putting in oven.

"Can be served over rice mixed with peas and mushrooms; or can be served over noodles."

Shirley Lankford
GFWC—London Bridge Woman's Club
Lake Havasu City, Arizona

Beef Stroganoff

- **1½ pounds beef (filet or sirloin)**
- **1 cup diced onions**
- **2 tablespoons butter or margarine**
- **1 small can tomato paste Plus equal amount of water**
- **1 tablespoon Worcestershire sauce**
- **1 tablespoon paprika Prepared mustard**
- **1 small can or 1 cup fresh, sliced mushrooms**
- **½ pint sour cream**

Cut meat into finger strips, then in half. Spread mustard on meat and let stand in refrigerator for at least 1 hour. Fry onions in butter. Sear meat in hot skillet. Add tomato paste, water, Worcestershire sauce, paprika, and onions. Simmer beef for about 1 hour or until tender, less time if using filet. Remove from heat, add mushrooms and sour cream. (If using fresh mushrooms, add about 15 minutes before cooking is completed.) Stir until well heated. Serve over rice.

Joann Hayden
GFWC—Twentieth Century Club
Atmore, Alabama

Stroganoff Steak Sandwiches

- **⅔ cup beer**
- **⅓ cup cooking oil**
- **1 teaspoon salt**
- **¼ teaspoon garlic powder**
- **¼ teaspoon pepper**
- **2 pounds beef flank steak (or round steak), cut 1 inch thick**
- **2 tablespoons butter or margarine**
- **½ teaspoon paprika**
- **4 cups sliced onion (sweet or mild variety)**
- **6 thick slices French bread, toasted**
- **1 cup dairy sour cream**
- **½ teaspoon horseradish**

In advance: Combine beer, oil, salt, garlic, and pepper. Pour over steak in shallow dish. Cover and marinate overnight in refrigerator.

Before serving: Drain steak; pat dry with paper towel. Broil under broiler or on barbecue grill to desired doneness. Melt butter adding paprika, dash salt and onions; cook until tender. Warm sour cream and stir in horseradish.

For each sandwich: Thinly slice meat on diagonal grain and place on top of bread slice. Top with onions, spoon sour cream mixture on top, and sprinkle with paprika if desired.

Ann Koelsch
GFWC—Gun Lake Area
Shelbyville, Michigan

Oven Stew

3 to 4 pounds chuck roast, cut in cubes
Potatoes
Carrots
Onions
Celery
Green beans, can be frozen
Peas, can be frozen
3 tablespoons tapioca
½ cup red wine
Large can tomato juice

Layer cubed meat in roasting pan. Add vegetables, salt, pepper, and marjoram if desired. Add tapioca. Cover all with tomato juice; add red wine. Cover and bake in 300 degree oven for approximately 4 to 5 hours.

Amounts of vegetables vary with number to be served.

Marguerite Miller
GFWC—Lotus Country Woman's Club
Spring Grove, Illinois

Apple Cider Stew

2 pounds beef stew meat (chuck)
Salad oil
3 tablespoons flour
2 teaspoons salt, or less to taste
¼ teaspoon pepper
¼ teaspoon thyme
2 cups apple cider
½ cup water
2 tablespoons vinegar
3 potatoes, quartered
4 carrots, sliced
1 stalk celery, sliced

In a large pan, brown meat in 1 tablespoon hot oil. Combine flour, salt, pepper, thyme and add to meat. Stir in cider, water and vinegar. Cook and stir until mixture comes to a boil. Reduce heat and simmer, covered for 1½ hours, or until meat is tender. Add potatoes, carrots and celery. Cook 30 minutes more or until vegetables are tender. Can also be made and long-simmered in a crock pot. Add vegetables, turn heat to high and cook until tender.

Paula Schaller
GFWC—Whitemarsh Junior Woman's Club
Lafayette Hill, Pennsylvania

Judy's Bar-B-Que

3 pounds ground beef
2 14 ounce bottles catsup
2 small onions, diced
1 green pepper, chopped
½ cup brown sugar
2 tablespoons dry mustard
1 tablespoon sugar
1 tablespoon salt
3 tablespoons vinegar

Brown onions, green pepper and ground meat in skillet. Drain fat. Add catsup, vinegar and dry ingredients, stirring well. Simmer 30 minutes over low heat. Crock pot or large kettle is ideal for this. Serve on hamburger buns.

Judy Broom
GFWC—Kinmundy Woman's Club
Kinmundy, Illinois

Barbecued Beef

4 pounds meat
2 cups chopped onion
1 chopped green pepper
2 chopped cloves garlic
1½ teaspoons chili powder
2 teaspoons cinnamon
2 tablespoons brown sugar
2 teaspoons salt
1 teaspoon black pepper
¼ to ½ teaspoon cayenne
4 cups catsup
2 tablespoons Worcestershire sauce
½ to 1 teaspoon tabasco sauce
3 tablespoons vinegar
3 cups stock or bouillon

Bring to boil, cover and simmer until meat falls to pieces. Serve with toasted buns and French fries. Serves 24.

Winifred Giroux
GFWC—Woman's Club of Allentown
Allentown, Pennsylvania

Short Ribs Supreme

3 pounds beef short ribs (2 pounds boneless chuck may be used)
2 teaspoons salt
½ cup water
½ cup chopped onion
1 6 ounce can tomato paste
1 cup catsup
¾ cup brown sugar
¼ cup vinegar
2 tablespoons mustard

Brown ribs in own fat, cover. Cook slowly one hour. Pour off drippings. Mix remaining ingredients and add to meat. Cover tightly. Cook for one hour and 30 minutes until tender.

Verna Mahrer
GFWC—Park River Fortnightly
Park River, North Dakota

Ono Hawaiian Steaks

- 6 medium steaks
- ¾ chopped fine dry onion
- 2 garlic buttons, chopped fine
- 1 small piece gingerroot, mashed
- ¼ ripe papaya, mashed
- 2½ tablespoons white sugar
- 2 parts water to one part soy sauce

Combine ingredients. Soak for 12 to 14 hours. Cook over charcoal fire.

"I've used this for at least 35 years."

Christian Deming Peterson
GFWC—Honolulu Woman's Club
Honolulu, Hawaii

Steak Continental

- 2 pounds flank steaks
- 1 tablespoon salt
- 1 tablespoon tomato paste
- ½ teaspoon pepper
- 1 clove garlic
- 2 to 3 tablespoons soy sauce
- 1 tablespoon vegetable oil
- ½ teaspoon oregano

Score both sides of steak with diagonal slices forming diamonds. Mash garlic with salt; add remaining ingredients. Mix well and rub into both sides of steak. Wrap in waxed paper, place in zip lock bag and refrigerate 5 to 6 hours. Grill over hot charcoal 5 to 8 minutes per side.

Joanne Meyer
GFWC—Elgin Junior Woman's Club
Elgin, Illinois

Soft Tacos with Homemade Flour Tortillas

Tortillas

- 3 cups flour
- ½ cup shortening
- 1 teaspoon baking powder
- 1½ teaspoons salt
- Scant 1 cup hot tap water

Meat Mixture

- 1½ to 2 pounds ground beef
- ½ cup bell pepper, chopped fine
- ½ cup celery, chopped fine
- ½ cup onion, chopped fine
- 1 teaspoon cumin
- Salt and pepper to taste
- 2 cloves garlic, minced

In food processor (or by hand), cut shortening into dry ingredients. Slowly add water until forms smooth dough. Roll into 1½ to 2 inch balls and roll out on cutting board into round shape. (Do not need extra flour on board.) Preheat iron skillet (use no shortening), cook on each side of tortilla about 30 to 45 seconds (medium to hi heat); keep warm in clean dish towel.

Fry and drain excess fat off meat; add other ingredients; simmer 20 minutes stirring occasionally. Serve tortillas with meat mixture, chopped lettuce and tomatoes and grated cheddar cheese.

"The tortilla recipe is one used by many Mexican cooks in the southwest."

Janice Ratliff
GFWC—Wednesday Study Club
Monahans, Texas

Western Style Bean Casserole

- 1 pound hamburger
- ½ pound bacon
- 1 onion, chopped
- 1 teaspoon salt
- ¼ teaspoon pepper
- 1 teaspoon dry mustard, optional
- ¾ cup brown sugar
- 1 cup catsup
- 2 tablespoons vinegar
- 1 tablespoon Worcestershire sauce
- ½ green pepper, chopped
- 1 clove garlic, chopped (optional)
- 1 pound can pork and beans
- 1 15 ounce can baby lima beans
- 1 15¼ ounce can large butter beans
- 1 15 ounce can dark red kidney beans
- (Drain last 3 cans of beans)

Fry bacon, drain and break into small pieces. Brown hamburger, onion, green pepper and garlic. Add salt, pepper, dry mustard, Worcestershire sauce, brown sugar, catsup, bacon, vinegar, and beans. Cover and bake in 350 degree oven about 1 hour or until bubbling and heated through. Remove cover and bake 15 minutes longer. This can also be prepared in a crock-pot approximately 3 to 4 hours or until heated thoroughly, and bubbling.

Dorothy L. Lechlitner
GFWC—General Federated Woman's Club of Goshen
Goshen, Indiana

Cornish Pasty

- 2 cups flour
- 1 teaspoon salt
- 1 teaspoon baking powder
- ⅔ cup shortening
- 1 teaspoon vinegar
- 1 beaten egg
- 3 cups diced sirloin
- 3 cups diced potatoes
- 6 tablespoons diced onion
- 3 tablespoons butter
- Salt and pepper to taste

Combine dry ingredients; blend vinegar, shortening, and egg into dry mixture. Put half of dough in 8 or 9-inch pie plate. Layer remaining ingredients. Cover with remaining dough. Seal edges of pie crust with water and crimp with fingers. Cut vents in top. Bake at 350 degrees for 1½ hours. Cover with dish towel after removing from oven and let stand 15 minutes before serving.

Marjorie Shelliam
GFWC—Hazel Green Woman's Club
Hazel Green, Wisconsin

Tourtiere

½ pound ground chuck
½ pound pork sausage meat
3 to 4 medium potatoes
1 onion
¾ cup water
Salt and pepper to taste
¼ teaspoon cinnamon, optional
¼ teaspoon allspice, optional
Pastry for 2-crust pie

Prepare pastry, wrap well and chill. Boil potatoes. While they cook, place beef and sausage in fry pan with thinly sliced onion. Partially cover with the water. Cook rapidly crumbling and stirring with a fork. When water has cooked off, salt lightly and drain excess fat. Drain and coarsely mash potato. Combine with meat, and spice if used. Cool. Taste, add pepper and more salt if needed. Fill pastry-lined pie plate. Make 1 inch triangular hole in top crust. Bake at 375 degrees until desired brown. Serve hot or cold.

"Tourtiere is the traditional French-Canadian pie served following Christmas midnight mass."

Helene Barton Loveless
GFWC—The Home Club
Cromwell, Connecticut

Italian Pie

Pie Crust

1 slightly beaten egg yolk (reserving white for filling)
1 cup biscuit mix
2 tablespoons milk

Filling

1½ pounds ground beef
½ cup onion, chopped
½ tablespoon flour
½ teaspoon salt
1 clove garlic, minced
½ teaspoon Italian seasoning
¼ teaspoon pepper
2 cups cottage cheese
1 slightly beaten egg
1 slightly beaten egg white
1 cup shredded Swiss cheese

Stir crust ingredients together and roll out on a floured surface to fit a 9-inch pie pan. Place in pie pan and flute edges. Brown the ground beef together with the onion and garlic. Drain excess fat. Add salt, pepper, Italian seasonings and flour; stir to coat meat with flour. Put into pie crust. Combine cottage cheese, egg and egg white, stirring to mix. Spoon on top the meat. Bake at 375 degrees for 15 minutes. Top with Swiss cheese and bake 10 more minutes. Let set 5 minutes before serving.

Mary Ann Sullivan
GFWC—Paris Junior Woman's Club
Paris, Illinois

Swedish Potato Sausage

- **1½ pounds pork shoulder, ground twice**
- **1½ pounds beef, ground twice**
- **3 pounds potatoes**
- **2 medium onions**
- **1 cup scalded milk**
- **1 teaspoon pepper**
- **3 tablespoons salt**
- **¾ teaspoon allspice**
- **¼ teaspoon ginger**
- **½ pound sausage casing**

Mix meat, spices and milk. Pare potatoes and peel onion. Force vegetables through food chopper, using medium knife. Add to meat mixture and mix all thoroughly. Cut casings into desired lengths. Fill each loosely with meat mixture. Tie each end securely with string. Place in bowl of slightly salted water (cold) until time to cook. To cook, cover sausage with boiling water. Bring to a hard boil. Cover and simmer for 45 minutes. Remove from water carefully to platter. Cut into 2-inch lengths for serving.

"This recipe originated in Sweden. My mother brought it to this country in 1900 when she came through Ellis Island. It has been in her family for over 200 years."

Cherrie J. Steinbach
GFWC—Dalecarlia Federated Woman's Club
Lowell, Indiana

Corned Beef

- **1 corned beef brisket**
- **6 peppercorns**
- **1 onion**
- **4 whole cloves**
- **1 stalk celery**
- **⅓ cup brown sugar**
- **1 tablespoon prepared mustard**
- **1 teaspoon horseradish**
- **⅓ cup catsup**
- **3 tablespoons vinegar**
- **2 tablespoons butter**

Place brisket in a deep pan and cover with water. Cook with peppercorns, sliced onion, cloves and celery for 2 hours or until brisket is tender. Cool and slice against the grain. Place in a baking dish. Heat together brown sugar, mustard, horseradish, catsup, vinegar and butter. Spoon on top of meat and in between slices. Heat at 350 degrees for 20 minutes and serve.

Rose M. Ditto
GFWC—Portia Club
Wamego, Kansas

Reuben Casserole

- 1 27 ounce can sauerkraut, drained
- 4 tablespoons thousand island dressing
- 1 tablespoon margarine
- 3 3 ounce packages sliced corned beef, chopped
- 2 cups Swiss cheese, shredded
- 2 cups rye bread crumbs
- ¼ teaspoon caraway seeds

Spread sauerkraut in a 13 × 9 × 2 baking dish. Spread with dressing and sprinkle with caraway seeds. Top with corned beef and cheese. Spread crumbs on top. Dot with butter. Bake at 375 degrees for 30 minutes.

Minnie D. Witchey
GFWC—Shadyside Woman's Club
Shadyside, Ohio

Corned Beef Pot

- 1 can corned beef (12 ounces)
- 8 medium-sized potatoes
- 2 medium-sized onions
- 1 stalk parsley

Refrigerate 1 can of corned beef until chilled. Pare, rinse, and dice potatoes and onions into 1-inch pieces. Barely cover with water and boil until just tender. Open can of corned beef. Dice meat into 1-inch pieces and fold into cooked potatoes and onions. Drain any excess broth into your "soup" saver jar. Add some fresh chopped parsley to top of serving dish, for color and added nutrition. Serve hot!

Mary Alice Dernberger
GFWC—Mutual and Civic Improvement Club
Hebron, Ohio

Corned Beef Casserole

- 1 8 ounce package noodles or shell macaroni
- 1 12 ounce can corned beef
- ¼ cup chopped celery
- ¼ pound grated cheese
- ¼ cup chopped onion
- ¾ cup buttered crumbs
- 1 can cream of chicken soup
- 1 cup milk
- 1 cup frozen peas

Cook macaroni according to directions and drain well. Break up the corned beef. Blend all ingredients except crumbs and spread into a 9 × 13-inch pan. Sprinkle the crumbs on top. Bake at 350 degrees for 45 minutes.

Marie Chocholousek
GFWC—Verdigre Woman's Club
Verdigre, Nebraska

Beer-Braised Loin of Pork

1 5 pound pork roast
3 large onions, chopped
1 pound carrots, peeled and diced
1 12-ounce bottle dark beer
2 teaspoons salt
¼ teaspoon pepper
1 bay leaf
5 whole cloves

Brown pork loin well on all sides in a kettle or heavy roasting pan. Remove from pan. Saute onions and carrots until soft in pork drippings. Stir in beer, salt, pepper, bay leaf and whole cloves. Return pork to kettle and cover. Braise in moderate oven (350) for 2 hours or until pork is tender when pierced with a fork. Place pork on platter and keep warm. Pour cooking liquid from kettle into a large bowl. Skim off fat; remove bay leaf, place liquid and solids in container of electric blender and whirl at low speed until smooth. Pour sauce into saucepan. Heat to boiling, stirring often. Stir in a little gravy coloring if needed. Generously spoon the sauce over the sliced pork.

Bonnie L. Pottinger
GFWC—Glendale Woman's Club
Glendale, Wisconsin

Company Casserole

1 6-ounce package seasoned long grain and wild rice
1 package frozen, chopped broccoli
1 12-ounce can chopped ham, cut into ½-inch cubes
1 can sliced mushrooms, drained
1 cup sharp cheddar cheese, cut into ½-inch cubes
1 can condensed cream of celery soup
2 teaspoons prepared mustard
1 cup mayonnaise
1 teaspoon curry, optional
¼ cup grated parmesan cheese

Cook rice and broccoli according to directions on packages. Spread rice on bottom of a buttered 13 × 9 × 2 pan, or larger. Top with broccoli, ham, mushrooms and cheese. Blend soup with mayonnaise, mustard and curry. Pour soup mixture over all. Sprinkle parmesan cheese on top. (You can stretch casserole by using more broccoli and/or 1 pound canned ham). Variation: Rice, broccoli, leftover chicken, cheese, mushroom soup, mayonnaise, curry, parmesan, plus a little salt. Bake at 350 degrees for 1 hour or until brown.

"I got this recipe from my mother-in-law about 20 years ago."

Nancy Lou Olson
GFWC—Woman's Club of Shillington
Shillington, Pennsylvania

Oslo Pork Chops

- 4 pork chops
- 2 tablespoons brown sugar
- 2 tablespoons vinegar
- 2 beef bouillon cubes
- 1 tablespoon Worcestershire sauce
- 1 teaspoon dry mustard or curry
- 1 cup hot water
- 1 medium onion

Flour pork chops in seasoned flour. Sear in pan. Combine sugar, vinegar, mustard and Worcestershire sauce. Add to hot water and bouillon. Pour over chops. Add sliced onion on top. Cook 10 minutes at 400 degrees; 1½ hours at 350 degrees. Sauce can be thickened with cornstarch. Pour over rice.

Grace Bradshaw
GFWC—Albany Woman's Club
Albany, Oregon

Bar-B-Q Pork Chops

- 6–8 lean center cut pork chops
- 1 16-ounce can tomatoes
- ½ cup brown sugar
- ¼ cup vinegar
- ½ teaspoon allspice
- 1 teaspoon cinnamon
- Salt and pepper

Brown pork chops in small amount of hot oil in large frying pan. Mix all other ingredients and pour over chops. Simmer over low heat until chops are tender, about 1 hour. Serve on large platter with mounds of rice between each chop. (Optional) Top each mound of rice with a circle of boiled slice of green pepper. Serve remaining sauce as gravy.

Doris M. Swearingen
GFWC—Hampden Township Civic Club
Hampden Township, Pennsylvania

Hecka (Oriental Dish)

- 1½ pounds pork butt (slice ¼ inch thick and cube)
- 1 clove garlic, chopped
- 1 stalk celery
- 3 onions, chopped
- 1 green pepper, cut in bite-size pieces
- ½ cup soy sauce
- 1 can bamboo shoots
- 1 can water chestnuts
- 1 package mushrooms
- 6–8 tablespoons sugar
- 2 tablespoons cornstarch
- ¼ cup water

In large skillet, cut fat off meat and melt. Use the grease to brown meat for 15 minutes. Add garlic the last few minutes. Add celery on top of meat; also a good swoop of soy sauce and two tablespoons of the sugar. Do not stir till it comes to a boil. After stirring, add onions, the same amount of soy sauce and sugar. Wait to boil, then stir. Then add green pepper, soy sauce and sugar. Wait to boil, then stir. Last comes mushrooms, shoots, chestnuts and remaining sugar and more soy sauce. Wait till boiling and stir. Thicken with cornstarch mixture

"I received this recipe over 30 years ago. It came from a Japanese American who has since passed away."

Helen M. Brace
GFWC—Bessemer Woman's Club
Bessemer, Michigan

Sweet-Sour Pork Chops

4 pork chops, 1 inch thick
2 tablespoons flour
½ teaspoon salt
1 tablespoon oil
1 3 or 4 ounce can mushrooms
1 large onion
2 tablespoons molasses
2 teaspoons soy sauce
2 tablespoons vinegar

Sprinkle pork chops with flour combined with salt. Brown in oil in skillet. Drain mushrooms, reserving the liquid. Cover chops with thinly sliced onion and mushrooms. Measure mushroom liquid and add enough water to make 1 cup. Add remaining ingredients. Pour over browned pork chops, mushrooms and onions. Cook over low heat for 45 minutes to an hour until pork chops are done. Serve over rice.

"This recipe was given to me over 30 years ago by a friend in Texas of whom I have long since lost track."

Lois C. Stanton
GFWC—Milwaukee-Suburban Woman's Club
Milwaukee, Wisconsin

American Chop Suey

3 pounds lean pork, diced
1 6 ounce package egg noodles
1 large green pepper, chopped fine
1 can pimiento, cut fine
1 can cream of chicken soup, thinned with pork broth
⅜ pound cheddar cheese, cut in small pieces
1 can cream style corn
Salt to taste
Buttered bread crumbs

Boil pork until tender (save broth). Cook noodles in slightly salted water (when done, drain and rinse with hot water). Mix all ingredients together, except corn, and place in buttered baking dish. Spread corn on top and cover with buttered crumbs. Bake about 1 hour in moderate oven; 350 degrees.

"This recipe has been in our family for more than 40 years."

Elizabeth M. Burton
GFWC—Suburban Woman's Club of Wauwatosa
Wauwatosa, Wisconsin

Mary's Barbecue

2–4 pound pork roast
1 cup liquid from roast
1 family-sized bottle of catsup
1 tablespoon brown sugar
1 teaspoon dry mustard
1 tablespoon Worcestershire
1 onion, chopped

In large pot, cover meat with water. Boil until tender. Remove meat from bone and shred. Add remaining ingredients and simmer until well mixed and thickened.

"I have served this to my family for 17 years and my mother-in-law served it to hers before that. This is truly a family recipe."

Alice M. Davidson
GFWC—Durham Junior Woman's Club
Durham, North Carolina

Old Virginia Ham

10–12 pound ham
Water
Brown sugar
Few cloves

Wash ham thoroughly and cover with cold water. Allow ham to soak in water overnight. Change water and cook slowly for three or four hours. Let cool in water used for cooking. Remove from water. Remove skin, sprinkle with brown sugar, and dot with cloves. Brown in oven.

Janie M. Townsend
GFWC—Keysville Woman's Club
Keysville, Virginia

Pork Szechwan

2 pounds boneless pork
¼ cup soy sauce
¼ cup cornstarch
1½ inches peanut oil for frying
1 clove garlic, mashed
1 egg, well beaten
2 tablespoons sherry

Sauce

2 tablespoons peanut oil
1 cup chopped green onions
1 4 ounce can chilies, chopped
Water
Salt
Tabasco as desired
1 clove garlic, chopped
1 can tomato sauce
2 tablespoons vinegar

Cut pork into thin slices, 2 inches long and ⅛ inch thick. Sprinkle with salt and pepper. Mix remaining ingredients until smooth; add pork strips and coat. (Best if left to marinate 8 hours or overnight.) Heat oil in wok or skillet and fry pork a few strips at a time until crisp. (About 2 to 3 minutes.) Drain strips on absorbent paper. Sauce: Heat oil and saute garlic and green onions until golden. Stir in tomato sauce, chilies and vinegar and stir until bubbly. Add water to thin if necessary and season with salt and tabasco to taste. Add pork strips and simmer to heat through. Serve with rice or noodles as entree or add water chestnuts and red pepper hunks to serve as hors d'oeuvre with toothpicks.

Tammy Guensler
GFWC—North Sacramento Woman's Club
Sacramento, California

Pork Chops and Rice

1 cup uncooked rice
6 pork chops
2 cans onion soup
2 cups cold water mixed with soup

Salt and pepper chops. Place on top of rice. Pour soup and water over rice and chops. (Pork chops may be browned in frying pan before placing on top of rice, if desired.) Bake in 350 degree oven for 1 hour.

Mary Margaret Roberson
GFWC—Presidents' Council of Dallas Federation of Woman's Clubs
Dallas, Texas

Grandmother's Holiday Ham

One half ham, six or seven pounds fully cooked (butt end)
2 quarts apple cider
1 cup brown sugar
2 teaspoons dry mustard
1 teaspoon ground cinnamon
Cloves to stud ham

Soak ham overnight in cider in a large pan, skin side down. Refrigerate. Remove ham from pan and drain cider into saucepan. Place ham on rack in roasting pan and bake at 350 degrees for about two hours (20 minutes per pound). Baste occasionally with cider. Remove ham from oven and strip off skin if necessary. Score ham. Mix brown sugar, mustard and cinnamon and spread over ham. Stud ham with cloves. Return to oven and continue to bake 30 minutes at 350 degrees, basting with cider. Let stand for 20 minutes before slicing.

Lee Klocko
GFWC—Wyoming Woman's Club
Wyoming, Pennsylvania

Fresh Sausage with Raisin Sauce

2 pounds fresh Polish sausage or mild Italian sausage
2 cups of stock (water from boiling sausage)
1 cup of raisins
2 tablespoons sugar
2 tablespoons water
1 tablespoon cornstarch

Boil sausage in 2 quarts of water for ½ hour. Save 2 cups of stock from saucepan. Place stock in a smaller saucepan and add 1 cup of raisins. Bring to a boil and simmer until raisins become plump. Caramelize sugar and water. Add to the raisin sauce and thicken by adding the cornstarch. Cut the sausage into links and place into the raisin sauce. Heat thoroughly. Serve with mashed potatoes.

Irene A. Benedict
GFWC—Tempe Woman's Club
Tempe, Arizona

Sausage and Peppers

2 large onions
6 peppers
2 pounds sausage (sweet)
½ cup white wine
2 tablespoons olive oil
2½ pounds white potatoes
Oregano, salt, pepper and garlic powder to taste

Coat bottom of roasting pan with olive oil. Cut onions, peppers and sausage into chunks. Put into roasting pan. Stir. Add wine and seasonings. Stir. Place in 300 degree oven for 1 hour. Stir often. Peel and quarter potatoes. Parboil potatoes. After 1 hour of cooking, add potatoes; stir. Cook covered ½ hour and then uncovered for ½ hour. Drain fat and serve.

Adrienne Ross
GFWC—Junior Woman's Club of River Edge
River Edge, New Jersey

Wild Rice and Sausage

- 1 pound bulk sausage
- 1 pound mushrooms, sliced
- 2 onions, chopped
- 2 cups wild rice, cooked
- 1/4 cup flour
- 1/2 cup cream
- 2 1/2 cups chicken broth (may use bouillon cubes)
- Oregano, thyme and pepper to taste

Saute sausage and break into small pieces. Saute mushrooms in sausage pan. Mix flour with cream until smooth and stir in chicken broth and seasonings. Combine all in 2 1/2 quart casserole and bake at 350 degrees for 25 to 30 minutes.

Tammy Guensler
GFWC—North Sacramento Woman's Club
Sacramento, California

Cavatini

- 1 green pepper
- 1 medium onion
- 1 large jar mushrooms
- 1 pound hot sausage
- 1 large jar spaghetti sauce
- 1 roll sliced pepperoni
- 1/2 box rotini noodles (cooked and drained)
- 1/4 to 1/2 cup water
- 1 large bag mozzarella cheese, shredded

Cook first four ingredients; put in very large casserole dish. Add sauce, water and noodles; stir. Cover with cheese. Bake at 400 degrees for 20 minutes.

Florence Blanton
GFWC—Jackson Junior Woman's Club
Jackson, Kentucky

Family Cheese and Egg Bake

- 1 12-ounce package pizza sausage
- 1 cup small curd cottage cheese
- 1/4 cup oil
- 1 3/4 cups pancake mix
- 3 cups cubed mozzarella cheese
- 6 eggs, well beaten

Brown sausage in skillet; drain. Add sausage, cottage cheese, oil, pancake mix and cheese to eggs; mix well. Pour into 9 × 13 baking pan. Bake at 350 degrees for 25–30 minutes or until set. Cut into squares. Serve warm with butter and syrup.

Ruth Janowicz
GFWC—Bay City Woman's Club
Bay City, Michigan

Baked Linguine

- **1 box linguine**
- **2 pounds regular sausage**
- **1 pound hot sausage**
- **1 large jar spaghetti sauce**
- **Sliced mozzarella cheese**
- **1 medium onion (chopped)**
- **Spices to taste**

Cook linguine according to package directions; drain. Fry sausages with chopped onion, drain. Mix sausages with spaghetti sauce and spices or seasonings you prefer. Add linguine. Put in 9 × 13 pan. Top with slices of mozzarella cheese. Bake at 350 degrees for 30–40 minutes or until cheese melts.

Brenda D. Taylor
GFWC—Batesburg-Leesville Woman's Club
Batesburg, South Carolina

Sausage-Lima Bean Bake

- **1 pound dried lima beans, large size**
- **1 pound sausage meat**
- **1 large onion, chopped**
- **1 large can tomato sauce**
- **4 tablespoons brown sugar**
- **4 slices bacon**

Soak lima beans overnight and cook till tender. Drain. Brown onion lightly, add sausage, and cook till sausage crumbles. Add to lima beans; then add tomato sauce and sugar. Top with bacon. Bake in casserole at 350 degrees for 45 minutes.

Alice Miller
GFWC—Woman's Club of Westwood
Westwood, New Jersey

Surprise Onions Italiano

- **4–6 large onions**
- **1 pound pork sausage**
- **1 cup soft bread crumbs**
- **8 tablespoons Italian or French dressing**
- **⅓ cup grated parmesan cheese and mozzarella cheese**
- **¼ cup chopped parsley**
- **1 cup tomato sauce**

Parboil onions for 20 minutes. Drain and peel when cool. Hollow out and reserve centers. Leave about ¼ inch thick shell. Chop reserved onion to make 2 cups. In medium skillet, brown sausage well, and drain. Add onion and cook 5 minutes. Stir in bread crumbs, 6 tablespoons Italian dressing, cheese and parsley. Spoon mixture into onion shells and place in baking dish. Top with tomato sauce and remaining dressing. Cover to bake. Bake at 375 degrees for 1 hour.

Margaret D. Thompson
GFWC—New Madrid Woman's Club
New Madrid, Missouri

Easter Pizza

1 pound boiled or baked ham, 1/4 inch slices cut in cubes
1 stick pepperoni, sliced thin
1 pound Swiss cheese, sliced thin
3 pounds ricotta cheese
Eggs, as needed

In a large glass baking dish or pan, make a layer of pepperoni to completely cover the inner surface. Add layers of ricotta, ham (press cubes into ricotta) and Swiss cheese. Keep repeating until the pan is full. Leave 1 inch of headroom. Beat eggs, one at a time, pouring into the pan, until the spaces between ingredients are full. A thin spatula can help distribute eggs. Bake until the eggs are completely set at 350 degrees, at least 45 minutes. Serve hot or cold.

Ava M. Biffer
GFWC—Bloomfield Woman's Club
Bloomfield, Connecticut

Meatballs with Sour Cream Sauce

1 1/2 pounds ground pork
1 egg
1/2 cup seasoned bread crumbs
1/2 cup milk
1/2 cup chopped onions
1 1/2 teaspoons salt
1/2 teaspoon marjoram
Pepper
4 tablespoons flour
2 tablespoons oil
1 cup water
1 beef bouillon cube
1/2 cup sour cream
2 teaspoons lemon juice
Mashed potatoes
1/4 cup parmesan cheese

Combine pork, eggs, bread crumbs, milk, onion, salt, marjoram and pepper; mix. Shape into balls, 1 1/2 inches round. Roll in 2 tablespoons flour. Brown in salad oil in skillet. Mound in center of 2-quart casserole. Measure drippings in skillet; add more oil to make 2 tablespoons. Stir in remaining flour. Gradually stir in water and bouillon cubes. Boil and remove. Add sour cream and lemon juice. Spoon mashed potatoes around meatballs. Sprinkle potatoes with cheese. Pour sour cream over meat balls. Bake at 350 degrees for 1 hour.

Sharon Peterson
GFWC—Wheaton Junior Woman's Club
Wheaton, Illinois

Pork Dinner

- **7–10 pork chops (use cutlet or cut meat off bone)**
- **1 tablespoon seasoned salt**
- **1 tablespoon paprika**
- **½ cup flour**
- **12 ounces gouda cheese**
- **1 cup whipping cream**

Grease a 9 × 12 baking dish. Put flour, salt and paprika in a bag to mix; add pork chops and shake to coat all pieces. Lay meat in baking dish and refrigerate for 12 to 24 hours. Remove from refrigerator and let warm a few hours before putting into oven (unless using a metal pan). Slice gouda cheese and cover meat. Whip cream and add ½ teaspoon seasoned salt. Pour over pork chops and bake one hour at 350 degrees. If too brown, cover with foil.

Janice Franklin May
GFWC—Flint Hills Federated Club
Manhattan, Kansas

Baked Pork Chops/Rice/Green Beans

- **6 thick pork chops**
- **1 10-ounce can cream of mushroom soup**
- **18 ounces frozen green beans**
- **Salt and pepper as desired**
- **1 cup chicken broth**
- **1 cup regular rice**
- **10 ounces milk**
- **½ teaspoon dill weed**

Bring chicken broth to boil, add rice and parboil. Put dill weed in mushroom soup diluted with 1 soup can of milk. Mix green beans with rice and place in baking dish. Brown pork chops and place on top of other ingredients. Cover; bake 45 minutes at 350 degrees.

Dorothy Zettler
GFWC—Mesquite Club
Las Vegas, Nevada

Williamsburg Pork

- **4 large pork chops**
- **1 onion, cut into 4 slices**
- **¼ cup smooth peanut butter**
- **½ can cream of mushroom soup**
- **¼ cup milk**
- **1 teaspoon Worcestershire**
- **1 teaspoon salt**
- **⅛ teaspoon pepper**

Trim fat from chops, then brown well. Place in flat casserole. Top each chop with slice of onion and ¼ of the peanut butter. Mix the remaining ingredients and pour over the chops. Bake at 300 degrees until the chops are tender, about 1 hour.

Helen C. Hammack
GFWC—Rossmoor Woman's Club
Los Alamitos, California

Stuffed Pork Chops with Apple Cornbread Dressing

6 10-ounce, center-cut pork chops, thick enough to cut a pocket in one side
Salt
Freshly ground pepper
3 tablespoons butter

Apple Corn Bread Dressing
½ cup dry bread crumbs
1 cup coarse cornbread crumbs
1¼ teaspoons salt
¼ teaspoon freshly ground pepper
3 eggs, beaten
¼ cup chopped walnuts
½ cup chopped apples

Preheat oven to 325 degrees. Stuff the pork chops with apple corn bread dressing and skewer the edge with toothpicks to keep closed. Season with salt and pepper; melt the butter in a heavy skillet; and cook chops until golden brown on both sides. Turn gently. Cook about 12 minutes. Place in a baking dish with 1½ cups water. Bake covered in preheated oven for 30 minutes. Before serving, spoon on hot tangy raisin sauce. Note: For best results, ask the butcher to cut the pockets for you. Toss bread crumbs and cornbread crumbs together. Add salt, pepper, beaten eggs and walnuts. Dressing should be light and fluffy. Add apples last.

Tangy Raisin Sauce
¼ cup brown sugar
¾ teaspoon prepared mustard
1½ teaspoons flour
¼ cup raisins
¼ cup red wine
¾ cup water

Mix brown sugar, mustard and flour together in a saucepan. Add raisins, wine and water. Bring to a boil. Lower heat and simmer about 10 minutes stirring constantly.

Bonnie Kellenberg
GFWC—Art and Literature Club
Parkville, Missouri

Mock Ham and Cheese Souffle

16 slices white bread
16 thin slices ham
8 ounces grated Swiss cheese
8 ounces grated cheddar cheese
6 beaten eggs
½ teaspoon onion salt
½ teaspoon dry mustard
3 cups milk
3 cups crushed corn flakes
½ cup melted butter

In 9 × 13 inch greased casserole, arrange ingredients in layers as follows: bread, ham, ½ of each of cheeses. Repeat. Combine beaten eggs, milk and dry ingredients. Pour over casserole. Refrigerate overnight. Sprinkle corn flakes and melted butter over top just before baking. Bake at 325 degrees for 45 minutes.

Helen Decibus
GFWC—Woman's Club of Avenel
Avenel, New Jersey

Etta's Expandable Pork Chop Casserole

Pork chops—as many as desired
Potatoes—enough for a 2-inch layer
Onions—enough for a 1-inch layer
Bread stuffing, seasoned—1-inch layer
Diluted cream of mushroom soup or just water
Butter

Slice peeled, raw potatoes into a greased casserole (casserole according to how many you want to serve: 1½ quart for 4 people; up to an electric or non-electric roaster for 20). Salt and pepper the potato layer. For the sliced onion layer, allow about 1 medium onion per person. Salt and pepper. Dot with butter. Mix your favorite bread dressing (stuffing) and layer over onions. Add required number of chops for top layer. Add water or diluted cream of mushroom soup to the top of the potato layer. Cover and bake at 350 degrees about 1–1½ hours to brown; longer if potatoes aren't done.

"This was my mother's recipe (she was born in 1880) and will accommodate any number of diners."

Jeanne Brooks Watkins
GFWC—Lawton Woman's Forum
Lawton, Oklahoma

Italian Stuffed Peppers

2 large or 3 medium green peppers
1 pound bulk pizza sausage
1 jar spaghetti sauce
Mozzarella cheese

Cut peppers in half, lengthwise and clean. Brown pizza sausage for about 4–5 minutes, breaking into small pieces. Divide among peppers, filling well. Spoon 2 tablespoons spaghetti sauce over each. Cover with aluminum foil and bake 1 hour at 350 degrees. Last 10 minutes, remove foil and sprinkle each pepper with shredded mozzarella.

Sandy Saily
GFWC—Bessemer Woman's Club
Bessemer, Michigan

Squash Casserole

1 pound sausage
2 cloves garlic
5 cups sliced yellow squash
¾ cup dry bread crumbs
¾ cup parmesan cheese
½ cup milk
2 tablespoons parsley
½ teaspoon oregano
½ teaspoon salt
2 eggs, beaten

Saute sausage and garlic until sausage is lightly browned; drain. Cook squash in a small amount of boiling, salted water until tender; drain. Combine sausage, squash and remaining ingredients; blend well. Spoon into lightly greased 10 × 6 × 1½ baking dish. Bake at 325 degrees for 20 minutes.

Margo Whitley
GFWC—Shakespeare Club
Lancaster, Texas

Acorn Squash with Sausage

- **2 medium acorn squash, halved and seeded**
- **Salt to taste**
- **½ pound bulk sausage**
- **1 medium onion, chopped**
- **¼ cup bread crumbs**

Place cut side of squash down in pan. Add ½ inch of boiling water to pan. Bake at 375 degrees for 35 minutes. Remove from oven and turn squash, cut side up. Sprinkle with salt if needed. Set aside. Cook sausage and onion until browned, stirring to break up meat. Drain off excess fat. Stir in bread crumbs. Fill squash. Bake at 375 degrees for 20 minutes more. Serve hot.

"This recipe is 35 years old and came from Midwest."

Beulah W. Sherman
GFWC—Woman's Club of Titusville, Inc.
Titusville, Florida

Rice and Sausage

- **1¼ pound hot sausage**
- **1 medium green pepper, chopped**
- **1 cup celery, chopped**
- **2 cups raw rice, rinsed in strainer**
- **2 cans chicken gumbo soup**
- **2 cans water**
- **1 package sliced almonds**
- **1½ cups sharp cheese, grated**

Brown sausage, celery and pepper. Drain off excess grease. Add rest of ingredients, cover and bake for 1 hour. Check at 45 minutes for doneness. You can also brown the ingredients, put in a crock pot and cook slowly for a longer time. It is a rich, satisfying dish.

Yvonne T. Rodgers
GFWC—Mothers' Club of DeWitt
DeWitt, Arkansas

Sausage Roll

- **2 cups flour**
- **½ teaspoon salt**
- **3 teaspoons baking powder**
- **5 tablespoons shortening**
- **⅔ cup milk**
- **1 pound hot pork sausage**

Sift flour, salt and baking powder; cut in shortening until mixture resembles coarse crumbs. Add milk all at once and mix. Divide dough into 2 parts. Roll out ¼ inch thick and spread with sausage. Roll like a jelly roll. Repeat for 2nd roll; wrap and chill. Slice in ¼ inch slices and bake in 400 degree oven for 5–10 minutes.

Gladys Fuller Pittman
GFWC—Sorosis
New Brockton, Alabama

Drunken Polish Sausages

8–10 Polish sausages
1 bay leaf (whole)
1 medium onion—quartered
2 cans beer

Cut Polish sausage in 1½–2-inch chunks. Place in 2-quart microwave dish. Add rest of ingredients. Microwave on high for 5 minutes. Rotate and turn to simmer for 5–7 minutes. Let stand, covered, 5 minutes. Serve with mashed potatoes and vegetables.

Maxine Slattery
GFWC—Rice Lake Federated Woman's Club
Rice Lake, Wisconsin

Frittata—Fresh Garden Variety

1 pound ground Italian sausage
½ cup chopped onion
½ cup chopped peppers
½ cup chopped zucchini
1 cup fresh spinach, finely torn
½ teaspoon sweet basil
Salt and pepper to taste
8 eggs, beaten
½ teaspoon lemon pepper
1 tomato, chopped
⅔ cup grated Swiss cheese
¼ cup parmesan cheese, or less to taste

Preheat broiler. Saute meat and vegetables (except tomato) in 10-inch cast iron skillet. Add butter if necessary. Sprinkle with basil, salt and pepper. Cook over medium heat until almost done. Whisk together the eggs and lemon pepper. Pour over meat mixture. Sprinkle with additional salt if desired. Cook over medium low heat; air bubbles will begin popping up. Sprinkle tomatoes over top. When eggs are almost cooked, place under broiler to finish off the top. Sprinkle with cheeses and return to broiler until melted. Cut like a pie. Serve from the skillet or ease onto serving platter.

Joan Krafka Meany
GFWC—Cedar Falls Junior Woman's Department
Cedar Falls, Iowa

Miniature Ham Pies

1 cup diced ham
½ cup diced salami or pepperoni
1 cup cheddar cheese, cubed (any sharp cheese)
1 tablespoon grated cheese
½ teaspoon salt
½ teaspoon pepper
1 egg
1 cup flour
½ teaspoon baking powder
1 cup milk

Grease miniature muffin tins well. Mix all ingredients and fill cups ¾ full. Bake at 375 degrees for 20–25 minutes or until slightly browned. Makes 3 dozen.

Sonny O'Neill
GFWC—Branford Woman's Club
Branford, Connecticut

Ham-Noodle Casserole

- 1½ cups homemade noodles
- 2 tablespoons butter
- 2 tablespoons flour
- 1 cup milk
- 1 cup grated cheese (sharp cheddar)
- 1 teaspoon salt
- 1 tablespoon catsup
- 1 tablespoon horseradish
- 2 cups chopped chunk ham
- 1 cup drained peas

Cook noodles; drain. Mix butter, flour and milk to make white sauce. Remove from heat, add cheese. Stir until melted. Add noodles, ham, peas and seasoning. Pour into 1¼ quart greased casserole. Top with ¼ cup of buttered bread crumbs. Bake at 350 degrees for 30 minutes.

Audrey McNutt
GFWC—Elquartelejo Study Club
Scott City, Kansas

Hawaiian Ham Loaves

- 8 whole graham crackers (32 sections)
- 1 pound ground ham
- 1 pound ground pork
- 1 pound ground beef
- 3 eggs
- 1 cup milk
- ⅔ cup tomato juice
- 2 15-ounce cans pineapple slices (16)
- 16 whole maraschino cherries

Sauce

- 1 cup brown sugar
- 2 teaspoons dry mustard
- ⅓ cup vinegar
- ½ cup water

Crush graham crackers; add meats, eggs, milk and tomato juice and mix well. Shape mixture into 16 portions (½ cup each) and place on a pineapple slice. Top with a cherry and place in baking dish. In a small saucepan, combine sauce ingredients and bring to a boil. Pour over ham loaves. Cover dish. Bake at 325 degrees, 45 minutes, basting occasionally. Remove cover and bake another 30 minutes.

Joan Krafka Meany
GFWC—Cedar Falls Junior Woman's Department
Cedar Falls, Iowa

Ham Rolls, Peaches In Raisin Sauce

½ cup light brown sugar, firmly packed
1½ teaspoons powdered dry mustard
1 tablespoon cornstarch
1 large can peach halves
¼ cup wine vinegar
½ cup seedless raisins
1 tablespoon butter or margarine
8 slices ready-to-eat, thin ham

Ahead of time: Blend sugar, mustard and cornstarch in small saucepan. Drain syrup from peach halves; measure and add enough water to make 1¼ cups. Stir this into sugar mixture. Add wine vinegar and heat to boiling, stirring occasionally; then cook until clear and thick. Remove from heat; stir in raisins and butter. Cool to room temperature. This may be used immediately or made the day before the party. If made ahead, store raisin sauce and peaches in covered dishes in refrigerator till ready to use. Roll up ham slices and fasten with toothpicks. To cook and serve: heat sauce, stirring occasionally. Add peach halves, ham rolls and continue heating, spooning sauce over peaches and rolls till all are piping hot. Serve at once in the dish it was heated in. Makes 4 or 8 servings, depending on your guests' appetites.

Dorothy L. Losio
GFWC—Woman's Club of Farmingdale
Farmingdale, New York

Breakfast Casserole

2 pounds sausage
9–12 eggs
1½ cups milk
1½ teaspoons dry mustard
1 teaspoon salt
1 pound bag potatoes O'Brien
1½ cup cheddar cheese, grated

Brown sausage, crumble and drain. Cook potatoes in sausage skillet about 15 minutes. Mix eggs, milk and seasonings. Place potatoes in 9 × 13 pan, cover with sausage; pour egg mixture over all and sprinkle cheese on top. Cover and refrigerate overnight. Bake at 350 degrees for 35 minutes or until firm. Let stand 10 minutes and serve.

Anita Mitchell
GFWC—Home Representative Club
Collinsville, Oklahoma

Sausage Casserole

2½ cups herbed croutons
1 pound bulk sausage, fried and well drained
2 cups sharp cheese, grated
6 eggs, well beaten
2 cups milk
1 can mushroom soup
1 small can mushrooms

Grease a glass dish, 9 × 9 × 4 or larger. Layer on bottom of dish the croutons, sausage and cheese. Make a mix of eggs and other ingredients. Pour over ingredients in dish. Bake on a cookie sheet in a preheated, 300 degree oven for 1½ hours.

Glennie Speed
GFWC—Parnassus
Jackson, Mississippi

Breakfast Casserole

- **4 slices bread**
- **½ pound sausage**
- **4 eggs**
- **½ cup milk**
- **½ cup shredded cheese**
- **Dash salt**
- **Butter**

Butter both sides of bread and place in casserole dish. Brown sausage until crumbly. Place on top of bread. Mix eggs, milk and salt. Pour over sausage. Top with cheese. Refrigerate overnight. Bake at 325 degrees for 30 minutes.

Betty Lou Graves
GFWC—Georgetown Woman's Club
Georgetown, Kentucky

Pigs in the Blanket

- **1 head of cabbage**
- **1 pound ground sausage**
- **1 small can sauerkraut**
- **1 cup uncooked rice**
- **1 quart tomato juice**

Boil cabbage until leaves will separate. Drain. Pull leaves off head of cabbage. Mix sausage, drained sauerkraut and rice well. Place sausage mixture in a cabbage leaf. Roll. Secure with toothpicks. Place in deep pan. Cover with 1 quart tomato juice on top of stove. Bring to boil. Put lid on pan and simmer about 2 hours.

"This recipe was given to my mother by a Hungarian friend in the 1940's."

Mrs. James H. Roberts
GFWC—Woman's Club of Elizabeth
Elizabeth, West Virginia

Kraut Supreme

- **2 16-ounce cans kraut**
- **1 can chicken broth**
- **¼ cup sugar**
- **½ teaspoon sage or oregano**
- **1 teaspoon caraway seed**
- **½–¾ pound smoked or summer sausage**
- **2 tablespoons chopped pimiento**
- **¼ cup chopped onion**
- **½ cup chopped celery**

Drain kraut well and rinse off juice. Add chicken broth and all other ingredients. Simmer slowly on top of stove until all flavors are blended—at least 1 hour. Variation to recipe: Brown ½ pound of pork sausage and add to above recipe before cooking.

Mae Adams
GFWC—Tuesday Study Club
Kincaid, Kansas

Ham Di Parma

- **1 8 ounce package spaghetti**
- **½ cup shredded parmesan**
- **⅓ cup butter or margarine**
- **6 ounces mushrooms, sliced**
- **1 small onion, chopped**
- **¼ cup flour**
- **2 cups cream**
- **¾ cup sauterne wine**
- **1 pound cooked ham, cut in strips**
- **⅓ cup sliced green olives**
- **Sliced pimiento strips**
- **¼ teaspoon oregano**
- **⅛ teaspoon black pepper**
- **¼ cup grated parmesan**

Melt butter in large skillet. Add mushrooms and onions. After sauteeing 5 minutes, remove mushrooms and onion. Cook spaghetti (al dente). Toss spaghetti with ½ cup parmesan cheese. Set aside. Blend flour with butter. Remove from heat and gradually add cream, stirring constantly. Bring mixture to a boil. Blend in wine, mushrooms, ham, olives, pimiento, oregano and pepper. Spoon over hot spaghetti in large baking dish. Sprinkle with parmesan and broil 4–6 inches from heat source until browned.

Jeanne Garvin
GFWC—Keystone A.O.K.
Muscatine, Iowa

Cauliflower-Ham Au Gratin

- **2 10 ounce packages frozen cauliflower, thawed and drained**
- **1¼ cups fully cooked ham, chopped**
- **1 can condensed cheddar cheese soup**
- **¼ cup milk**
- **⅔ cup biscuit mix**
- **2 tablespoons firm butter**
- **2 tablespoons shredded cheddar cheese**
- **½ teaspoon ground nutmeg**

Heat oven to 400 degrees. Arrange cauliflower in ungreased 2-quart baking dish; sprinkle with the ham. Beat soup and milk until smooth; pour over ham. Mix remaining ingredients until crumbly; sprinkle over soup mixture. Sprinkle with paprika, if desired. Bake at 400 degrees for 20–25 minutes, or until topping is golden brown.

Cindy Stanek
GFWC—Longmont Woman's Club
Longmont, Colorado

Mandarin Ham Rolls

- **11 ounces mandarin orange sections, drained**
- **1½ cups cooked rice**
- **½ cup mayonnaise**
- **2 tablespoons chopped pecans**
- **2 tablespoons snipped parsley**
- **1 tablespoon sliced green onion**
- **8 slices boiled ham**
- **¼ cup orange marmalade**
- **4 tablespoons lemon juice**
- **¼ teaspoon ground ginger**

Reserve 8 orange sections. Chop remainder and combine with cooked rice, mayonnaise, pecans, parsely and onion. Divide mixture among ham slices. Roll up ham around filling. Combine marmalade, lemon juice and ginger; brush over ham. Bake uncovered at 350 degrees for 20–25 minutes. Brush occasionally with remaining sauce. Garnish with orange sections.

Dortha V. Tucker
GFWC—Searchlight Club
Overbrook, Kansas

Schnitz and Knepp

Schnitz

- **1 quart dried sweet apples**
- **3 pounds smoked ham**
- **2 tablespoons brown sugar**

Dumplings (knepp)

- **2 cups flour**
- **4 teaspoons baking powder**
- **1 egg, well beaten**
- **3 tablespoons melted butter**
- **½ cup milk**
- **1 teaspoon salt**
- **¼ teaspoon pepper**

Soak apples overnight. Cook ham; add apples and water in which they soaked, and simmer one more hour. Add sugar. Dumplings: Sift together flour, baking powder, salt and pepper. Quickly stir in mixture of beaten eggs, milk and butter. Drop by tablespoons into simmering ham and apples. Cover kettle tightly and cook 20 minutes.

Evelyn B. Lichtenwalner
GFWC—Woman's Club of Macungie
Macungie, Pennsylvania

Ruth A. Rhoads
GFWC—Woman's Club of Fleetwood
Fleetwood, Pennsylvania

Hawaiian Spareribs

- **2 sides of spareribs, cut into serving pieces**
- **2 tablespoons brown sugar**
- **2 tablespoons cornstarch**
- **½ teaspoon salt**
- **¼ cup vinegar**
- **½ cup catsup**
- **1 9 ounce can crushed pineapple with juice**
- **1 tablespoon soy sauce**

In saucepan, combine sugar, cornstarch and salt. Stir in vinegar, catsup, pineapple and soy sauce. Cook till slightly thickened, about 5 minutes, stirring constantly. Arrange a layer of ribs in roasting pan. Cover with part of pineapple mixture. Add another layer of ribs and top with remaining sauce. Cover tightly (with top or aluminum foil). Bake at 350 degrees for 1½ hours. This recipe can be multiplied to fit the number of guests. Serves 4.

Sylvia Lewis
GFWC—Past Presidents Ltd. Second District
Long Island, New York

Sausage and Rice Casserole

- **1 pound bulk sausage**
- **1 cup onion, chopped**
- **1 clove garlic, chopped**
- **1 cup celery, chopped**
- **1 cup rice, uncooked**
- **1 can cream of mushroom soup**
- **2 cans cream of chicken soup**
- **1 green pepper, chopped**

Brown sausage in fry pan and pour off grease. Add onions, garlic, celery and green pepper to sausage. Simmer until tender. Wash rice and add to mixture along with soups. Bake at 350 degrees for 1½ hours, stirring occasionally.

Maisie Davis
GFWC—Panorama Woman's Club
Fort Wayne, Indiana

Johnny Mazetti Hot Dish

- **1½ pounds lean pork**
- **3 tablespoons fat**
- **3 small onions**
- **2 teaspoons dry parsley**
- **½ cup green pepper**
- **½ cup celery**
- **10½ ounces tomato soup**
- **1½ cups water**
- **2 teaspoons salt**
- **¼ teaspoon pepper**
- **1 4 ounce can mushrooms**
- **1 4 ounce package noodles**

Cook noodles according to package. Brown cubed pork in 3 tablespoons fat with the onions (chopped) until tender. Add the parsley, green pepper (diced), celery (cut small), tomato soup, 1½ cups water, salt, pepper and mushrooms to the cooked noodles and pork. Bake at 350 degrees for 1 hour.

Faith Marshek
GFWC—Clintonville Woman's Club
Clintonville, Wisconsin

Veal with Green Peas

- 1 3 pound veal roast
- 1 carrot, sliced
- 2 small tomatoes or 1 teaspoon tomato puree
- 1 head garlic, unpeeled
- ¼ cup cognac
- ¾ cup dry white wine
- 1 cup stock of beef bouillon
- 1 pound green peas
- 3 tablespoons olive oil
- 1 rounded tablespoon butter
- 1 rounded tablespoon flour
- 1 branch fresh thyme or ⅓ teaspoon dried thyme
- 1 bay leaf
- ½ stick cinnamon or ⅛ teaspoon powdered cinnamon
- 6 black pepper grains
- Salt to taste

Heat olive oil in casserole. When oil is hot, put in thyme, bay leaf, garlic, cinnamon, pepper grains, carrot and tomatoes (if you use puree, add it later with the wine). Brown meat well on all sides with the herbs and vegetables over a moderate flame. When meat is brown, add cognac, wine and bouillon or stock. Salt to taste and simmer over low fire, covered, for about 2 hours or until meat is very tender. Turn meat from time to time while cooking. Add water in small amounts if sauce becomes scarce or dry. Before meat is done, boil peas in small amount of water until just tender; drain and set aside. When meat is tender, remove it and strain sauce. Melt butter, stir in flour, dilute with a little sauce and add to body of sauce to thicken it. Cook over low fire, stirring frequently until it thickens. Remove string from roast. Cut into slices and reheat it in sauce with cooked peas. Serve meat on platter with peas and sauce over it. Note: Make day before and slowly reheat. Can substitute vegetables for peas (artichoke hearts, tiny onions or lima beans, for example).

Constance Bernschein
GFWC—Norwalk Woman's Club
Norwalk, Connecticut

Veal Parmigiana

- 1½ pounds veal round steak
- 1 slightly beaten egg
- 2 tablespoons milk
- 1 teaspoon salt
- ⅓ cup dry bread crumbs
- ¼ cup grated parmesan cheese
- 2 tablespoons butter
- 1 8 ounce can tomato sauce
- ¼ teaspoon Italian seasoning
- ⅛ teaspoon instant minced garlic
- 16 slices or 3 cups shredded mozzarella cheese

Cut steak into 6 serving pieces. Pound with meat mallet. Combine egg, milk and salt in shallow dish. Combine crumbs and cheese on waxed paper. Dip meat into egg mixture. Then coat with crumbs. Preheat 9½-inch browning skillet in microwave oven for 4½ minutes. Add 1 tablespoon butter and half of meat. Cook in microwave oven for 5 minutes, turning meat halfway through cooking time. Return all meat to skillet. Combine tomato sauce, seasoning and garlic. Spoon over meat. Cook, covered, in microwave oven 12 minutes or until meat is tender. Top with cheese. Cook, covered, 3 to 4 minutes or until cheese is melted.

Dorothy Oberhellmann
GFWC—Fairview Heights Woman's Club
Fairview Heights, Illinois

Veal Scallopini

1 pound veal cutlets
3 tablespoons flour
Salt and pepper
¼ cup margarine
¼ pound mushrooms, chopped
¼ cup onions, chopped
⅓ cup chicken broth (can dilute 1 teaspoon chicken bouillon granules in ⅓ cup hot water)
¼ cup white wine, dry
½ teaspoon marjoram

Flatten cutlets to ¼ inch thickness. Combine flour, salt and pepper; dredge cutlets, coating well. Saute in margarine for 3 minutes each side until browned. Remove cutlets to 1-quart casserole; reserve pan drippings. Saute mushrooms and onion in drippings; remove from heat. Add broth, wine and marjoram; pour over cutlets. Cover and bake at 325 degrees for 25 to 30 minutes.

Beverly D. Martin
GFWC—Westwood Junior
Richmond, Virginia

Veal Casserole

1 pound diced veal
1 6 ounce can mushrooms
1 large diced onion
1 10 ounce package noodles
1 cup sour cream
4 tablespoons butter
½ teaspoon salt
¼ teaspoon paprika
1 cup hot water

Brown the diced veal in butter. Add 1 cup hot water and simmer till tender. Brown the mushrooms with the diced onion and add to veal. Cook the noodles and add to veal mixture. Season with salt and paprika. Add the sour cream, mix, cover and bake in oven-proof casserole dish at 350 degrees for 30 minutes.

Kathy Vogelsang
GFWC—Hartford Junior Women
Hartford, Wisconsin

Lamb Curry

2 cups "leftover" lamb
1 tablespoon fat
3 tablespoons onion
1 tablespoon curry powder
1 tablespoon flour
2 bouillon cubes
2 cups hot water
¼ cup catsup
½ teaspoon salt
½ cup chopped apple
1 cup diced celery

Brown meat in fat; add onion and cook until yellow. Add curry mixed with flour; allow to bubble. Add bouillon cubes dissolved in water, catsup, salt, apple and celery. Simmer 1¼ hours over medium heat. Serve over hot rice.

Jean T. Rice
GFWC—Bedford Woman's Club
Bedford, New Hampshire

Venison/Wild Rice Casserole

- **1½ cups wild rice (raw)**
- **6 to 8 slices bacon, browned and crumbled**
- **2 pounds venison or red steak**
- **1 medium onion, chopped**
- **1 small jar mushrooms**
- **1 tablespoon oleo or butter**
- **1 can cream of mushroom soup**
- **1 can cream of chicken soup**
- **1 can beef consomme**
- **¼ teaspoon thyme**
- **⅛ teaspoon pepper**
- **¼ cup Worcestershire sauce**
- **4 ounces sliced water chestnuts**

Wash and cook wild rice. Brown bacon; drain and crumble. Brown venison (sliced thin as for stroganoff) in bacon fat and drain well. Saute onion and mushrooms in butter. Mix all together with wild rice. Mix remaining ingredients well and add to rice mixture. Bake in 9 × 13 casserole at 325 degrees for 1½ hours.

Connie Thienes
GFWC—Blackduck Tri Sigma Club
Blackduck, Minnesota

Venison Meatloaf

- **1½ pounds chopped venison**
- **1 pound sausage meat**
- **2 small eggs, beaten or 1 large**
- **¼ cup chopped onion**
- **1 teaspoon salt**
- **¼ teaspoon pepper**
- **Sage**
- **¾ cup oats**
- **1 cup milk**

Piquant Sauce

- **½ cup brown sugar**
- **½ cup ketchup**
- **½ teaspoon mustard**

Soak oats in milk; add eggs, meat, onion and seasonings. Mix well. Press into loaf pan. Pour half of sauce over. Bake 1 to 1½ hours at 350 degrees. Serve with extra sauce. Piquant Sauce: Mix all ingredients well.

Muriel W. Hawkins
GFWC—Woman's Club of River Edge
River Edge, New Jersey

Marinated Venison Roast

- **1 4 pound venison roast**
- **½ cup red wine**
- **1 cup tomato juice**
- **¼ cup sugar**
- **2 bay leaves**
- **½ lemon, sliced thin**
- **1 onion, sliced**
- **2 carrots, cut up**
- **3 stalks celery, cut up**
- **2 cloves garlic, chopped**
- **1 tablespoon tenderizer**
- **Salt and pepper to taste**

Place roast in deep dish not much larger than the piece of meat. Combine remaining ingredients and pour over meat to cover. Cover dish and marinate overnight. The day of serving, roast at 350 degrees for 2½ to 3 hours or until tender, in covered roasting pan, basting frequently with marinade. Remove heat, strain juices and thicken with flour for gravy.

Kathy Albert
GFWC—Manchester Junior Woman's Club
Manchester, New Hampshire

Liver Knaefly

- **3 cups flour**
- **1 teaspoon allspice**
- **1 teaspoon salt**
- **¼ pound liver**
- **Little parsley**
- **2 eggs**
- **1 teaspoon pepper**
- **½ teaspoon cloves**
- **1 small onion**

Grind liver, onion and parsley. Mix all together. Use water to make a stiff dough. Scrape or cut into boiling water. Boil, then drain and fry in butter. Serve with gravy.

Juanita Holst
GFWC—The Woman's Club of Ste. Genevieve
Ste. Genevieve, Missouri

Liver Dish (for those who think they hate liver)

- **4 thin slices tender beef liver**
- **6 tablespoons butter**
- **1 heaping tablespoon chopped onion**
- **¾ cup dry white wine (or cooking wine)**
- **1 tablespoon lemon juice**
- **1 egg yolk**
- **2 pinches salt**
- **1 pinch nutmeg**

Wash liver and blot with toweling. Melt butter in medium skillet. Add onion; cook for 1 minute. Add wine and nutmeg. Cook for 2 minutes more. Add lemon juice; turn flame low. In large skillet, sear liver on both sides over fairly high heat. Remove; keep warm. Beat yolk and add to sauce with salt. Stir until slightly thick. Place on serving plate. Cover with sauce.

Fran Hensley
GFWC—Historical Club
Coshocton, Ohio

Creamy Chicken Livers

- **1 pound fresh chicken livers**
- **2 tablespoons bacon drippings**
- **Salt and pepper to taste**
- **1 can cream of mushroom or cream of celery condensed soup**
- **¼ cup half and half**
- **⅓ pint sour cream**
- **2 tablespoons sherry**
- **¼ teaspoon dried onion flakes**

Place chicken livers in large skillet with hot bacon drippings and brown on medium heat, turning occasionally, for about 10 minutes. Push the livers to one side of the skillet. Mix the soup, sour cream, sherry, onion flakes and half and half; add to skillet. Stir, heat and mix in the livers. Cover and simmer 20 minutes. Serve over toast points, noodles or cooked rice. Salt and pepper may be added to the chicken livers while they are browning.

Shirley Rankin
GFWC—Saturday Club
Cotter, Arkansas

All Purpose Barbecue Sauce

- **¼ cup molasses**
- **½ cup brown sugar**
- **2 teaspoons dry mustard**
- **Tabasco to taste**
- **1 tablespoon wine vinegar**
- **⅓ cup cider vinegar**
- **1 teaspoon chili powder**
- **1 teaspoon salt**
- **½ teaspoon pepper**
- **1 tablespoon Worcestershire sauce**
- **¼ cup catsup**
- **½ teaspoon onion powder**
- **¼ teaspoon garlic powder**

Put all ingredients in saucepan. Stir over medium heat to blend. Bring to boil, stirring as needed. Simmer 20 minutes, stirring occasionally. Can be stored in refrigerator indefinitely.

"In 1945 as newlyweds, my husband and I experimented to make a good sauce for basting meats and for serving at the table as a meat accompaniment."

Linda B. Setliff
GFWC—Cary Woman's Club
Cary, North Carolina

Plum Good Ribs

Sauce

2 tablespoons butter
1 medium onion, chopped
1 2 pound can purple plums
1 6 ounce can frozen lemonade
1/4 cup chili sauce
1/4 cup soy sauce
1 teaspoon Worcestershire sauce
2 teaspoons prepared mustard
1 teaspoon ground ginger
2 dashes tabasco sauce

For sauce, prepare ahead. Saute onion in butter. Pit plums and puree in blender with their juice. Add to onion mixture with lemonade, chili sauce, soy sauce, Worcestershire sauce, mustard, ginger and tabasco. Simmer uncovered for 15 minutes. Refrigerate.

Meat

8–10 pounds spare-ribs (about 4 racks)
1 tablespoon salt

For meat, cut ribs into serving-size pieces. Simmer 1½ hours in salted water until fork tender. Drain. Put in flat roasting pan and spoon some sauce over them. Bake at 375 degrees about one hour or until nicely browned, basting often, and turning as necessary.

Shirley Potter
GFWC—Parkersburg Woman's Club
Parkersburg, West Virginia

Barbecued Ribs—Island Style

1 cup orange marmalade
1 can consomme
2 teaspoons salt
1/3 cup catsup
1/3 cup mild vinegar
4 to 5 pounds ribs

Marinate all day or overnight 4 to 5 pounds ribs, either beef or pork. Bake in a 300 degree oven until nicely browned and well done, about 3 hours.

Helen McConnell
GFWC—Afternoon Home and Garden No. 1
Burlington, Iowa

Spaghetti Sauce

- **30 ounces tomato sauce**
- **15 ounces tomato paste**
- **1 cup red wine**
- **1 cup water**
- **1 pound ground beef**
- **1 onion**
- **1 teaspoon basil**
- **1 teaspoon oregano**
- **1 teaspoon marjoram**
- **1 teaspoon sage**
- **1 teaspoon thyme**
- **1 teaspoon salt**
- **½ teaspoon pepper**
- **½ teaspoon garlic**
- **1 pound spaghetti**

Brown ground beef in a dutch oven. Chop onion and add to meat. Add tomato sauce, paste, water, wine and seasonings. Cover and simmer for 1 to 2 hours over low heat. Cook spaghetti according to package instructions. Serve with parmesan cheese.

Sherry Connally
GFWC—Junior Ebell Club of Irvine
Irvine, California

Spicy Spaghetti Sauce

- **4 tablespoons cooking oil**
- **1 pound ground meat (turkey)**
- **2 large onions**
- **7 cloves garlic, chopped or pressed**
- **1 teaspoon hot paprika**
- **½ teaspoon black pepper**
- **1 large carrot, grated**
- **4 15 ounce cans tomato sauce**
- **¼ teaspoon salt**
- **1 whole medium hot red pepper**
- **2 tablespoons parsley**
- **1 teaspoon basil leaves**
- **1 teaspoon sugar**
- **1 cup diced celery**

Brown ground meat with onions, garlic and celery in a 5-quart stainless steel pot. Add spices and cook a few minutes before adding the tomato sauce. Heat to boiling. Reduce heat and simmer for ½ hour. Serve over cooked spaghetti. Yield: 2½ quarts of spaghetti sauce.

Lillian Wefald
GFWC—West Suburban Woman's Club
Hopkins, Minnesota

Cranberry-Orange Chutney

- **1 cup fresh orange sections**
- **¼ cup orange juice**
- **4 cups (1 pound) cranberries**
- **2 cups sugar**
- **1 cup chopped, unpeeled apple**
- **½ cup seedless raisins**
- **¼ cup chopped walnuts**
- **1 tablespoon vinegar**
- **¼ cup chopped celery**
- **½ teaspoon ground ginger**
- **½ teaspoon ground cinnamon**
- **⅛ teaspoon allspice**
- **¼ teaspoon cloves**

Combine all ingredients in a large saucepan and bring to a boil. Reduce heat and simmer for 5 minutes or until the berries are soft. Chill until serving. Yield: 5½ cups.

Julia K. Shew
GFWC—Louisville Woman's Club
Louisville, Ohio

Idaho Fresh Prune Chutney

- **1 cup light brown sugar, firmly packed**
- **1 cup granulated sugar**
- **¾ cup cider vinegar**
- **1½ teaspoons red peppers, crushed**
- **2 teaspoons salt**
- **2 teaspoons mustard seed**
- **2 fat cloves of garlic, thinly sliced**
- **¼ cup thinly sliced onion**
- **½ cup preserved ginger, thinly sliced**
- **1 cup seedless white raisins**
- **3½ cups fresh Italian prunes, halved and seeded, about 20**

Mix together sugars and vinegar and bring to the boiling point. Add remaining ingredients, except prunes, and mix well. Stir in prune halves. Simmer until thickened, about 50 minutes, stirring frequently and gently. Refrigerate. Yield: 1½ cups.

"This recipe was developed by Mrs. Robert E. Smylie, a first lady of Idaho. It appeared in the New York Times when Clementine Paddleford was 'This Week Food Editor'."

Ann Waters
GFWC—Marshfield Woman's Club
Marshfield, Wisconsin

Mustard Sauce

- **1 10¾ ounce can tomato soup**
- **1 9 ounce jar prepared mustard**
- **9 ounces vinegar**
- **4 whole eggs, beaten**
- **1 cup sugar**
- **½ pound margarine**

Cook in double boiler until thick. (I stir constantly in regular saucepan over medium heat until thick.) This sauce will keep a long time in refrigerator. Good to use wherever you use mustard.

Grace Donnenwirth
GFWC—Twentieth Century Club of Clyde
Clyde, Ohio

January Chili Sauce

- **6 cups drained, canned tomatoes**
- **5 medium onions, chopped very fine**
- **5 sweet green peppers, chopped very fine**
- **1 16 ounce can pears, drained and chopped**
- **1 16 ounce can peaches, drained and chopped**
- **1 teaspoon hot pepper sauce or ½ teaspoon hot pepper**
- **1 pint vinegar**
- **2 tablespoons salt**
- **4 cups sugar**
- **4 sticks cinnamon**
- **2 tablespoons whole cloves**

Bring tomatoes to a boil over medium heat. Add finely chopped onions and peppers, salt, sugar, hot sauce, spices that have been placed in a cheese cloth "bag" and vinegar. Return to a boil and immediately add chopped fruit (coarsely chopped). Return again to a boil, continue to cook for 3 to 5 minutes, stirring with a wooden spoon enough to keep from burning. Pour immediately into jars and refrigerate.

Elizabeth H. Lasselle
GFWC—Stoneham Woman's Club
Stoneham, Massachusetts

Raisin Sauce

- **½ cup brown sugar**
- **1 teaspoon dried mustard**
- **2 tablespoons cornstarch**
- **1½ cups water**
- **½ cup white wine**
- **1 cup crushed pineapple**
- **½ cup raisins**

Mix brown sugar, dried mustard and cornstarch in saucepan. Add all other ingredients and cook. Stir over medium temperature until thickens (about 20 minutes).

Ellen Davis
GFWC—Gun Lake Area
Shelbyville, Michigan

Picante Sauce

- 1 gallon tomatoes, chopped and peeled
- 4 medium green peppers, seeded and chopped
- 4 medium onions, diced
- 4 medium fresh jalapeno peppers, chopped
- 4 to 8 cloves garlic
- 2 cups cider vinegar
- 4 teaspoons salt
- 4 teaspoons sugar
- ½ teaspoon cayenne pepper
- ½ teaspoon ground cumin

Grind vegetables coarsely. Stir vinegar, salt and sugar into vegetable mixture. Transfer vegetables to a 12-quart pan. Simmer, uncovered, in 300 degree oven, after bringing to a boil at medium heat on top of stove. Cook until liquids are reduced and mixture reaches desired consistency (about 30 minutes). Stir in cayenne and ground cumin. Seal in hot, sterile pint jars. Makes about 8 pints. Note: Food processor will puree vegetables too fine.

Hilda Van Valkenburg
GFWC—North Park Woman's Club
Walden, Colorado

Pesto Genovese (Green Sauce)

- 5 or 6 garlic cloves, peeled and minced
- ¼ cup snipped basil or 2 tablespoons dried basil
- ¼ cup grated parmesan cheese
- 2 tablespoons finely chopped California walnuts
- ½ teaspoon salt
- 6 tablespoons olive or salad oil

In mortar (or small bowl) with pestle (or back of spoon) mix garlic, basil, cheese, walnuts, salt; pound mixture to smooth paste. Gradually add oil, working mixture to make smooth pesto. On each heated dinner plate, arrange mound of hot noodles (allow ½ pound for 6 servings); top with pat of butter, then with 1 tablespoon pesto. Just before eating, each person tosses noodles with pesto.

Erminia S. Costa
GFWC—Farmingbury Woman's Club
Wolcott, Connecticut

Mushroom Sauce for Ham

- 4 tablespoons margarine
- 1 pound fresh mushrooms
- 1 medium onion, sliced thin
- 2 tablespoons flour
- 1 6 to 8 ounce carton sour cream
- Salt and pepper to taste
- 1 tablespoon prepared mustard
- 1 tablespoon finely chopped parsley

Saute onion and mushrooms in margarine until tender. Add flour and stir to thicken. Add sour cream, salt and pepper to taste. If too thick, add milk. Variation: Add 1 tablespoon prepared mustard or 1 tablespoon finely chopped parsley. Serve warm baked ham with ¼ to ½ cup mushroom sauce over each slice.

Peggy T. Singleton
GFWC—Veritas Club
Greensboro, Alabama

Fish & Seafood

Nantucket Scallops

3 tablespoons butter
1 teaspoon chopped chives
½ teaspoon parsley
½ teaspoon tarragon
Dash of garlic salt
Dash of black pepper
¾ teaspoon lemon juice
¼ teaspoon salt
2 pounds bay scallops
½ cup bread crumbs
3 tablespoons melted butter

Melt butter and mix with herbs and spices. In a shallow, buttered pan (or individual dishes) put scallops in bottom. Top with herbed butter, then bread crumbs. Pour 2nd melted butter over all. Bake in preheated 500 degree oven for 5 minutes.

Sandy Wing
GFWC—Framingham Woman's Club
Framingham, Massachusetts

Photo features: Shrimp Fandango—Page 185
Fantastic Fish Fillets—Page 176

Pescatore (The Fisherman)

- **1 cup cooked, diced sausage**
- **1 cup diced ham**
- **1 cup diced, sweet red pepper**
- **1 cup diced onions**
- **1 cup crushed tomatoes**
- **½ pound diced mushrooms**
- **½ pound crisp bacon, crumbled**
- **1 pound precooked shrimp**
- **1 pound lobster meat, cooked**
- **1 pound cooked crab claws**
- **1 teaspoon coriander powder**
- **1 tablespoon garlic powder**
- **1 cup brown gravy**
- **1 cup red wine**
- **Pepper and salt to taste**

Mix all ingredients together and cook over medium-low flame for ½ hour. Have 2 cups of rice cooked in chicken broth ready to mix with the meat and fish. Mix together and let stand for 10 minutes. Serve in large casserole garnished with shrimp or lobster pieces.

Raphael Serbelle
GFWC—Woman's Club of Lodi
Lodi, New Jersey

Golden Seafood Casserole

- **4 tablespoons butter**
- **4 tablespoons flour**
- **3 hard cooked eggs, sliced**
- **1 can shrimp (cut in half, lengthwise)**
- **1 can tuna**
- **2 cups milk**
- **¼ teaspoon pepper**
- **1 can mushrooms**
- **1 can crabmeat**
- **¼ pound cheddar cheese**
- **2 cups soft bread crumbs**
- **4 tablespoons melted butter**

Melt 4 tablespoons butter; add flour and blend. Gradually add milk and stir constantly until mixture thickens. Add pepper. In a greased baking dish, arrange a layer of tuna; cover with small amount of white sauce. Follow with a layer of eggs, shrimp, mushrooms, crab meat, separating each layer with small amount white sauce. Add remaining white sauce; sprinkle grated cheddar cheese on top. Mix bread crumbs with melted butter (4 tablespoons) and place on top. Cook at 300 degrees for 1½ hours.

"Dates back to '50's! When our children were small just about everyone had milk delivered to their home. This recipe came from a calendar given to us by our milkman."

Bernice Goldsmith
GFWC—Sleepy Eye Woman's Club
Sleepy Eye, Minnesota

Seafood Lasagna

9 lasagna noodles
1 10 ounce package frozen, chopped spinach, thawed
1 large onion, chopped
2 tablespoons vegetable oil
3 ounces cream cheese, at room temperature
1 cup creamy cottage cheese
1 egg, beaten
2 teaspoons Italian herb seasoning, salt and pepper
1 can condensed cream of celery soup
½ cup milk
1 8 ounce bag frozen cooked shrimp
1 to 2 pounds frozen fish fillets, thawed and cubed
3 tablespoons Parmesan cheese
2 tablespoons seasoned bread crumbs
½ cup shredded sharp cheddar cheese
Butter or margarine

Cook and drain noodles according to package directions. Arrange 3 noodles in bottom of greased, oblong 2-quart baking dish. Press thawed spinach in a strainer. Cook onion in hot oil until soft. Blend in spinach, cream cheese, cottage cheese, egg and herb seasoning. Add salt and pepper to taste. Spread about ⅓ of this mixture over noodles in dish. Combine soup, milk, shrimp and fish. Spread about ⅓ of this over cheese layer. Repeat layers. Mix Parmesan cheese and bread crumbs; sprinkle on top. Bake at 350 degrees for 45 minutes and top with shredded cheese; dot with butter; bake 5 more minutes. Let stand 20 minutes before cutting.

J. Barbara Kluding
GFWC—Sarasota Junior Woman's Club
Sarasota, Florida

Scallops Supreme

2 tablespoons butter
3 ounces softened cream cheese
½ cup chopped onions
1 can cream of mushroom soup
1 can milk (use soup can)
1 6 ounce jar artichoke hearts, chopped
1 pound scallops—large, cut into halves
⅛ teaspoon red pepper

In a large frying pan, melt butter, add onions and saute until tender. Add mushroom soup, milk and softened cream cheese. Stir and cook until creamy and well blended. Add scallops (chopped up roughly) and artichoke hearts. Season with salt and pepper and red pepper to taste. Heat thoroughly over medium heat for 20 to 25 minutes. Serve over toast or pastry shells.

Cheryl Gereau
GFWC—Junior Woman's Club of Green Bay, Inc.
Green Bay, Wisconsin

Seafood Gruyere Supreme

- ½ cup butter
- ¾ cup onion, chopped
- ¾ cup green pepper, chopped
- 6 ounces sliced mushrooms and liquid
- ⅔ cup flour
- 1 to 2 teaspoons salt
- ⅛ teaspoon pepper
- ¾ cup milk
- 1½ cups or 8 ounces Swiss Gruyere cheese
- 1 tablespoon lemon juice
- 1 teaspoon dry mustard
- ½ teaspoon Worcestershire sauce
- 1½ cups crabmeat, cooked
- 1½ cups lobster meat, cooked
- 1 cup shrimp, cooked

Melt butter and stir in onions and green pepper. Cook 3 minutes; add mushrooms and cook a few minutes longer until tender, but not brown. Remove from heat and stir in flour, salt and pepper. Gradually add milk; cook until thickened. Stir in cheese, lemon juice, dry mustard and Worcestershire sauce. Stir until cheese melts. Break the cooked shellfish into pieces; add to the sauce and heat thoroughly. Sprinkling of paprika or pimiento adds a nice touch. Serve over party shells, rice or toast points.

Thelma Iverson
GFWC—Bowie Woman's Club
Bowie, Maryland

Nantucket Seafood Casserole

- 2 cups sliced zucchini
- ¾ cup thin carrot strips, 1 inch long
- ½ cup flour
- 2 tablespoons Parmesan cheese
- ½ pound fresh or frozen flounder, haddock or cod
- 3 tablespoons margarine
- 2 tablespoons dry white wine
- ⅔ cup half and half cream
- ½ cup milk
- ½ pound cleaned, uncooked shrimp
- ½ pound bay scallops

Cut fish into 2-inch pieces. Rinse shrimp and scallops and drain on paper towel. In a large skillet, saute the carrots and zucchini in margarine until crisp tender, 3 to 4 minutes. Sprinkle the flour over the vegetables and toss lightly to coat; cook 1 minute. Add half and half and milk; stir and cook until mixture thickens. Add the seafood and Parmesan cheese. Cook until mixture comes to a boil. Remove from heat and add wine; salt and pepper to taste. Spoon into buttered casserole. Top with buttered soft bread crumbs. Sprinkle with a little Parmesan cheese and paprika. Bake at 350 degrees for 20–30 minutes until mixture is bubbly.

"This is my attempt at copying an entree we enjoyed at Nantucket Restaurant several years ago. It has become a Christmas buffet special."

Doris Blyler
GFWC—Woman's Club of Moorestown
Moorestown, New Jersey

Shrimp and Scallop Pilaf

- **2 tablespoons butter or margarine**
- **¼ teaspoon turmeric**
- **1 cup uncooked long-grain white rice**
- **1 medium size onion, chopped**
- **1 clove garlic, minced**
- **½ teaspoon salt**
- **1 13¾ ounce can chicken broth (plus enough water to measure 2½ cups)**
- **8 ounces sea scallops, halved crosswise**
- **8 ounces peeled and deveined shrimp**
- **1 10-ounce package frozen green peas, partially thawed**
- **Pepper to taste**

In large skillet melt butter over medium heat. Stir in turmeric; add rice, onion and garlic. Cook about 3 to 5 minutes, until onion is translucent—stirring often. Pour in broth mixture and bring to boil. Reduce heat; cover and simmer for 15 minutes. Add scallops, shrimp and peas. Simmer covered 5–7 minutes longer or until scallops are opaque, shrimp turn pink and peas are heated. Taste and season with pepper and salt.

Glenda Degenhardt
GFWC—White Columns Woman's Club
Waynesboro, Georgia

Creamy Fish and Cheese Chowder

- **1 pound fish fillets, fresh or frozen**
- **2 tablespoons butter**
- **6 tablespoons chopped onion**
- **1 cup chopped carrots**
- **6 tablespoons chopped celery**
- **¼ cup flour**
- **½ teaspoon salt, optional**
- **Dash paprika**
- **2 10-ounce cans chicken broth, undiluted**
- **2 cups milk**
- **1 cup grated processed cheese**

Thaw frozen fish fillets enough to allow cutting, about 30 minutes. Cut fish in 1 inch cubes. Melt butter in large saucepan; add onions, carrots and celery. Cook until onion is transparent. Blend in flour, salt and paprika. Cook 1 minute, stirring constantly. Gradually add chicken broth and milk. Cook, stirring constantly until thickened. Add fish; simmer until fish flakes easily (5 minutes for fresh, 10 for frozen). Add cheese; stir until melted. Serve hot. Yield: 2½ quarts.

Katherine Von Ahnen
GFWC—Reedsburg Federated Woman's Club
Reedsburg, Wisconsin

Fantastic Fish Fillets

- **3 10-ounce packages frozen, chopped spinach**
- **1 pint sour cream**
- **3 tablespoons flour**
- **Juice of 1 lemon**
- **½ cup finely minced onion**
- **2 teaspoons salt**
- **½ teaspoon nutmeg**
- **Pepper to taste**
- **6 to 8 flounder (or any other whitefish) fillets**
- **2 tablespoons butter**

Cook spinach according to package directions. Drain and mix with salt, pepper and nutmeg. Spread on surface of shallow 9 × 13 inch baking dish. Place fish on spinach and top with sauce made with sour cream, flour, lemon juice and onion which have been mixed together. Melt butter and pour over all. Bake at 375 degrees for 25 minutes or until fish flakes easily with a fork.

Bobby Ruth Bjork
GFWC—Madison Valley Woman's Club
Ennis, Montana

Codfish A La Vizcaina

- **1 pound codfish fillets**
- **½ cup olive oil**
- **2 onions pared and sliced**
- **½ cup tomato sauce**
- **1 pound potatoes, pared and sliced**
- **½ cup olives**
- **1 can pimientos, chopped**
- **2 cloves garlic, peeled and crushed**
- **¼ cup raisins**

Place the codfish fillets in hot water. Remove any skin and bones; shred flesh. In baking dish or casserole, layer the ingredients in this order: shredded codfish, sliced onions and sliced potatoes. Add the tomato sauce, olives, pimientos, raisins and garlic. Pour the olive oil over it; place in the oven and bake at 375 degrees for 30 minutes.

"This recipe has been in my family for many years; it is a genuine Spanish recipe."

Amalia J. Rodriguez
GFWC—Puerto Rican American Woman's League
Washington, D.C.

Baked Fish Au Gratin

1 pound fish fillets
8 slices American cheese
1/4 cup chopped parsley
1 teaspoon oregano
Basil or thyme
1/4 cup corn oil
1 cup chopped onion
2 tablespoons cornstarch
1/8 teaspoon salt
1/8 teaspoon pepper
1 1/2 cups milk

Layer fish and cheese alternately in lightly greased 8 × 8 inch baking dish. Sprinkle with parsley, oregano, and basil or thyme. Cook onion in hot oil in skillet until tender, but not brown. Stir in cornstarch, salt and pepper. Remove from heat; slowly pour in milk. Bring to boil, stirring constantly; boil 1 to 2 minutes. Pour over fish. Bake at 400 degrees for 20 to 30 minutes until fish flakes easily with fork.

"This recipe was given my husband on a fishing trip to Lake Michigan."

Agnes M. Simms
GFWC—Loda Federated Woman's Club
Loda, Illinois

Oven Fried Fish-N-Chips

4 small round potatoes, unpeeled
1 tablespoon corn-sunflower oil
Salt/pepper as allowed
No-stick cooking spray
1 pound fish fillets
1/4 cup 1 percent milk
1/2 cup English muffin crumbs
1 tablespoon corn oil margarine

Scrub unpeeled potatoes and slice in 1/4-inch rounds. Soak the potato rounds in ice water for 20 minutes. Preheat oven to 450 degrees. Spray a shallow, non-stick baking pan with cooking spray. Drain and dry potatoes; place a few at a time in a plastic bag with oil and shake to coat well. Arrange potatoes in a single layer on the baking pan. Bake uncovered for 10 minutes. In the meantime, in food processor, make very fine English muffin crumbs. Place crumbs in flat dish; put milk in another dish. Prepare fish fillets; cut in serving pieces. Dip in milk and roll in crumbs. Spray baking dish with cooking spray. Place fillets close together, but not overlapping. Sprinkle with salt and pepper as allowed. Drizzle melted margarine over fillets. Remove potatoes from oven. Increase oven temperature to 500 degrees. Place fish in oven and bake for 10 to 12 minutes. Turn potato rounds over and return to oven. Continue baking until potatoes are a golden brown and fish flakes easily with a fork. Remove potatoes to serving dish; salt and pepper as allowed. Serve fish fillets in baking dish. Serve all with a garden salad.

Mrs. William A. Gwaltney
GFWC—The Woman's Club of Windsor
Windsor, Virginia

Salmon Crunch Casserole

- **1 pound canned salmon (or 2 or more cups baked or boiled salmon)**
- **¼ cup broth drained from salmon (or water)**
- **1 envelope dry onion soup mix**
- **2 cans mushroom soup**
- **1 5-ounce can water chestnuts, sliced**
- **1 3-ounce can chow mein noodles**
- **2 tablespoons diced pimiento**
- **⅓ cup toasted sliced almonds**

Blend soups and broth or water and set aside. Mix all other ingredients, except almonds, and put in buttered 9 inch × 13 inch pan. Bake at 325 degrees for 40 minutes. Sprinkle on almonds and bake 10 minutes more to brown. If unexpected company arrives, cook a little rice to serve with or under it.

Elisabeth S. Hakkinen
GFWC—Haines Woman's Club
Haines, Alaska

Salmon Loaf

- **1 pound can red salmon, drained and flaked**
- **½ cup light Miracle Whip**
- **½ cup chopped onion**
- **1 can condensed cream of celery soup**
- **1 tablespoon lemon juice**
- **1 cup dry bread crumbs**
- **1 teaspoon salt**
- **1 beaten egg**

Combine all ingredients. Bake at 350 degrees in a greased 8½ × 4½ loaf pan for 1 hour. Serve with cucumber sauce (optional).

Cucumber Sauce

- **¼ cup light Miracle Whip**
- **½ cup dairy sour cream**
- **¼ chopped cucumber**

Fold light salad dressing and cucumber into sour cream.

Doris L. Kiddey
GFWC—Fern Creek Woman's Club
Louisville, Kentucky

Doris's Salmon Salad Pie

1 15-ounce can salmon
1 10-ounce package frozen, chopped broccoli
2 unbaked 9-inch pie crusts
½ cup diced celery
⅓ cup sliced green onions
3 hard-cooked eggs (diced)
¾ teaspoon dill weed
⅓ teaspoon pepper
1 cup grated Swiss cheese
1½ cups mayonnaise

Drain and flake salmon; remove bony cartilage. Cook broccoli according to package directions and arrange in bottom of pie crust. Mix salmon, celery, onions, eggs, seasonings and cheese with mayonnaise (a little less mayonnaise may be used if mixture appears to be becoming somewhat too moist). Spoon mixture over broccoli. Cover all with top crust; slit openings. Bake at 375 degrees for 30 minutes.

Betty Ruff
GFWC—Rolling Hills Woman's Club of Catonsville
Catonsville, Maryland

Salmon Pot Pie

1 can red salmon, flaked
1½ cups diced, cooked potatoes
3 hard-cooked eggs, sliced
3 tablespoons melted oleo
3 tablespoons flour
1 can chicken with rice soup
½ cup milk
¼ teaspoon salt
½ teaspoon Worcestershire sauce
Paprika

Put salmon into buttered casserole dish. Add potatoes and eggs. Combine oleo, flour, soup, milk, salt, Worcestershire sauce and simmer over low heat until thickened. Pour over casserole ingredients. Top with small biscuits; dust with paprika. Bake at 350 degrees for 30 minutes.

Verna MacArthur
GFWC—Katahdin Club
Island Falls, Maine

Caviar Pie

8 large eggs; hard cooked, peeled and chopped
4 tablespoons butter or margarine, melted
¼ teaspoon dry mustard
⅛ teaspoon pepper
1 large onion, chopped
1 cup sour cream
1 jar caviar

Mix melted butter or margarine with the chopped eggs, mustard and pepper. Press in 9-inch pie plate to form shell. Cover bottom of shell with chopped onion; layer with sour cream and cover top with caviar. Garnish as desired and serve with mild crackers.

Mary Isabel Laroque
GFWC—The Saturday Club of Wayne—Evening Section
Wayne, Pennsylvania

Tuna Burgers

- 1 small can tuna or salmon
- ½ pound sharp cheese, grated (2 cups)
- ¼ cup minced onion
- ¼ cup pickle relish
- ¼ cup catsup
- ¼ cup salad dressing
- 1 cup chopped celery
- ½ teaspoon salt
- ¼ teaspoon pepper
- 2 tablespoons pimiento
- 12 hamburger buns

Mix all ingredients together well. Fill hamburger buns. Wrap buns in foil if they are to be baked in the oven. Wrap in waxed paper if they are to be cooked in microwave. Bake in 350 degree oven for 20 minutes or microwave on high 1½ to 2 minutes, cooking 4 buns at a time.

"This was a Saturday lunch favorite when I was growing up. The recipe is probably close to 20 years old."

Patricia Lynn Luber
GFWC—Carlock Junior Woman's Club
Carlock, Illinois

Tuna Florentine

- 2 10-ounce packages frozen, chopped spinach, thawed
- 2 tablespoons instant minced onion
- 1 12½ ounce can tuna, drained
- 6 hard-boiled eggs
- 2 10¾ ounce cans cream of mushroom soup
- 1 cup sour cream
- Salt and pepper
- ¼ cup melted butter
- 2 cups soft bread crumbs

Squeeze spinach to remove water. Spread spinach evenly in a greased 2-quart casserole. Sprinkle with onion, tuna and eggs. Mix mushroom soup and sour cream. Pour mixture evenly over eggs. Mix melted butter, crumbs and sprinkle evenly over top of casserole. Bake in preheated moderate oven (350 degrees) for 30 to 35 minutes or until golden brown and bubbly.

Golda Tobler
GFWC—Mesquite Club
Las Vegas, Nevada

Oyster Pie

- **1 quart oysters (drain)**
- **Butter flavored crackers (crushed)**
- **1 stick butter**
- **Mace**
- **½ to 1 pint whipping cream (not whipped)**
- **Salt and pepper**

Alternate layers of oysters and crushed crackers in oblong casserole dish (greased with butter). Sprinkle a little mace seasoning lightly, a little salt and pepper, and dot each layer with butter. Top last layer with cracker crumbs. Cover with whipping cream. Bake at 350 to 375 degrees for about 30 minutes or until bubbly.

"This recipe was passed down to me by a Welch family living on James Island."

Sissy Welch
GFWC—Woman's Club of Charleston
Charleston, South Carolina

Deviled Oysters

- **3 dozen oysters (1 pint)**
- **2 cups celery, chopped**
- **2 onions, chopped**
- **½ cup butter or margarine**
- **1 large pod garlic**
- **3 eggs, hard boiled**
- **About 6 slices of bread, toasted**
- **4 sprigs fresh parsley, chopped**
- **Worcestershire sauce**

Cook onions, celery and garlic 20 minutes with butter or margarine. Cut oysters with scissors, then add to seasoning—cook 5 minutes. Remove from heat. Mash hard boiled eggs with fork, then add eggs with parsley to mixture. Add salt, Worcestershire sauce to taste, and crumbled bread crumbs to mixture (you may need more bread to get the right consistency). Fill oyster shells or casserole and sprinkle crumbs on top. Bake at 350 degrees for 30 minutes.

"I have been using this recipe for more than 35 years."

Winona Broussard
GFWC—Attakapas Study Club
Crowley, Louisiana

Crab on English Muffins

- **¼ pound butter (1 stick)**
- **2 tablespoons mayonnaise**
- **2 shakes garlic powder or 1½ teaspoons garlic salt**
- **1 jar Old English sharp cheese spread**
- **1 can crabmeat or ½ pound crabmeat**
- **6 English muffins, split**

Mix all ingredients together, spread on English muffins. Put in freezer until firm. Cut into wedges, broil until golden brown.

Kim Roberge
GFWC—Franklin Junior Woman's Club
Franklin, New Hampshire

Dorothy Seabold
GFWC—Woman's Club of Glyndon
Glyndon, Maryland

Crab Pelau

- **2 tablespoons oil**
- **1 tablespoon butter**
- **1 medium onion, minced**
- **2 tomatoes, peeled and chopped**
- **1 cup shredded or flaked coconut**
- **1¼ cup milk**
- **1 cup long-grain rice**
- **1 cup water**
- **1½ teaspoons salt**
- **Pinch of curry powder**
- **2 cups crabmeat**
- **2 tablespoons Jamaica rum**

Saute onion in oil and butter; add tomatoes. Cook until soft. Soak coconut in milk; strain, squeeze coconut dry and discard, saving coconut milk. Add rice to onions, stir to blend; add coconut milk, water, salt and curry powder. Cover and cook on very low heat for 25 to 30 minutes. Add crabmeat and rum to rice during last 5 minutes.

Llewellyn Reed
GFWC—Literary and Civic Club
Ridgeville, South Carolina

Bowler's Wharf Crab Cakes

- **1 pound lump crabmeat, all shell removed**
- **Crushed saltine crackers (2 per cake)**

Filler

- **3 slices bread, crusts removed, cubed**
- **Dash of nutmeg**
- **3 tablespoons mayonnaise**
- **1 teaspoon Dijon mustard**
- **1 teaspoon Old Bay seasoning**
- **Small handful chopped fresh parsley**
- **½ small sweet red pepper, finely diced (optional)**
- **1 beaten egg white, folded in last**

First, mix filler ingredients in bowl until doughy and thoroughly mixed. Adjust seasonings to taste. Gently fold in crabmeat. Divide into four sections approximately the size of tennis balls and gently form into a flattened ball about 1½ inches thick. Do not mash it to death! Roll the sticky balls in the crushed saltines and refrigerate until ready to cook. May be prepared as much as a day in advance. Saute in butter over medium to medium-low heat approximately 12 to 15 minutes per side; or until golden brown and crisp on the outside and thoroughly heated.

Kay A. Kauffman
GFWC—The Woman's Club of Essex County
Tappahannock, Virginia

Salmon Corn Cakes

- **3 eggs**
- **2 teaspoons flour**
- **2 teaspoons lemon juice**
- **1 can salmon, drained and flaked**
- **1 can whole kernel corn, drained**
- **Minced onion (according to taste)**
- **Dash pepper**
- **½ teaspoon salt**
- **6 crackers, crumbled**

Mix eggs, flour, lemon juice, pepper and salt until foamy. Stir in corn and salmon. Drop mixture by generous spoonfuls onto hot griddle. Flatten slightly. Cook until golden brown, about 3 minutes on each side. Grease griddle if necessary. Serve with pimiento sauce.

Pimiento Sauce

- **½ cup dairy sour cream**
- **¼ cup grated cheese**
- **2 tablespoons chopped pimientos**

Heat all ingredients just to boiling over low heat, stirring constantly.

Dorothy Davis
GFWC—Home Culture Club
Mount Vernon, Missouri

Maryland Crab Imperial

- **1 pound back-fin crab**
- **1 egg, beaten lightly**
- **1 hard-cooked egg, mashed**
- **2 tablespoons mayonnaise**
- **1 slice bread, fine crumbs**
- **1 tablespoon minced pimiento**
- **1 tablespoon capers**
- **1 tablespoon minced parsley**
- **1 tablespoon minced chives**
- **¼ teaspoon dry mustard**
- **1½ teaspoon lemon juice**
- **1 teaspoon Worcestershire sauce**
- **¾ teaspoon salt**
- **¼ teaspoon pepper**

Save some large lumps of crab for top. Mix all ingredients except topping together. Pile in greased shells and garnish with large lumps.

Topping

- **½ cup mayonnaise**
- **2 tablespoons dry sherry**
- **Paprika**

Mix mayonnaise and sherry and pour some over each crab shell. Sprinkle with paprika.

Bake at 350 degrees for 15 minutes.

Juanita A. Eagles
GFWC—Rossmoor Woman's Club
Silver Spring, Maryland

Deviled Crab Casserole

- **4 tablespoons butter**
- **2 tablespoons flour**
- **½ cup milk**
- **2 cups crabmeat**
- **½ teaspoon salt**
- **¼ teaspoon pepper**
- **¼ teaspoon prepared mustard**
- **2 tablespoons chopped parsley**
- **1 tablespoon lemon juice**
- **2 hard-cooked eggs, chopped**
- **½ cup buttered bread crumbs**

Make white sauce with first 3 ingredients. Add crabmeat, seasonings and eggs. Pour into buttered casserole. Cover with crumbs. Bake in 400 degree oven 10 minutes or until crumbs are brown.

"I've been making it for at least 40 years."

Marguerite E. Witt
GFWC—Woman's Club of Catasauqua
Catasauqua, Pennsylvania

Shrimp Fandango

- **2 tablespoons peanut oil (or other)**
- **1 cup each, large-diced yellow and green peppers**
- **1 garlic clove, minced**
- **1¼ pound large shrimp, shelled and deveined**
- **½ cup vermouth (optional)**
- **1 cup snow peas**
- **1 cup julienne carrots (steamed crisp)**
- **1 cup sliced scallions**
- **1 dash salt**
- **1 dash hot sauce**
- **2 cups cooked rice**

In 10-inch skillet heat oil over medium heat; add peppers, garlic, and saute until tender, about 2 minutes. Increase heat to high; add shrimp and cook, stirring constantly, until shrimp begins to turn pink. Add vermouth; continue to stir and cook until liquid is reduced. Add remaining ingredients except rice, and cook, stirring constantly, until heated through. Serve over hot rice.

"Only 277 calories per serving."

Dorothy C. Ellis
GFWC—Tampa Civic Association
Tampa, Florida

Baked Stuffed Shrimp

- **1 pound of large shrimp**

Stuffing

- **1 can drained crabmeat**
- **1 cup medium white sauce**
- **1 dash Worcestershire sauce**
- **1 ounce sherry wine (optional)**
- **1 dash Tabasco sauce**

Peel, devein and split open, almost through, (butterfly) shrimp. Add crabmeat to white sauce, Tabasco, Worcestershire and wine. Mix together lightly. Place opened shrimp on a buttered baking sheet and place spoonfuls of the crab mixture on each shrimp. Sprinkle lightly with paprika. Bake at 350 degrees for 15 to 20 minutes. Sprinkle with chopped parsley before serving.

Mary Ann Clark
GFWC—Flagler Woman's Club
Flagler Beach, Florida

Shrimp Delight

1 pound raw medium-sized shrimp (approximately 20 count)
1 egg
¾ cup milk
¼ cup firmly packed light brown sugar
1¼ cups all-purpose flour
2 to 4 ounce packages shredded coconut

Cut each shrimp in half lengthwise. In small bowl combine egg, milk and brown sugar; beat until well blended. Gradually add flour, beating until batter is smooth. Heat one inch of oil until it reaches 375 degrees. Place coconut in separate bowl. Dip each half shrimp in batter; then coat thoroughly with coconut. Drop in hot oil and fry about 5 minutes or until golden brown. Serve hot. May be reheated in 350 degree oven for 5 minutes. Note: If using precooked shrimp, reduce oil heat to 350 degrees and just pop in and out to heat. May be served with chutney.

"I obtained this recipe in the 70's as a member of the Gourmet Group, American Woman's Club, Bogota, Colombia, South America."

Sue Jean Armstrong
GFWC—San Dieguito Woman's Club
Encinitas, California

Shrimp Pie

1 pound shrimp, cooked and cut into bite-size pieces
8 ounces Monterey Jack cheese, cut into cubes
1 egg, slightly beaten
Salt and pepper to taste
1 can crescent rolls

Open rolls. Press five rolls (points to center) into 9-inch pie plate to form crust. Mix all other ingredients. Pour into pie shell. Place remaining 3 rolls over the top (points to center). Seal edges. Bake at 350 degrees for 35 minutes, or until crust is golden brown and cheese melted.

Jeannine Faubion
GFWC—Woman's Club of Ft. Myers
Ft. Myers, Florida

Doris' Shrimp in Garlic Sauce

- **2 tablespoons salad oil**
- **2 pounds uncooked shrimp**
- **2 small cloves garlic, chopped fine**
- **1 6-ounce can tomato paste**
- **2 teaspoons salt**
- **½ teaspoon pepper**
- **½ teaspoon dried basil leaves**
- **½ cup chopped onion**

Using hot oil in large skillet over medium heat, saute shrimp, turning several times until they just turn pink. Remove from heat. Stir in other ingredients, along with 1 cup water. Simmer covered until heated through. Add mushrooms and pimiento if desired. Serve over a bed of cooked rice.

Mary Hjelle
GFWC—Barrett Study Club
Barrett, Minnesota

Shrimp and Artichoke Divan

- **1½ sticks butter**
- **9 tablespoons flour**
- **1½ cups milk**
- **1½ cups heavy cream**
- **Salt and pepper to taste**
- **2 cans artichoke hearts, or 1 package frozen**
- **2 pounds fresh mushrooms, sliced**
- **½ cup dry sherry (or dry white wine)**
- **2 tablespoons of Worcestershire sauce**
- **½ cup grated Parmesan cheese**
- **Paprika**

Heat oven to 375 degrees (if using frozen artichoke hearts, cook according to package directions first). Melt 9 tablespoons of the butter and stir in flour. When blended, gradually add the milk and cream, stirring constantly with a wire whisk. When mixture is thickened and smooth, season to taste with salt and pepper. Arrange artichoke hearts and shrimp over bottom of a buttered baking dish. Cook the mushrooms in remaining butter and spoon over the shrimp and artichokes. Add wine and Worcestershire sauce to cream sauce and pour over casserole. Sprinkle with Parmesan and paprika. Bake 30 minutes and serve over cooked wild rice or if you prefer, over white rice.

Margaret Saetre
GFWC—Zehlian Club
Thief River Falls, Minnesota

Clam Sauce with Linguine

- **1 clove garlic, finely chopped**
- **4 tablespoons butter**
- **1 tablespoon flour**
- **1 7-ounce can minced clams**
- **4 tablespoons parsley**
- **Pinch of thyme**
- **Salt and pepper to taste**

In a skillet, saute garlic in butter for one minute. Stir flour in the juice from the canned clams. Add the parsley, salt, pepper and thyme; simmer gently for 5 minutes. Add minced clams; if additional liquid is needed, add 2 tablespoons white wine. Simmer for one minute and serve with linguine cooked according to directions on the box. Serve with freshly ground Parmesan cheese.

Trudy Farrington
GFWC—Woman's Club of Laguna Beach
Laguna Beach, California

Mom's Deviled Clams

- **2 dozen large sea clams**
- **6 stalks celery**
- **4 medium onions**
- **3 teaspoons mustard**
- **3 to 4 dashes of hot sauce**
- **3 tablespoons butter**
- **2 to 3 packages no salt crackers**

Grind together sea clams, celery and onions. Cook slow for 1 hour. Cool. Add mustard, hot sauce, butter, Worcestershire sauce and enough crackers to soak up liquid. Put into cleaned-out clam shells. Dot with butter. Bake at 375 degrees for 10 minutes or until crunchy on top. These can be frozen.

Bonnie B. Hornung
GFWC—Junior Woman's Club
Salisbury, Maryland

Lobster or Crabmeat Bisque

- **¼ cup butter or margarine**
- **¼ cup minced scallion**
- **½–1 pound lobster or crabmeat, chopped**
- **⅓ cup dry white wine**
- **2 cups water**
- **1 pint all purpose cream**
- **2 egg yolks, lightly beaten**
- **Salt to taste**
- **Pinch white pepper**
- **Scant ¼ teaspoon dried thyme**

In heavy saucepan, melt butter and cook onion. Add all crabmeat or lobster meat and quickly saute for several minutes. Add wine and water; cover and simmer for 10 minutes. Stir in cream and heat for about 5 minutes. Pour a small amount of hot mixture into beaten egg yolks and return to pan stirring constantly. Heat while stirring until slightly thickened. Add seasonings. Heat for 5 minutes more and serve.

Grace Peschel
GFWC—Woman's Club of Northford
Northford, Connecticut

Treadway Inn Style Individual Lobster Pie

2 tablespoons butter
1 cup lobster meat
¼ cup sherry
3 tablespoons butter
1 tablespoon flour
¾ cup thin cream
2 egg yolks

Topping

¼ cup cracker meal
¼ teaspoon paprika
1½ teaspoons Parmesan cheese
2 tablespoons melted butter
1 tablespoon finely crushed potato chips

Melt 2 tablespoons butter. Add sherry and boil 1 minute. Add lobster and let stand. Melt 3 tablespoons butter and add flour. Stir until it bubbles (1 minute). Remove from heat. Slowly stir in cream and wine, drained from lobster. Return to heat and cook, stirring until sauce is thick and smooth. Beat egg yolks well, adding 4 tablespoons sauce, 1 tablespoon at a time. Add to sauce, mixing well. Heat over hot water (not boiling) in double boiler. Sauce should be stirred constantly while heating (about 3 minutes). Add lobster. Turn in small, deep pie plate. Sprinkle with mixed topping. Bake 300 degrees for 10 minutes.

"This recipe came from the Publick House and published in Sturbridge Kitchens, Sturbridge Federated Church, 1957. Also excellent made with crabmeat or crabmeat substitute."

Marjorie F. Campbell
GFWC—Ogunquit Woman's Club
Ogunquit, Maine

Stuffed Lobster Supreme

8 frozen rock lobster tails
1 stick butter
4 tablespoons flour
1 teaspoon salt
1 teaspoon paprika
2 cups cream
¼ cup cracker crumbs
¼ cup grated Parmesan cheese
1 teaspoon melted butter
2 tablespoons lemon juice
Few grains cayenne

Cook tails in salted boiling water; drain. Using scissors, cut meat away from shells; dice meat, save shells. Saute lobster meat in butter, remove from heat. Blend in flour, salt, paprika and cayenne. Slowly stir in cream; cook, stirring constantly, until mixture thickens and boils (1 minute). Stir in lemon juice, spoon filling into lobster shells and sprinkle tops with mixture of cracker crumbs, melted butter and parmesan cheese. Bake in 450 degree oven for 10 to 12 minutes.

Jane Lee Nosal
GFWC—Woman's Club of Farmingdale
Farmingdale, New York

Poultry

Chicken Asparagus Casserole

- 2 **chicken breasts, skinned, boned and cut into 1-inch cubes**
- ¼ **teaspoon pepper**
- ½ **cup cooking oil**
- 2 **10 ounce packages frozen asparagus**
- 1 **10½ ounce can cream of chicken soup**
- ½ **teaspoon curry powder or to taste**
- ½ **cup mayonnaise**
- 1 **teaspoon lemon juice**
- 1 **cup cheddar cheese, shredded**

Heat oil in fry pan over medium heat. Add chicken, sprinkle with pepper and saute slowly about 6 minutes or until white and opaque. Remove and drain and place on paper towel. Cook asparagus by package directions, drain and place on bottom of 9 × 9 × 2 inch baking pan or casserole. Place chicken on top of asparagus. Mix together chicken soup, mayonnaise, lemon juice and curry powder (we prefer just a dash), pour over chicken and asparagus. Bake in 375 degree oven for 30 minutes or until done. Sprinkle with cheese last 5 minutes. Serves 4.

Ann Koelsch
GFWC—Gun Lake Area
Shelbyville, Michigan

Photo features: Chicken, Almonds & Peaches—Page 203

Curry in a Hurry

- **1 cup diced apple**
- **1 teaspoon curry powder**
- **1 can cream of chicken soup**
- **1 cup diced, cooked chicken or pork**
- **2 cups cooked rice**
- **¼ cup chopped onion**
- **2 tablespoons margarine**
- **½ cup water**
- **Shredded coconut**

In saucepan cook apple, onion and curry in butter until onion is tender. Stir in soup, water and meat. Heat, stirring now and then. Serve over rice. Garnish with coconut.

Esther Mary Crane
GFWC—Raleigh Woman's Club
Memphis, Tennessee

Chinese Walnut Chicken

- **1 cup walnuts—large pieces**
- **¼ cup salad oil**
- **2 chicken breasts, cut in thin strips**
- **½ teaspoon salt**
- **1 cup onion slices**
- **1½ cups bias cut celery**
- **1¼ cups chicken broth**
- **1 teaspoon sugar**
- **2 tablespoons cornstarch**
- **1 5 ounce can water chestnuts, sliced and drained**
- **1 green pepper, cut up**
- **1 tablespoon soy sauce**
- **2 tablespoons cooking sherry**
- **Pineapple chunks (optional)**

In skillet, toss walnuts in hot oil, stirring constantly. Remove walnuts to paper towel; put chicken in skillet, salt, cook 5 minutes until tender. Remove chicken, put onion, celery and ½ cup chicken broth into skillet; cook uncovered. Combine sugar, cornstarch, soy sauce, sherry. Add remaining chicken broth; pour over vegetables and cook until thickens. Add walnuts and chicken. Heat through. Serve over rice.

Grace L. Riffer
GFWC—Philomathean
Apple Creek, Ohio

Turkey Rice Casserole

- **1 6 ounce package long grain and wild rice mix**
- **½ cup chopped onion**
- **½ cup chopped celery**
- **2 tablespoons butter**
- **1 can cream of mushroom soup**
- **¼ cup parsley**
- **½ cup dairy sour cream**
- **⅓ cup water**
- **½ teaspoon curry powder**
- **2 cups cubed turkey or chicken**

Prepare rice according to package directions. Cook onion and celery in butter until tender. Stir in soup, sour cream, water and curry. Add turkey/chicken and rice mixture. Pour into 12 × 7 × 2 baking dish. Bake uncovered at 350 degrees for 40 minutes. Stir before serving; garnish with parsley.

June Riskedahl
GFWC—Tuttle Mater Cara
Tuttle, North Dakota

Turkey and Broccoli Hot Dish

- **2 pounds cooked turkey or chicken**
- **1 package chopped broccoli (thawed and drained)**
- **½ cup sliced Velveeta cheese**
- **½ cup rice, cooked**
- **½ cup mayonnaise**
- **1 can cream of mushroom soup**
- **1 can French fried onion rings**

Dice turkey; sprinkle cooked rice in 2½-quart casserole. Place broccoli on top of rice. Cover with turkey or chicken. Lay Velveeta slices over poultry. Mix soup and mayonnaise. Spread over cheese. Bake at 350 degrees for 40 minutes. Remove to add onion rings. Bake 15 minutes more.

Nancy J. Svendsen
GFWC—Federated Women for the Arts
Rushford, Minnesota

Oven Fried Chicken

- **3 pounds chicken**
- **½ cup oil**
- **2 teaspoons salt**
- **1 teaspoon dry mustard**
- **1 teaspoon paprika**

Cut chicken into serving pieces. Combine oil, salt, paprika and dry mustard in a pie plate. Dip chicken into mixture, coating well on each side. Bake, uncovered, in shallow baking dish in a very hot oven, 450 degrees, for 50 minutes or until tender, turning once.

Mary Kell
GFWC—Pompton Lakes Woman's Club
Pompton Lakes, New Jersey

Old-Fashioned Fried Chicken

- **1 2 or 2½ pound frying chicken**
- **1 cup flour**
- **1 teaspoon baking powder**
- **½ teaspoon salt**
- **1 egg**
- **½ cup milk**

Cut chicken into serving portions and steam until tender in water to cover with 1 teaspoon salt added. Drain and cool. Mix and sift dry ingredients. Beat egg and add dry mixture. Dip each piece of chicken in batter and fry in about 1 inch of hot fat. Turn each piece so that it will brown evenly.

Janie M. Townsend
GFWC—Keysville Woman's Club
Keysville, Virginia

Crispy Cajun Chicken

- **1 2–3 pound broiler-fryer, cut up**
- **½ cup salad dressing**
- **1 teaspoon ground cumin**
- **1 teaspoon onion powder**
- **½ teaspoon red pepper**
- **½ teaspoon garlic powder**
- **1½ cups crushed sesame crackers**

Remove skin from chicken and brush pieces with combined salad dressing and seasonings. Coat with crumbs. Place on rack of broiler pan and bake at 400 degrees for 45 minutes.

Dollie Cretsinger
GFWC—Spencer Federated Woman's Club
Spencer, Iowa

Chicken Kabobs

- **12 skewers**
- **3 pounds chicken, cut in 1-inch cubes**
- **1 large pineapple, cut in chunks**
- **2 green peppers, cut in 1-inch squares**
- **1 package cherry tomatoes**
- **½ cup chutney**
- **⅓ cup soy sauce**
- **1 sliced clove garlic**
- **¼ cup lemon juice**
- **2 tablespoons vegetable oil**
- **½ teaspoon black pepper**
- **½ cup ketchup**

In a blender, combine chutney, soy sauce, garlic, lemon juice, vegetable oil, pepper and ketchup. Blend until smooth. Pour into glass container and marinate overnight in refrigerator or for 1 hour at room temperature. Drain, reserving marinade. Thread chicken on several skewers. Thread all the pineapple on skewers. Thread peppers and tomatoes on remaining skewers. Brush all with marinade. Grill chicken skewers for 10 minutes, pineapple skewers for 8 minutes, peppers and tomatoes for 5 minutes. Heat remaining marinade for sauce.

Doreen Hickey Lindley
GFWC—Robinson Junior Woman's Club
Robinson, Illinois

Bicentennial Chicken

- **1 chicken, cut into pieces**
- **1 cup orange juice**
- **½ cup raisins**
- **¼ cup slivered almonds**
- **1 tablespoon curry**
- **1 teaspoon cinnamon**
- **½ cup marmalade**
- **1 teaspoon ginger**

Cut the chicken into quarters or eighths. Cook the ingredients for 10 minutes and spread over the chicken. Bake at 350 degrees for 1 hour.

Elizabeth W. McClave
GFWC—Lebanon Valley Woman's Club
New Lebanon, New York

Fantastic Chicken Breast

- **3 whole chicken breasts, deboned, skinned and split**
- **1 package dry onion soup mix**
- **1 8 ounce bottle Russian dressing**
- **1 8 ounce jar raspberry preserves**

Place chicken in a 10-inch casserole. Combine soup mix, dressing and preserves; pour over chicken. Bake uncovered at 350 degrees for 30 minutes. Cover and bake additional 30 minutes.

Delphine D. Hermer
GFWC—Hempfield Woman's Club
Lancaster, Pennsylvania

Orange Glaze Chicken

- **3 pounds frying chicken, cut up**
- **1 6 ounce can frozen orange juice concentrate, thawed**
- **1 4 ounce can mushrooms, stems and pieces, drained**
- **½ tablespoon cornstarch**
- **1 teaspoon dry or prepared mustard**
- **1 teaspoon paprika**

Cut larger pieces of chicken in half. Arrange chicken in 2-quart baking dish. Combine juice, mushrooms, cornstarch, mustard and paprika. Spoon over chicken. Cover with waxed paper and microwave on high for 28 minutes or until chicken is done, spooning glaze over chicken during last 10 minutes.

Violet L. Hardin
GFWC—Wapakoneta Woman's Club
Wapakoneta, Ohio

Gingered Chicken

- **4 chicken breasts, skinned**
- **⅓ cup honey**
- **⅓ cup chili sauce**
- **⅓ cup soy sauce**
- **1 teaspoon fresh grated ginger**
- **1 tablespoon cornstarch**
- **2 tablespoons water**

Mix honey, chili sauce and ginger together in an 8 × 11 microwave-safe pan. Lay chicken in pan, turning so both sides are covered with the mixture. Cover pan with wax paper, microwave on high 15 minutes. Mix cornstarch and water, pour over chicken and microwave uncovered, for 2 minutes, stirring a few times. Serve over rice.

Sue Lawrence
GFWC—Duarte Woman's Club
Duarte, California

Honey Lemon Chicken Breasts

- **4 large chicken breasts, boned and halved**
- **4 slices of bread, diced**
- **4 tablespoons minced scallions**
- **1½ cups fresh mushrooms, chopped fine**
- **8 tablespoons butter**
- **¾ cup honey**
- **1 cup lemon juice**

Heat oven to 350 degrees. Saute bread cubes, scallions and mushrooms in butter. Flatten chicken breasts and slit down the center to create a "pocket" opening. Fill opening with stuffing. Place breasts (stuffed side up) in buttered baking dish. Bake for 15 minutes. Mix honey and lemon and brush chicken with mixture. Bake 30 minutes more; baste occasionally.

Nona Maher
GFWC—The Woman's Club of Upper Saddle River
Upper Saddle River, New Jersey

Easy Baked Chicken Breasts

- 8 chicken breast halves, skinned and boned
- 8 slices Swiss cheese, 4 × 4 inches
- 1 10¾ ounce can cream of chicken or cream of mushroom soup
- ¼ cup dry white wine
- 1 cup herb-seasoned stuffing mix, crushed
- 2–3 tablespoons butter or margarine, melted

Arrange chicken in a lightly greased 12 × 8 × 2-inch baking dish. Top with cheese slices. Combine soup and wine; stir well. Spoon sauce over chicken; sprinkle with stuffing mix. Drizzle butter over crumbs. Bake at 350 degrees for 45 minutes.

Carolyn R. Wentworth
GFWC—Willimantic Woman's Club
Willimantic, Connecticut

Chicken and Noodle Cacciatore

- 4–5 pounds stewing chicken, cooked and boned
- 3½ cups tomatoes, chopped
- 14 green stuffed olives
- 3 4 ounce cans sliced mushrooms
- ½ cup green pepper, cut in strips
- ¼ cup chopped onion
- 1 teaspoon salt
- ⅛ teaspoon pepper
- ¼ teaspoon basil
- 1 1 pound package medium-width noodles
- 2 tablespoons oil
- 1 clove garlic, minced

Reserve broth after cooking chicken. Combine in skillet oil, onion and garlic. Cook until soft, about 10 minutes. Add remaining ingredients except chicken and noodles and cook for 20 minutes. Skim fat from chicken broth. Measure broth and add water to make 5 cups. Pour into 4-quart pan. Bring to boil. Add 1 tablespoon salt and noodles. Bring to boil and cook 15–20 minutes until tender. Drain. Place in 3-quart shallow casserole. Arrange chicken on noodles. Pour sauce over chicken and noodles and bake at 350 degrees for 20 minutes.

Marilyn J. Karber
GFWC—New Athens Woman's Club
New Athens, Illinois

Chicken Lasagna

- 3 cups cooked chicken, cut up
- 9 lasagna noodles
- 2 cans cream of mushroom soup
- ⅔ cup milk
- ½ teaspoon salt
- ½ teaspoon poultry seasoning
- 1 cup cottage cheese
- 6 ounces softened cream cheese
- ⅓ cup sliced olives
- ⅓ cup chopped onion
- ⅓ cup chopped green pepper
- ¼ cup chopped parsley

Cook noodles and rinse. Cream together cottage cheese and cream cheese. Add the other ingredients. Layer noodles, chicken and sauce in lasagna pan, putting some sauce in bottom. On top layer, spread just the sauce, no chicken. Cover with foil and refrigerate if not ready to bake. May be kept in refrigerator 1–3 days, if needed. Top with enough coarse bread crumbs and grated sharp cheese to cover. Bake in a 375 degree oven for 30 minutes.

Renee B. Wilson
GFWC—South Arundel Junior Woman's Club
Friendship, Maryland

Green Noodles and Chicken

- 4–5 pounds chicken, cooked and cut into bite-size pieces
- 1 package spinach noodles, cooked according to directions

Sauce

- 1 stick oleo
- 1 cup chopped celery
- 1 cup chopped onion
- 1 cup chopped green pepper
- 1 8 ounce can mushrooms
- 1 pound Velveeta cheese, cubed
- 2 cans mushroom soup, undiluted
- 1 small jar olives, sliced

Saute first five ingredients for sauce. Add Velveeta cheese; stir until smooth, then add soup and olives. Combine noodles, sauce and chicken, mixing well. Pour into buttered casserole. Top with crushed crackers. Bake at 300 degrees until bubbly.

Mrs. T. Stratton Jones, Jr.
GFWC—Book Lovers Study Club
Russellville, Alabama

Chicken Casserole

- 2 cups cooked chicken
- 2 cups brown rice
- ½ cup shredded almonds
- 2 cups cream of mushroom soup
- 1 large onion, diced
- 1 cup mayonnaise
- 1 teaspoon salt
- 1 tablespoon lemon juice
- ½ cup sliced celery
- 4 hard-boiled eggs, diced

Mix all ingredients. Put in a greased 9 × 13-inch 2-quart casserole. Add crushed potato chips on top. Add liquid from chicken. Bake at 350 degrees for 1 hour.

Emma S. Thompson
GFWC—Raymond Woman's Club
Raymond, Nebraska

Washington Square Special

- 4 ounces noodles
- 3 cans cooked chicken, 1½–2 cups
- ¼ teaspoon orange rind
- 2 cups sour cream
- 1 tablespoon butter
- ¼ teaspoon lemon rind
- Parsley
- 1 cup water
- 2 chicken bouillon cubes
- 2 teaspoons salt
- ½ teaspoon pepper

Cook noodles. In skillet, add butter and chicken; heat gently. Add bouillon cubes to water, add to chicken along with rinds, salt and pepper. Drain noodles, mix gently. Cook for 10 minutes over medium heat. Stir in sour cream. Heat quickly. Do not boil. Sprinkle with parsley.

Voni Lindgren
GFWC—Rochester Woman's Club
Rochester, Illinois

Company Chicken (Microwave)

- 1 2½ ounce package corned beef
- 3 whole chicken breasts, skinned, halved and flattened to ¼-inch thickness
- 12 ounces fresh mushrooms, thinly sliced
- 1 can cream of mushroom soup
- ½ cup dairy sour cream
- ⅓ cup sliced almonds

Cut each half of flattened breast in order to have 12 smaller rolls. Then place 2 slices of corned beef on each, roll up, spreading the slices of beef to go around. Secure with toothpick. Place mushrooms in 8 × 11-inch (2 quart) glass dish. Arrange chicken rolls on top of mushrooms. Combine soup and sour cream and pour over chicken. Cover with plastic wrap or wax paper and microwave on high 8–14 minutes. Rearrange chicken rolls halfway through cooking. Sprinkle almonds over to serve. Serves 6.

Margaret Leimer
GFWC—Burlington Woman's Club
Burlington, Iowa

Enchilada Delight

- ¼ cup butter or margarine
- ¼ cup all-purpose flour
- 2 cups chicken broth
- 1 8 ounce carton sour cream
- 2 canned jalapeno peppers, seeded and chopped
- 12 corn tortillas
- 1 whole chicken breast, cooked and chopped
- 2 cups shredded Monterey Jack cheese, divided
- ¾ cup chopped onion
- Chopped fresh parsley
- 2 tablespoons vegetable oil

Melt butter in a heavy saucepan over low heat; add flour, stirring until smooth. Cook 1 minute, stirring constantly. Gradually add chicken broth; cook over medium heat, stirring constantly until mixture is thickened and bubbly. Stir in the sour cream and chopped peppers. Pour half of sour cream sauce into a lightly greased 12 × 8 × 2 baking dish; set aside dish and remaining sour cream sauce. Fry tortillas in oil, one at a time, in a medium skillet, 5 seconds on each side, or just until tortillas are softened. Add additional oil, if necessary. Drain on paper towel. Place about 1 tablespoon each of chicken, cheese and onion on each tortilla; roll up each tortilla and place seam side down in reserved baking dish. Pour remaining sour cream sauce over top. Bake at 425 degrees for 20 minutes. Sprinkle remaining cheese on top; bake an additional 5 minutes or until cheese melts. Garnish with parsley and serve with spicy sauce.

Spicy Sauce

- 1 large tomato, finely chopped
- ½ cup onion, finely chopped
- 2 canned jalapeno peppers, seeded and chopped
- ¼ cup tomato juice
- ½ teaspoon salt

Combine all ingredients, stir well; chill until serving time.

Rubye Alexander
GFWC—Fortnightly Club of Durant
Durant, Oklahoma

Lo-Cal Chicken Casserole

- 3 pounds chicken
- 1 cup zucchini
- 1 medium onion
- 1 cup cottage cheese
- 2 tablespoons lemon juice
- 2 tablespoons Parmesan cheese—optional
- Dill weed
- Tarragon

Boil chicken and debone. Arrange pieces in 2 quart microwaveable casserole. Layer zucchini, onion, cottage cheese atop. Sprinkle with lemon juice, Parmesan, dill weed and tarragon. Microwave on 5 power for 10 minutes. Turn and continue on 10 power until done (about 10 minutes more). Any other high water content vegetable may be substituted for zucchini, including potatoes.

Sara Y. Sharadin
GFWC—McClure Woman's Club
McClure, Pennsylvania

Stuffed Chicken Breast A La Lou Ella

- **8 chicken breasts**
- **1¼ sticks oleo or butter**
- **1 onion, chopped**
- **1 medium bell pepper, chopped**
- **½ cup celery, chopped**
- **1½ pounds shrimp, fresh and chopped**
- **3–4 cups fresh bread crumbs**
- **4–6 tablespoons parsley, minced**
- **4–6 tablespoons onion top, minced**
- **Salt to taste**
- **Red pepper to taste**
- **Black pepper to taste**
- **1 can mushroom soup or cream of chicken soup**
- **2 cups chicken stock or canned chicken broth**
- **½ pound shrimp**
- **¼–½ cup oleo or butter**

Debone chicken breast, saving bones and skin for broth or you may use canned chicken broth. Place each half of chicken breast between wax paper or in a plastic bag. Carefully flatten chicken to ¼-inch thickness by using a meat mallet or rolling pin. Sprinkle chicken with seasoning to taste. Melt ¼ stick oleo or butter in a heavy aluminum pot. Saute onions, bell pepper and celery until wilted or transparent. Add chopped shrimp and let cook approximately 10 minutes or until done. Season to taste. Add bread crumbs to desired texture for stuffing. Put in parsley and onion tops. Fill each breast with stuffing and fold over. Fasten edges with toothpicks or tie securely with a string. Melt the remaining 1 stick of oleo or butter in a heavy skillet and brown chicken on all sides. Remove from skillet and place seam side down in baking dish. Mix chicken broth and soup. Cover chicken breasts with soup and broth mixture. Cover baking dish with aluminum foil and bake at 350 degrees for 45 minutes to one hour or until tender. While chicken bakes, make medium white sauce.

White Sauce

- **4 tablespoons oleo or butter**
- **4 tablespoons flour**
- **¼ teaspoon salt**
- **2 cups milk**

Melt butter over medium heat. Add flour, salt, pepper and stir until well blended. Remove from heat. Gradually stir in milk and return to heat. Cook, stirring constantly until thick and smooth. Makes 2 cups. Prepare shrimp in ¼–½ cup butter until done. Season to taste. Remove chicken from oven. Arrange on platter and remove toothpicks or string. Pour white sauce over chicken breast and top with sauteed shrimp.

Lou Ella S. Lognion
GFWC—Unique Club
Opelousas, Louisiana

Savoury Chicken Rolls

- **2 pounds chicken breasts**
- **8 pieces canned pineapple spears**
- **8 strips cheddar cheese**
- **4 whole pickles, cut into strips**
- **1 carrot, pared, blanched and cut into long strips**
- **2 tablespoons brown sugar**
- **½ cup bread crumbs**
- **1 egg, slightly beaten**

Marinade

- **Juice of pineapple spears**
- **1 teaspoon Worcestershire sauce**
- **1–1½ teaspoons salt**
- **½ teaspoon pepper**

Debone chicken. Slice meat thinly and marinate for one hour. Lay chicken slices on a clean chopping board. Sprinkle with brown sugar and place strips of pineapple, cheese, pickles and carrot on one end. Roll chicken to cover fillings. Tie with a string. Do the same for the rest of the chicken slices to make 8 rolls. Dip each roll in egg, then in bread crumbs. Heat cooking oil in a suitable pan. Deep fat fry each roll until golden brown. Serve with catsup or any desired dip.

Carmina P. Catapang
GFWC—Centro Escolar University Woman's Club
Manila, Philippines

Easy Chicken

- **6–8 chicken breasts, skinned**
- **1 pound peeled carrots**
- **1 green pepper, cut up**
- **2 stalks celery, chopped**
- **6–8 potatoes**
- **½ cup wine or water**
- **1 package onion soup mix**
- **4 tablespoons butter**
- **Pepper to taste**

Line broiler pan or large pan with foil and add ingredients. Sprinkle soup mix over ingredients and dot with butter. Bake in oven for 3–4 hours at 325 degrees.

Kathy Rugg
GFWC—Woman's City Club, Portsmouth
Portsmouth, New Hampshire

Three Cheese Chicken

- **6 chicken breasts**
- **1 8 ounce package cream cheese**
- **1 cup ricotta cheese**
- **1 cup mozzarella cheese**
- **1 egg**
- **½ cup milk**
- **Bread crumbs**

Flatten chicken as much as possible. Make a paste of the 3 cheeses and put in center of chicken. Roll or wrap chicken around the cheese mixture. Dip in egg, milk, and finally add bread crumbs. Put in greased baking dish. Bake at 350 degrees for 45 minutes.

Catherine T. Brown
GFWC—Powhatan Junior Woman's Club
Powhatan, Virginia

Chicken, Almonds, 'N Peaches

- **4 whole broiler-fryer chicken breasts, halved and skinned**
- **⅔ cup flour, divided**
- **1½ teaspoons paprika**
- **1 teaspoon salt**
- **½ teaspoon ground black pepper**
- **½ cup corn oil**
- **½ cup slivered almonds**
- **1 29 ounce can peach halves, drained, liquid reserved**
- **Water to make 1½ cups liquid using peach liquid**
- **1 10½ ounce can beef broth**
- **2 tablespoons ketchup**
- **1 cup sour cream**
- **½ cup grated Parmesan cheese**

Mix ⅓ of flour with paprika, salt and pepper. Roll chicken pieces in flour. Heat corn oil in frying pan over medium heat; add chicken and cook to brown on all sides, turning as needed. Remove chicken and place in a large casserole or baking dish. Slightly brown almonds in frying pan; stir in remaining ⅓ cup flour. Add water-peach juice mixture and broth, stirring constantly. Add ketchup; cook until thickened. Remove from heat and stir in sour cream; pour over chicken. Cover with foil. Bake in 350 degree oven for 1 hour. Remove from oven; uncover. Arrange peach halves, cut side up, over top of chicken; sprinkle with cheese. Return to oven; bake uncovered for 10 minutes or until chicken is done. Serve with egg noodles; garnish with parsley.

Kathryn J. Wendell
GFWC—Fayetteville Junior Woman's Club
Fayetteville, West Virginia

Chicken Asparagus Rolls

- **¼ teaspoon garlic powder**
- **¼ teaspoon rosemary**
- **½ teaspoon salt**
- **2 boneless chicken breasts, halved, skin removed and pounded thin enough to roll up**
- **2 1 ounce slices mozzarella cheese, cut in half**
- **1 10 ounce package frozen asparagus spears, defrosted and drained**
- **¼ teaspoon paprika**
- **4 teaspoons grated Parmesan cheese**

Combine garlic powder, rosemary and salt in small bowl. Sprinkle over flattened chicken. Lay slice of cheese on each piece. Top each with four asparagus spears. Fold long edge of chicken breast over asparagus and roll up. Secure with toothpicks. Sprinkle paprika over all. Place seam side down on microwave pie plate in pinwheel design with asparagus tips facing in. Cover with wax paper. Microwave on high 3 minutes; turn pieces in opposite direction and sprinkle with Parmesan. Cover with wax paper. Microwave on high 3 minutes until chicken is opaque and tender.

Shirley J. Parks
GFWC—Edmore Woman's Club
Edmore, Michigan

Chicken Supreme

- **4 chicken breasts, halved and boned**
- **8 slices bacon**
- **1 4 ounce package chipped beef**
- **1 can cream of chicken soup**
- **½ pint sour cream**

Wrap each piece of chicken with a bacon strip. Cover bottom of greased, oblong baking dish with chipped beef. Arrange chicken breasts on top of the beef. Mix the soup (undiluted) with the sour cream and spoon mixture over the chicken. Refrigerate (can be overnight). Bake uncovered at 275 degrees for 3 hours.

Julia Wolfe
GFWC—Wapakoneta Woman's Club, Inc.
Wapakoneta, Ohio

Creamy Baked Chicken Breasts

- **4 whole chicken breasts, split, skinned and boned**
- **8 4 × 4 inch slices Swiss cheese**
- **1 10¾ ounce can cream of chicken soup, undiluted**
- **¼ cup dry white wine**
- **1 cup herb-seasoned stuffing mix, crushed**
- **¼ cup butter or margarine, melted**

Arrange chicken in lightly greased 9 × 13 × 2 inch baking dish. Top with cheese slices. Combine soup and wine, stirring well. Spoon sauce evenly over chicken and sprinkle with stuffing mix. Pour butter over crumbs; bake at 350 degrees for 40–45 minutes.

Billie Hall
GFWC—Aglaian Study Club
Galveston, Texas

Chicken in a Stuffing Nest

- **3 tablespoons flour**
- **3 tablespoons butter or margarine**
- **1½ cups chicken broth**
- **½ cup light cream**
- **2 cups cooked chicken or turkey, cut up**
- **1 cup boiling water**
- **1 cup cooked peas**
- **⅔ cup shredded carrots**
- **½ cup chopped green onions**
- **¼ teaspoon thyme**
- **⅛ teaspoon sage**
- **½ cup margarine**
- **1 8 ounce package herb-seasoned stuffing mix**

In a saucepan, melt butter. Add flour and cook, stirring until bubbling and smooth. Remove from heat. Gradually blend in chicken broth and heat, stirring until thickened and smooth. Add cream, chicken, peas, carrots, onion, thyme and sage. Prepare stuffing according to package directions, using butter and water. Press against sides and bottom of 1½-quart baking dish. Pour hot mixture into center of prepared dish. Bake at 400 degrees for 15 minutes or until hot and bubbly. Can be modified to cook in a microwave. Microwave high for 6–8 minutes, turning once during the cooking time.

"I found this recipe in a newspaper column about 10 years ago."

Judy Denniston
GFWC—Michiana Junior Woman's Club
South Bend, Indiana

Apple and Herb Stuffed Chicken Breast

3 whole chicken breasts (split, boned, skinned and pounded thin)
¼ cup onions, chopped fine
1 small clove garlic
1 large apple, peeled and cored
1½ tablespoons butter or margarine
½ cup soft bread crumbs
¼ teaspoon rosemary
¼ teaspoon basil
¼ teaspoon salt
Flour
3 tablespoons butter or margarine
¾ cup apple juice
2 tablespoons cognac or sherry

Chop onions and garlic; use press. Grate apples. Melt butter in small skillet, saute onion and garlic until golden; add grated apple, bread crumbs, rosemary, basil and salt. Stir over low heat until thoroughly mixed. Spoon 1½ tablespoons apple mixture on boned side of chicken breast. Roll up, tuck in ends and secure with toothpicks. Coat with flour. Heat 3 tablespoons butter in pan and brown rolls well. Add apple juice and cognac; cover and simmer 30 minutes. Cover and place in oven to keep warm until serving time.

Louise C. Henson
GFWC—Brookside Woman's Club
Brookside, New Jersey

Chicken (Turkey) Scallop

1 8 ounce package seasoned stuffing
3 cups cubed chicken or turkey, cooked or baked
½ cup butter
½ cup flour
4 cups chicken broth, cooled
6 eggs, slightly beaten
¼ teaspoon salt
Dash of pepper
1 can mushroom soup
¼ cup milk
1 cup sour cream
¼ cup chopped pimiento

Prepare stuffing according to package directions. Spread in greased 9 × 13 × 2 pan. Top with chicken. Melt butter; add seasoning and flour. Add cooled broth and stir until mixture thickens. Stir small amount of hot mixture into slightly beaten eggs. Return to hot mixture and pour over chicken. Bake in a 325 degree oven for 45 minutes. Let stand for 5 minutes before cutting in squares. Sauce: Mix 1 can mushroom soup with milk, sour cream and pimiento. Heat and stir until hot. Pour over cut squares when serving.

"This was served at a church gourmet luncheon 30 years ago."

Helen V. Lane
GFWC—Wicomico Woman's Club
Salisbury, Maryland

Jamaican Chicken

- 1 20 ounce can pineapple slices
- 6 boned, skinned ½ breasts of chicken
- 1 teaspoon chicken bouillon
- ½ cup boiling water
- 1 teaspoon dry instant coffee
- 1 10¾ ounce can condensed cream of chicken soup
- ¼ pound shredded sharp cheddar cheese

Place pineapple slices in bottom of a square 2-quart baking dish. Save any extra for garnish. Top with chicken breasts. Dissolve bouillon in water and combine with coffee and soup. Pour over chicken and bake at 375 degrees for 40 minutes. Sprinkle with cheese and return to oven until cheese melts.

Cindy Stanek
GFWC—Longmont Woman's Club
Longmont, Colorado

Hawaiian Chicken

- 4 chicken breasts (raw)
- ¼ cup brown sugar
- ½ cup ketchup
- ¼ cup vinegar
- 2 tablespoons flour or cornstarch
- 1 small green pepper, chopped
- 1 can pineapple chunks with juice

Lay chicken breasts in casserole. Mix all ingredients together and pour over chicken. Cover with foil. Bake at 375 degrees for 1½ hours.

Nancy Shanks
GFWC—Mocksville Woman's Club
Mocksville, North Carolina

Italian Boneless Chicken

- **4–6 chicken breast halves (skinned and boned)**
- **3 tablespoons olive oil**
- **1 finely minced clove garlic (optional)**
- **1 chopped onion**
- **1 28 ounce can tomatoes (break up into pieces)**
- **1¼ teaspoons salt**
- **¼ teaspoon pepper**
- **1 8 ounce can tomato sauce**
- **¼ teaspoon dried thyme**
- **1 egg**
- **½ cup packaged dried bread crumbs (Italian style)**
- **1 cup Parmesan cheese**
- **2 tablespoons olive oil**
- **½ pound mozzarella cheese, sliced**

In 3 tablespoons of hot olive oil, saute garlic and onion until golden. Add tomatoes, salt, pepper and simmer uncovered 10 minutes. Add tomato sauce, thyme; simmer uncovered 20 minutes. Beat egg well with fork. Combine bread crumbs with ½ cup Parmesan cheese. Dip each piece of chicken into egg, then into crumbs and cheese mixture. Saute in one tablespoon of hot olive oil (2 or 3 pieces of chicken at a time) in skillet until golden brown, turning once. Repeat until all pieces of chicken are done. Place chicken side by side in a 9 × 13 baking dish. Pour two-thirds of tomato mixture over chicken. Arrange slices of mozzarella on top of chicken. Spoon rest of tomato mixture over chicken. Sprinkle with ½ cup Parmesan cheese. Bake at 350 degrees for 30 minutes.

Kay Galm
GFWC—Gainesville Woman's Club
Gainesville, Florida

Coq-Au-Vin

- **½ cup flour**
- **2 teaspoons salt**
- **¼ teaspoon cracked pepper**
- **3–4 pounds frying chicken, cut in pieces**
- **4 slices bacon**
- **3 small onions**
- **1 clove garlic, finely minced**
- **1 stem celery, cut up**
- **1 pound fresh mushrooms, sliced**
- **¾ cup red wine**
- **1 bay leaf**
- **1 tablespoon chopped parsley**

Combine flour, salt and pepper in bag. Add chicken; shake to coat. Cut bacon in 1-inch pieces. Place in bottom of cooker and microwave, uncovered, 3½ minutes on full power. Stir after half the time. Do not drain. Stir in flour from bag. Place all remaining ingredients in cooker. Microwave 15 minutes, full power or until chicken is tender. Stir gently and microwave 10 minutes. For conventional oven, 350 degrees for 1 hour 10 minutes.

Dorothy Galloway
GFWC—History Club
Celina, Ohio

Chicken Breast Supreme

- 8 chicken breasts—skinned
- 2 cans cream of mushroom soup
- 1 cup sour cream
- 3/4 cup sherry
- Paprika
- Salt to taste

Salt chicken, place in baking dish. Combine soup, sour cream and sherry. Pour over chicken, totally covering it. Sprinkle with paprika. Bake at 325 degrees for 1 hour and 15 minutes. Serve with long grain and wild rice.

Gloria M. Durchsprung
GFWC—Woman's Club of Southampton
Southampton, Pennsylvania

Chicken with Cashews

- 4 large half chicken breasts
- 1/4 cup water
- 1/4 cup sherry
- 2 tablespoons dark corn syrup
- 1 tablespoon vinegar
- 4 teaspoons cornstarch
- 1/4 cup peanut oil
- 1/2 cup green pepper cubes
- 1/2 cup cashews
- 2 tablespoons sliced green onions
- 2 minced cloves garlic
- 1/4 teaspoon ground ginger
- 1 4 ounce can sliced mushrooms

Remove skin from chicken. Cut meat from bone into 1-inch cubes. Combine water, sherry, soy sauce, syrup, vinegar and corn starch. Blend thoroughly and set aside. Preheat pan or wok over high heat, about 2 minutes. Add oil, pouring it around the sides of pan; heat 2 minutes. Add chicken cubes; stir fry 2 to 3 minutes or until chicken turns white; push to side of pan. Add peppers, cashews, mushrooms and stir fry 2 to 3 minutes; push to side. Add onions, garlic and ginger and stir fry 1 minute; push to side. Add stirred sauce mixture, bring to boil, stirring gently. Boil 1 minute, stirring rest of ingredients with sauce.

Rose Mary Phelleps
GFWC—Camp Hill Civic Club
Camp Hill, Pennsylvania

Chicken Dijon

- 1 fryer chicken, cut up
- 1 tablespoon butter
- 1 tablespoon green onion or shallots, chopped
- 1/4 cup dry white wine
- 2 tablespoons Dijon mustard
- 1 can cream of chicken soup

Brown chicken in butter in heavy skillet. Lower heat, cover and continue cooking until tender; 1/2–3/4 hour. Remove to heated serving platter. Add onion to drippings in skillet. Saute until tender, but not brown. Pour in wine. Cook over high heat until reduced by 1/3. Stir in mustard and soup and heat thoroughly. Pour over chicken and serve. (Speed cooking time by using microwave to cook chicken.)

Gretel Ruppert
GFWC—Woman's Club of Allentown
Allentown, Pennsylvania

Chicken Tetrazzini

- 2 tablespoons butter or margarine
- ⅓ cup seasoned dry bread crumbs
- ¼ cup butter or margarine
- ¼ cup flour
- ½ teaspoon Italian seasoning
- ½ teaspoon salt
- ¼ teaspoon pepper
- 1 cup chicken broth
- 1 cup half and half
- 8 ounces spaghetti, cooked
- 2 cups cut-up chicken, cooked
- 1 4 ounce can sliced mushrooms, drained
- ¼ cup grated Parmesan cheese

Place 2 tablespoons butter in small bowl. Microwave on high for 45 to 60 seconds, or until butter melts. Stir in bread crumbs. Set aside. Place butter in 2-quart casserole. Microwave at high for 45 seconds to 1¼ minutes, or until butter melts. Blend flour, Italian seasoning, salt and pepper into butter. Stir in broth and half and half. Microwave at medium for 8 to 9 minutes, or until mixture thickens, stirring every 2 minutes. Stir in spaghetti, chicken, mushrooms and Parmesan cheese. Cover. Microwave at medium power level for 5–6 minutes, or until heated through, stirring once. Sprinkle with bread crumbs mixture. Microwave, uncovered, for two minutes or until hot.

Tina Honican
GFWC—Cumberland Woman's Club
Cumberland, Kentucky

Scalloped Chicken and Spaghetti

- ⅓ cup butter
- ¼ cup chopped onion
- 1 clove garlic, cut up
- 1 cup sliced mushrooms
- ¼ cup flour
- 2 cups chicken stock
- Salt
- Pepper
- 3 cups cooked chicken, diced
- 1 cup tomatoes
- ¼ pound grated American cheese
- 1 8 or 9 ounce package thin spaghetti
- ½ cup buttered crumbs for top

Heat butter. Add garlic, onion and mushrooms. Cook 10 minutes or until soft. Add flour. Add chicken stock and cook until thick and smooth. Season to taste with salt and pepper. Add chicken, tomatoes and cheese. Cook a little longer to melt cheese. Pour mixture over cooked spaghetti and mix. Put in buttered casserole. Sprinkle bread crumbs on top. Cover and warm 25 to 60 minutes at 375 degrees, depending on how cold it is.

Lee Crippen
GFWC—Woman's Club of Bethesda
Bethesda, Maryland

Buttermilk Pecan Chicken

2 broiler-fryer chickens
½ cup margarine
1 cup buttermilk
1 egg, slightly beaten
1 cup flour
1 cup ground pecans
1 tablespoon paprika
1 tablespoon salt
⅛ teaspoon pepper
¼ cup sesame seeds (optional)
⅛ cup pecan halves

Melt margarine in 9 × 13 baking dish. Mix buttermilk and egg in shallow dish. Mix flour, ground pecans, paprika, salt, sesame seeds and pepper together. Dip each piece of chicken first into the buttermilk, then into the flour mixture. Place skin side down in melted margarine in baking dish. Then turn chicken pieces to coat each side. Place a pecan half on each piece of chicken. Bake until tender and golden brown, about 1¼ hours at 350 degrees.

Edna Koontz
GFWC—Twentieth Century Club
Clyde, Ohio

Roast Duck (with Dried Fruit Stuffing)

1 4 pound duckling
¼ cup butter
1 cup dry bread crumbs
1 large onion, chopped
1 pound mixed dried fruit, pitted and chopped
Salt and pepper to taste

Thaw frozen duckling. Salt and pepper inside and out. Chop liver. Melt butter and saute onion and liver for 5 minutes. Chop fruit and mix with onion, liver and bread crumbs. Use this mixture to stuff neck and body cavities of duckling. Sew or skewer openings and tie legs together. Roast on rack set in foil-lined baking pan in preheated oven at 350 degrees for 1–1¼ hours, or until leg can be moved up and down easily.

Adelaide V. Rees
GFWC—Woman's Club of Prospect Park
Prospect Park, Pennsylvania

Pheasant in Apricot Sauce

3 pheasants
12 ounces apricot preserves or jam
1 teaspoon tarragon
1 cup white wine
1 cup whipping cream
4 teaspoons cornstarch
1 16 ounce can apricot halves

Halve breasts; cut legs and thigh sections from pheasants. Salt pieces and put in baking dish. Mix together apricot jam, tarragon and wine. Pour mixture over pheasant. Bake covered for 1–1½ hours at 325 degrees. Remove pheasant pieces. To pan juices add cream and boil. Mix cornstarch with a little water. Stir into sauce. Return to boiling, stirring constantly. Add apricot halves. Pour over pheasant and serve.

Bea Beckley
GFWC—Arlington Heights Woman's Club
Arlington Heights, Illinois

Lemon-Honey Barbecued Chicken

⅓ cup honey
⅓ cup lemon juice, freshly squeezed
⅓ cup soy sauce
1 clove garlic, minced
1 whole chicken, cut into serving pieces and skinned
Barbecue sauce

In blender, combine the first 4 ingredients and pour over chicken. Allow chicken to marinate in refrigerator for at least 3 hours (the longer the better). Make sure the pieces are marinated on both sides. Place chicken pieces in a pan lined with foil and bake at 400 degrees for 1 hour. During this time, baste chicken with reserved marinade several times until all liquid has been used. Reduce oven to 350 degrees. Remove pan from oven and drain. Rearrange chicken and apply barbecue sauce to each piece. Cook for additional 30 minutes. Add more sauce if you desire and cook a little longer. Cooking time may vary due to size of chicken and basting time.

Judith H. Burch
GFWC—Brussels Woman's Club
Brussels, Illinois

Bar-B-Q Sauce for Chicken

1 cup water
2 cups vinegar
½ cup cooking oil
1 tablespoon salt
1 tablespoon garlic powder
¼ pound margarine

Bring all ingredients to a rolling boil. Marinate chicken in sauce all day or overnight. Cook slowly over low heat on grill approximately 1 hour, turning every 15 minutes. May also be used to broil chicken. Makes enough sauce for 3 usages. Stores 6 months in refrigerator.

Debbie L. Harris
GFWC—Nelly Custis Junior Woman's Club
Quinton, Virginia

Turkey Cornbread Dressing

1 pan cornbread
6 slices stale bread
1 cup onions, chopped
1 cup celery, diced
2 eggs, slightly beaten
2 cups rich chicken broth
1 cup turkey drippings
1½ teaspoons poultry seasoning
1 tablespoon butter
Salt and pepper to taste

Saute onion and celery in butter until tender. Combine bread, vegetables, broth drippings and seasonings. Mix well. (Should be mushy. If not, add broth or water.) Add eggs. Pour into hot, greased iron skillet and bake 400 degrees for 45 minutes. Stir two or three times during cooking to mix in brown crust.

"This was my mother's recipe—now about 50 years old."

Lillian R. Johnson
GFWC—Lithonia Woman's Club
Lithonia, Georgia

Celery Stuffing for Turkey

2 medium onions, finely chopped
1½ cups celery, chopped
½ cup margarine
1 small jar sliced mushrooms (approximately 1 cup)
1 package bread stuffing
2 eggs
Poultry seasoning to taste
1 teaspoon salt
2 cups chicken broth
Dried parsley

Saute onions and celery in margarine until transparent. Add mushrooms and cool slightly. Add this mixture to bread stuffing. Add eggs, poultry seasoning, salt and chicken broth. You can add a little dried parsley if you desire.

Mary Connell
GFWC—Junior Woman's League of Canfield, Inc.
Canfield, Ohio

Turkey with Ham Dressing

18–22 pound turkey
Salt and pepper
5 pounds potatoes

Dressing

6 onions
1½ sticks butter
4 slices dry bread (toasted)
2 pounds ham (ground)
1 tablespoon sage
1 teaspoon salt
1 teaspoon pepper

Wash turkey, salt and pepper inside and out. Prepare dressing. Brown onions, sliced, in butter. Add salt and pepper. Dampen bread and mix with ground ham. Add to browned onions. Add sage and mix well. Stuff turkey with dressing. Add 1 cup water to roasting pan. Bake at 350 degrees for 4–5 hours. Remove turkey from pan. Peel potatoes, cut in quarters, salt and cook in turkey-ham drippings in uncovered roasting pan. Add water if necessary to cover potatoes. Cook until tender.

"My father originated this recipe over 60 years ago."

Toni Themis
GFWC—The Woman's Club of Joliet
Joliet, Illinois

Sausage Stuffing

3 medium onions, chopped fine
½ stalk celery, chopped
2 loaves stale bread, regular size
1 pound sausage
Pinch of thyme
Pinch of sage
Salt and pepper to taste
1 raw egg

Mix together first 4 ingredients. Add remaining ingredients. Stuff 12 pound turkey and cook according to directions on label. If some of the stuffing does not fit into turkey, just bake separately in oven until crisp; about 20–25 minutes at 325 degrees.

Dorothy M. Constants
GFWC—Woman's Club of Oakland, Inc.
Oakland, New Jersey

Chestnut Dressing for Turkey

3 cups chestnuts
½ cup butter
1 teaspoon salt
Few grains pepper
¼ cup sweet cream
1 cup cracker crumbs

Shell and blanch chestnuts. Mash. Add ¼ cup butter, salt, pepper and sweet cream. Mix well and add the cracker crumbs, mixed with the other ¼ cup of butter. Stuff turkey and bake at 325 degrees according to directions on label.

"This is a 3-generation recipe brought from France by my grandmother."

Barbara D. Davis
GFWC—Buechel Woman's Club
Louisville, Kentucky

Wild Rice Dressing

¼ cup wild rice
1 cup gravy stock or beef broth
½ cup sliced mushrooms
⅓ cup white rice
1 minced onion
½ teaspoon salt

Put wild rice, salt and liquid in a 4-cup measuring cup. Cover, place in microwave. Bring to a boil on high. Cook for 8 minutes on 20% power. Uncover and add onions, mushrooms and white rice. Cover and bring to a boil on high. Cook for 12 more minutes at 20% power. Let stand for 5 minutes to absorb liquid.

Dorothy B. Skinner
GFWC—Kingston Woman's Club
Kingston, Tennessee

Pineapple Dressing

½ cup butter or oleo
1 cup sugar
4 eggs
1 1 pound 4 ounce can crushed pineapple
5 slices cubed white bread

Cream butter and sugar, beat in eggs one at a time. Stir in pineapple, fold in bread cubes and place in greased 1½-quart casserole. Bake at 350 degrees for 1 hour.

Adrienne Groves
GFWC—Woman's Club of Berkley
Berkley, Michigan

Vegetables

Baked Artichoke and Cheese

1 cup mayonnaise
1 cup grated parmesan cheese
2 cups (8 ounces) shredded mozzarella cheese
2 8 ounce cans artichoke hearts (drain)
2 teaspoons garlic powder

Combine first 5 ingredients in a bowl; pour into a lightly greased casserole. Bake at 350 degrees for 25 minutes. Serve hot with crackers.

Sharon Peterson
GFWC—Wheaton Junior Woman's Club
Wheaton, Illinois

Photo features: Okra Supreme—Page 225
Best Ever Cauliflower With Cheese Sauce—Page 222

Asparagus Dish

- **⅔ cup white vinegar**
- **½ cup sugar**
- **Cinnamon and cloves to taste**
- **½ teaspoon salt**
- **½ cup water**
- **1 tablespoon celery seed**
- **2 large cans asparagus, drained**
- **1 hard-boiled egg**

Place asparagus in dish. Bring to a boil all ingredients except asparagus. Pour vinegar mixture over asparagus. Refrigerate 24 hours. Before serving, pour off liquid and grate a hard-boiled egg over asparagus for garnish.

Cathy Hunt
GFWC—Brandywine Woman's Club of Old Hickory
Old Hickory, Tennessee

Dotty's Tex-Mex Beans

- **3 cups dry pinto beans**
- **4 small cloves garlic, minced**
- **½ cup bacon, diced**
- **1 8 ounce can tomato sauce**
- **1 tablespoon chili powder**
- **Pinch of baking soda**
- **Salt and pepper to taste**

Sort and rinse pinto beans. Cover with at least 2 inches of water and let soak overnight. Drain water. Barely cover beans with fresh water. Add garlic, bacon, tomato sauce, chili powder and baking soda. Bring to a boil. Let simmer 2 to 3 hours until tender. Salt and pepper to taste. To make refried beans, drain off bean juice and mash beans. Add bean juice as needed for correct consistency.

Catherine S. Cabinian, R.D.
GFWC—Morgan County Woman's Club
West Liberty, Kentucky

Dried Lima Beans and Tomatoes Casserole

- **½ pound dried lima beans**
- **½ cup olive oil**
- **Parmesan cheese**
- **1 No. 2 can tomatoes**
- **4 spring onions, tops and bulbs chopped**
- **2 teaspoons salt**
- **½ teaspoon sugar**
- **Dash cayenne**
- **½ green pepper, chopped without seeds**

Soak beans overnight. Cook until just tender, about 15 minutes. Cook onions in oil until yellow; add beans, which have been drained, and green pepper with seasonings. Toss a few minutes in pan to add flavor, then put in greased casserole and cover with the whole can of tomatoes. Sprinkle with parmesan cheese. Cook uncovered in 350 degree oven for 30 minutes.

Mary Elizabeth Allen
GFWC—Lancaster Shakespeare Club
Lancaster, Texas

Four Bean Casserole

- 2 cans pork and beans
- 1 can green beans, drained
- 1 can butter beans, drained
- 1 can kidney beans, drained
- 8 slices bacon, fried crisp and broken
- 1 large onion, chopped
- 1 cup brown sugar
- 1 can tomato paste
- 1 teaspoon salt, pepper to taste
- 2 teaspoons dry mustard

Brown bacon; remove to drain on paper. Saute onion in bacon drippings. Add sugar and brown. In a 4-quart casserole, combine beans, mustard, salt, pepper, tomato paste and broken bacon. Mix well, adding onions and grease. Bake covered at 350 degrees for one hour.

Elna Welsh
GFWC—Sacramento Woman's Club
Sacramento, California

Green Beans with White Sauce

- 2 cans green beans
- 1 cup mayonnaise
- 2 hard-boiled eggs
- 1 tablespoon horseradish
- 1 teaspoon Worcestershire sauce
- Salt to taste
- Pepper to taste
- Garlic salt to taste
- Onion salt to taste
- 1½ teaspoons parsley flakes
- 1 lemon, juiced

Season and heat (do not cook) beans. Drain and place in serving dish. Mix all other ingredients to make white sauce. Pour over beans before serving.

Ms. Owen De Angelo
GFWC—Fortnightly
Moss Point, Mississippi

Italian Green Beans

- 1 15 ounce can French style green beans, drained
- 1 14 ounce can artichoke hearts, drained
- ⅓ cup parmesan cheese
- ⅓ cup olive oil
- ⅓ cup bread crumbs
- 2 tablespoons bread crumbs for topping

Chop artichoke hearts and mix with green beans. Add the remaining ingredients to the artichoke-green bean mixture and stir. Put in an ovenware pan (loaf size or 8 × 8), or a microwave pan if cooking in the microwave. Top with a sprinkling of bread crumbs. Heat until bubbly. Bake at 350 degrees for 30 minutes in oven or high for 15 minutes in microwave (turn halfway through cook time).

Colleen J. Ehlenbeck
GFWC—Tallahassee Junior Woman's Club
Tallahassee, Florida

Aunt Elsie's Oven Green Beans

1 tablespoon butter
½ cup cheddar cheese
½ cup buttered bread crumbs
1 tablespoon flour
Pinch of salt
2 tablespoons chopped pimiento
½ teaspoon Worcestershire sauce
1 can mushroom soup
1 quart drained, cooked green beans (can use canned beans)

Make white sauce of butter, flour, seasoning and can of mushroom soup. Add cheese and pimiento and blend. Pour over 1 quart drained, cooked green beans. Cover with buttered crumbs and bake ½ hour at 350 degrees.

"This recipe was given to me, when I was a new bride 38 years ago, by Aunt Elsie who was a great aunt of my husband."

Janice A. Stambaugh
GFWC—Phoedalian Woman's Club
Glendale, Arizona

Chinese Vegetables

3 carrots, peeled
3 stalks celery
1 bunch green onions or 1 large white one, sliced
Cornstarch mixed with water, as needed
Salt and pepper to taste
Sugar, if desired
2 large green peppers, sliced
½ cup cashews
½ cup chicken bouillon
Small amount of oil

Heat oil in frying pan until hot. If you have a wok, this should be used. When the oil is hot, add the vegetables. Be careful not to get spattered. Stir but do not brown. When about ¼ of way cooked, add cashews, chicken bouillon, salt, pepper and sugar. Simmer and cook until the vegetables are cooked to your liking, preferably crispy. Add cornstarch to thicken.

Sophia Spencer
GFWC—Meadville Woman's Club
Meadville, Pennsylvania

Boston Baked Beans

1 pound beans, pea beans preferably
1 teaspoon baking soda
1 medium onion
3 tablespoons brown sugar
3 tablespoons molasses
3-inch square of chunk bacon or 1/4 inch sliced bacon
6 tablespoons catsup
1 teaspoon dry mustard
1 teaspoon salt
Water enough to cover beans

Pick over beans, checking for stones, etc. Soak overnight in cold water. Drain and parboil with 1 teaspoon baking soda for 15 minutes. Drain; cover with hot water and return to boil (to remove soda). Drain. In bottom of bean pot or casserole, slice the onion. Add the beans and the bacon (or salt pork if desired). Add the sauce of molasses, brown sugar, catsup, mustard, salt and water. Cover and bake at 225 degrees for 5 to 6 hours.

"I got this recipe during the Depression from a First National Store's publication."

Ida A. Vanderpoel
GFWC—Granby Woman's Club
Granby, Massachusetts

Cranberry Beets

1 cup water
1 cup sugar
2 cups cranberries
1 teaspoon cornstarch
1 tablespoon cold water
1 No. 303 can cubed or sliced beets, drained

Mix water and sugar; boil for 5 minutes. Add cranberries; cook, without stirring, until cranberries pop open or for 5 minutes. Drain, reserving juice. Heat reserved juice. Mix cornstarch with cold water, making smooth paste; add to juice. Cook until clear and thickened or for about 3 to 4 minutes. Add cranberries and beets. Yield: 8 servings. Can be served hot or cold.

Jayne Johnson
GFWC—Civic League
Indianola, Mississippi

Honeyed Beets

1/2 cup honey
2 tablespoons vinegar
2 1 pound cans sliced beets
2 tablespoons butter
1 medium onion, sliced and separated into rings

In a saucepan, blend honey, vinegar and 2 tablespoons beet liquid. Add butter, drained beets and onion rings. Simmer until heated through, stirring occasionally. Do not overcook as onion rings should remain crisp.

Ruth Pedersen
GFWC—Northwood Literary
Northwood, North Dakota

Marinated Broccoli

3 bunches broccoli (cleaned and separate)
1 cup vinegar
½ cup oil
1 tablespoon dill weed
1 teaspoon pepper
1 tablespoon MSG
1 teaspoon garlic powder
1 tablespoon sugar

Mix all ingredients together and marinate in refrigerator for 24 hours. Mix occasionally to insure even saturation.

Jeanette Jester
GFWC—Vista
Camas, Washington

Aunt Helen's Broccoli/Corn Casserole

1 10 ounce package chopped broccoli (thawed)
1 16 ounce can cream-style corn
1 egg, beaten
Dash salt
Dash pepper
1 cup stuffing mix, flavored
1 small onion, chopped
3 tablespoons melted butter

Mix together broccoli, cream-style corn, egg, salt, pepper and onions in a bowl. Melt butter and add stuffing, stirring to coat. Add ¾ cup stuffing mix to broccoli mixture and put into buttered casserole dish; top with remaining crumbs. Bake at 350 degrees for 30 to 40 minutes.

V. Elaine Proctor
GFWC—Poultney Woman's Club
Poultney, Vermont

Broccoli Casserole

2 packages broccoli flowerets or 1 large package broccoli cuts
1 can mushroom soup
1 cup mayonnaise
2 eggs, beaten
2 tablespoons chopped onion
1 cup grated sharp cheese
½ cup crushed cheese crackers

Cook broccoli and drain. Mix mayonnaise, soup, eggs, onion and cheese. Put broccoli into a 1½ quart casserole dish. Sprinkle with crackers. Bake at 350 degrees for 30 minutes.

Elizabeth Proctor
GFWC—Gordon Woman's Club
Gordon, Georgia

Cabbage Crunch

4 tablespoons sesame seeds
1 cup slivered almonds (toasted)
1 head cabbage, chopped
4 green onions, chopped fine
2 packages Ramen noodles (chicken flavor)

Dressing

4 tablespoons sugar
1 cup salad oil
6 tablespoons vinegar
1 teaspoon salt
2 packages chicken flavoring from noodles

Put cabbage in large bowl, then onions, broken-up noodles, sesame seeds and almonds. Pour dressing on salad and mix.

Mrs. Fred Geiger
GFWC—Cozad Woman's Club
Cozad, Nebraska

Carrots with Herbs

1 bunch carrots
2 tablespoons butter
½ teaspoon sugar
2 tablespoons cream
½ teaspoon salt
2 sprigs parsley
¼ teaspoon thyme

Scrape carrots and cut in long thin strips. Put in saucepan with butter, sugar, salt and chopped parsley; cover tightly. Cook over very low heat about 20 minutes. Add thyme and cream and simmer 2 minutes longer. Serves 4.

Alice Eubank
GFWC—Mesquite Club
Las Vegas, Nevada

Apple-Carrot Bake

6 apples
2 cups cooked carrots—sliced
⅓ cup brown sugar
2 tablespoons flour
Salt to taste
¾ cup orange juice

Peel, core and slice thinly the apples and layer half in a 2 quart, greased baking dish. Layer half the carrots. Mix brown sugar, flour, salt and spread half over the apple-carrots. Repeat layers of each and pour the orange juice evenly on top. Bake at 350 degrees for 45 minutes. Perfect for pork or ham.

Verna G. Farmer
GFWC—Tucker Woman's Club
Tucker, Georgia

Spicy Cauliflower

- **3 tablespoons peanut oil**
- **1 tablespoon mustard seed**
- **1 inch fresh ginger, cut into match sticks**
- **1 medium onion, sliced**
- **1½ teaspoons turmeric**
- **1 large cauliflower, separated into small florets**
- **½ teaspoon salt**
- **Juice of ½ lemon**
- **¼ cup water**

In a large saucepan (or skillet with cover), heat the oil and add the mustard seed. Cover; when seeds stop popping, remove lid and add ginger, onion and turmeric. Stir fry for 3 minutes. Add cauliflower, salt, lemon juice and water. Stir to coat cauliflower evenly. Cover and simmer for 15 to 20 minutes or until florets are tender.

For spicier dish, 1 green chili may be chopped and added with ginger.

Celeste Jacobs
GFWC—Randolph Township Woman's Club
Randolph, New Jersey

Cauliflower Casserole

- **1 large head cauliflower**
- **½ pint sour cream**
- **1 can cream of shrimp soup**

Break cauliflower into serving-size pieces. Cook in small amount of water until tender. Put in casserole and pour well-mixed shrimp soup and sour cream over cauliflower. Bake at 350 degrees for 25 minutes and serve hot.

Mildred Fisher
GFWC—Philomathean
Apple Creek, Ohio

Best Ever Cauliflower with Cheese Sauce

- **1 head cauliflower**
- **1 teaspoon lemon juice**
- **8 ounces grated cheese, sharp or mild**
- **4 to 5 tablespoons butter**
- **2 cups milk**
- **¼ teaspoon salt**
- **⅓ cup flour**
- **4 to 6 drops tabasco sauce**
- **½ to 1 teaspoon catsup**
- **Sprinkle paprika**
- **Chopped parsley**

Cut cauliflower into florets of desired size but not too small. Rinse well. Bring cauliflower to boil in water to cover. Flavor with 1 teaspoon lemon juice. Boil gently until fork tender; drain before adding cheese sauce. Meanwhile, grate cheese and set aside. In small saucepan, melt over low heat the butter, adding salt. Add plain flour, making a thick roux. Gradually add milk, stirring constantly. Add grated cheese, stirring constantly. Stir in tabasco sauce and catsup. Pour cheese sauce over cauliflower. Keep warm until ready to serve.

Ruth M. Frederick
GFWC—Somo Sala Circle
Morristown, Tennessee

Corn and Tomato Casserole

- **6 ears fresh corn**
- **1 medium onion, chopped**
- **1 medium green pepper, chopped**
- **2 tablespoons butter**
- **4 medium potatoes, sliced**
- **Salt and pepper**
- **Buttered crumbs**

Combine cut fresh corn, onions, green pepper; saute in butter for 5 minutes. Spoon half of corn mixture in buttered casserole and top with half of tomato slices. Repeat layers and top with buttered crumbs. Bake in 375 degree oven for 30 minutes.

Ruth J. Woodruff
GFWC—Woman's Club of Bethlehem
Bethlehem, Pennsylvania

Corn Casserole

- **1 can whole kernel corn**
- **1 can creamed corn**
- **1 cup sour cream**
- **1 package cornbread mix**
- **1 stick butter, melted**
- **2 eggs, beaten**

Mix all ingredients together and bake in large baking dish for 15 minutes in 350 degree oven. Remove from oven and add grated cheese over top. Return to oven until melted.

Carolyn Taylor
GFWC—Twentieth Century Club
Mammoth Spring, Arkansas

Grandmother's Corn Pudding

- **1 2 pound can creamed corn**
- **3 tablespoons sugar**
- **3/4 cup milk**
- **2 tablespoons margarine or salad oil**
- **2 eggs, slightly beaten**
- **2 tablespoons flour**

Mix all ingredients together and bake in oven at 350 degrees for 40 minutes.

Becky Johnson
CFWC Vcrnon Study Club
Vernon, Alabama

Different Marinated Mushrooms

- **8 ounces mushrooms, sliced**
- **2 tablespoons margarine**
- **2 tablespoons grenadine**
- **1 tablespoon finely chopped green onions**
- **1 clove garlic, crushed**

Combine all ingredients in small saucepan over low heat and cook until mushrooms are tender. Serve with all meats. Makes approximately four servings.

Judy Daniels
GFWC—El Dorado Woman's Club
Long Beach, California

Oven Fried Sesame Eggplant

- **¾ cup saltine cracker crumbs (12 double)**
- **½ cup grated parmesan cheese**
- **¼ cup sesame seeds**
- **¼ teaspoon pepper**
- **1 medium eggplant**
- **Mayonnaise**

Preheat oven to 400 degrees. Grease 2 baking sheets. Mix cracker crumbs, cheese, sesame seeds and pepper together in small bowl. Cut off stem and peel the eggplant. Cut into ½-inch thick slices. Spread both sides of each slice with mayonnaise. Dip each side into crumbs pressing lightly so they adhere. Cut each slice into quarters, making 4 triangles. Place on sheets and bake in 400 degree oven for 10 to 12 minutes until undersides are golden. Turn the triangles over and bake for 5 to 7 minutes longer until golden on both sides. Serve warm or at room temperature. Can be frozen and used as hors d'oeuvre or vegetable dish.

Jo Waters
GFWC—Mesquite Club
Las Vegas, Nevada

Eggplant Parmesan

- **3 medium-sized firm eggplants**
- **2½ cups tomato sauce**
- **2½ cups shredded mozzarella**
- **2 eggs**
- **2 cups instant mashed potato flakes**
- **2 tablespoons seasoned salt**
- **4 tablespoons olive oil (or cooking oil spray)**

Slice eggplant into ¼-inch slices. Soak in water 30 minutes, cover and then drain. Dip into beaten egg, dredge into potato flakes and seasoned salt. Place on shallow, greased pan and bake in 450 degree oven for 8 to 10 minutes on each side until golden brown. Drain on paper. Layer in baking dish, eggplant slices with tomato sauce and cheese. Bake 30 to 40 minutes at 350 degrees.

Joann Clarke
GFWC—Junior Woman's Club of Portsmouth
Portsmouth, Virginia

Mushrooms Divine

- **½ pound fresh mushrooms, quartered**
- **1 tablespoon butter**
- **1 beef bouillon cube**
- **½ cup hot water**
- **2 tablespoons flour**
- **Dash of black pepper**
- **½ cup whipping cream**
- **¼ cup dried bread crumbs**
- **¼ cup grated parmesan cheese**

Saute mushrooms in butter for 8 to 10 minutes at medium heat. Let set about 10 minutes. Dissolve bouillon in hot water; set aside. Melt 1 tablespoon butter, then add flour and stir until smooth. Blend in pepper, cream and bouillon. Stir into mushrooms. Pour into one-quart greased casserole. Top with bread crumbs and parmesan cheese. Bake uncovered at 350 degrees for 30 minutes.

Lynda Pasqueretta
GFWC—Junior Woman's Club of Wyckoff
Wyckoff, New Jersey

Okra Supreme

2 cups sliced okra
1 large or 2 medium onions, chopped
½ cup chopped red and/or green bell pepper
1 cup celery, sliced
4 to 5 ears of corn, cut off cob (approximately 1 cup)
3 tomatoes, skinned and chopped
¾ cup water
2 cloves garlic
1 teaspoon seasoned salt
2 tablespoons fresh parsley, chopped
1 bay leaf (remove before serving)
2 tablespoons Worcestershire sauce
2 tablespoons soy sauce
½ teaspoon black pepper
3 tablespoons bacon drippings
Salt (if needed)

Mix all ingredients and cook over medium heat approximately 15 to 20 minutes. Note: May be served over rice. Seasonings may be adjusted to your taste.

Ann Combs
GFWC—Jackson Woman's Club
Jackson, Kentucky

Onion Pie

8 or 9-inch unbaked pie shell
2 tablespoons butter
2 cups thinly sliced onions
2 eggs, beaten
1 cup sour cream
Salt to taste
Pepper to taste

Saute onions until soft (about 10 minutes) and spoon into pie shell. Mix sour cream with beaten eggs and salt and pepper to taste. Pour over onions. Mix gently so pastry will not be pierced.

Bobbie Shira
GFWC—San Diego Woman's Club
San Diego, California

Black-Eyed Peas Texican

- **16 ounce frozen black-eyed peas**
- **⅔ cup peanut or olive oil**
- **3 tablespoons red wine vinegar**
- **1 small onion, chopped**
- **1 to 2 cloves of garlic**
- **Handful of parsley**
- **Cracked pepper**
- **Salt free seasoning**

Place peas in a large saucepan; cover with water. Blend together with oil, vinegar, onion, garlic and parsley. Season with pepper and seasoning. Bring to a boil and simmer only till peas are tender.

Patricia Siegfreid-Giles
GFWC—Lancaster Shakespeare Club
Lancaster, Texas

Company Peas

- **¼ cup water**
- **1 10 ounce package green peas**
- **2 cups sliced celery**
- **½ teaspoon salt**
- **½ teaspoon crushed rosemary**
- **½ cup slivered toasted almonds**
- **½ cup sour cream**
- **Garlic**

Bring water to boil adding peas and celery. Cover and boil about 5 minutes. Drain liquid, if necessary. Mix sour cream, salt, rosemary, garlic. Mix peas, celery and almonds. Heat together and serve.

Beverly Olson
GFWC—Marquette Woman's Literary
Marquette, Kansas

Peas A L'Orange

- **1 package frozen peas**
- **2 tablespoons butter or margarine**
- **1 tablespoon sugar**
- **1 teaspoon cornstarch**
- **½ teaspoon salt**
- **½ teaspoon grated orange rind**
- **½ cup orange juice**

Cook peas according to package directions. Drain; add butter. Mix together sugar, cornstarch, salt, orange rind and orange juice. Add peas and heat until sauce is slightly thickened. Serve at once.

"Old family recipe."

Claudia F. Kahn
GFWC—The Glen Rock Woman's Club
Glen Rock, New Jersey

Potato Dumplings

3 cups cooked and mashed potatoes
2 eggs
⅓ cup cream of wheat
1 teaspoon salt
1 tablespoon butter
2 cups flour

Boil potatoes till tender; mash, adding 2 beaten eggs, ⅓ cup cream of wheat, 1 teaspoon salt, butter and flour. Stir together. Put flour on a board and knead dough a little to shape. Cut in 2 pieces and roll into a long roll. Cut in ¾-inch pieces and drop in boiling, salted water. Cook 8 to 10 minutes. Serve with sauerkraut.

Mrs. Ed Callies
GFWC—Leigh Woman's Club
Leigh, Nebraska

Colcannon

6 medium cooked potatoes
5 tablespoons butter
2 teaspoons salt
⅛ teaspoon black pepper
½ cup finely chopped onion
3 cups cooked, shredded cabbage

Preheat oven to 350 degrees. Mash potatoes with 3 tablespoons butter, salt, pepper and onion. Add cabbage and mix well. Place in 2-quart buttered casserole dish. Bake for 15 minutes. Remove from oven and dot with remaining butter. Return to oven. Bake 5 minutes longer. Serve hot.

Lucille Dolan
GFWC—Brookside Woman's Club
Brookside, New Jersey

Lemon Potatoes

2½ pounds potatoes, peeled and cut into chunks
⅓ cup chopped onion
Juice of 2 or 3 lemons
1 teaspoon oregano
32 ounces canned chicken broth, heated

Put all ingredients in a 7 × 11 baking dish and bake uncovered in 350 degree oven for 1½ hours. Check after an hour for more broth and lemon juice.

Barbara A. Peterson
GFWC—Minnesota Valley
Richfield, Minnesota

Swiss Fried Potatoes

1 medium onion
3 tablespoons butter or margarine
4 medium-sized potatoes, boiled in jacket and cooled
1 teaspoon caraway seeds
½ teaspoon salt

Chop onion and saute in butter; grate potatoes on medium-sized grater (not necessary to peel new potatoes). Spoon grated potatoes on top of sauteed onions. Sprinkle caraway seeds and salt on top. Cut remaining butter into small pieces and place on top. Cover; turn heat to low for 20 to 25 minutes. Do not disturb. Bottom is crusty—serve a portion of this crust with each serving.

"My father was born in Switzerland. His mother cooked potatoes in this fashion."

E. Dorothy Strachan
GFWC—Woman's Club of Fleetwood
Fleetwood, Pennsylvania

Kugeli (Potato Loaf)

1 cup chopped onion
2 eggs, beaten
½ cup milk
2 teaspoons salt
⅛ teaspoon black pepper
Pinch parsley
7 slices bacon
2 tablespoons melted shortening
6 large potatoes, grated
½ teaspoon Worcestershire sauce
⅛ teaspoon sage
1 cup flour

Fry onions and bacon. Crumble cooked bacon. Combine all ingredients. Put in 2 loaf pans (greased). Bake at 350 degrees for 1 to 1½ hours until browned and mixture separates from sides of pan.

"This old Lithuanian recipe was served as a main dish or as a side dish. Has been in my family for generations. Leftovers fried (sliced) are fantastic."

Veronica Ann Howland
GFWC—Wendell Woman's Club
Wendell, North Carolina

Hash Brown Potatoes

15–20 pounds unpeeled potatoes
1 cup butter or margarine
1 pound onions
¼ cup Worcestershire sauce
3 tablespoons salt
3 tablespoons paprika
1 teaspoon pepper

Cook potatoes and cool. Peel and chop onions. Cube cold, peeled potatoes. Melt butter in a large pan and add onions. Saute 5 minutes. Remove from heat and add Worcestershire, salt, paprika and pepper; add to potatoes. Put in well-greased pan (17 × 12 × 2 inch). Bake at 375 degrees about 1 hour or until brown.

Virginia S. Maunder
GFWC—The Fortnightly Club of Leominster
Leominster, Massachusetts

Brandied Sweet Potatoes and Apples

6 large sweet potatoes
3 to 4 cooking apples
2 teaspoons cornstarch
½ teaspoon nutmeg
2 teaspoons salt
½ cup granulated sugar
1 cup water
1 tablespoon lemon juice
⅓ cup brandy

Cook unpared potatoes in boiling, salted water to cover about 25 to 30 minutes or until tender. Drain and cool. Peel and slice crosswise, about ½ inch thick. Mix cornstarch, nutmeg, salt, sugar and water, adding water gradually. Cook over low heat, while stirring, until a clear sauce is formed. Stir in lemon juice and brandy. Arrange sweet potato slices and pared apple wedges in a single layer in a shallow baking pan. Pour on sauce. Bake until glazed, basting occasionally.

Clarice Kronquist
GFWC—Newberry
Newberry, Michigan

Ambrosia Sweet Potato Bake

6–7 cups sliced, cooked yams
½ orange and ½ lemon, sliced
1 cup crushed pineapple
½ cup brown sugar
½ cup melted butter
½ teaspoon salt
½ cup coconut

Place yams, lemon and orange in 11 × 7 pan. Combine other ingredients and pour sauce over yams. Sprinkle coconut over all. Bake 350 degrees for 30 minutes.

Dorothy K. Moon
GFWC—Montrose Woman's Club
Montrose, Colorado

Royal Spinach and Artichoke

- **1 8½ ounce can artichoke hearts**
- **1 8 ounce can water chestnuts, sliced**
- **1 8 ounce package cream cheese**
- **1 stick butter**
- **¼ teaspoon garlic powder (optional)**
- **Salt and pepper to taste**
- **1 teaspoon lemon juice**
- **3 3 ounce packages frozen chopped spinach, cooked and drained**
- **Seasoned bread crumbs or cracker crumbs**

Cut artichoke hearts in half and place in buttered casserole. Add water chestnuts. Mix cream cheese and butter together in the top of a double boiler (or in a microwave on low speed). When melted, stir to blend well and add garlic, salt, pepper, lemon juice and spinach. Pour over artichokes and water chestnuts. Bake at 350 degrees for 30 minutes. Sprinkle top with seasoned bread crumbs or crushed crackers. Bake a few more minutes until toasted. Serves 6 to 8.

Carolyn Glascoe Woodall
GFWC—Roxboro Woman's Club
Roxboro, North Carolina

Squash Casserole

- **1½ pounds yellow squash**
- **2 medium-sized carrots**
- **1 medium-sized onion**
- **1 can pimiento pieces**
- **1 can cream of chicken soup**
- **1 cup dairy sour cream**

Topping

- **1 package stuffing mix**
- **1 stick margarine**

Cook squash until tender. Drain; cook carrots (sliced thin) until tender. Season with margarine. Mix together with onion (chopped), pimiento, soup and sour cream. Place in casserole and top with 1 package stuffing mix tossed in melted stick of margarine. Bake at 350 degrees for 30 minutes.

"This casserole freezes well."

Polly Moore
GFWC—Tri-Community Woman's Club
Henrietta, North Carolina

Skillet Squash

- **2 tablespoons water**
- **½ teaspoon salt**
- **2 small sliced zucchini**
- **2 small sliced yellow squash**
- **1 small bunch broccoli (cut stalk in ¼ and cut into 1-inch pieces)**
- **½ pound fresh mushrooms**
- **¼ teaspoon lemon pepper**
- **2 to 3 tablespoons butter**

Combine salt and water. Add squash, broccoli and mushrooms. Toss to blend. Sprinkle with pepper; dot with butter. Microwave (high) covered, 10 to 12 minutes, stirring halfway through cooking. Rest, covered, 5 minutes.

Carol Braden
GFWC—Bullitt County
Shepherdsville, Kentucky

Squash Puff

- **4 cups cooked, mashed winter squash**
- **2 tablespoons margarine**
- **2 tablespoons brown sugar**
- **2 eggs, separated**
- **⅛ teaspoon nutmeg**
- **½ teaspoon salt**
- **½ cup pecans**
- **Bran**

Measure squash. Add other ingredients, including egg yolks. Beat egg whites until stiff. Fold into squash mixture. Mix gently and pour into a greased baking dish. Garnish with a mixture of ½ cup of chopped pecans and bran. Bake at 350 degrees for 30 minutes and serve at once.

"This recipe came from my Pennsylvania-Dutch ancestors."

Lois Brown
GFWC—Boscobel Woman's Club
Boscobel, Wisconsin

Zucchini Lasagna

- **6 to 8 large zucchini, sliced ¾ inch thick**
- **1 large can tomato puree**
- **1 1-pound container ricotta cheese**
- **Chopped onion**
- **¼ pound sliced fresh mushrooms**
- **1 tablespoon oregano**
- **1 tablespoon basil**
- **Pepper to taste**
- **1 pound mozzarella cheese, sliced**
- **½ cup parmesan cheese**

In 9 × 13 casserole dish, layer tomato puree, zucchini slices, ricotta cheese, chopped onion, mushrooms, oregano, basil, pepper, mozzarella cheese. End layers with mozzarella cheese. Top with parmesan cheese. Bake at 350 degrees for 45 minutes.

Cynthia McMahon
GFWC—Swift Creek Woman's Club
Colonial Heights, Virginia

Zucchini and Rice Provencal

1 cup uncooked, converted, long grain rice
½ cup chopped onion
1 tablespoon butter
1 tablespoon olive oil
3 medium zucchini (1½ pounds) diced
1 cup chicken broth
¾ cup half and half cream
¼ cup snipped parsley
½ teaspoon salt
⅛ teaspoon nutmeg
½ cup shredded Swiss cheese (2 ounces)

Cook butter, oil and onion until golden. Add all other ingredients except cheese. Using large skillet, cook 25 minutes (simmer) or until done. Sprinkle cheese on top. Let set about 5 minutes until cheese melts. Can be covered during cooking.

Dorothy Cole
GFWC—Oshkosh Woman's Club
Oshkosh, Wisconsin

Zucchini Zest

3 small zucchini
1 can zesty tomato soup
1 small onion
1 tablespoon margarine
¼ cup water

Wash and slice zucchini; add chopped onion, margarine, water and soup. Cook on top of stove until tender and liquid is somewhat absorbed.

Virginia N. Ulrich
GFWC—Beechmont
Louisville, Kentucky

Tomato Surprise

1 16 ounce can tomato sauce
1 package sweetener
2 packages plain gelatin
½ cup water
2 tablespoons chopped onion
12 ounces lowfat cottage cheese
1 teaspoon Worcestershire sauce
¼ to ½ cup mayonnaise (lowfat if desired)
½ cup chopped bell pepper
¾ cup chopped celery
8 to 10 sliced olives

Soften gelatin in ½ cup water. Combine with tomato sauce, onion and sweetener. Bring to boil and cool to room temperature. Blend cottage cheese in food processor. Add tomato mixture and process till smooth. Pour in mixing bowl and add Worcestershire sauce and mayonnaise; add pepper, celery and olives. Pour in 9 × 9 inch dish. Chill till firm. Cut in 9 squares.

Henrietta S. Ellis
GFWC—Marietta Woman's Club
Marietta, Georgia

Eastern Sho' Tomato Pudding

1 2 pound can tomatoes
1 cup brown sugar
1/4 cup white sugar
1 teaspoon salt
3/4 cup boiling water
3 cups white bread, cubed
1/2 cup melted butter
1/2 teaspoon pepper or to taste

Preheat oven at 375 degrees. Put tomatoes, sugars, salt and pepper together in saucepan, stir well. Add boiling water and boil for about 5 to 7 minutes. While tomatoes are cooking, cut bread into 1/2-inch cubes (fresh or stale bread) and put into a medium-sized casserole. Pour melted butter over cubes, stir and add the boiling tomato mixture. Stir again. Bake for 50 to 60 minutes, depending upon your oven temperature. These are even better when warmed over. They also freeze well. Can be made ahead of time.

"This is an old Eastern shore recipe."

Hilda Ott Micari
GFWC—Woman's Club of Glenhill
Baltimore, Maryland

Tomatoes Rockefeller

6 large tomatoes
4 tablespoons butter
1/2 cup onion, finely chopped
2 10 ounce packages frozen chopped spinach, cooked and drained well
1/2 teaspoon garlic salt
1 tablespoon MSG
1/2 teaspoon thyme
1 teaspoon salt
1/4 teaspoon pepper
1/2 cup seasoned bread crumbs
2 eggs, slightly beaten
1/4 cup grated parmesan cheese
1/2 teaspoon Worcestershire sauce

Slice the top off the tomatoes and gently scoop out approximately 1/3 of the inside. Turn upside down to drain. Melt butter and add onion. Cook until tender. Add spinach, seasonings and bread crumbs; mix well. Add eggs and cook, stirring constantly, until well combined. Stuff tomatoes with spinach mixture. Sprinkle cheese over top and dot with additional butter. Bake at 350 degrees for 10 minutes, covered.

Bonnie L. Pottinger
GFWC—Glendale Woman's Club
Glendale, Wisconsin

Hawaiian Vegetables

5 cups raw carrots, peeled, slivered on diagonal
1 cup green pepper, cut in 1-inch cubes
1 small can peeled water chestnuts, slivered
1 medium can crushed pineapple, drained—save juice
1/8 cup diced onion
1 cup slivered celery

Sauce

1 cup sugar
1/2 cup vinegar
1/2 cup water (include juice of pineapple)
1/2 teaspoon salt
3 tablespoons cornstarch

Cook carrots, peppers, onions, and celery until barely done. Drain and add drained pineapple and water chestnuts. Cover with a sweet and sour sauce.

For sauce, combine and simmer 5 minutes sugar, vinegar, water with juice of pineapple and salt. Mix cornstarch with 2 tablespoons cold water. Remove sauce from heat and stir in cornstarch. Cook until thick. Add to drained vegetables and heat in 300 degree oven for 30 minutes.

Madalyn Bennett
GFWC—Adrian Woman's Club
Adrian, Michigan

Banh Xeo

Filling

Bean sprouts
Sliced white onion
Carrots, shredded with potato peeler
Bacon, cut in 1-inch pieces
Tiny peas, optional

Crepe

4 eggs
1 teaspoon salt
5 tablespoons flour
Water to thin
(Mix above)

Coat fry pan with oil. Fry bacon and small amount of vegetables. Pour 1 ladle of crepe mix to coat vegetables. Put pan lid over mixture a few minutes. Put some more vegetables in center and turn like an omelet. Does not save well—eat the same day.

"I got the recipe 8 years ago from some Vietnamese 'boat people' of Chinese ancestry."

Dianne Lundquist
GFWC—Ebell Club of Irvine
Irvine, California

Vegetable Chili Con Frijoles

¼ cup (½ stick) soft margarine
2 large onions, chopped (2 cups)
2 cloves garlic, minced
4 medium-size tomatoes, chopped (4 cups)
3 medium zucchini, chopped (4 cups)
½ pound fresh mushrooms, sliced (2 cups)
2 medium-size green or red bell peppers, sliced (2 cups)
¾ cup water
3 tablespoons chili powder
2 teaspoons ground cumin
1 teaspoon dried leaf oregano, crumbled
1 teaspoon sugar
¾ teaspoon salt
¼ to ½ teaspoon hot pepper sauce
3 cups cooked red kidney beans, without salt, drained
3 cups cooked rice, without salt
¾ cup lowfat plain yogurt
½ cup chopped scallions

In large pot or dutch oven, melt margarine; saute garlic and onion until tender, about 2 minutes. Add tomatoes, zucchini, mushrooms, bell pepper, water, chili powder, cumin, oregano, sugar, salt and hot pepper sauce. Mix well and bring to boil. Cover. Simmer about 25 minutes or until vegetables are crisp-tender. Stir in beans; cook 5 minutes longer until heated through. Serve with rice, yogurt and scallions.

A. Wasson
GFWC—Philomathean Club
Shreveport, Louisiana

Sour Cream Succotash

1 package frozen lima beans
1 can Mexicorn niblets
Sprinkling of onion flakes
Butter, salt and pepper to taste
¼ cup sour cream

Cook lima beans as directed on package. Drain. Add heated niblets and onion flakes. Reheat together and add butter, salt and pepper to taste. Stir in sour cream.

Gail Birket
GFWC—Gainesville Woman's Club
Gainesville, Florida

Pasta

Cottage Cheese Noodle Florentine

- **6 ounces medium egg noodles, cooked by directions on package**
- **1 10 ounce package frozen spinach, thawed and drained**
- **1 16 ounce carton creamed cottage cheese**
- **½ cup grated parmesan cheese**
- **½ cup sour cream**
- **1 teaspoon hot pepper sauce**
- **3 teaspoons fresh sweet basil, minced**
- **5 teaspoons fresh thyme leaves**
- **1 tablespoon melted butter**
- **¼ cup bread crumbs**

Combine all ingredients except butter and bread crumbs and place in a 1½ quart casserole. Combine butter and bread crumbs and sprinkle over casserole. Bake at 350 degrees for 45 minutes.

Anita Brown
GFWC—Woman's Club of Live Oak
Live Oak, Florida

Photo features: Garden Fettuccine—Page 239

Corned Beef Egg Noodle Casserole

- **2 tablespoons margarine**
- **2 tablespoons chopped onion**
- **1 can cream of mushroom soup**
- **½ can milk**
- **2 teaspoons prepared mustard**
- **½ teaspoon salt**
- **½ cup bread crumbs (buttered)**
- **8 ounces egg noodles (cooked)**
- **2 12 ounce cans corned beef**
- **⅛ teaspoon black pepper**

Cook noodles as directed on bag. Saute onions in margarine. Add soup, milk, mustard, salt and black pepper to the onion mixture. Simmer until bubbly. In a buttered casserole, make alternate layers of noodles, corned beef and soup mixture. Top with buttered bread crumbs. Bake at 350 degrees for 20 minutes.

Mary B. Willis
GFWC—Springdale Woman's Club
West Columbia, South Carolina

Macaroni Cheese Souffle

- **1½ cups cooked elbow macaroni (¾ cup uncooked)**
- **1 cup soft bread crumbs (2 slices)**
- **6 tablespoons melted oleo (or butter)**
- **1½ cups scalded milk**
- **1½ cups cut up cheese (sharp cheddar—½ pound)**
- **3 eggs**
- **½ jar pimiento**
- **1 tablespoon chopped onions**
- **Salt and pepper to taste**

Cook macaroni and drain. Add bread to macaroni. Melt oleo or butter and add to milk. Add grated cheese, stirring until melted. Beat egg yolks until light. Add to macaroni. Beat egg whites until stiff and add pimiento and onion. Fold egg whites last into 3-quart casserole. Bake in 350 degree oven for 1 hour. Reduce heat and cover if it starts to brown. Put pan of water under casserole in oven.

Kristian Skotland
GFWC—Waltham Woman's Club
Waltham, Massachusetts

Pierogi

- 4 cups sifted flour
- 1 egg
- 1 cup lukewarm water
- 1 teaspoon salt
- 2 tablespoons melted butter

Filling

- 1 pound ricotta cheese
- 2–3 cooked, mashed potatoes
- Salt, pepper to taste
- ½ teaspoon thyme
- Mix together.

Mix flour, egg, water, salt and butter together lightly and knead in bowl. Let rest for ½ hour covered. Knead dough on floured board and roll to ⅛″ thickness. Cut out circles with a glass or cup. Fill with favorite filling, pressing edges together well. Drop Pierogis gently into boiling, salted water. When they come to the top, reduce heat to slow boil. Boil ten minutes. Remove with slotted spoon; place in colander. Rinse with cold water lightly. Drain. Saute in butter.

"These freeze very well. After boiling, drain, cool and freeze. To reheat, place in pan in single layer. Drizzle with melted butter; bake at 350 degrees for about 45 minutes."

Kathi White
GFWC—Hudson Junior Woman's Club
Hudson, New Hampshire

Garden Fettuccine

- ½ pound fettuccine
- ½ bunch broccoli (cut in pieces)
- ¼ pound carrots, sliced
- ¼ pound or 2 small zucchini, sliced
- 4 large mushrooms, sliced
- ¼ cup chopped onions
- 1 clove garlic, finely minced
- 3 tablespoons butter
- 3 tablespoons flour
- ½ tablespoon dried oregano leaves
- 2 cups milk
- 6 slices processed cheese, cut up
- 1 tablespoon salt

In large saucepan, cook onion and garlic in butter until tender. Stir in flour, salt and oregano. Gradually stir in milk. Cook and stir over medium heat, until mixture thickens. Add in cheese; stir until melted. Add vegetables that have been cooked to just tender. Prepare fettuccine according to package directions. Drain. Serve sauce over hot, cooked fettuccine.

Pat Galusha
GFWC—Omaha Woman's Club
Omaha, Nebraska

Spaghetti-Broccoli Casserole

- **1 8 ounce package vermicelli**
- **2 10 ounce packages frozen broccoli**
- **6 scallions or green onions**
- **4 tablespoons butter or oleo**
- **1 teaspoon salt**
- **Dash ground pepper**
- **1 pound pasteurized processed cheese, divided**
- **½ cup milk or light cream**
- **Parmesan cheese and Butter**

Cook vermicelli; drain. Cook frozen broccoli; drain. Chop onion including green tops; saute in butter. Put vermicelli into 9 × 13 buttered baking pan. Cut cheese into slices and arrange half on top. Pour milk over cheese and vermicelli; arrange broccoli, sauteed onions and seasoning on top. Arrange remaining cheese on top and sprinkle with parmesan cheese. Dot with butter. Bake 350 degrees for 25–30 minutes.

Betty Jo Carl
GFWC—Mid-Century Panorama Club
Pacific, Missouri

Fettuccine Primavera

- **½ pound fettuccine (wide flat pasta)**
- **1 bag frozen mixed vegetables**
- **¼ cup sour cream**
- **¼ cup parmesan cheese**
- **1 clove minced garlic**
- **Dash nutmeg, salt, pepper**
- **2 tablespoons butter**

Cook pasta as directed on package; drain. Steam vegetables. Add butter to drained pasta and vegetables. Fold in sour cream, cheese, garlic, nutmeg, salt and pepper. Chill.

Rita Quin
GFWC—Olympia Fields Woman's Club
Olympia Fields, Illinois

Spinach Lasagna

- **1 pound ricotta**
- **2 cups mozzarella (separated)**
- **1 egg**
- **1 10 ounce package frozen, chopped spinach (thawed)**
- **1 teaspoon salt**
- **1 teaspoon oregano**
- **Dash pepper**
- **3 cups tomato sauce**
- **9 lasagna noodles, uncooked**

In large bowl, mix ricotta, 1 cup mozzarella, egg, spinach, salt, oregano and pepper. In a greased 9 × 13 inch pan, layer 1 cup sauce, 3 noodles and half of the cheese mixture. Repeat. Top with remaining noodles and sauce. Sprinkle with remaining 1 cup mozzarella. Pour ¾ cup water around the edges of the pan (less if you use more sauce). Cover tightly with foil and bake at 350 degrees for 1 hour, 15 minutes. Let stand for 15 minutes before serving.

Carol Dizio
GFWC—Barrington Junior Woman's Club
Barrington, Rhode Island

Spaghetti In A Loaf

- **1½ pounds ground beef**
- **½ cup chopped onion**
- **1 egg**
- **2 teaspoons salt**
- **1 cup uncooked spaghetti (broken in 2″-3″ pieces)**
- **½ teaspoon pepper**
- **6 ounces tomato paste**
- **6 ounces water**

Sauce

- **¼ cup chopped onion**
- **2 tablespoons salad oil**
- **6 ounces tomato paste**
- **6 ounces water**

Mix meat, onions, egg, seasonings, spaghetti, paste and water. Place in 8 × 8 × 2 Pyrex dish. Bake 375 degrees for 50 minutes. Prepare sauce by sauteing onion in oil; add paste and water until heated through. Pour over baked loaf and bake 20 minutes longer. Serve with Parmesan cheese and garlic bread.

Jean L. Mumm
GFWC—Durant Federated Woman's Club
Durant, Iowa

Laurie's Spaghetti Pie

- **6 ounces spaghetti**
- **2 tablespoons margarine**
- **⅓ cup grated parmesan cheese**
- **2 eggs, well beaten**
- **1 cup cottage cheese**
- **1 pound ground beef or bulk sausage**
- **½ cup chopped onion**
- **¼ cup chopped green pepper**
- **1 8 ounce can tomatoes, cut up**
- **1 6 ounce can tomato paste**
- **1 teaspoon sugar**
- **1 teaspoon oregano**
- **½ teaspoon garlic salt**
- **½ cup shredded mozzarella cheese**

Cook spaghetti according to directions on package; drain. Stir in parmesan cheese and eggs. Form into pie-crust shape in a 10-inch buttered pie plate. Spread cottage cheese over it. In skillet, cook ground beef, onion and green pepper until vegetables are tender and meat is browned. Drain off excess fat. Stir in undrained tomatoes, tomato paste, sugar, oregano and garlic salt; heat through. Turn meat mixture into spaghetti crust. Bake uncovered in 350 degree oven for 20 minutes. Remove and sprinkle with mozzarella cheese. Bake 5 minutes longer, or until cheese melts.

Laurie Roberts Cramer
GFWC—Junior Woman's Club of Charlotte
Charlotte, North Carolina

Susan's Poppy-Onion Pasta

- **16 ounces vegetable pasta spirals or spinach noodles**
- **1 onion, quartered and sliced**
- **1 4.5 ounce jar sliced mushrooms, rinsed & drained**
- **6 tablespoons butter or margarine**
- **2 teaspoons poppy seeds**

Prepare pasta per package instructions. Saute onion and mushrooms over medium heat in butter. When onion begins to color but not brown, add poppy seeds and mix well. Pour over freshly cooked (and drained) pasta. Toss and serve immediately

Susan R. Moyer
GFWC—Woman's Study Club
Dugger, Indiana

Homemade Manicotti with Cheese

- **3 eggs, room temperature**
- **¾ cup all-purpose flour**
- **⅛ teaspoon salt**
- **¾ cup water**
- **1 pound ricotta cheese or small curd cottage cheese**
- **8 ounces mozzarella cheese, diced**
- **½ cup grated parmesan cheese**
- **1 egg**
- **½ teaspoon salt**
- **2 teaspoons chopped parsley**
- **2½ cups prepared spaghetti sauce**

To make manicotti pasta: In blender, combine eggs, flour, salt, and water until smooth. Let stand at least ½ hour. Heat 8-inch skillet. Pour in 3 tablespoons batter, rotating skillet quickly to spread batter over bottom. Cook over medium heat until top is dry, but bottom is not brown. Turn out on wire rack to cool. Continue until all batter is used.

Filling: Combine ricotta, mozzarella, ¼ cup parmesan, egg, salt and parsley. Spread ¼ cup filling down the center of each manicotti and roll up. To assemble: Pour 1½ cups sauce into an 8 × 12-inch baking dish. Arrange manicotti, seam side down, in dish. Top with remaining sauce, sprinkle with remaining parmesan. Bake uncovered at 350 degrees for ½ hour, or until bubbly.

Diane P. H. Williams
GFWC—Melbourne Area Junior Woman's Club
Melbourne, Florida

Manicotti Parmigiana

- 1 1½ ounce package spaghetti sauce mix
- 1 1 pound 12 ounce can tomatoes
- 1 8 ounce can tomato sauce
- 1 teaspoon garlic powder
- 1 pound ground beef
- ¼ cup chopped green pepper
- ½ pound mozzarella cheese, diced
- 1 box of large stuffing shells (or 8 manicotti shells)
- Parmesan cheese

Mix the first four (4) ingredients in a large saucepan. Cover and simmer for 20 minutes. Meanwhile, cook manicotti shells in boiling, salted water per directions on package; drain. Brown ground beef and green pepper in a skillet; drain fat. Remove from heat and stir in mozzarella cheese. Stuff manicotti shells with meat-cheese mixture. Pour ¾ of sauce in bottom of a 12 × 8 × 2 inch baking dish. Place stuffed shells over sauce; top with remaining sauce. Sprinkle with parmesan cheese. Bake at 375 degrees for 30 minutes.

Nancy Latoza
GFWC—Johnston City Woman's Club
Johnston City, Illinois

Microwave Lasagna

- 1 32 ounce jar spaghetti sauce
- 1 pound ground chuck
- ¼ cup grated parmesan cheese
- 12 ounces cottage cheese
- 2 eggs
- 1 package mozzarella cheese
- Lasagna noodles

Mix together eggs, cottage cheese and parmesan cheese. Set aside. Brown ground chuck and drain off fat. Mix with spaghetti sauce. Layer, beginning with sauce mixture, then noodles, then cottage cheese mixture, then noodles, ending with sauce. Cover with plastic wrap and cook on full power for 10 minutes. Turn ½ turn and continue cooking for 10 more minutes. Remove from oven and sprinkle with mozzarella cheese. Cover with foil (shiny side down) and let stand for 20 minutes or until firm. Use 9 × 13 glass dish.

Grace Smith
GFWC—Woman's Club of Shadyside
Shadyside, Ohio

Stuffed Rigatoni

Sauce

- 1 28 ounce can tomatoes
- 1 6 ounce tomato paste
- 1/4 teaspoon sugar
- 2 onions, chopped
- 1 bay leaf
- 1 cup water
- Salt
- 1 package rigatoni

Stuffing

- 1 onion, chopped
- 1 clove garlic, minced
- 1 1/2 pounds ground meat
- 1 package frozen chopped spinach, defrosted and drained
- 1 egg, beaten
- 1 cup bread crumbs
- 1 cup romano cheese, grated
- 2 tablespoons chopped parsley
- Pinch of sweet basil or Italian spice

The sauce: Brown onions in a little oil. Add all other ingredients and simmer 45 minutes.

The stuffing: Brown onion and garlic in oil; add meat and fry slowly until cooked. Drain. Combine meat mixture with spinach and other stuffing ingredients. Cook rigatoni (large size macaroni) until half done (about 7 minutes). Drain, rinse, cool and stuff with meat mixture. Grease baking dish. Make one layer of stuffed rigatoni and cover with sauce; if enough for second layer, make it and top with sauce. Cover and bake at 300 degrees for 1 hour.

Evie Gloistein
GFWC—Monticola Club
Susanville, California

Mom's Spaghetti and Steak

- 1 onion, sliced
- 1/2 cup green pepper, sliced
- 1 crushed garlic clove
- 3 teaspoons oil
- 2 8 ounce cans tomato sauce
- 1/2 cup hickory barbeque sauce
- 1 bay leaf
- 1/2 teaspoon basil
- 1/2 teaspoon oregano
- 1 flank steak
- 1 package spaghetti

Cook onion, green pepper and garlic in oil until crisp. Stir in tomato sauce, barbeque sauce, salt and pepper to taste and bay leaf. Cover; simmer 30 minutes. During last 10 minutes, add oregano and basil. Cook spaghetti. Treat steak with tenderizer. Broil 3–5 minutes on each side. Slice and arrange on spaghetti; add sauce and serve.

"This recipe is about 30 years old."

Bette Jameson
GFWC—Walnut Valley Woman's Club
Walnut, California

Lasagna

- **1 pound ground beef**
- **1 teaspoon garlic chips**
- **1 6 ounce can tomato paste**
- **1 8 ounce can tomato sauce**
- **1 15 ounce can stewed tomatoes**
- **1 teaspoon salt**
- **1 small onion (chopped)**
- **¾ teaspoon pepper**
- **½ teaspoon oregano**
- **¼ cup sugar**
- **8 ounces Swiss cheese**
- **¾ pound mozzarella**
- **8 ounces cooked wide lasagna noodles**

Brown beef, garlic and onion together; drain off grease. Add tomato products, 2 cups water and seasonings. Simmer 2 hours, stirring often. Preheat oven to 350 degrees. In 9 × 13 baking dish, alternate layers of cooked noodles, cheese (broken in small pieces) and meat mixture. Cover with foil and bake at 350 degrees for 45 minutes.

Sandy German
GFWC—Milford Junior Woman's Club
Milford, Illinois

Erin's Lasagna

- **1 medium onion, chopped**
- **1 pound ground beef**
- **1 pound ground pizza or Italian sausage**
- **2 15 ounce cans tomato puree**
- **1 12 ounce can tomato paste**
- **1 tablespoon oregano**
- **½ cup parmesan cheese**
- **2 teaspoons basil flakes**
- **2 teaspoons garlic powder**
- **1 teaspoon salt**
- **½ cup water**
- **½ cup red cooking wine**
- **2 pounds mozzarella cheese**
- **½ pound provolone cheese**
- **8 ounces lasagna noodles (9 noodles)**

Brown onion and ground beef; in separate pan, brown sausage. Drain both. Combine meats in dutch oven and add puree, paste, oregano, parmesan, basil, garlic, salt, water and wine. Bring to slow boil. Simmer for 45 minutes. Cook noodles according to box directions. Slice cheeses. Reserve ½ of sauce for top layer. In 13 × 9 pan, layer sauce, noodles and cheese 3 times. Top with reserved sauce. Sprinkle with more parmesan. Bake at 350 degrees for ½ hour. Let set 10 minutes before cutting.

Erin L. Epping
GFWC—Brown Deer Junior Woman's Club
Brown Deer, Wisconsin

Rice & Other Grains

Rice and Chili Pepper Casserole

- **1 cup uncooked long grain rice**
- **1 pint sour cream**
- **2 packages muenster cheese (2 long plastic packages)**
- **5 cans green (whole) chili peppers**
- **Grated parmesan cheese and butter**

Cook and drain rice. Deseed and rinse peppers well and drain. Mix sour cream and rice. Work in layers in a casserole dish. Start with rice and sour cream mixture, then layer of cheese, then peppers. Repeat (3) times. End with cheese and peppers on top. Sprinkle grated parmesan cheese on top and lay several pats of butter on top. Bake in 400 degree oven until slightly brown and bubbly.

"Freezes very well. Is very good with beef dishes and can be prepared in advance."

Peggy A. Couch
GFWC—Dunwoody Woman's Club
Dunwoody, Georgia

Photo features: Rice Italiano—Page 251

Wild Rice Casserole

- ½ cup wild rice
- ½ cup long grain or brown rice
- ¼ cup chopped chives or dry onions
- 1 can sliced mushrooms and juice
- 1 stick butter, melted
- 2 cans chicken broth
- ½ cup blanched, slivered almonds
- 1 can water chestnuts, chopped

Place almonds and water chestnuts in butter and cook together about 15 minutes until slightly browned. Mix all ingredients together in 2-quart casserole. Bake 1 hour at 350 degrees, uncovered, or until liquid is absorbed. Will "hold" in 200 degree oven, if covered.

"Outstanding accompaniment for seafood or poultry entrees."

Bobby Ruth Bjork
GFWC—Madison Valley Woman's Club
Ennis, Montana

Wild Rice Hot Dish

- 1 cup wild rice (raw)
- 1 cup white rice (raw)
- 1 onion diced (large)
- 1 cup chopped mushrooms
- ¼ cup butter
- 1 pound pork sausage
- 1 teaspoon salt
- 1 can cream of mushroom soup
- ½ can of water or chicken broth

Boil each rice separately in 3 quarts water for 20 minutes. Drain. Saute onion in butter. Saute mushrooms in butter. Brown and drain pork sausage. Mix everything in a greased 5-quart casserole dish. Bake at 300 degrees for 1½ hours. Do not let rice get dry. Add more water or broth if needed.

To cook in microwave, put rice and 3 cups water in 3-quart covered casserole. Microwave on high for 10 minutes. Let stand 10 minutes, stir, cover. Microwave again about 10 minutes—let stand 5 minutes. Stir and drain.

Dorothy Rakow
GFWC—Breckenridge Woman's Study Club
Breckenridge, Minnesota

Cheese Grits Casserole

- 3 cups water
- 1 cup grits
- 2 cups grated cheddar cheese
- 1 stick margarine, melted
- 3 eggs
- ½ teaspoon garlic powder
- ½ teaspoon salt
- ¼ tcaspoon pepper

Cook grits in salted boiling water until thick. Add cheese to grits and stir until melted. Add melted margarine and mix evenly. Beat eggs, then add seasoning. Gradually add eggs to cheese grits mixture. Pour into 1-quart casserole. Bake 40–45 minutes at 350 degrees. Great when served with black-eyed peas.

Jean Van Bebber
GFWC—Lutz/Land O' Lakes Woman's Club
Lutz, Florida

Fried Rice

6 or 7 slices bacon
1 or 2 stalks celery—1 inch pieces
2 carrots—sliced
1 green pepper—chunks
1 bunch green onions —1 inch pieces
Small can sliced mushrooms—drain
1½ cups raw rice (cooked)
Peppers
Soy sauce to taste
2 beaten eggs

Cut bacon in ½-inch pieces and fry in large frying pan until grease begins to come out. Then add celery, sliced carrots, green pepper, green onions and mushrooms. Allow to cook until degree of doneness you like is reached. Add cooked rice and soy sauce to taste. Mix. Push to one side and add beaten eggs. When eggs have set a bit, mix altogether and serve.

Do not drain bacon fat. Cook in a large frying pan. Amount of vegetables can be adjusted according to your personal taste. Good served with teriyaki steak.

Barbara A. Peterson
GFWC—Minnesota Valley
Richfield, Minnesota

Chinese Fried Rice

5 cups long grain brown rice, cooked
2 eggs
1 cup steamed bean sprouts
1 can cocktail shrimp
¼ cup soy sauce
2 tablespoons cooking oil
1 cup chopped ham

Cook rice and let set for 24 hours. Start rice frying with 2 tablespoons oil. Add rice, ham, bean sprouts, shrimp; cook until it starts to brown. Make a well in center of rice. Add eggs and cook until only slightly done. Then mix into rice. Continue cooking and add soy sauce slowly until all is mixed. Cook until browned and rice separates easily.

Delores Schulte
GFWC—Yanktown Federated Woman's Club
Yanktown, South Dakota

Barley Pilaf

½ cup butter or margarine
1 large onion
2 cups barley
5 cups hot chicken broth
1½ teaspoons salt
½ teaspoon pepper
½ cup finely chopped green onion
¼ cup parsley
1 cup cashews

Heat butter in heavy skillet. Add onion and cook until soft and golden. Add barley and stir over high heat till coated with butter and lightly tan. Transfer to 2-quart casserole and add ⅔ of the boiling chicken broth. Season. Cover dish and bake at 350 degrees for 25–30 minutes. Stir in green onion, parsley and remaining broth. Cook 15 minutes longer or until broth is absorbed and grains puffed and tender. Adjust seasoning. Keep warm in slow oven till ready to serve. Toss with whole cashews before serving. Makes 12 servings.

Christine Callaway
GFWC—Burlington Junior Woman's Club
Burlington, Iowa

Aruba Sunshine Rice

- **½ cup celery, sliced**
- **¼ cup onions, sliced**
- **2 tablespoons butter or margarine**
- **2 teaspoons orange peel, grated**
- **½ teaspoon poultry seasoning**
- **1 cup orange juice**
- **1 cup chicken broth or water**
- **1 cup uncooked rice**

Saute celery and onions in butter until tender crisp, add remaining ingredients. Bring to boil and stir well. Reduce heat, cover and simmer about 20 minutes or until rice is tender and liquid is absorbed. Season to taste.

May Geerman
GFWC—Woman's Club of Aruba
Aruba

Sherried Rice

- **1½ cups rice**
- **1 cup sherry**
- **2 beef bouillon cubes dissolved in 2 cups hot water**
- **1½ teaspoons salt**
- **½ cup butter, melted**
- **½ cup sliced fresh mushrooms, sauteed**

Use a baking dish with lid. Mix all ingredients together in dish. Cover with lid and bake in 350 degree oven for 1 hour.

Deanna Alfeld
GFWC—La Canada Junior Woman's Club
Flintridge, California

Spicy Rice

- **¼ cup margarine**
- **½ cup chopped onions**
- **1½ cups regular rice**
- **½ teaspoon allspice**
- **¼ teaspoon curry powder**
- **¾ teaspoon salt**
- **½ teaspoon turmeric**
- **⅛ teaspoon pepper**

Saute margarine and onion together. Add to other ingredients. Place all in 2-quart casserole. Add 3½ cups chicken broth (or use 3 bouillon cubes with water) which has been heated to boiling. Optional—You can add ¼ cup chopped almonds. Cover. Bake 30–40 minutes at 350 degrees. Can serve as substitute for potatoes.

Carolyn M. Warren
GFWC—Olla Podrida
Rittman, Ohio

Festive Rice Casserole

- **1 6 ounce can sliced mushrooms**
- **2 teaspoons minced onion**
- **½ cup chopped almonds**
- **1 cup shredded cheddar cheese**
- **1¼ cups uncooked rice**
- **½ teaspoon pepper**
- **Water**
- **3 beef bouillon cubes**
- **4 teaspoons soy sauce**
- **2 teaspoons chopped parsley**
- **2 teaspoons chopped pimiento**
- **Add salt to taste**

Drain mushrooms; reserve liquid. In a greased 2-quart casserole, combine mushrooms, onion, almonds, cheese, rice and pepper. Add enough water to reserved mushroom liquid to make 1¼ cups. Heat this liquid to simmer, add bouillon cubes and stir until dissolved. Add soy sauce. Pour over rice mixture. Cover. Bake until all of the liquid has been absorbed. Before serving, stir in parsley, pimiento and salt to taste. Bake at 375 degrees for 45–55 minutes.

Gippa Kendall
GFWC—De Witt Mother's Club
De Witt, Arkansas

Rice Italiano

- **¼ cup butter**
- **1 large onion, diced**
- **½ pound Italian sweet sausage, cut up**
- **1 can artichoke hearts, drained and sliced**
- **½ package frozen peas**
- **1 small can chopped mushrooms, drained**
- **1 can beef bouillon**
- **3 cups cooked rice**
- **½ cup shredded parmesan cheese**

Preheat oven to 375 degrees. In a large skillet, saute onion and sausage in butter till slightly brown. Add artichokes and peas. Cook slightly. Add mushrooms and ½ can bouillon; simmer 10 minutes, uncovered. Stir in rice and remaining bouillon. Put in buttered 1½-quart casserole. Sprinkle with parmesan cheese. Bake 15–20 minutes until cheese is slightly browned.

Syliva Lewis
GFWC—Floral Park Woman's Club, Inc.
Floral Park, New York

Oven Croquettes

- **1 cup cooked rice**
- **1 tablespoon margarine**
- **1 tablespoon flour**
- **½ cup skimmed or low-fat milk**
- **1 cup mixed vegetables, slightly mashed**
- **2 tablespoons minced onion**
- **½ teaspoon salt**
- **1 cup chopped meat (chicken, turkey, roast beef, pork, tuna) (cooked meat only)**
- **Other ingredients listed below for coating**

Melt margarine, stir in flour; gradually add milk. Cook until thick. Add onions and cook about 1 minute. Add meat, vegetables, rice and salt. Mix well. Chill. Shape into 10 croquettes. Combine one beaten egg and 3 tablespoons milk. Roll croquettes in bread crumbs (1½ cups dry), egg mixture, and again in crumbs. Dip in melted margarine (about ⅓ cup). Bake in 400 degree oven for 45 minutes.

"This uses left-over items and can be served with mushroom (soup) sauce. Any type of vegetable (peas, squash, etc.) could be substituted."

Peggy Sandidge
GFWC—Beta Delphian Study Club
Crowley, Louisiana

Dee's Polenta

- **1½ cups yellow corn meal**
- **½ teaspoon salt**
- **5½ cups cold water**
- **4 tablespoons (½ stick) butter or margarine**
- **¼ cup flour**
- **½ teaspoon dry mustard**
- **2 cups milk**
- **1 cup (¼ pound) processed American cheese, cut up**
- **1 jar pimientos, diced**
- **10 slices crisp bacon**

Blend corn meal, salt and water in large pot. Bring mixture to boil. Cook, stirring often, until thick. Cover. Cook over very low heat 15 minutes. Pour into loaf pan (9 × 5 × 3). Chill about 2 hours, or till firm. Cook bacon till crisp, set aside. Melt butter in sauce pan. Remove from heat. Stir in flour and mustard. Add milk slowly. Cook over low heat, stirring constantly, till sauce thickens and boils 1 minute. Add cheese and pimientos, stirring till cheese is melted. Cut chilled corn meal into 1″ cubes. Layer half in bottom of buttered shallow baking dish (8–10 cup size). Crumble 5 slices of crisp bacon over cubes; top with second layer of corn meal cubes. Pour cheese sauce over cubes. Halve remaining bacon slices; arrange checkerboard style on top. Bake 45 minutes in 375 degree oven or until top is bubbly.

Dorothy L. Losio
GFWC—Woman's Club of Farmingdale
Farmingdale, New York

Barley-Pine Nut Casserole

- **½ cup pine nuts**
- **½ cup butter, divided**
- **1 cup chopped onions**
- **1 cup pearl barley**
- **1 cup finely chopped parsley**
- **1 cup finely chopped chives**
- **2 cups canned beef consomme**
- **1 teaspoon salt and pepper to taste**

Saute pine nuts in butter until golden and set aside. Saute onion in remaining butter until golden. Add barley and brown lightly. Stirring constantly, add parsley, chives and consomme. Salt and pepper half the pine nuts and pour pine nuts and barley into 2-quart casserole. Bake at 350 degrees for 1 hour, stirring once after 30 minutes. Sprinkle the remaining pine nuts on top and bake 20 minutes more. If it is too dry, add a little more liquid; the barley seems to soak up liquid at different rates from time to time.

Virginia Barham
GFWC—Dunsmuir Federated Woman's Club
Dunsmuir, California

Gnocci

- **2½ cups boiled potatoes (mashed, plain, no skins)**
- **2 eggs, lightly beaten**
- **½ teaspoon salt—to taste**
- **2¼ cups flour**

Mix all ingredients except flour on cutting board or in bowl. Add 1½ cups flour to mixture. Knead dough for 3–4 minutes. Add remaining flour, kneading until dough is no longer sticky. Divide dough and roll into long strips (like making clay snakes in kindergarten) about ¾ inch in diameter. Cut into pieces 2–3 inches long. Drop into boiling salted water. Pasta is done when it floats to the top. Serve with your favorite spaghetti sauce.

"An old family recipe from Italy—Great Grandmother's."

Karen Zumpft
GFWC—Mesquite Club
Las Vegas, Nevada

Santa Fe Souffle

- **1¼ cups grits (quick cooking but not instant)**
- **½ teaspoon tabasco**
- **1 pound Velveeta cheese, grated**
- **3 beaten eggs**
- **1 stick oleo**
- **2 small cans chopped green chiles**

Cook grits according to directions on package, adding tabasco. When cooked, add cheese, eggs, oleo and green chiles. Stir until cheese and oleo melt. Pour into a large, greased casserole. Bake at 350 degrees until puffy and brown, 25–30 minutes.

Joyce Saub
GFWC—De Ridder Study Club
De Ridder, Louisiana

Eggs & Cheese

Chili Rellenos Casserole

8 ounces cheddar and Jack cheese, mixed
10 eggs
1 teaspoon baking powder
¾ teaspoon cumin
Taco sauce
2 4 ounce cans whole chilies
½ cup flour
2 cups cottage cheese
1 large avocado

Grease 9 × 13 pan. Cut cheese in finger-size pieces and stuff each kind in whole chilies. Place chilies in greased pan. In large bowl, whip eggs, flour, baking powder and cumin till blended well. Stir in cottage cheese and pour over stuffed chilies. Shred a little extra cheese on top. Bake at 350 degrees for 30–35 minutes. To serve you may top each square with avocado and taco sauce. May be made a day ahead and also freezes well.

Elizabeth Mueller
GFWC—Suburban Woman's Club of Tucson
Tucson, Arizona

Photo features: Chicken 'n Biscuit 'n Eggs—Page 261

Cheese Flan

- **6 egg yolks**
- **8 ounces cream cheese**
- **1 can condensed milk**
- **1 13½ ounce can evaporated milk**
- **1 teaspoon vanilla extract**

Coating

- **½ cup sugar**
- **1 tablespoon water**

Blend all ingredients thoroughly in blender. Pour into caramelized loaf pan and bake at 400 degrees for 1 hour. Allow to cool enough to refrigerate. Refrigerate for several hours till very cold. Run a knife along pan edges and unmold onto serving plate. Garnish with strawberries, raspberries or fruit of your choice.

To coat mold:
Put sugar and water in small pan and cook over medium-high heat until sugar melts and comes to golden caramel color. Stir to prevent burning. Pour mixture into mold and turn to coat bottom and part of sides.

C. Edna Rios Sissman
GFWC—Latham Woman's Club
Latham, New York

Swiss-Gruyere Fondue

- **2 cups shredded gruyere cheese**
- **2 cups shredded Swiss cheese**
- **3 tablespoons all-purpose flour**
- **½ teaspoon dry mustard**
- **Dash garlic powder**
- **¾ cup dry white wine**
- **½ teaspoon Worcestershire sauce**
- **Vegetable dips or bread cubes**

Toss together cheeses, flour, mustard and garlic powder. In a 1½-quart microwave-safe casserole, cook wine, Worcestershire sauce and ½ cup water, uncovered, on 100% power for 1–1½ minutes or until hot. Add cheese mixture to hot liquid; microwave uncovered on 50% power 7–9 minutes or until cheese is melted, stirring every two minutes. Serve with vegetable dips or bread cubes. Reheat as necessary on medium high.

Barbara Trimble
GFWC—Woman's Club of Westview Park
Catonsville, Maryland

Enchiladas

1 dozen corn tortillas
½ cup cooking oil
Almonds
2 cups shredded Monterey Jack cheese
¾ cup chopped white onion
¼ cup butter or margarine
¼ cup flour
2 cups chicken broth or bouillon
1 cup sour cream
1 4 ounce can jalapeno peppers

Cook tortillas in small skillet in ½ cup cooking oil until soft. Drain on paper towel. Fill with 2 tablespoons cheese and 1 tablespoon onion and 1 teaspoon almonds. Roll tortilla and put in pan seam side down. Make white sauce out of remaining ingredients on top of stove. Whisk melted butter, flour, chicken broth and sour cream. Top with jalapeno peppers and ½ cup cheese. Bake 425 degrees for 20 minutes.

Virginia Crain
GFWC—Alpha Literary and Improvement Club
Lompoc, California

Italian Meat Pie

1½ pounds ricotta
8 ounces mozzarella, diced
½ pound provolone, sliced
¾ cup grated romano cheese
½ pound salami, minced
½ pound cooked sweet sausage, casing removed
5 large eggs
Salt and pepper to taste
1 box pie crust or your own

Use large-size casserole dish that is heat proof or two 9-inch pans; grease pans or dish. Put in ¾ pie crust that was rolled out first, save rest for lattice top. Combine all ingredients; stir well to mix, put in pie pan or casserole. Lattice top, brush with beaten egg yolk. Bake at 325 degrees for 1½ hours. I have always used a deep-dish casserole dish.

Agnes Jenners
GFWC—Red Oak Woman's Club
Wall Township, New Jersey

Surprise Quiche

- **1 unbaked 9-inch pie shell**
- **1 package spinach souffle**
- **2 eggs, beaten**
- **3 tablespoons milk**
- **2 teaspoons chopped onion**
- **¾ cup grated cheese, any kind**
- **¾ cup cooked, crumbled sausage**
- **½ cup sliced mushrooms, drained**

Thaw spinach about 2–3 hours. Mix all ingredients except cheese. Add ½ cup cheese and mix. Pour into a 9-inch unbaked pie shell. Sprinkle the rest of the cheese on top. Bake at 400 degrees for 25–30 minutes. Let stand for 15 minutes before serving. I like to use different meats—ham, chicken or whatever you have. Shrimp is a nice change too.

Hilde T. Kline
GFWC—Pocono Mountain Woman's Club
Pocono Lake, Pennsylvania

Zucchini Pie

- **3 cups shredded or sliced zucchini**
- **1 large onion, chopped**
- **½ cup grated parmesan cheese**
- **½ cup cheddar cheese**
- **½ cup salad oil**
- **1 cup biscuit mix**
- **4 eggs, beaten**
- **3 tablespoons minced parsley**
- **1 teaspoon salt**
- **½ teaspoon pepper**

Grease 9-inch pie plate or 9 × 9 baking dish. Mix all ingredients together in large bowl until lightly coated with batter. Pour into greased pan and bake until golden brown at 350 degrees for 35–40 minutes. Serve warm or cold.

Janet Parisi
GFWC—Cresskill Woman's Club
Cresskill, New Jersey

Scrambled Egg Casserole

3 strips bacon, fried crisp and crumbled
Parsley flakes
4 ounces dried beef, cut up
1 large can mushroom pieces, drained
3 tablespoons butter or margarine
¼ cup plus 2 tablespoons flour
3 cups milk
Dash pepper
12 eggs, beaten
¼ teaspoon salt
¾ cup evaporated milk or milk to which some dried milk powder has been added
2 tablespoons butter or margarine

Saute beef and mushrooms in butter or margarine; stir in flour till well mixed. Gradually add milk, stirring until smooth and thickened. Add pepper. Set aside. Mix eggs, salt, milk and scramble lightly in butter or margarine. Layer eggs and sauce in greased 9 × 13 pan, ending with sauce. Bake covered at 275 degrees for one hour. Garnish with bacon and parsley. Refrigerate overnight.

Ruth Monte
GFWC—Woman's Club of Newtown Square
Newtown Square, Pennsylvania

Confetti Egg 'N Cottage Casserole

1 6 ounce package spinach noodles, cooked and drained
6 hard-cooked eggs, coarsely chopped, one reserved
1 16 ounce container cottage cheese
1 8 ounce container sour cream
2 tablespoons chopped pimiento
2 teaspoons chicken flavor instant bouillon
5 teaspoons creamy ranch-style salad dressing mix
1 cup soft buttered bread crumbs

Preheat oven to 350 degrees. Lightly grease 11½ × 7 inch baking dish. Set aside. In large bowl, thoroughly combine noodles, chopped eggs, cottage cheese, sour cream, pimiento, bouillon and dressing mix. Pour mixture into greased baking dish. Top with buttered bread crumbs. Bake 25 minutes. Remove from oven and let stand 5 minutes. Slice remaining egg. Place egg slices on casserole as garnish.

Robin Dickson
GFWC—Phoenix Society
Gainesville, Georgia

Deviled Eggs Hawaiian

- **2 pounds frozen or fresh cooked broccoli**
- **12 hard-boiled eggs**
- **4½ ounces deviled ham**
- **½ teaspoon dry mustard**
- **2 teaspoons lemon juice**
- **4 tablespoons mayonnaise**
- **Salt and pepper**

Cream Sauce

- **6 tablespoons melted margarine**
- **6 tablespoons flour**
- **3 cups milk**
- **2 cups grated sharp cheese**
- **1 teaspoon mustard**
- **Salt and pepper**

Cook chopped broccoli; arrange in bottom of 12–15 inch casserole dish. Cut hard-boiled eggs in half. Combine deviled ham, dry mustard, lemon juice, mayonnaise, salt and pepper with egg yolks. Fill egg whites and place on top of broccoli. Make a cream sauce of margarine, flour, milk, grated sharp cheese, mustard, salt and pepper. Pour over broccoli and eggs. Top with corn flakes and butter. Bake at 350 degrees for 20–25 minutes.

Hazel Epps
GFWC—Seattle Federated Coterie
Seattle, Washington

Never Fail Omelette

- **¼ cup butter**
- **1½ dozen eggs—18**
- **1 cup sour cream**
- **1 cup milk**
- **2 teaspoons salt**

Heat oven to 325 degrees. Melt butter in pan or glass dish 9 × 13 inch, tilting dish so butter coats sides of dish. Mix together eggs, sour cream, milk and salt. Blend well with a spoon but do not beat. Bake 35 minutes. Test for doneness with a knife (should come out clean). Cut in squares to serve. Very rich.

Marion Van Norman
GFWC—Woman's Club of Hellertown
Hellertown, Pennsylvania

Chicken 'N Biscuit 'N Eggs

- **1 cup chicken, cooked and chopped**
- **¼ cup onion, chopped**
- **1 tablespoon green pepper, chopped**
- **¼ cup water chestnuts, chopped**
- **½ cup sour cream**
- **1 teaspoon salt**
- **½ teaspoon pepper**
- **1 cup sharp cheddar cheese, grated**
- **4 hard-boiled eggs, chopped**
- **8 canned biscuits**
- **1 10¾ ounce can cream of mushroom or chicken soup**
- **⅓ cup milk**
- **½ cup sharp cheddar cheese, grated, for garnish**
- **Sliced tomatoes for garnish**
- **1 hard-cooked egg for garnish**

Mix first eight ingredients until thoroughly mixed. Set aside. Using 2 pieces waxed paper, sprayed with cooking spray, place 2 biscuits side by side in row of 4 on the paper. Cover top with other paper and roll as thin as possible. Place in 9 × 13 × 2 inch baking dish sprayed with cooking spray. Add chicken and egg filling down center of biscuit dough. Roll the biscuit sides over to center of mixture and press to seal dough. Bake at 450 degrees for 10 minutes. Heat one can of either cream of mushroom or chicken soup with milk. Pour over crust and bake an additional 10 minutes or until soup mixture bubbles. Remove from oven. Sprinkle with cheddar cheese and garnish with sliced tomatoes and eggs. Place an egg slice on top of each tomato slice. Serves four.

Reesa Byrd
GFWC—Enterprise Literary Club
Enterprise, Alabama

Single's Quiche

- **1 egg**
- **1 tablespoon flour**
- **1 cup milk**
- **½ teaspoon Worcestershire sauce**
- **Salt and pepper to taste**
- **2 slices Swiss cheese**

Combine egg and flour and beat well. Add Worcestershire sauce, milk, salt and pepper. Pour over 2 slices of Swiss cheese in a greased pan. Bake at 325 degrees until knife comes out clean. Length of time depends on depth of pan. Quiche will rise almost double.

Ida Vivian McCulley
GFWC—Saturday Club
Cotter, Arkansas

Savory Souffle Roll

4 tablespoons butter
½ cup flour
½ teaspoon salt
⅛ teaspoon white pepper
2 cups milk
5 eggs, separated

Preheat oven to 400 degrees. Grease, line with waxed paper and grease again a jelly roll pan. Dust lightly with flour. Melt butter in saucepan, blend in flour, salt and pepper. Gradually stir in milk. Bring to a boil, stirring and cook one minute. Beat egg yolks just to mix. Add a little hot sauce while beating. Return all to pan and cook over medium heat one minute longer, stirring. Do not boil. Cool to room temperature, stirring occasionally. Beat whites till stiff but not dry. Fold into cooled sauce and spread in pan. Bake 25–30 minutes till well puffed and browned. Turn immediately onto a clean towel. Spread with warm filling and roll up. Place on serving platter, seam side down. After rolling and placing on platter, can be kept warm at 200 degrees for 30 minutes.

Filling

2 tablespoons butter
4 shallots, finely chopped
4 medium mushrooms, chopped
1 cup cooked chopped spinach
1 cup chopped cooked ham
1 tablespoon mustard
¼ teaspoon nutmeg
6 ounces cream cheese, softened
Salt and pepper to taste

Melt butter in skillet and saute shallots till tender. Add mushrooms and cook until they give up their moisture and it evaporates, about 3 minutes. Add spinach, ham, mustard and nutmeg; heat, stirring. Stir in cheese. Add salt and pepper. Spread on warm souffle and roll up.

Mercedes Brunner
GFWC—Woman's Club of Danbury/New Fairfield
Danbury, Connecticut

Apple Puffed Pancake

6 eggs
1½ cups milk
1 cup flour
3 tablespoons sugar
1 teaspoon vanilla
½ teaspoon salt
¼ teaspoon cinnamon
¼ pound butter or oleo
2–3 apples, peeled, thinly sliced
4 tablespoons brown sugar

In blender or mixer bowl, mix eggs, milk, flour, sugar, vanilla, salt and cinnamon until well blended. Batter will be lumpy. Melt butter in 13 × 9 × 2 pan in oven. Add apple slices to pan (should sizzle). Return to oven until butter sizzles. Do not let brown. Remove dish from oven and immediately pour batter over apples. Sprinkle with brown sugar. Bake in middle of 425 degree oven for 20 minutes until puffed and brown. Serve immediately.

Doris Baker Hadad
GFWC—Trumbull Community League
Trumbull, Connecticut

Armadillo Eggs

- **1 jar jalapeno peppers—about 15 peppers**
- **½ pound Monterey Jack cheese, grated**
- **½ pound bulk sausage, hot (optional)**
- **1½ cups buttermilk biscuit mix**
- **Pork flavored coating mix**
- **1 beaten egg**

Using rubber gloves, split and seed 15 jalapeno peppers. Stuff with a small piece of Monterey Jack cheese. Pinch pepper closed. Make dough of sausage, cheese and biscuit mix. Divide into 3 equal parts. Wrap dough around pepper about ¼ inch thick. Completely cover pepper. Roll in pork coating mix, then in beaten egg and then again in coating mix. Bake at 300–325 degrees for 20–25 minutes.

Betty Jean Pelt
GFWC—Cosmopolitan Woman's Club of Mobile
Mobile, Alabama

Scotch Eggs

- **1 pound Italian sausage**
- **1–2 cups Italian bread crumbs**
- **8 eggs, hard boiled, peeled**
- **1 egg, beaten**

Divide sausage into eight 2-ounce portions. On surface sprinkled with Italian-style bread crumbs, pat each portion to ⅛ inch thick. Wrap each portion completely around a hard-boiled egg, pressing edges together to seal. Roll sausage and coated eggs in ⅓ cup Italian crumbs. Dip in beaten egg. Bake in preheated oven at 375 degrees for 20 minutes. Serve with mustard sauce.

Lorene Wasinger
GFWC—Study Club
Hannibal, Missouri

Chili Egg Puff

- **10 eggs**
- **½ teaspoon salt**
- **½ cup flour**
- **1 teaspoon baking powder**
- **1 pint creamed small curd cottage cheese**
- **1 pound shredded Monterey Jack cheese**
- **2 4 ounce or 1 7 ounce can diced green chilies**
- **½ cup melted oleo**

Beat eggs with electric mixer. Add flour, baking powder, salt, cheeses and oleo. Stir in chilies. Pour mixture into a buttered 9 × 13 inch baking dish. Bake 350 degrees for 35 minutes or until top is browned. The mixture may be made and stored in the refrigerator overnight.

Dorothy Thomas
GFWC—Patagonia
Patagonia, Arizona

Linda Moerdyke
GFWC—Sunset-Hacienda Junior Woman's Club
Hacienda Heights, California

Cakes

English Tea Cake

1½ cups sugar
½ cup butter
2 eggs, well beaten
1 cup sweet milk
½ teaspoon baking soda
2 level cups flour
¼ teaspoon nutmeg

Cream sugar and butter, add beaten eggs and beat before adding half the milk. Sift in the flour, baking soda and nutmeg. Beat well and add the remaining milk. Bake at 400 degrees for 50 minutes, in a loaf pan or small tube pan. Delicious served warm with tea.

"My grandmother's mother brought this recipe with her when the family moved from England to the USA in 1852."

Evelyn Finke
GFWC—Syracuse Federated Woman's Club
Syracuse, Nebraska

Photo features: Strawberry Cake—Page 286
Dirt Cake—Page 272

Hot Milk Sponge Cake

- **4 eggs, beaten well**
- **2 cups sugar**
- **2 cups flour**
- **1 cup just boiling milk**
- **1 teaspoon baking powder**
- **1 teaspoon lemon extract**
- **1 teaspoon vanilla**
- **½ cup chopped black walnuts**

Beat together eggs and sugar. Add flour slowly. Add milk, baking powder and extracts until blended. Mix in nuts. Pour into well greased tube pan. Bake 350 degrees for 45–50 minutes. When cake is done, reverse pan and cool about 1 hour. Remove carefully from pan and cool completely. After cool, sprinkle with powdered sugar.

"This is a very old family recipe from Northern Burlington County in New Jersey. My husband's grandmother made this family favorite without a written recipe. My mother-in-law recently wrote it down as accurately as she could remember it."

Barbara Vanzandt
GFWC—Metuchen Woman's Club
Metuchen, New Jersey

Angel Food Cake

- **1⅔ cups egg whites**
- **1 cup plus 2 tablespoons sifted cake flour**
- **1¾ cups granulated sugar**
- **½ teaspoon salt**
- **2 teaspoons cream of tartar**
- **1 teaspoon vanilla**
- **½ teaspoon almond extract**
- **1 cup sifted granulated sugar**

Sift together 4 times sifted flour and ¾ cup sugar. In large mixer bowl, combine egg whites, salt, cream of tartar and flavorings. Beat at high speed until whites form stiff peaks. Add 1 cup sugar gradually and beat at medium speed until sugar is thoroughly mixed. With hand whip, gradually add sugar-flour mixture until thoroughly mixed. Pour into ungreased tube pan; use knife to cut evenly into pan. Bake 350 degrees for 35 minutes. Turn upside down and cool and cut around edges.

V. Berniece Heath
GFWC—Litchfield Woman's Club
Litchfield, Illinois

Ture Cake

- **8 ounces butter**
- **9 ounces honey**
- **9 ounces flour**
- **5 ounces sugar**
- **2 ounces chocolate**
- **5 ounces nutmeats, chopped fine**

Put flour, butter and nuts in saucepan. Cook, stirring constantly until nuts are brownish; about one hour. Add chocolate melted in a little water and sugar. Stir quickly; add honey. Mix all and pack in a mold. Do not use for at least 24 hours.

"This recipe was given to my mother on the prairie in Alberta in 1910."

Edna M. Brown
GFWC—Milton Woman's Improvement Club
Milton-Freewater, Oregon

Chocolate Angel Food Cake

- **3/4 cup sifted cake flour**
- **1 1/4 cups sifted powdered sugar**
- **1/4 cup cocoa**
- **2 teaspoons instant coffee**
- **1 1/2 cups egg whites, 12–14**
- **1/4 teaspoon salt**
- **1 1/2 teaspoons cream of tartar**
- **3/4 cup granulated sugar**

Combine sifted flour with powdered sugar, cocoa and powdered coffee and sift together three more times. Set aside. Preheat oven to 375 degrees. In large bowl of electric mixer, beat egg whites until foamy. Sprinkle cream of tartar and salt over surface and beat at high speed until soft, moist peaks form. Continue beating egg whites, gradually adding the granulated sugar, 2 tablespoons at a time, until stiff peaks form. Sift 1/4 of the flour-sugar mixture at a time over the meringue and gently fold in each addition. Do not overmix. Turn into 10 × 4 ungreased 2-piece tube pan. Gently cut through the batter with a knife twice to break up air bubbles. Bake 375 degrees for 35–40 minutes or until the cake springs back when lightly touched. Invert the pan to cool completely, about 1 1/2–2 hours. To remove from pan, run thin sharp knife around sides, remove outside pan rim. Run knife under cake and around inside rim to separate from bottom of pan.

"This is an excellent dessert for persons watching their cholesterol and also is relatively low in calories if eaten without icing or other sauces. It is a recipe adaptation I completed for a culinary hearts cooking class taught by the American Heart Association. You can save up egg whites in a freezer container and freeze them until you have enough to make angel food cakes. Just thaw and measure when ready to use."

Joan Krafka Meany
GFWC—Cedar Falls Woman's Club, Junior Department
Cedar Falls, Iowa

Coconut Cake

- **1 yellow cake mix**

Icing and Filling

- **2 cups sour cream**
- **2 cups sugar**
- **18 ounces frozen coconut**

Bake cake according to instructions on box making two layers either 8 or 9 inches. When cool, divide into four layers.

Mix sour cream, sugar and coconut in a bowl. Cover and let set in the refrigerator overnight. Ice 4 cooled layers and put in refrigerator for 3–5 days before eating.

Peggy A. Couch
GFWC—Dunwoody Woman's Club
Dunwoody, Georgia

Burnt Sugar Black Walnut Cake Frosting

- **3 cups sugar**
- **2 cups milk**
- **½ cup white corn syrup**
- **1 tablespoon butter**
- **1 cup black walnuts**
- **1 teaspoon vanilla**
- **1 2-layer yellow cake mix or favorite yellow cake recipe**

Prepare your favorite yellow cake recipe.

Frosting:
Place 1 cup sugar in a 6-quart saucepan. Heat, stirring constantly, until sugar becomes a dark brown syrup. Remove from heat. Put 2 cups sugar, milk and corn syrup in another saucepan. Bring to a boil. Return burnt sugar to heat. Mixture will flare up so be careful to pour slowly. Slowly pour milk mixture over hot burnt sugar. Cook to soft ball stage, 235 degree on candy thermometer. Remove from heat, add vanilla, walnuts and butter. Mix. Punch several holes in cake layers with toothpick before frosting. This causes frosting to be absorbed into cake layer. Apply slowly to top of yellow cake layers or 9 × 13 cake.

"My mother made this cake in the 1940's from homegrown black walnuts in Marion County, Alabama."

Jean C. Dyar
GFWC—The Lamplighters Woman's Club
Germantown, Tennessee

Burnt Sugar Cake

- **½ cup sugar**
- **½ cup boiling water**
- **1½ cups sugar**
- **⅔ cup butter**
- **2 beaten egg whites**
- **1 cup cold water**
- **3 cups flour, or 2½ cups if using a mixer (sift 6 times—then measure)**
- **1 teaspoon baking soda**
- **1 teaspoon vanilla**

Burn ½ cup sugar in skillet, stir constantly. Add boiling water and boil to a syrup, then set aside. Cream sugar and butter; add cold water and beat thoroughly. Add flour and baking soda and mix. Add the sugar syrup and beat. Fold in beaten, but not dry, egg whites and the vanilla. Mix well and pour into cake pans. Bake at 350 degrees for 30–40 minutes.

Frosting

- **1 cup sugar**
- **1 cup cream**
- **1 teaspoon salt**

Mix sugar and cream in skillet and cook to a caramel consistency. Add salt and beat to a beautiful caramel.

"I am 91 years old and most of my cooking has always been done without a written recipe."

Darlie Cook
GFWC—Peoria Woman's Club
Peoria, Arizona

Rum Cake

- 1 cup chopped pecans or walnuts
- 1 box yellow cake mix
- 1 3¾ ounce package vanilla instant pudding and pie filling
- 4 eggs
- ½ cup cold water
- ¼ cup oil
- ½ cup rum

Grease and flour 10-inch tube or 12-cup bundt pan. Sprinkle nuts over bottom of pan. Mix all cake ingredients together. Pour batter over nuts. Bake at 325 degrees for 1 hour. Invert on serving plate.

Glaze

- 1 stick butter
- ¼ cup water
- 1 cup granulated sugar
- ½ cup rum

Prick top of cake. Mix butter in saucepan. Stir in water and sugar. Boil 5 minutes, stirring constantly. Remove from heat and stir in rum. Drizzle and smooth glaze evenly over top and sides. Allow cake to absorb glaze. Repeat until glaze is used up.

Allyrae Wallace
GFWC—Camden Study Club
Camden, Alabama

Oatmeal Cake

- 1 cup quick oatmeal
- ½ cup chopped dates
- 1½ cups boiling water
- 1 cup white sugar
- 1 cup brown sugar
- ½ cup butter or oleo
- 2 eggs, beaten
- 1 teaspoon vanilla
- 1½ cups flour
- 1 teaspoon baking soda
- ½ teaspoon salt
- ½ cup chocolate chips
- ½ cup chopped English walnuts

Mix oatmeal, dates and boiling water together. Let stand while you prepare the batter. Beat sugars and oleo until well creamed. Add eggs and vanilla. Beat again until creamed. Sift flour, baking soda and salt. Add flour mixture to sugar, oleo and egg mixture and blend in. Add date-oatmeal mixture and blend. Pour into greased 9 × 13 pan. Sprinkle over the top chocolate chips and chopped English walnuts. Bake at 350 degrees for 40 minutes. Can be eaten plain, iced or served with whipped topping.

Mrs. Edward Cole
GFWC—Cadiz Woman's Civic Club
Cadiz, Ohio

Filbert Cake and Frosting

- **1/3 cup shortening**
- **1 1/2 cups firmly packed brown sugar**
- **2 eggs**
- **1 tablespoon grated lemon peel**
- **2 cups sifted cake flour**
- **1 teaspoon baking powder**
- **1/2 teaspoon baking soda**
- **1/2 teaspoon salt**
- **1 cup sour cream**
- **2/3 cup chopped filberts**

Combine first four ingredients in mixing bowl and beat for two minutes. Sift dry ingredients and beat alternately with sour cream into shortening mixture. Beat two minutes. Stir in filbert nuts. Bake in two greased and floured 8-inch pans at 350 degrees for 30–40 minutes. When cool, frost with filbert nut frosting.

Filbert Nut Frosting

- **1/4 teaspoon cream of tartar**
- **1 cup firmly packed brown sugar**
- **2 egg whites**
- **1/4 cup water**
- **1 teaspoon vanilla**

Combine first four ingredients in top of double boiler. Beat over boiling water until frosting will stand in peaks. Add vanilla. Frost cake and sprinkle sides with chopped filbert nuts.

Peggy Hughes
GFWC—Woman's Club of Waycroft
Arlington, Virginia

Hattie's Shortcake

- **2 cups all-purpose flour**
- **3 teaspoons baking powder**
- **1 teaspoon salt**
- **4 heaping "silver" teaspoons of sugar (scant 1/4 cup)**
- **3/4 cup milk**
- **1 egg**
- **7/8 cup shortening (1 cup minus 2 tablespoons or 14 tablespoons)**
- **Any fruit; strawberries, raspberries, etc., washed and sugared**

Sift dry ingredients together. Mix in shortening with a fork and fingers. Add milk mixed well with egg. Do not beat egg separately. Do not sift flour when measuring. Spread in 8 × 8 × 2 aluminum pan and dot with butter to bake. Bake at 400 degrees for 20–25 minutes. Cut in 9 equal pieces, split, butter and layer with fruit. Good with milk or whipped cream.

"This was my great-grandmother's recipe."

Grace Wiseman
GFWC—Rochester Junior Woman's Club
Rochester, Michigan

Old Hickory Nut Cake

1 cup sugar
½ cup butter or margarine
3 egg yolks
2 cups all-purpose flour
½ teaspoon baking soda
½ teaspoon ground nutmeg
⅓ cup bourbon
⅓ cup milk
1 cup chopped hickory nuts or pecans
1 cup raisins
3 stiffly beaten egg whites
3 tablespoons bourbon
1 teaspoon cinnamon
¼ teaspoon salt

Cream sugar and butter together until fluffy. Add egg yolks, one at a time, beating well after each. Stir together flour, cinnamon, soda, nutmeg and salt. Add to creamed mixture alternately with bourbon and milk. Stir in nuts and raisins. Gently fold in egg whites. Bake in greased 9 × 5 × 3-inch loaf pan at 350 degrees for 60 to 65 minutes. Cool. Brush entire cake surface with 3 tablespoons bourbon. Wrap in foil; store overnight.

"This recipe was served by President Jackson, or Old Hickory, during his term at a Christmas party."

Valley E. Ricks
GFWC—Le Bonte Woman's Club
Greenwood, Mississippi

Black Walnut Sheet Cake

2 cups flour
2 cups sugar
1 teaspoon baking soda
½ teaspoon salt
1 cup butter or margarine
4 tablespoons cocoa
1 cup water
½ cup buttermilk
2 eggs

Sift dry ingredients into bowl. Melt butter and mix with cocoa and water. Bring to a rapid boil and pour over dry ingredients. Add buttermilk and eggs. Bake in cookie sheet pan with edge at 350 degrees for 20 minutes. Spread with icing while still hot.

Icing

½ cup butter
4 tablespoons cocoa
6 tablespoons buttermilk
1 pound powdered sugar
1 cup chopped black walnuts or pecans

Melt butter; add cocoa and buttermilk. Bring to a boil. Add powdered sugar and walnuts. Pour over cake.

Dorothy M. Crank
GFWC—Independence Study Club
Independence, Missouri

Dirt Cake

- **1 large package chocolate sandwich cookies or choco-mint cookies**
- **1 8 ounce package cream cheese**
- **½ cup butter or margarine**
- **1 cup powdered sugar**
- **1 9 ounce carton whipped topping**
- **2 3½ ounce packages instant French vanilla pudding**
- **3 cups milk**
- **1 teaspoon vanilla**

Crush cookies and put half of the crumbs in a 9 × 13 pan. Mix cream cheese and butter until smooth with a mixer. Fold in powdered sugar and then the whipped topping. In a separate bowl, mix pudding, milk and vanilla. Fold cream cheese mixture and pudding mixture together and pour into pan with the cookie crumbs. Sprinkle remaining crumbs over the top. Whipped cream may be used instead of the whipped topping if a richer dessert is desired. This may be frozen or will be nice just chilled.

Donna Elvin
GFWC—Marquette Woman's Literary Club
Marquette, Kansas

Margaret Knott
GFWC—Palm Beach Gardens Woman's Club
Palm Beach Gardens, Florida

German Jam Cake

- **2 cups sugar**
- **¾ cup oleo**
- **4 eggs**
- **1 teaspoon vanilla**
- **1 cup pecans, chopped**
- **3 cups flour**
- **1 teaspoon allspice**
- **1 teaspoon cinnamon**
- **1 teaspoon nutmeg**
- **1 teaspoon baking soda**
- **1 cup buttermilk**
- **⅔ cup cherry preserves**
- **⅔ cup apricot preserves**
- **⅔ cup pineapple preserves**

Cream sugar, oleo and eggs. Sift flour and spices. Dissolve soda into buttermilk, then add slowly. Fold in vanilla and preserves. Add nuts. Pour in greased and floured 10-inch tube pan. Bake in 325 degree oven for 1½ hours. Cool in pan 15 minutes. Remove to plate.

Irene K. Knipling
GFWC—Woman's Study Club
Port Lavaca, Texas

Paradise Cake

- **2 cups whole wheat flour**
- **1½ cups sugar**
- **1½ teaspoons baking powder**
- **1½ teaspoons baking soda**
- **2 eggs, well beaten**
- **2 cups crushed pineapple with juice**
- **1 tablespoon vegetable oil**

Topping

- **1 cup sugar**
- **1 6 ounce can evaporated milk**
- **¼ cup butter**
- **1 tablespoon vanilla**
- **1 cup coconut, flaked**
- **1 cup broken pecans**

Combine dry ingredients in bowl. Add eggs, pineapple and oil. Use wooden spoon; do not use electric mixer. Pour into greased and floured 9 × 12 pan. Bake at 350 degrees for 30–35 minutes. While cake bakes, prepare topping. Combine in saucepan sugar, milk and butter. Bring to boil for 2 minutes. Remove from flame and add vanilla, coconut and pecans. When cake is baked, immediately pour hot topping over hot cake. Can be served warm or cold. Delicious either way!

Rose C. Mader
GFWC—Woman's Club of New Brunswick
New Brunswick, New Jersey

Punch Bowl Cake

- **1 yellow cake mix**
- **1 can blueberry pie filling**
- **1 can cherry pie filling**
- **3–4 bananas**
- **1 large can crushed pineapple and juice**
- **1 large whipped topping**
- **1 small whipped topping**

Bake cake according to package; cool and divide into four parts. Layer ¼ crumbled cake in bottom of punch bowl. Spread with ½ can blueberry pie filling. Spread with whipped topping. Repeat layers 2 times, alternating cherry and blueberry pie filling. Next spread with sliced bananas. Spread with pineapple and juice. Repeat layering with remainder of cake, cherry filling and whipped topping. Garnish with cherries, nuts and coconut.

Verna D. Turk
GFWC—Cosmopolitan Woman's Club of Mobile
Mobile, Alabama

Ferncrest Pound Cake

- **1 pound butter**
- **1 pound sugar (2 cups)**
- **1 pound eggs (8 extra large)**
- **1 pound unsifted flour (2⅔ cups)**

All must be room temperature. Cream butter thoroughly. Add sugar and beat. Fold in eggs and do not overbeat. Fold in flour until smooth or evenly blended. Pour batter into large greased bundt or angel food pan. Bake in a slow oven 325 degrees for about one hour and 10–15 minutes. Remove pan from oven, place on rack. Cool ½ hour and remove cake from pan. Serve plain, iced or sprinkled with powdered sugar.

Ferne Smith Hetrick
GFWC—Camp Hill Civic Club
Camp Hill, Pennsylvania

Coconut Cream Cheese Pound Cake

- **½ cup butter, softened**
- **½ cup shortening**
- **1 8 ounce package cream cheese, softened**
- **3 cups sugar**
- **6 eggs**
- **3 cups all-purpose flour**
- **¼ teaspoon baking soda**
- **¼ teaspoon salt**
- **1 6 ounce package frozen coconut, thawed**
- **1 teaspoon vanilla extract**
- **1 teaspoon coconut flavoring**

Cream butter, shortening and cream cheese. Gradually add sugar, beating at medium speed of an electric mixer until light and fluffy. Add eggs, one at a time, beating after each. Combine flour, baking soda and salt. Add to creamed mixture, stirring just until blended. Stir in coconut and flavorings. Spoon batter into greased and floured 10-inch tube pan. Bake at 350 degrees for 1 hour and 15 minutes or until done. Cool in pan 10–15 minutes. Remove from pan. Cool completely.

Anne Adkins
GFWC—Ravenswood Civic Club
Ravenswood, West Virginia

Fruit Cocktail Cake

- **2¼ cups all-purpose flour**
- **2 teaspoons baking soda**
- **1 teaspoon salt**
- **1 cup brown sugar**
- **2 eggs**
- **¼ cup soft butter**
- **1 16 ounce can fruit cocktail**

Put all ingredients in a large bowl and beat at low speed to moisten. Then 2 minutes at medium speed. Grease 9 × 13 pan on sides only, flour the sides also. Bake at 350 degrees for 30–40 minutes. Sometimes I like to sprinkle ½ cup semi-sweet chocolate bits and ½ cup chopped nuts on top just before baking.

Beverly A. Goodrich
GFWC—Wolfeboro Woman's Club
Wolfeboro, New Hampshire

Black Walnut Pound Cake

- **1 cup shortening**
- **1 stick butter or margarine**
- **1 cup white sugar**
- **2 cups light brown sugar**
- **½ teaspoon vanilla**
- **½ teaspoon black walnut flavoring**
- **½ teaspoon salt**
- **1 cup milk**
- **6 eggs**
- **3 cups plain flour**
- **½ teaspoon baking powder**
- **1 cup walnuts, chopped fine**

Mix first seven ingredients well. Add milk and eggs, one at a time. Mix well. Add plain flour, one cup at a time, adding baking powder with last cup, and fine chopped walnuts. Spoon into pan and bake for one hour or until top has cracked open and dried in a 350 degree oven.

Bessie J. Cogdill
GFWC—Sylva Woman's Club
Sylva, North Carolina

Five Flavor Pound Cake

Cake

- **2 sticks margarine**
- **½ cup oil**
- **3 cups sugar**
- **5 eggs**
- **3 cups flour**
- **½ teaspoon baking powder**
- **1 cup milk**
- **1 teaspoon vanilla**
- **1 teaspoon lemon extract**
- **1 teaspoon coconut flavoring**
- **1 teaspoon rum flavoring**
- **1 teaspoon butter flavoring**

Glaze

- **½ cup sugar**
- **½ teaspoon vanilla**
- **½ teaspoon coconut flavoring**
- **¼ cup water**
- **½ teaspoon butter flavoring**
- **½ teaspoon lemon extract**
- **½ teaspoon rum flavoring**
- **½ teaspoon almond flavoring**

Cream margarine, oil and sugar well. Add eggs, one at a time, beating well after each. Add flour alternately with milk—begin and end with flour. Add flavorings, beat well. Bake in tube pan at 325 degrees for 1½ hours. Cool in pan for 15 minutes. For glaze, mix all ingredients, heat and pour over warm cake.

Virginia Darnell
CFWC—Pamunkey Evening Woman's Club
Mechanicsville, Virginia

Cream Cheese Pound Cake

- ½ pound butter or margarine
- ½ pound cream cheese
- 2 cups sugar
- 2 cups all-purpose flour
- 2 teaspoons baking powder
- 6 eggs
- 2 teaspoons vanilla

Cream butter and cream cheese together. Gradually add sugar. Sift flour and baking powder together. Add flour mixture and eggs alternately. Mix well. Add vanilla. Grease and flour tube pan. Bake at 350 degrees for one hour.

"This recipe was given to me almost thirty years ago by my first neighbor when we moved into our first house as newlyweds."

Helen S. Wood
GFWC—West Essex Woman's Club
Caldwell, New Jersey

Honey Chocolate Cake and Frosting

Cake

- 2 cups sifted cake flour
- 1½ teaspoons baking soda
- ½ teaspoon salt
- ½ cup butter
- 1¼ cups honey
- 2 eggs, unbeaten
- 3 squares unsweetened chocolate, melted
- ⅔ cup water

Frosting

- 3 ounces cream cheese
- ¼ cup milk
- 3 cups sifted confectioners' sugar
- ⅛ teaspoon salt
- 1 teaspoon vanilla
- 3 ounces chocolate, melted

Sift flour once, measure, add soda and salt and sift together three times. Cream butter, add honey gradually, by tablespoons, beating after each addition to keep mixture thick. Add ¼ of flour and beat until smooth. Add eggs, one at a time, beating after each one. Add chocolate and blend. Add remaining flour in thirds, alternately with water, beating well after each addition. For best results, beat very well at each stage of mixing. Add vanilla. Bake in two greased 8-inch layer pans. Bake at 350 degrees for 30 minutes.

Frosting: Blend cream cheese with milk. Add confectioners' sugar, salt and vanilla. Beat in chocolate. Spread on cake.

Louise H. Smith
GFWC—Molly Pitcher Woman's Club
Freehold Township, New Jersey

White Chocolate Cake

- **2 cups sugar**
- **½ cup butter**
- **4 eggs, separated**
- **¼ pound white chocolate**
- **½ cup hot water**
- **1 cup buttermilk**
- **1 teaspoon baking soda**
- **1 cup coconut, optional**
- **2½ cups cake flour, sifted**
- **1 cup chopped nuts, optional**

Cream butter and sugar, beat in egg yolks one at a time. Melt chocolate in water, let cool. Add to creamed mixture. Add buttermilk, soda, flour, coconut and nuts. Beat egg whites until stiff and fold into mixture. Pour into three layer pans. Bake 35 minutes at 350 degrees. Makes three layers. Frost with white chocolate icing or butter frosting.

Sandra K. Powell
GFWC—Itasca Junior Woman's Club
Itasca, Illinois

Chocolate Zucchini Cake

- **3 cups flour**
- **½ cup cocoa**
- **2 teaspoons baking soda**
- **½ teaspoon salt**
- **1½ cups sugar**
- **1 cup vegetable oil**
- **3 eggs**
- **½ cup milk**
- **2 cups zucchini, finely shredded**
- **2 teaspoons vanilla**
- **1 cup nuts, chopped, optional**

Sift dry ingredients together in small bowl and set aside. Beat sugar and oil until smooth, then add eggs one at a time, beating well after each addition. Combine with dry ingredients, alternating with milk and zucchini. Mix well. Add vanilla and chopped nuts. Bake in two greased and floured 9 × 5 loaf pans, or use greased and floured bundt pan, at 350 degrees for 50–60 minutes. For variety you may glaze tops or serve with ice cream or whipped cream.

Mary Ellen Gallagher
GFWC—Mesquite Club
Las Vegas, Nevada

Fruit Torte

- **1 20 ounce can crushed pineapple—do not drain**
- **1 can peach pie filling**
- **1 package yellow cake mix—without pudding**
- **1 cup nuts**
- **1 cup flaked coconut**
- **1 cup melted butter or oleo**

Place pineapple in 9 × 12 pan and smooth over bottom of pan. Spread peach filling over this. Sprinkle cake mix over the top, then nuts and coconut. Pour the melted butter over the top. Bake 55 minutes to one hour at 350 degrees. Keeps well and may be prepared well ahead of serving.

Delores B. Roskens
GFWC—Spencer Federated Woman's Club
Spencer, Iowa

Grandma Jackie's Devil's Food Cake and Frosting

Cake

- **2 cups sugar**
- **1/4 cup butter**
- **2 tablespoons lard or shortening**
- **2 heaping tablespoons cocoa**
- **1 cup boiling water**
- **2 egg yolks**
- **1/2 cup sour milk**
- **1 1/2 teaspoons soda**
- **1 tablespoon vanilla**
- **2 cups flour**
- **2 beaten egg whites**

Boil first five ingredients together one minute. Cool thoroughly. Then beat next three ingredients together thoroughly with rotary beater. Add vanilla and flour. Fold in beaten egg whites. Bake at 350 degrees for about 40 minutes.

Frosting

- **1 one pound box powdered sugar**
- **2/3 cup cocoa**
- **1 cube butter (one stick)**
- **1 tablespoon vanilla**
- **3 tablespoons hot coffee**

Frosting: Mix all ingredients together using enough coffee to make spreading consistency.

"This recipe is at least seventy-five years old and is a family favorite—well worth making from scratch."

Bobby Ruth Bjork
GFWC—Madison Valley Woman's Club
Ennis, Montana

Quick and Sinful Double Chocolate Cake

- **1 devil's food cake mix**
- **1 3 1/2 ounce package chocolate instant pudding**
- **1 cup peanut butter chips**
- **1 can chocolate fudge topping**
- **1 can ready-to-spread chocolate frosting**
- **4 eggs**
- **1/2 cup oil**
- **1 cup water**

Grease and flour 9 × 13 pan. Mix dry pudding with cake mix before adding the eggs, oil and water. Blend on low speed until moistened. Mix at medium speed for two minutes. Scrape bowl often. Add peanut butter chips and mix for 30 seconds more. Bake at 350 degrees for 35–40 minutes. When done, let cake sit on cooling rack for 5 minutes. Poke holes all over with long-tined fork. While still hot, cover the whole top of the cake with chocolate fudge topping. Let cool completely, then frost with chocolate frosting. Swirl to decorate and serve.

Stephanie Sidella
GFWC—Junior Woman's Club of Rockville, Inc.
Rockville, Maryland

Persian Nut Torte and Frosting

Torte

12 eggs, separated
¾ cup sugar
6 tablespoons flour
1 teaspoon baking powder
1 bar German sweet chocolate, grated

Beat egg yolks until light; add sugar gradually. Beat until light yellow. Sift flour and baking powder. Add flour mixture and chocolate to creamed mixture. Beat egg whites until stiff, not dry. Fold into creamed mixture. Pour into 3 greased 9-inch round cake pans. Bake at 350 degrees for 40 minutes. Invert pans on rack to cool. Fill layers and frost.

Frosting

1 pound unsweetened butter
1⅛ cups powdered sugar
1 cup boiling milk
½ pound finely chopped walnuts
1 teaspoon vanilla

Beat butter and powdered sugar in electric mixer for five minutes, until looks like whipped cream. Pour boiling milk over nuts. When cool, add to butter mixture. Add vanilla. Frost torte. Best made day before and stored in refrigerator overnight.

Edythe J. Nommensen
GFWC—Junior Woman's Club of Waukesha
Waukesha, Wisconsin

Fresh Apple Cake

Cake

2 cups sugar
1½ cups cooking oil
2 teaspoons vanilla
2 well-beaten eggs
3 tablespoons lemon juice
1 teaspoon salt
3 cups flour
1 teaspoon cinnamon
1 teaspoon nutmeg
1 teaspoon baking soda
1½ cups chopped pecans
3 cups peeled, chopped apple

Combine sugar, oil, vanilla, eggs, lemon juice and salt in mixing bowl. Beat well. Mix flour and baking soda. Add to first mixture; beat well. Add pecans, apples, cinnamon and nutmeg. Mix well. Bake in greased and floured bundt pan for 1½ hours at 325 degrees. Put hot cake on plate. Pour hot glaze over cake.

Glaze

1 cup sugar
½ cup buttermilk
½ teaspoon baking soda
2 tablespoons corn syrup
½ cup butter
½ teaspoon vanilla

Combine ingredients in saucepan. Bring to rolling boil over low heat. Boil 10 minutes, stirring occasionally. Glaze may run off cake, so I sometimes save ½ of it to heat and put on each slice of cake along with whipped topping.

Karen Schlenz
GFWC—Junior Woman's Club of Ladd
Ladd, Illinois

Date Nut-Orange Slice Cake

- **2 sticks butter**
- **2 cups granulated sugar**
- **4 eggs**
- **1 cup buttermilk**
- **1 teaspoon baking soda**
- **3½ cups sifted flour**
- **½ pound diced dates**
- **1 pound bag orange slice candy, chopped**
- **1 can coconut—optional**
- **2 cups chopped nuts**
- **1 cup orange juice**
- **2 cups confectioners' sugar**

Cream butter and sugar until fluffy. Add eggs, beating well after each addition. Combine buttermilk and baking soda, then add alternately to butter-sugar mixture with flour, setting aside enough flour to dredge dates, orange slices, nuts and coconut. Then add to cake batter. Pour into tube pan lined with wax paper. Bake at 300–325 degrees for 2–2½ hours. When cake is done, mix orange juice and powdered sugar; heat this and pour over cake immediately. Let cake stand in pan for about 30 minutes. Remove from pan.

Catherine Sellers
GFWC—Mother's Club
Montgomery, Alabama

Black Walnut Cake

- **1 pound flour—4 cups before sifting**
- **1 pound butter**
- **9 eggs**
- **1 pound sugar—2 cups**
- **1 pound black walnuts**
- **1 teaspoon vanilla**
- **1 glass white wine—8 ounces**

Flour the nuts. Cream butter and sugar. Add eggs, flour and wine alternately. Add vanilla; add floured nuts. Cook in greased and floured large cake mold at 275 degrees for 2–3 hours.

"This was my grandmother's recipe. It is an old Virginia recipe—well over 100 years old."

Mrs. Curtis L. Rudolph
GFWC—Woman's Club of Bon Air
Richmond, Virginia

Turtle Cake

- **1 German chocolate cake mix**
- **½ cup canned milk**
- **¾ cup melted oleo**
- **1 14 ounce package caramel candy**
- **⅓ cup canned milk**
- **1 16 ounce package chocolate chips**
- **1½ cups chopped pecans**

Mix together cake mix, milk and oleo. Spread ½ of batter into 9 × 13 greased pan. Bake at 350 degrees for 5 minutes. Cool. Batter will be gooey. Melt together caramel candy and milk. Drizzle over cooled cake. Top with chocolate chips and pecans. Spoon the remainder of the cake batter on the top. Bake 20 minutes at 350 degrees. Cool before cutting. Do not overbake.

Bobbi Gose
GFWC—Marie Anderson Achievers
Fayette, Missouri

Irresistible Chocolate Cheesecake

- **24 chocolate wafers**
- **1/4 teaspoon cinnamon**
- **1/4 cup melted butter**
- **1 1/3 cups semi-sweet chocolate bits**
- **3 8 ounce packages softened cream cheese**
- **1 cup sugar**
- **2 eggs**
- **2 teaspoons cocoa**
- **1 teaspoon vanilla**
- **1 1/2 cups sour cream**

Crush wafers. Add melted butter and cinnamon. Press over bottom of 8-inch springform pan. Melt chocolate bits over hot (not boiling) water. In large bowl, beat cream cheese and gradually beat in sugar. Add eggs one at a time, beating after each. Beat in melted chocolate, cocoa, vanilla and sour cream. Pour into springform pan. Bake at 350 degrees for 45–50 minutes. Cool at room temperature 1 hour. Refrigerate 5–6 hours before serving. Quite rich, but you become addicted!

Nancy Bregar
GFWC—Bedford Junior Woman's Club
Bedford, New Hampshire

Crustless Cheesecake

- **1 pound cream cheese**
- **1 pound ricotta cheese**
- **2 cups sugar**
- **1 teaspoon vanilla**
- **1/2 cup soft butter**
- **4 eggs**
- **1/2 cup flour**
- **1 1/2 tablespoons lemon juice**
- **1 pint sour cream**

Put all ingredients in bowl and beat with mixer on medium speed for 20 minutes or until light and creamy. Pour into buttered 9-inch spring pan. Bake at 350 degrees for 1 hour. Turn off oven and let set in oven 2 hours.

Margaret Ann Wakefield
GFWC—Fairmont Junior Woman's Club
Fairmont, West Virginia

Raspberry Cheesecake

- **1 8 ounce package cream cheese, softened**
- **1/2 cup sugar**
- **1/2 cup sour cream**
- **1 teaspoon vanilla**
- **1 8 ounce container of whipped topping**
- **2 pints raspberries**
- **2 tablespoons sugar**
- **1 graham cracker crust**

Mix one pint of raspberries with one tablespoon sugar. Let set until juicy and crush lightly. Set aside. Beat cream cheese until smooth. Blend in sugar. Stir in sour cream, vanilla and raspberries until blended. Fold in whipped topping. Spoon into crust and chill until set. Slice second pint of raspberries and combine with sugar. Spoon over pie and top with whipped cream.

Edith S. Doscher
GFWC—Hightstown Woman's Club
Hightstown, New Jersey

Precious Prunie

Cake

1½ cups white sugar
1 cup salad oil
3 eggs
2 cups flour
1 teaspoon nutmeg
1 teaspoon allspice
1 teaspoon cinnamon
1 teaspoon baking soda
1 teaspoon salt
1 cup buttermilk
1 cup shelled walnuts
1 cup prunes, cooked, cooled and cut up
1 teaspoon vanilla

Combine sugar, oil and eggs. Beat one minute. Sift together flour, spices, salt and baking soda. Add flour mixture alternately with buttermilk to first mixture. Add prunes, nuts, and vanilla. Pour into greased 10 × 14 pan and bake at 300 degrees for 40–50 minutes.

Sauce

1½ cups white sugar
¾ cup buttermilk
1½ sticks butter
3 teaspoons vanilla
2 tablespoons corn syrup
¾ teaspoon baking soda

Place all ingredients in saucepan and cook. Stir over medium heat until it forms a soft ball when dropped in cold water. Do not overcook. Do not beat. Pour over hot cake in pan.

"This cake should stand at least 8 hours before serving to absorb sauce."

Martha E. Steadman
GFWC—The Woman's Club of Grafton
Grafton, West Virginia

Plum Cake

Cake

2 cups self-rising flour
2 cups sugar
3 eggs
1 cup oil
1 teaspoon ground cloves
1 teaspoon cinnamon
2 jars baby plum with tapioca

Mix together and pour in greased and floured tube pan. Bake at 325 degrees for 1 hour 15 minutes.

Glaze

1 cup powdered sugar
Juice of one lemon

Mix sugar with juice and pour over cake while warm.

Carolyn Sellers
GFWC—Cosmopolitan Woman's Club of Mobile
Mobile, Alabama

Maraschino Cherry Cake

- **2¼ cups flour**
- **1⅓ cups sugar**
- **3 teaspoons double-action baking powder**
- **½ cup vegetable shortening**
- **½ cup milk**
- **¼ cup maraschino cherry juice**
- **16 maraschino cherries—cut in eighths**
- **2 large eggs**
- **½ cup chopped nuts**

Sift together flour, sugar and baking powder. Add shortening, milk, maraschino cherry juice and cherries. Beat 2 minutes. Add eggs and beat 2 minutes. Fold in chopped nuts. Bake at 350 degrees for 30–35 minutes in 2 round layer pans, 8-inch diameter, or oblong pan. Frost with white icing and decorate with maraschino cherries.

Helen M. Jauert
GFWC—Wapakoneta Woman's Club
Wapakoneta, Ohio

Aunt Hattie's Blackberry Cake

Cake

- **3 eggs**
- **2 cups sugar**
- **2 sticks butter**
- **3½ cups all-purpose flour**
- **1 cup buttermilk**
- **1 can blackberries (juice and all)**
- **½ teaspoon cloves**
- **1 teaspoon cinnamon**
- **2 teaspoons baking powder**
- **½ jar (9 ounces) blackberry preserves**

Cream eggs, sugar and butter in small bowl. In large bowl mix flour, buttermilk, blackberry juice, cloves, cinnamon, baking powder and blackberry preserves. Mix in creamed mixture thoroughly. Grease and flour 3 cake pans. Pour in cake mixture. Bake at 350 degrees for 30–35 minutes. Cool.

Filling

- **1 cup sugar**
- **½ cup milk**
- **1 tablespoon butter**

Cook all ingredients until thick. Punch cake layers with fork. Pour filling over cake layers. Ice with favorite icing.

Jane D. Brown
GFWC—Raceland Woman's Club
Raceland, Kentucky

Pina Colada Cake

Cake

- 1 package yellow or white cake mix
- 1 15¼ ounce can crushed pineapple, drained
- ⅔ cup sour cream
- Whipping cream
- 1 8½ ounce can cream of coconut
- ¼ cup dark rum

Pour box of cake mix into bowl and forget about package directions. Add can of drained, crushed pineapple and sour cream. Mix 100 strokes by hand until smooth and pour into greased and floured tube pan, or 9 × 5-inch loaf pan or layer pans. Bake at 350 degrees for 35–40 minutes. It comes out very, very moist when removed from oven. Cool slightly. Punch holes into cake with tester or toothpicks and sprinkle rum over it—just enough to flavor it, not drown it.

Frosting

- Cold whipping cream
- Half can of cream of coconut

Whip some very cold whipping cream until stiff and add half a can of cream of coconut. Spoon that over the cake to frost it.

Lynda Swetz
GFWC—Arlington Junior Woman's Club
Jacksonville, Florida

Orange Cake

- 1¼ cups granulated sugar
- 1 orange, juiced and peeled
- ½ cup shortening
- 2 eggs
- ½ teaspoon salt
- 1 cup chopped pecans
- 1 teaspoon baking soda
- 1 cup dates or raisins
- 2 cups cake flour
- 1 cup sour milk
- ½ teaspoon baking powder

Grind and mix dates or raisins with orange rind as you grind. Work in pecans. Combine orange juice and ¼ cup sugar and set aside. Cream 1 cup sugar with shortening. Add eggs and cream well. Sift flour, measure and sift with baking soda, baking powder and salt. Add alternately with milk to first mixture. Add dates or raisins, rind and pecans to batter. Mix until well blended. Pour into large bundt pan, well oiled and floured on bottom only. Bake at 325 degrees for 1 hour or until done. When half cooled, spoon orange juice and sugar mixture over cake which has been pierced with a fork. Refrigerate if kept for a long period of time.

Wanda R. Atkinson
GFWC—Woman's Club of Steubenville
Steubenville, Ohio

Banana Split Cake

1 stick margarine, melted
2 cups graham cracker crumbs
2 eggs
2 sticks margarine
1 teaspoon vanilla
2 cups powdered sugar
3–5 bananas, sliced
1 20 ounce can crushed pineapple, well drained
1 large container whipped topping
½ cup chopped maraschino cherries
¾ cup chopped pecans

Combine graham cracker crumbs and 1 stick margarine. Pack into a 9 × 13 pan. Beat eggs, 2 sticks margarine and powdered sugar together no less than 15 minutes. Spread over the unbaked crumb crust. Add the sliced bananas and pineapple. Add layer of whipped topping. Top with cherries and pecans. Drizzle chocolate syrup over cream topping. Refrigerate overnight.

Ruth A. Ashmore
GFWC—Flint Hills Club
Manhattan, Kansas

Mincemeat Cake

1 cup mincemeat
¾ cup sugar
1 tablespoon shortening
1 cup water
1½–2 cups flour
1½ teaspoons baking soda
½ teaspoon salt

Cream sugar and shortening. Add mincemeat and water. Mix. Add dry ingredients. Bake 350 degrees in 10-inch greased pan for 30 minutes.

Marguerite Gustafson
GFWC—Mytle Grove Woman's Club
Pensacola, Florida

Fresh Cherry Cake

1⅓ cups sugar
1 cup salad oil
3 cups fresh cherries
3 eggs
3 cups flour
1 teaspoon salt
1 teaspoon baking soda
2 teaspoons vanilla extract
1 cup walnuts

Combine sugar, oil, fruit, nuts and eggs. Sift together flour, salt and baking soda and add to first mixture. Add vanilla. Mix well. Pour in 9 × 13 × 2 pan. Bake at 325 degrees for 45 minutes or until done. May be served as is or frosted with a cream cheese frosting. Other fruits such as rhubarb, blueberries, strawberries or apples may be used in place of cherries. Frozen sweet or sour cherries may be used without thawing, bake a little longer. Sunflower seeds may be used instead of nuts.

Mary Helen Stewart
GFWC—Maquoketa Tuesday Club
Maquoketa, Iowa

Strawberry Cake

- **1 package strawberry flavored gelatin**
- **3 tablespoons flour**
- **1 yellow cake mix**
- **1 cup oil**
- **½ cup water**
- **4 eggs**
- **1 cup nuts, chopped**
- **1 teaspoon almond flavoring**
- **½ box frozen strawberries, thawed**

Mix gelatin and flour. Add remaining ingredients using only enough strawberries for proper batter consistency. Pour into prepared greased and floured, 2 layer, 9-inch pans. Bake in 350 degree oven for 25–30 minutes. Turn layers onto cake rack to cool. Frost with strawberry frosting.

Frosting

- **½ stick oleo**
- **1 box powdered sugar, sifted**
- **Strawberries**

Cream oleo, add sugar and enough strawberries for proper frosting consistency.

Shirley Simmons
GFWC—Lutz-Land O' Lakes Woman's Club
Lutz, Florida

Low Sugar Banana Cake

- **¾ cup sugar**
- **½ cup butter or shortening**
- **2 eggs**
- **2–3 bananas**
- **1 cup buttermilk**
- **1 teaspoon baking soda**
- **1 teaspoon vanilla**
- **2¼ cups flour**
- **1 teaspoon baking powder**
- **½ teaspoon salt**
- **⅔ cup nuts**

Cream sugar and butter together. Add eggs, beating well. Add dry ingredients, sifted together, alternately with buttermilk. Add bananas chopped in chunks, not mashed. Add broken nuts and fold into batter. Add vanilla. Bake in 2 loaf pans or 4 smaller ones that have been sprayed with shortening. Bake 350 degrees for 35 minutes.

Mrs. Charles D. Leonard
GFWC—Progressive Study Club
Normangee, Texas

Orange Slice Candy Fruit Cake

- **3½ cups sifted all-purpose flour**
- **½ teaspoon salt**
- **1 pound orange slice candy, cut in small pieces**
- **8 ounces pitted dates, chopped**
- **2 cups chopped nuts**
- **3¼ ounces flaked coconut**
- **1 cup butter or oleo**
- **2 cups sugar**
- **4 eggs**
- **1 teaspoon baking soda**
- **½ cup buttermilk or ½ cup milk and 1 teaspoon vinegar**
- **1 cup orange juice**
- **2 cups sifted powdered sugar**

Sift together flour and salt and set aside. Combine the orange candy, dates, nuts and coconut. Add to candy mixture ½ cup of flour mixture, mixing well and then set it aside. Cream oleo, adding sugar gradually and then the eggs, one at a time. Beat well. Combine baking soda with the buttermilk. Add flour mixture and buttermilk to sugar alternately, blending well after each addition. Add candy mixture and blend thoroughly. Turn into 10-inch tube pan or 2 loaf pans or 5 small loaf pans 3½ × 7½ which have been greased and floured. Bake at 300 degrees for 1 hour and 45 minutes. Remove from oven. Combine orange juice and powdered sugar. Mix well. Pour over cakes while hot. Let cool in pans. Remove and wrap in plastic wrap and foil. Keep in refrigerator.

Audrey M. Dodge
GFWC—Bradenton Woman's Club, Inc.
Bradenton, Florida

Italian Petal Torte

- **1 package yellow cake mix**
- **1 pound ricotta cheese (Italian cottage cheese)**
- **¼ cup sugar**
- **1 cup heavy cream**
- **1 teaspoon vanilla**
- **1 4 ounce jar red cherries**
- **¼ cup candied orange peel (4 ounce jar)**
- **¼ cup finely diced toasted almonds**
- **½ square semi-sweet chocolate, grated**
- **¼ cup dark rum**

Prepare yellow cake as per printed instructions in two 9-inch layer cake pans. Bake at 350 degrees for 35–40 minutes. Cool completely. Beat ricotta cheese with sugar, 2 tablespoons of the heavy cream and vanilla until smooth. Set remaining cream aside for topping. Set aside eight of the cherries for garnish, then chop remaining. Stir into cheese mixture with orange peel, almonds and grated chocolate. Chill for at least one hour. Split cooled layers, drizzle each with 1 tablespoon rum. Spread 3 layers with cheese mixture, stack together, top with remaining layer. Cover and chill overnight. Just before serving beat remaining cream. Swirl on top of cake. Sliver remaining cherries and arrange in petal fashion on top.

Mary L. Thorne
GFWC—Woman's Club of Easton
Easton, Pennsylvania

Grandma's Irish Christmas Cake

- **1 pound currants**
- **1 pound raisins**
- **1 pound golden raisins**
- **½ pound mixed peel fruit cake mix**
- **4 ounces almonds, chopped**
- **4 ounces cherries, halved**
- **1 apple, diced well**
- **Juice and rind of an orange and lemon**
- **1 pound brown sugar**
- **1 pound butter**
- **Glass whiskey**
- **8 eggs**
- **20 ounces flour**
- **1 teaspoon allspice**
- **½ teaspoon cinnamon**
- **Pinch salt**
- **Vanilla essence**

Wash fruit in warm water and dry well. Put all fruit in a large bowl. Pour all juices and ½ glass of whiskey over fruit and leave overnight. Sift flour and add spice, cinnamon and salt. Beat sugar and butter until soft and creamy. Transfer to a large bowl. Break 1 egg into the mixture. Beat with your fingertips and coat the mixture. Add about 3 large spoonfuls of flour and mix well. Continue alternating until all the eggs and flour have been added to the mixture. This must be done with your fingertips. Now add bowl of fruits and juices and beat entire mixture with a wooden spoon until you feel that you've lost your right arm! Grease an 11-inch square pan or angel food pan. Line with brown paper, then waxed paper; only bottom and sides. Cover mixture in pan with a sheet of brown paper. Bake at 300 degrees for the first 3½ hours. Remove brown paper cover. Reduce heat to 275 degrees and bake an additional 2–2½ hours. Check center with a knitting needle to be sure it's properly baked. Pour ½ glass whiskey on cake when you remove it from the oven. Leave cake in tin overnight. Remove from tin, wrap firmly in foil and store in a cool, dry place until ready to use.

Deirdre M. Schoenster
GFWC—Bethel Woman's Club
Bethel, Connecticut

Rhubarb Cake

- **2 cups diced rhubarb**
- **½ cup sugar**
- **½ cup shortening**
- **1½ cups sugar**
- **1 egg**
- **2 cups flour**
- **½ teaspoon salt**
- **1 teaspoon baking soda**
- **1 teaspoon cinnamon**
- **½ teaspoon nutmeg**
- **1 cup sour milk**
- **1 teaspoon vanilla**

Mix rhubarb and ½ cup sugar together, set aside. Cream sugar and shortening together. Add egg and beat. Sift flour, baking soda, salt and spices. Add to creamed mixture a half cup at a time alternating with ¼ cup of sour milk and the vanilla. Stir well. After the dry ingredients are well mixed, stir in sugared rhubarb mixture. Mix well and pour into greased and floured 13 × 9 × 2 cake pan. Bake for 60 minutes or until done at 375 degrees. Test with toothpick inserted in thickest part of cake. Serve with or without a sour cream frosting.

"My mother gave this recipe to me over 25 years ago and her mother gave it to her—may be 100 years old."

Gloria J. Gregory Gardner
GFWC—Belleville Area Intermediate Study Club
Belleville, Michigan

Fresh Apple Cake

Cake

- **3 eggs**
- **1¼ cups oil**
- **2 cups sugar**
- **2½ cups self-rising flour**
- **2 medium apples, peeled, cored and chopped**
- **1 cup shredded coconut**
- **1 cup chopped walnuts or pecans**

Blend eggs, oil and sugar until creamy. Add flour a little at a time. Blend well. Batter will be stiff. Fold in apples, coconut and nuts. Pour in tube pan and bake for 1 hour at 350 degrees. Remove from pan after 30 minutes.

Topping

- **½ stick oleo**
- **½ cup brown sugar**
- **⅓ cup milk**

Combine all ingredients in a saucepan and bring to a boil for 3 minutes. Pour over cake.

Marie Wilkes
GFWC—Woman's Civic Club of Birmingham
Birmingham, Alabama

Applesauce Cake

- **1 cup shortening**
- **2 cups sugar**
- **2 eggs**
- **3 cups sifted flour**
- **1½ teaspoons nutmeg**
- **1 tablespoon cinnamon**
- **½ teaspoon salt**
- **1 teaspoon cloves**
- **1 tablespoon baking soda**
- **2½ cups applesauce**
- **2 tablespoons white corn syrup**
- **1 cup raisins**
- **1 cup nuts**

Cream shortening, sugar and eggs. Sift together flour, nutmeg, cinnamon, salt, cloves and baking soda. Add alternately with applesauce and white corn syrup. Fold in raisins and nuts. Pour into greased and floured tube or bundt pan and bake at 300 degrees for 1½ hours.

Kathryn Coble
GFWC—Sebastian Junior Woman's Club
Sebastian, Florida

Applesauce Honey Cake

- **¾ cup butter or margarine**
- **½ cup brown sugar, packed**
- **½ cup honey**
- **2 teaspoons baking soda**
- **1 cup all-purpose white flour**
- **1 cup whole wheat flour**
- **1 teaspoon baking powder**
- **2 eggs**
- **2 teaspoons cinnamon**
- **¼ teaspoon nutmeg**
- **⅛ teaspoon cloves**
- **1 cup raisins (soak in hot water a while)**
- **1 cup walnuts**
- **1 1 pound can warm applesauce**

Cream butter and brown sugar. Add honey and mix well. Beat in eggs. Stir together white flour, wheat flour, baking powder, baking soda, cinnamon, nutmeg and cloves several times. Wash and dry raisins on paper towel. Add dry ingredients alternately with warm applesauce to a creamed mixture. Add raisins and nuts. Bake in 9 × 13 pan or glass dish at 310 degrees for 45 minutes.

Lois C. Mills
GFWC—Norwalk Woman's Club
Norwalk, California

Great-Grandmother's Carrot Cake

- **1⅓ cups sugar**
- **1⅓ cups water**
- **1 cup raisins or chopped candied fruit**
- **1 tablespoon butter**
- **2 large finely grated carrots**
- **1 teaspoon cinnamon**
- **1 teaspoon cloves**
- **1 teaspoon nutmeg**
- **1 cup chopped nuts**
- **2½ cups sifted flour**
- **½ teaspoon salt**
- **1 teaspoon baking soda**
- **2 teaspoons baking powder**

In a saucepan combine sugar, water, raisins, butter, carrots and spices. Simmer it together for 5 minutes. Cover and let stand for 12 hours; then add nuts, flour, salt, baking soda and baking powder. Mix well. Bake it in 2 oiled loaf pans or 1 tube pan (9 or 10 inches) at 275 degrees for 2 hours. Cool. Foil wrap. It's fun to make—very different.

Ann E. Kennedy
GFWC—Milford Woman's Club
Milford, New Hampshire

Ruth J. Hafel
GFWC—The Woman's Club of Springfield
Springfield, Illinois

Molasses Zucchini Cake

½ cup oleo
½ cup cooking oil
1¼ cups sugar
2 eggs
1 teaspoon vanilla
¾ cup molasses
½ cup buttermilk
2 cups unpeeled, shredded zucchini
1 cup chopped raisins
2½ cups sifted flour
1 teaspoon baking soda
½ teaspoon baking powder
¼ teaspoon salt
¾ teaspoon cinnamon
½ teaspoon cloves
½ teaspoon nutmeg

Mix oleo, oil, sugar, eggs, vanilla and molasses. Add buttermilk (or whole milk with 1 teaspoon vinegar) and zucchini. Sift dry ingredients and add to mixture. Add chopped raisins. Pour into greased and floured 9 × 13 pan. Sprinkle top with mixture of sugar and cinnamon. Bake at 325 degrees for 45 minutes.

Shirley C. Atwood
GFWC—Norumbega
Bangor, Maine

Zucchini Cake

3 eggs
1 cup oil
2¼ cups sugar
2 cups grated zucchini
1 teaspoon vanilla
3 cups flour
1 teaspoon cinnamon
1 teaspoon salt
1 teaspoon baking soda
1¼ teaspoons baking powder
⅛ teaspoon allspice
Confectioners' sugar

Beat eggs until stiff and foamy. Add oil, sugar, zucchini and vanilla. Mix well. Add flour, cinnamon, salt, baking soda, baking powder and allspice. Mix well. Grease and flour 2 loaf pans or 1 oblong; put in pans and bake at 325 degrees for 1 hour or until done. When completely cooled, sprinkle with confectioners' sugar.

Mary Jo Dellomo
GFWC—Junior Woman's Club of Asbury Park
Asbury Park/Ocean, New Jersey

Candy

Highland Toffee

- 1/3 cup butter
- 2 cups rolled oats
- 1/2 cup brown sugar, packed
- 1/4 cup light corn syrup
- 1/2 teaspoon salt
- 1 1/2 teaspoons vanilla

Melt butter in an 8-inch square pan; add oats and mix well to coat. Mix in sugar and salt, add syrup and vanilla; mix with hands. Pat down solid. Bake at 400 degrees for 10–12 minutes. Cool and cut.

Carlene Garner
GFWC—Woman's Club of Tacoma
Tacoma, Washington

Photo Features: Strawberries (Candy)—Page 297
Lemon or Lime Slice Cookies—Page 316
Truly Fruity Cookies—Page 333

Old English Nut Toffee

- **1 pound butter**
- **1 pound granulated sugar (about 2 cups)**
- **½ cup coarsely chopped almonds**
- **Milk chocolate, optional**

Combine all ingredients in a heavy 3-quart saucepan. Heat slowly over medium heat to boiling point and boil gently until mixture reaches 305 degrees or until golden brown. Stir constantly while candy is cooking. When required temperature is reached, pour out on a well-oiled marble slab or baking sheet. Spread flat with an oiled knife. Let stand several minutes, loosen bottom and mark into squares. Then, if desired, candy may be covered with a thin layer of melted dipping chocolate and sprinkled with finely chopped additional almonds. When cool, carefully break into pieces.

Jean Ness
GFWC—Woman's Club of Falls Church
Falls Church, Virginia

Jean Dawson
GFWC—Franklin Park Woman's Club
Franklin Park, Illinois

Carol Oakland
GFWC—Vistarian
Bisbee, North Dakota

Barbara Cornell
GFWC—Sorosis Club
Starkville, Mississippi

Cracker Jack

- **8 quarts popped popcorn, unsalted (make sure there are no unpopped kernels)**
- **2 cups brown sugar**
- **2 cubes margarine, melted (1 cup)**
- **½ cup white corn syrup**
- **1 teaspoon salt**
- **½ teaspoon baking soda**
- **Unsalted peanuts, optional**

Boil sugar, margarine, syrup and salt for 5 minutes. Add baking soda and stir. Keep popcorn warm in 200 degree oven while making candy. Pour candy over popcorn. Place in roaster pan in 200 degree oven for 1 hour. Stir every 15 minutes to coat and break up. After baked, put on waxed paper to cool.

Corrine Hieb
GFWC—Kirkland Woman's Club
Kirkland, Washington

Microwave Caramel Popcorn

16–20 cups popped corn
1 cup brown sugar
1/4 cup light corn syrup
1/2 teaspoon salt
1/2 cup butter or oleo
1 teaspoon vanilla
1/2 teaspoon baking soda

Spray inside of large paper bag with cooking spray. Add popped corn. Combine sugar, syrup, salt and butter in an 8-cup glass measuring cup. Microwave on high for 2 minutes. Stir and microwave for 3 more minutes. Add vanilla and baking soda; stir well. Pour mixture over popcorn and stir well. Fold top of sack. Place in microwave and cook for 1 minute. Shake and cook for 1 minute. Shake and cook for 30 seconds, shake again and cook for 30 seconds. Pour onto aluminum foil and let cool.

Peggy Hansen
GFWC—Mediapolis Junior Woman's Club
Mediapolis, Iowa

Debra Seeton
GFWC—Knoxville Junior Woman's Club
Knoxville, Illinois

Kathy Countryman
GFWC—Elan Junior Federated Club
Lone Tree, Iowa

Swedish Nuts

3 cups pecan halves
1/2 cup butter
2 egg whites
1 cup sugar
Dash of salt

Melt butter on a cookie sheet in a 325 degree oven. Beat egg whites until stiff. Add sugar and salt. Fold in nuts. Spread this mixture on top of melted butter. Bake at 325 degrees for about 30 minutes, stirring and turning over every 10 minutes until mixture is browned and all butter is used up.

Peggy Carney
GFWC—Woman's Club of Springfield
Springfield, Pennsylvania

Homemade Granola

4 cups rolled oats
1/2 cup sunflower seeds
1/4 cup honey or maple syrup
1/4 cup corn oil
1 teaspoon vanilla
1/2 cup raisins
1/2 cup chopped dates
1/2 cup pecans

In large bowl combine oats, seeds and pecans, mixing well. In another bowl mix syrup, oil and vanilla; add to dry mixture. Mix well and spread out in a shallow baking pan. Set in 325 degree oven and bake for 20 minutes, stirring after 10 minutes. When baking is complete, remove from oven and add raisins and dates.

Lucinda A. Dyer
GFWC—Contemporary Woman's Society of Kingsport
Kingsport, Tennessee

Date Loaf

- **2 cups finely ground pecan meats**
- **¾ cup milk**
- **1 8 ounce package pitted dates**
- **2½ cups sugar**
- **2 tablespoons butter**

Cook sugar and milk to soft ball stage. Add finely chopped dates and stir until well melted. When soft ball stage is reached again, remove the candy from the heat. Add the nuts and butter and stir as long as possible; pour it on a thin cloth that has been wet in cold water. Roll from side to side and work with hands into a long roll. When cold, cut into thin slices.

Marion E. Bedsaul
GFWC—Woman's Club of Lead
Lead, South Dakota

Elsie S. Barnes
GFWC—De Leon Shakespeare Club
De Leon, Texas

Sugarplums

- **1 15 ounce package seedless raisins**
- **1 11 ounce package dried mixed fruits**
- **1 8 ounce package dried figs or pitted prunes**
- **1½ cups chopped walnuts**
- **Sugar**

Chop raisins, mixed fruits, figs or prunes and walnuts in food grinder using coarse blade. Mix thoroughly. Shape mixture into 1-inch balls and roll in sugar. Place in waxed paper and let dry at room temperature 4 hours or overnight. Store tightly covered. If desired, roll in additional sugar just before serving. Makes about 72 balls.

Betty Dance
GFWC—We Moderns Club
Lewistown, Missouri

Unbaked Coconut Drops

- **2 cups brown sugar, packed**
- **½ cup milk**
- **½ cup oleo**
- **3½ cups quick oats**
- **1 teaspoon vanilla**
- **2 cups coconut**
- **1¼ cups English walnuts**

Bring the sugar, milk and oleo to a boil. Remove from stove and add oats, vanilla, coconut and walnuts. Stir well. Drop by spoonfuls on waxed paper and cool. Makes 4 dozen drops.

"This is my own personal recipe and is about 15 years old."

Janice Summers
GFWC—Adrian Woman's Club
Adrian, Michigan

Strawberries

1 cup ground nuts (pecans or English walnuts)
1 can coconut, ground
3/4 cup sweetened, condensed milk
1 teaspoon vanilla
1 6 ounce package strawberry flavored gelatin
Green food coloring
Slivered almonds
Red sugar

Mix green food coloring in small amount of water; add almonds. Soak until green; Spread on paper to dry. Do the day before making the strawberries.

Mix nuts, coconut, condensed milk, vanilla and dry gelatin; refrigerate for at least 1 hour. Roll into ball and form into strawberry shape; roll in red sugar. Insert the green almond slivers into the strawberries. Makes about 50 strawberries. Store in an airtight container.

Florence G. Darnell
GFWC—Rossmoor Woman's Club
Silver Spring, Maryland

Blanch's Texas Amber

22 ounces candied orange slices
2 cups chopped pecans
2 cans sweetened condensed milk
2 small cans coconut
1 teaspoon orange extract
1 teaspoon vanilla extract
1 pound powdered sugar, sifted

Mix all ingredients together, except powdered sugar. Pour into a 13 × 9 × 2 inch glass baking dish, sprayed with cooking spray. Bake at 275 degrees for 30 minutes. Remove from oven; add powdered sugar and mix well. Drop by teaspoons on waxed paper and cool.

Jean Fischer
GFWC—Fairfield History Club
Fairfield, Texas

Pulled Butter Mints

1 cup water
1/4 cup butter
2 cups sugar
8 drops oil of peppermint
3–4 drops food coloring (optional)

Heat water and butter in heavy deep pot over high heat until butter melts. Add sugar and stir until sugar dissolves. Do not stir. Boil rapidly until temperature reaches 260 degrees on candy thermometer or forms a medium-hard ball when dropped into cold water. Pour over buttered marble slab or cold tray. Do not scrape pan. Sprinkle peppermint oil and coloring on syrup. As it cools, pull edges and fold into center of candy. When cool enough, with well-buttered hands, pull and cut with scissors.

Emogene V. Hensley
GFWC—Mooresville Woman's Club
Mooresville, North Carolina

Carrot Fudge

- **1½ cups grated carrots**
- **½ teaspoon lemon extract**
- **3½ cups sugar**
- **½ cup sweetened condensed milk**
- **½ cup water**

Cook carrots, sugar, milk and water to soft ball stage (235 degrees). Remove from stove; add lemon extract and cool to room temperature. Beat until creamy. Pour into buttered pan, pat to 1-inch depth. When firm, cut into squares.

Delva Powers
GFWC—Wichita Delta Hypatia
Wichita, Kansas

Cracker Jack Squares

- **24 saltine crackers**
- **7 tablespoons peanut butter**
- **¼ teaspoon dry ginger**
- **2 cups sugar**
- **⅔ cup milk**

Butter a 9 × 9 inch pan. Crush crackers into fine crumbs with rolling pin. Add peanut butter and ginger; set aside. Boil sugar and milk for just 5 minutes. Remove from heat and add cracker mixture. Mix well. As mixture starts to thicken, pour into prepared pan and cool. Cut into squares.

"Our children discovered this recipe in the United Methodist Jr. Sunday School paper on July 7, 1962."

Alma G. Josbena
GFWC—Towanda Woman's Club
Towanda, Pennsylvania

Hawaiian Fudge

- **2 cups granulated sugar**
- **½ cup crushed pineapple, undrained**
- **½ cup cream (may use half and half or evaporated milk)**
- **1 tablespoon butter or margarine**
- **¼–½ cup nuts, chopped**

Boil together everything but nuts until mixture forms a soft ball in cold water. Tint mixture a pale green. Cool; beat until creamy. Add chopped nuts and pour into a buttered 9 × 11 inch dish. Cool; cut into squares.

"My mother found this recipe in a magazine in 1930 and it has always been a favorite."

Jerrye Jackson
GFWC—Century Study Club
Quanah, Texas

Dream Fudge

- **1 cup chopped nuts or coconut**
- **1 stick oleo**
- **1 12 ounce package real chocolate chips**
- **1 teaspoon vanilla**
- **2 cups sugar**
- **16 marshmallows**
- **1 cup evaporated milk**

In large mixing bowl, combine nuts or coconut, oleo, chocolate chips and vanilla. Set aside. In large, heavy saucepan, combine sugar, marshmallows and milk and bring to boil. Stir constantly for 10 minutes. Combine with other mixture and beat until thick. Drop by teaspoon onto waxed paper; cool in refrigerator.

Carolyn S. Warbritton
GFWC—Gateway Woman's Club
Jacksonville, Florida

Heavenly Fudge

- **½ cup cocoa**
- **3 cups sugar**
- **⅛ teaspoon salt**
- **1½ cups milk**
- **¼ cup margarine**
- **1 teaspoon vanilla**
- **3 pounds peanut butter**

Combine dry ingredients in a heavy 4-quart saucepan. Stir in milk; bring to a bubbly boil on medium heat, stirring constantly. Boil without stirring to 234 degrees (soft ball stage). Remove from heat and stir in peanut butter until fudge is cool and getting thick. Pour onto a lightly buttered platter. With greased hands, push fudge into a 1-inch thick large square.

Lucille Chandler
GFWC—Clay County Woman's Club
Clay, West Virginia

Rena's Peanut Butter Fudge

- **2 cups sugar**
- **⅔ cup evaporated milk**
- **1 cup marshmallow cream**
- **1 cup peanut butter (creamy)**
- **1 teaspoon vanilla**

Mix sugar and evaporated milk in a heavy saucepan, cook until soft ball stage. Remove from heat and add marshmallow cream, peanut butter and vanilla. Mix until well blended. Pour into a buttered 8 × 8 inch pan. Cool and cut into desired size squares. Hint: Try not to scrape sugar crystals into candy while cooking.

Although this is a fairly modern recipe, it has been used every holiday season for about 30 years.

Hannesina Gates Shafer
GFWC—Woman's Literary Club
Shubert, Nebraska

Marie's Chocolate Fudge

- **2 cups sugar**
- **1 block German sweet chocolate**
- **2 tablespoons white syrup**
- **½ cup milk**
- **1 stick butter**
- **2 teaspoons vanilla**
- **1 cup chopped pecans or walnuts (optional)**
- **Pinch of salt**

Combine sugar, chocolate, syrup, milk and ½ stick butter. Cook, stirring constantly, until all ingredients are dissolved and mixture starts boiling. Reduce heat and cook until it forms a hard ball in cold water (about 15 minutes). Add vanilla and ½ stick butter. Add nuts and beat until it loses glossy look; pour into a greased pan. Cool and cut into squares.

"My Aunt Marie has made this fudge since the 1930's."

Alice R. Robertson
GFWC—Norlina Woman's Club
Norlina, North Carolina

Microwave Fudge

- **1 12 ounce package chocolate chips**
- **1 can sweetened condensed milk**
- **1½–2 cups chopped pecans**

Combine chocolate chips and milk; heat in microwave on high for 20 to 30 seconds. Stir; return to oven for another 30 seconds. Stir; add pecans and spread hurriedly into a buttered 9-inch square pan. Cool and cut into squares. Makes about 20 squares.

Bonnie Warth
GFWC—Ozona Woman's Forum
Ozona, Texas

Nut Goodie Bars

- **1 12 ounce package chocolate chips**
- **1 12 ounce package butterscotch chips**
- **2 cups peanut butter (crunchy)**
- **1 cup margarine**
- **½ cup evaporated milk**
- **1 3 ounce package vanilla pudding**
- **2 pounds powdered sugar**
- **1 pound peanuts**
- **1 teaspoon vanilla**
- **1 tablespoon maple flavoring**

Butter a 15 × 10 × 1 inch jelly roll pan. Melt both kinds of chips in microwave. Stir in peanut butter. Spread half of mixture in bottom of pan and chill. Keep remaining mixture over hot water or in oven. Melt margarine in saucepan; slowly add evaporated milk; stir in pudding mix, cook, stirring constantly until slightly thickened (do not boil). Remove from heat; stir in flavorings and powdered sugar. Carefully spread mixture over chilled chocolate layer. Put peanuts on top. Chill 30 minutes. Spread reserved chocolate mixture over to cover. Chill; cut into 1-inch squares. Refrigerate.

Adalyn Schoonover
GFWC—Lisbon Woman's Club
Lisbon, North Dakota

Butterscotch Candy Lollipops

- **2 cups granulated sugar**
- **1 cup cold water**
- **⅔ cup light corn syrup**
- **¼ teaspoon salt**
- **6 tablespoons butter**
- **1 teaspoon vanilla**

Mix sugar, water, corn syrup and salt. Place in large pot over medium/high heat and boil to 270 degrees on candy thermometer. Stir in butter. Stir until temperature reaches 300 degrees. Remove from heat. Add vanilla. Pour immediately into greased, small metal molds or onto baker's parchment. Add sticks and remove from molds while still warm. If using parchment, butterscotch may be marked into small squares while hot then broken when cooled.

"During the Depression years, a neighbor made and sold these lollipops at Eastertime."

Petey Semmens
GFWC—Escanaba
Escanaba, Michigan

Foolproof Pastel Divinity

- **3 cups sugar**
- **¾ cup white corn syrup**
- **¾ cup water**
- **2 egg whites**
- **1 3 ounce package desired flavored gelatin**
- **1 cup chopped nuts**
- **½ cup grated coconut**
- **1 teaspoon vanilla**

Mix sugar, syrup and water. Cook over medium heat, stirring until sugar dissolves. Cook to a hard ball stage. Beat egg whites until they fluff up. Gradually add dry gelatin, beating until mixture holds peak. Pour syrup into egg white mixture, beating constantly until candy holds shape and loses gloss. Fold in nuts, coconut and vanilla. Drop from spoon onto waxed paper or quickly pour into an 8-inch square, buttered pan. Let stand until set. Cut into pieces with knife dipped in hot water.

Zoie McClendon
GFWC—Mothers Study Club
Weatherford, Oklahoma

Cinnamon Candy—Firestick

- **4 cups white sugar**
- **2 cups water**
- **1½ cups white corn syrup**
- **1½ teaspoons red food coloring**
- **1 teaspoon cinnamon oil**

Combine sugar, water and syrup. Do not stir before or during cooking. Boil rapidly to hard crack stage. Add food coloring and cinnamon oil. Pour mixture quickly onto lightly greased pan (jelly roll pan with sides can be used). Score as soon as candy sets. When it hardens, break along score lines. You may also use green food coloring and mint or anise flavoring.

Leila Pelton
GFWC—X—Junior Woman's Club
Cheyenne, Wyoming

Chocolate Truffles

- ⅔ cup whipping cream
- 3 tablespoons unsalted butter
- 1 tablespoon sugar
- 6 1 ounce squares semi-sweet chocolate, chopped
- 2 tablespoons desired liqueur
- Cornstarch
- 1 pound dipping chocolate, cut up

In a 1-quart pan, combine cream, butter and sugar. Cook and stir until butter is melted and mixture is very hot. Remove from heat and stir in chocolate. Mix until melted. Stir in liqueur. Transfer mixture to a chilled bowl, cover and chill 1 hour or until completely cool, stirring often. Drop mixture from rounded teaspoon onto baking sheet lined with waxed paper. Chill 30 minutes or until firm. Roll balls in cornstarch, brush off excess and dip in melted dipping chocolate.

Carlene Garner
GFWC—Woman's Club of Tacoma
Tacoma, Washington

Martha Washington Creams

- 2 sticks butter, melted
- 2 boxes confectioners' sugar
- 1 can sweetened condensed milk
- 1 teaspoon vanilla
- 1 cup coconut
- 2 cups chopped pecans
- 1 cup chopped cherries
- 1 block paraffin wax
- 2 6 ounce packages chocolate chips

Mix all ingredients except wax and chocolate and place in refrigerator overnight. Next morning, melt in top of double boiler, paraffin wax and chocolate chips. Roll refrigerated mixture into balls and dip in chocolate. Place on waxed paper until dry. Store in airtight containers in the refrigerator. Makes 5–6 dozen balls.

Lynda Swetz
GFWC—Arlington Junior Woman's Club
Jacksonville, Florida

Cherry Drops

- 4 tablespoons melted butter
- 2 cups powdered sugar
- 1 cup chopped walnuts
- 1 cup shredded coconut
- 1 cup maraschino cherries, drained and chopped
- ⅔ cup peanut butter
- 2½–3½ tablespoons paraffin
- 1 package chocolate chips

Mix together butter, sugar, walnuts, coconut, cherries and peanut butter. Shape into small balls. In a double boiler, melt paraffin and chocolate chips. Dip balls into melted wax and chocolate. Put on waxed paper to harden.

Bonnie J. Walden
GFWC—Battle Ground
Battle Ground, Washington

Peanut Butter Delights

- 1 2½ pound jar of creamy peanut butter
- 2 pounds powdered sugar
- 1 pound softened butter
- 2 semi-sweet chocolate squares
- 1 12 ounce bag chocolate chips
- 1 German sweet chocolate bar
- ½ square paraffin

Cream butter and peanut butter. Add powdered sugar a little at a time until mixture will form a small ball without sticking to your hands. Roll into small balls. Place on a cookie sheet and refrigerate. Melt chocolate and paraffin over double boiler. Insert a toothpick into a ball and dip into chocolate, leaving the top free of chocolate. Return ball to cookie sheet and place in refrigerator to harden chocolate. Makes about 200 balls.

Louise A. Martin
GFWC—Kewaskum Junior Woman's Club
Kewaskum, Wisconsin

Peanut Butter Balls

- 2 cups peanut butter
- 2 cups powdered sugar
- 4 tablespoons butter or margarine
- 3 cups rice cereal
- 1 cup shredded coconut
- 1 12 ounce package chocolate chips
- ⅓ bar paraffin, grated

Mix peanut butter, sugar and butter as you would pie dough. Add cereal and coconut. Make into balls the size of a walnut and cool in refrigerator several hours or overnight. Melt chocolate chips and wax in top of double boiler over hot water. Dip balls in melted chocolate and let set on waxed paper. Store in covered container. Makes about 5 dozen balls.

Grace Kelley
GFWC—Centralia Reading Circle
Centralia, Kansas

Firm Ball Caramels Candy

- 2 cups sugar
- 2 cups cream
- 1¾ cups corn syrup
- 1 cup butter or butter substitute
- 1 cup chopped nuts (optional)
- Few grains salt

Boil all ingredients together except the nuts and 1 cup cream. Boil 30 minutes. Add the second cup of cream and boil to a firm ball stage, 248 degrees. Add nuts and pour without stirring into well-buttered pan. When cold, cut into squares.

Edith Fuller
GFWC—Tuesday Study Club
Saginaw, Michigan

Kentucky Bourbon Pralines

- **2 cups white sugar**
- **1 cup buttermilk**
- **1 teaspoon baking soda**
- **2 tablespoons margarine or butter**
- **2½ cups pecans**
- **5 tablespoons Kentucky bourbon**

Dissolve sugar in the buttermilk to which has been added the baking soda. Bring to boil, 210 degrees on candy thermometer. Add margarine and pecans. Again, bring to a boil and boil to 230 degrees. Remove from fire and let set 1 minute. Add bourbon. Stir vigorously until alcohol burns off from heat of sugar mix. Drop onto waxed paper with a soup spoon or tablespoon. Makes about 36.

Elizabeth H. Espinosa
GFWC—Takoma Park Woman's Club
Washington, D.C.

Donna F. G. Corrado
GFWC—Mexico Civic Club
Mexico, Missouri

Pralines

- **1 cup light brown sugar**
- **1 cup white sugar**
- **⅔ cup evaporated milk**
- **1 cup pecans, broken into pieces**
- **2 tablespoons butter**
- **½ teaspoon vanilla**

Mix sugars and milk in heavy saucepan and cook to thread stage over medium heat, 25 minutes. Add pecans, butter and vanilla and cook to soft ball stage. Remove from heat and beat with spoon until creamy. Drop by spoonfuls on foil sprayed lightly with cooking spray. Test first praline; if it hasn't set, beat a little longer.

Linda P. Bruggers
GFWC—Cary Juniors
Cary, North Carolina

Unusual Pecan Clusters

- **1 pound white almond bark**
- **1 pound chocolate almond bark**
- **1 12 ounce package semi-sweet chocolate chips**
- **6 cups coarsely chopped pecans**

Melt white bark, chocolate bark and chocolate chips in the top of a double boiler. When melted, stir in pecans and drop on waxed paper.

Janice R. Elliott
GFWC—Hiawatha Progressive Club
Hiawatha, Kansas

Pecan Cream Candy

- 3 cups white sugar
- 1 cup white corn syrup
- 1 pint cream
- ½ pound whole pecans
- ½ teaspoon salt

Mix all ingredients together. Bring to a boil, reduce heat to low and cook slowly for about an hour, or until a little dropped in cold water forms a firm, soft ball. Remove from heat and beat immediately until very stiff. Turn out on table and knead until smooth. It may be pressed into a buttered pan and cut in squares or formed into rolls and sliced when cool. Rolls wrapped in foil will keep indefinitely in refrigerator. Remove as needed, bring to room temperature and slice. Makes about 3½ pounds.

"This is a very old recipe, collected by Ruth Dawson and published in a candy making bulletin she put out while a foods extension specialist at North Dakota State University. Miss Dawson, now deceased, served in that post for many years and was a GFWC member in Fargo."

Lois E. Trapp
GFWC—Clio Club
Enderlin, North Dakota

Peanut Brittle Candy

- 2 cups white sugar
- 1 cup water
- 1 cup white corn syrup
- 1 pound raw peanuts
- ½ teaspoon salt
- 1 heaping teaspoon baking soda
- 1 tablespoon butter
- 1 teaspoon vanilla

Mix sugar, water and syrup and bring to a boil at 250 degrees on a candy thermometer. Put peanuts in candy mixture and boil to 290 degrees. Remove from heat and add salt, baking soda, butter and vanilla. Pour on greased baking sheet.

Edith Fuller
GFWC—Tuesday Study Club
Saginaw, Michigan

Yummy Nut Brittle

- **1 cup sugar**
- **½ cup white corn syrup**
- **1 cup nuts (may use peanuts, almonds, pecans or walnuts)**
- **1 teaspoon butter**
- **1 teaspoon vanilla extract (use almond extract if using almonds)**
- **1 teaspoon baking soda**

In 1½-quart casserole, stir together sugar and syrup. Microwave on high for 4 minutes. Stir in nuts. Microwave on high 3–5 minutes or until light brown. Add butter and vanilla; blend well. Microwave on high 1–2 minutes. Nuts will be lightly browned and the syrup very hot. Add baking soda; stir gently until mixture is light and foamy. Pour onto a lightly greased cookie sheet. Let cool ½ to 1 hour. When the brittle is completely cooled, break into small pieces. Store in an airtight container.

Gloria J. Gregory Gardner
GFWC—Belleville Area Intermediate Study Club
Belleville, Michigan

Sauerkraut Candy

- **2 cups light brown sugar, firmly packed**
- **2 cups white sugar**
- **¼ cup light corn syrup**
- **1⅓ cups half and half**
- **½ stick butter**
- **¼ teaspoon salt**
- **1 teaspoon vanilla**
- **1½ cups shredded coconut**

Combine sugars, syrup, half and half in a 3-quart saucepan with buttered sides. Cook over medium-high heat, stirring until sugar is dissolved. Continue cooking to the soft ball stage (242 degrees). Remove from heat and add butter and salt. Cool to lukewarm. Add vanilla and beat until creamy; mixture becomes opaque and loses gloss. Fold in coconut all at once. Pour into a buttered and chilled platter or into an 8 inch square pan. Makes about 2¼ pounds.

"This candy was very popular in the Midwest during the Gay Nineties and was sold from barrels in grocery stores. After World War I, for reasons unknown, it disappeared. This recipe was given to me by my mother and from her mother."

Mary Alice Day
GFWC—The Woman's Club of New Port Richey
New Port Richey, Florida

Cookies

Overnight Macaroons

- 4 cups quick-cooking oatmeal
- 2 cups brown sugar
- 1 cup salad oil
- 2 beaten eggs
- 1 teaspoon salt
- 1 teaspoon almond extract

On the night before, mix the first 3 ingredients. The next morning mix in the remaining ingredients. Drop them from a teaspoon onto a greased baking sheet and bake at 325 degrees for 15 minutes.

"They have a chewy texture, almond-macaroon taste."

Suzanne Fain
GFWC—Willows Monday Afternoon Club
Willows, California

"Almond Joy" Bars

- 1 6 ounce package chocolate chips
- 1 8 ounce package cream cheese
- ⅔ cup evaporated milk
- 1 cup coconut
- ½ teaspoon almond extract
- 4 cups flour
- 1½ cups sugar
- 1 teaspoon baking powder
- ½ teaspoon salt
- 1 cup softened margarine
- 2 eggs
- Additional ½ teaspoon almond extract

Combine chocolate chips, cream cheese, and evaporated milk in a glass bowl and microwave until chips melt. Add coconut and ½ teaspoon almond extract; mix well. Combine flour, sugar, baking powder, salt, margarine, eggs and other ½ teaspoon almond extract. Mix until crumbly. Place ½ of crumbly mixture in a greased 9 × 13-inch pan. Spread chocolate mixture over first layer, then top with the rest of the crumbly mixture. Bake at 375 degrees for 35 minutes. Cool and cut into bars.

Carole E. Ellingsworth
GFWC—Durant Woman's Club
Durant, Iowa

Double Chocolate Crumb Bars

- ½ cup butter or margarine
- ¾ cup sugar
- 2 eggs
- 1 teaspoon vanilla
- ¾ cup all-purpose flour
- ½ cup chopped pecans
- 2 tablespoons unsweetened cocoa powder
- ¼ teaspoon salt
- ¼ teaspoon baking powder
- 2 cups tiny marshmallows
- 1 6 ounce package (1 cup) semi-sweet chocolate pieces
- 1 cup peanut butter
- 1½ cups crisp rice cereal

Cream butter or margarine and sugar; beat in eggs and vanilla. Stir together flour, chopped nuts, cocoa, baking powder and ¼ teaspoon salt—stir into egg mixture. Spread in bottom of greased 13 × 9 × 2-inch baking pan. Bake in a 350 degree oven for 15 to 20 minutes or until bars test done. Sprinkle marshmallows evenly on top; bake 3 minutes more. Cool. In small saucepan, combine chocolate pieces and peanut butter; cook and stir over low heat until chocolate is melted. Stir in cereal. Spread mixture on top of cooled bars, chill, and cut into bars. Refrigerate. Makes 3 to 4 dozen.

Edna Sokolich
GFWC—Woman's Club of Lacey
Forked River, New Jersey

Pineapple Brownies

- **1½ cups flour, sifted**
- **1 teaspoon baking powder**
- **½ teaspoon salt**
- **½ teaspoon cinnamon**
- **¾ cup butter or margarine**
- **1½ cups sugar**
- **3 eggs**
- **1 teaspoon vanilla**
- **1 cup pineapple chunks**
- **2 squares unsweetened chocolate**

Cream butter with sugar and add eggs one at a time; add vanilla. Blend in dry ingredients and mix well. Put 1 cup batter in second bowl and add to it: 1 cup well-drained pineapple chunks cut in two. To first bowl add: 2 squares unsweetened chocolate, melted. Put 1½ cups of chocolate mixture in greased 9 × 13-inch pan, cover with white mixture. Drop remaining chocolate dough over it. Bake at 350 degrees for 45 minutes. Frost with chocolate frosting. Freezes well.

Barbara S. Brubakken
GFWC—Monday Night Study Club
Hoople, North Dakota

Peppermint Brownies

- **2 eggs**
- **½ cup buttermilk**
- **¼ teaspoon cinnamon**
- **Dash of salt**
- **2 cups sugar**
- **2 cups flour**
- **1 teaspoon baking soda**
- **1 teaspoon vanilla**
- **1 stick margarine**
- **1 cup water**
- **½ cup oil**
- **4 tablespoons cocoa**

Beat together first 4 ingredients. Add sugar, flour, soda and vanilla. Bring to a boil the margarine, water, oil and cocoa. Add to first mixture. Put in an 18 × 12 × 1-inch pan or 13 × 8½ × 2-inch and 8 × 5½ × 2-inch pans (2 pans). Bake in a 400 degree oven for 20 minutes or until done to touch.

Topping

- **8 tablespoons butter**
- **4 cups powdered sugar**
- **4 tablespoons cream**
- **1 teaspoon peppermint flavoring**
- **A few drops green food coloring**
- **4 squares semi-sweet chocolate**
- **4 tablespoons melted butter**

Mix butter, powdered sugar, cream, peppermint flavoring and green food coloring. Mix until creamy and spread on cooled brownies. Refrigerate after topping. Melt together semi-sweet chocolate and melted butter. Cool slightly to prevent melting of peppermint layer. Spread quickly and evenly on peppermint frosting. Chill partially and then cut in desired pieces. Store in refrigerator until ready to use or it may be frozen.

Melva Splitter
GFWC—Lyons Li-Ar-Mu
Lyons, Kansas

Peanut Butter Bars

- **1 cup flour**
- **1 cup quick-cooking oats**
- **1 cup chocolate chips**
- **¼ cup brown sugar**
- **½ cup butter or margarine**

Preheat oven to 350 degrees. In medium bowl, combine flour, oats, and brown sugar. Cut in butter until mixture resembles a fine meal. Press into bottom of a 9-inch square pan. Bake at 350 degrees for 20–25 minutes or until slightly browned. Sprinkle chocolate chips over hot crust; return to oven until chips have softened, about 1 minute. Spread chips over crust. Cool slightly.

Topping

- **½ cup sugar**
- **½ cup honey**
- **½ cup instant nonfat dry milk powder**
- **¾ cup peanut butter**
- **2 cups rice cereal**
- **1 cup chopped peanuts**

Topping: In medium saucepan, combine sugar and honey; heat to rolling boil. Remove from heat; stir in nonfat dry milk powder and peanut butter until smooth. Stir in rice cereal and ½ of the peanuts. Spread topping over chocolate layer. Sprinkle with remaining peanuts. Let bars set before cutting.

Martha Phillips
GFWC—Pierson Study Club
Pierson, Iowa

Lemon Love Notes

- **¼ cup butter**
- **¼ cup powdered sugar**
- **½ teaspoon baking powder**
- **1 cup flour**
- **2 tablespoons lemon juice**
- **2 eggs**
- **1 teaspoon grated lemon rind**
- **¼ teaspoon salt**
- **2 tablespoons flour**
- **1 cup sugar**

Cream butter and powdered sugar; add flour and baking powder to make a stiff batter. Press into an unbuttered, nine-inch square pan. Bake 15 minutes at 350 degrees. Cool. Beat eggs with 1 cup sugar, mix well with remaining ingredients. Pour over crust and bake 25 minutes at 350 degrees. Cool.

Frosting

- **¾ cup powdered sugar**
- **2 teaspoons milk**
- **½ teaspoon vanilla**

Frost with powdered sugar, milk and vanilla. Cut into 16 small squares.

Leona Berry
GFWC—Manlius Woman's Club
Manlius, Illinois

Coconutty Oat Bars

¾ cup soft butter
⅔ cup packed brown sugar
1 egg
1 teaspoon vanilla
⅔ cup flour
½ teaspoon baking powder
½ teaspoon salt
2 cups oats, uncooked
1 3½ ounce can flaked coconut
½ cup chopped walnuts
½ cup chopped dates

Beat soft butter and sugar until light and fluffy. Blend in egg and vanilla. Add combined flour, baking powder and salt; mix well. Stir in remaining ingredients. Spread into well-greased 15 × 10 × 1-inch jelly roll pan. Bake in 350 degree oven for 20 minutes or until golden brown. Cool; cut into 2 × 3-inch bars.

Jane Pickens
GFWC—Newton Junior Woman's Club
Newton, Illinois

Easy Almond Bars

2 sticks oleo
1 cup or 8 ounce can almond paste
2 eggs, beaten
2 cups sugar
¼ teaspoon salt
¼ teaspoon almond flavoring
2 cups flour
¼ teaspoon vanilla

Melt oleo, add almond paste and beat well. Add eggs and beat again. Stir in sugar, salt, almond flavoring, flour, and vanilla. Spread into 9 × 13-inch pan and sprinkle with sugar. Bake at 300 degrees until golden brown, 40 to 45 minutes. Cool and cut into bars.

"I received this recipe from an elderly lady whose parents came from the Netherlands."

Arvonne Van Hemert
GFWC—Pella Woman's Federated Club
Pella, Iowa

Ho-Made Heath Bar Cookies

2 sticks or ½ pound butter, not margarine
1 cup brown sugar
35 soda crackers
1 12 ounce package semi-sweet chocolate chips
⅓ cup chopped pecans

Line jelly-roll pan, or cookie sheet with sides, with whole crackers. Over low heat, melt butter and stir in brown sugar. Mix thoroughly. Pour mixture over crackers and spread to cover completely. Bake at 350 degrees for 7 minutes. Remove from oven, sprinkle with chocolate chips and return to oven for 1 minute. Remove, spread chocolate evenly and sprinkle with nuts. Chill and cut into bars.

Sarah A. Higginbotham
GFWC—The Friday Literary Club of Saint Louis
Saint Louis, Missouri

Spicy Apple Bars

1½ cups flour
½ cup oatmeal
¾ cup brown sugar
½ cup butter, softened

Filling

1½ cups brown sugar
¼ teaspoon salt
1 teaspoon cream of tartar
1 teaspoon cinnamon
½ teaspoon nutmeg
¼ teaspoon cloves
½ cup quick cooking oats
¼ cup butter, softened
2 cups apples, diced
½ cup chopped pecans

Blend crust ingredients; press in bottom of 9 × 13-inch pan.

Combine first 8 filling ingredients; add apples and nuts. Toss to coat with mixture. Spread evenly on top of crust. Bake in 350 degree oven until brown, about 40–45 minutes. Cool slightly; cut into bars.

Dorothy Englund
GFWC—Golden Valley Woman's Club
Golden Valley, Minnesota

Sour Cream Raisin Bars

2 cups raisins
1 cup brown sugar
1 cup butter
1¾ cups quick cooking oats
1 teaspoon soda
1¾ cups flour
3 egg yolks
1½ cups sour cream
1 cup sugar
2½ tablespoons cornstarch
1 teaspoon vanilla

Cook raisins in water to cover for 10 minutes. Drain and let cool while mixing remainder of bars. Cream together brown sugar and butter. Add oats, soda and flour. Mix well. Put one-half of mixture into a greased 9 × 13-inch pan. Press down and bake for 7 minutes at 350 degrees. In a heavy saucepan, combine egg yolks, sour cream, sugar and cornstarch. Cook, stirring constantly, until mixture boils and thickens. Add raisins and vanilla. Pour over crust and top with remaining crumbs. Bake 30 minutes at 350 degrees. Cool and cut into bars. Refrigerate to store.

Anita Hamm
GFWC—Nemaha Federated Woman's Club
Nemaha, Iowa

Betty Peterson
GFWC—Semper Fidelis
Northwood, Iowa

Loretta Engelbart
GFWC—Leigh Woman's Club
Leigh, Nebraska

Cheryl Christianson
GFWC—Halstad Woman's Club
Halstad, Minnesota

Ardis Tunberg
GFWC—Zehlian Art & Book Club
Thief River Falls, Minnesota

Chocolate-Peanut Butter-Oatmeal Bars

- **1 cup butter**
- **1⅓ cups dark brown sugar**
- **¾ cup white corn syrup**
- **5⅓ cups quick-cooking oats**
- **2 teaspoons vanilla**

Grease 13 × 9-inch baking pan. Heat oven to 350 degrees. Beat butter and sugar until fluffy. Stir in corn syrup, oatmeal and vanilla. Butter hands and pat mixture evenly in pan. Bake 16 minutes. Don't overbake. Mixture will still look moist in center. Cool pan on rack until lukewarm; spread warm glaze over top. Cool completely before cutting.

Glaze

- **1 12 ounce package semi-sweet chocolate bits**
- **1 cup creamy peanut butter**

In a small saucepan, over low heat, melt chocolate until smooth and add peanut butter. Blend until smooth.

Irene Paysou
GFWC—Woman's Community Club of Union
Union, Maine

Nutritious Chocolate Chip Bars

- **2½ cups flour (half regular, half whole wheat)**
- **2 cups brown sugar**
- **1 teaspoon baking soda**
- **½ teaspoon salt**
- **1 cup margarine, softened**
- **2 teaspoons vanilla**
- **2 eggs**
- **2 cups quick-cooking oats**
- **1 12 ounce package chocolate chips**
- **½ cup nuts or sunflower seeds**

Optional

- **½ cup peanut butter**
- **½ cup flaked coconut**
- **½ cup nonfat dry milk**
- **½ cup wheat germ**

Grease a 15½ × 10½-inch jelly roll pan. In large bowl, combine all ingredients except oats, chocolate chips and nuts. Beat at medium speed until well blended. Stir in oats. Stir two of the optional ingredients into dough. Add remaining ingredients. Bake at 375 degrees for 15–20 minutes or until edges are golden brown (center is soft). Cool. Cut into bars.

Kay Walter
GFWC—Keystone AOK
Muscatine, Iowa

Walnut Chews

1 cup flour
½ cup butter
2 tablespoons sugar

Filling

2 eggs
1½ cups brown sugar
½ tablespoon vanilla
1 cup maraschino cherries, cut and drained
1 cup broken English walnuts
½ cup flaked coconut
2 tablespoons flour
½ teaspoon baking powder
Pinch of salt

These cakes are made in two parts. Mix flour, butter and sugar and pack in baking pan (8 × 10). Bake at 250 degrees for 20 minutes.

Mix eggs, brown sugar, vanilla, cherries, walnuts, coconut, flour, baking powder and salt. Pour over baked ingredients. Return to oven at 350 degrees for an additional 30 minutes. Cool for ½ hour and cut in squares of desired size.

"Old family recipe."

Marie J. Hammond
GFWC—Woman's Club of Columbia
Columbia, South Carolina

Pecan Surprise Bars

1 package yellow cake mix
½ cup butter, softened
1 egg
1 cup chopped pecans

Grease bottom and sides of 13 × 9-inch pan. Reserve ⅔ cup dry cake mix for filling. In large mixing bowl, combine remaining dry cake mix, butter and egg; mix until crumbly. Press in prepared pan. Bake at 350 degrees for 20–30 minutes, until light golden brown. Meanwhile, prepare filling. Pour filling over partially baked crust; sprinkle with pecans. Return to oven and bake for 30–35 minutes, until filling is set. Cool, cut into 36 bars.

Filling

⅔ cup reserved cake mix
½ cup packed brown sugar
1½ cups dark corn syrup
1 teaspoon vanilla
3 eggs

In large mixing bowl, combine all ingredients; beat at medium speed 1–2 minutes.

Voni Lindgren
GFWC—Rochester Woman's Club
Rochester, Illinois

Eunice C. Crocker
GFWC—Fort Jones Federated Woman's Club
Fort Jones, California

Raspberry Marzipan

1¼ cups flour
⅓ cup brown sugar, packed
½ cup butter, softened

Filling
¾ cup flour
½ cup brown sugar
¼ cup butter
½ teaspoon almond extract
¾ cup raspberry jelly

Glaze
¾ cup powdered sugar
1 tablespoon milk
1 teaspoon almond extract

Grease and flour 9-inch square pan and preheat oven to 350 degrees. Combine bottom layer ingredients and press into pan. Bake 15–20 minutes or until edges are lightly browned. Spread jelly on hot bottom layer.

Mix filling ingredients and sprinkle over jelly. Return to oven 20–25 minutes.

When marzipan is completely cool, mix glaze and drizzle over marzipan. Cut into about 12 bars and enjoy.

Eileen J. Shaw
GFWC—South Arundel Junior Woman's Club
Harwood, Maryland

Cottage Cheese Cookies

2 cups sifted flour
1 cup butter, no substitutes
1 cup plus 2 tablespoons creamed style, small curd cottage cheese
Raspberry jam

Glaze
1 cup confectioners' sugar
⅛ teaspoon almond extract
Milk

Place flour in medium-sized mixing bowl. Cut in butter as for pie crust. Add cottage cheese until mixture forms a ball. Chill for one hour. Roll out ⅛ inch thick. Cut with a 3-inch cookie cutter. Place ¼ teaspoon jam in the center. Moisten edges. Fold in half. Seal with a fork. Place on greased cookie sheets, prick top with fork. Bake 15 minutes at 400 degrees.

Make glaze with enough milk to spread thinly. Cool cake on rack, then glaze.

Irene Dauphin
GFWC—Altrusa Club
Mooreland, Oklahoma

Rugelach

- 2 cups all-purpose flour
- ½ cup sugar
- 1 8 ounce package cream cheese, well chilled and cut into small pieces
- 1 cup or 2 sticks unsalted butter, well chilled and cut into small pieces

Nut Filling

- ¼ cup sugar
- 2 teaspoons ground cinnamon
- 1 cup chopped nuts
- 2 tablespoons confectioners' sugar for topping

Combine flour and sugar in large bowl. Scatter pieces of cream cheese and butter on top, cut in with pastry blender until texture of fine meal. Rub mixture gently in hands until it forms a soft dough. Shape into ball. Divide dough into 5 equal parts; shape each part into ball. Wrap individually in plastic wrap and chill overnight in refrigerator. Roll balls of dough, one by one, on well-floured pastry cloth with well-floured, stockinette-covered rolling pin into circles slightly larger than 8½ inches in diameter. With well-floured, large, sharp knife, cut each circle into 8 pie-shaped wedges; leave circle intact.

Stir together sugar, cinnamon and nuts in small bowl until well mixed. Sprinkle about 3 tablespoons of filling over each circle. Roll each wedge toward point, pressing point into dough to secure. Arrange cookies, points down, on ungreased baking sheet, spacing about 1 inch apart. Bake in top third of preheated moderate oven, 350 degrees, for 15–18 minutes until light tan. Remove at once to wire rack to cool. Lightly dust cookies with powdered sugar, if you wish. Store in airtight container.

Gussie L. Saperstein
GFWC—Lutz-Land O' Lakes Woman's Club
Lutz-Land O' Lakes, Florida

Lemon or Lime Slice Cookies

- 1 cup softened butter or margarine
- 1 cup sifted powdered sugar
- ¼ teaspoon salt
- ¼ teaspoon yellow or green food coloring
- 2 tablespoons grated lemon rind
- 2½ cups sifted flour

Preheat oven to 375 degrees. Mix butter, sugar, salt, food coloring and lemon rind thoroughly. Add flour and blend well. Roll ¼ inch thick on floured board. Cut into 2-inch circles. Cut circle in half, put on ungreased cookie sheet for 6 minutes in 375 degree oven. Do not brown.

Icing

- 1 egg white
- Lemon juice
- 1 cup powdered sugar

Mix egg white and lemon juice into powdered sugar. With decorator put section lines on half cookie to resemble lemon or lime sections. To make them even more life-like, roll edge in yellow sugar for a rind.

Kay Linton
GFWC—Past AFWC President's Club
Anchorage, Alaska

Hungarian Cookies

3 cups flour
¾ teaspoon cinnamon
1 teaspoon cocoa
1½ cups butter or margarine
1½ cups confectioners' sugar
1½ teaspoons lemon juice
2 cups ground almonds
Raspberry jam

Cream the butter with sugar and lemon juice. Stir in the almonds. Mix in the cinnamon and cocoa and half the flour. Mix in remaining flour. Chill dough for 30 minutes. Roll out on floured surface, one-half at a time, to ¼-inch thickness. Cut with a 2-inch round cookie cutter. Bake on greased cookie sheet in a 325 degree oven for 12 minutes. Cool. Put pairs together sandwich fashion with raspberry jam.

Topping

1 12 ounce package semi-sweet chocolate chips
Slivered almonds, garnish

Melt chocolate chips over hot, not boiling, water and cool slightly. Spread on tops of cookies and garnish with almond slivers.

Betty Silvani
GFWC—Woman's Club of Secaucus
Secaucus, New Jersey

Fold Overs

1 cup butter
1½ cups light brown sugar
2 eggs
1 teaspoon vanilla
1½ cups rolled oats
3¼ cups flour
1 teaspoon soda
1 teaspoon cream of tartar
½ teaspoon salt

Cream butter and brown sugar. Beat in eggs, one at a time. Stir in vanilla and oatmeal. Sift flour, soda, salt and cream of tartar. Add to above and mix in. Chill dough 2 hours or overnight. Roll dough ⅛ inch thick on floured board. Cut with 2½-inch round cookie cutter; scalloped is prettiest. Spread half of each cookie with filling. Fold other half of cookie over filling. No need to seal edges. Bake 8 to 10 minutes at 375 degrees.

Filling

1 8 ounce package dates, chopped
1 cup sugar
1 cup water
1 teaspoon grated orange rind
¾ cup walnuts or pecans

Mix dates, sugar and water. Boil 2 minutes. Beat smooth. Add orange rind and nuts. Cool.

"Have had this recipe for many years."

Grace Anderson
GFWC—Woman's Club of Greene
Greene, Iowa

Original Girl Scout Cookies

- **6 cups flour**
- **2 cups sugar**
- **3 eggs**
- **1½ cups butter**
- **2 teaspoons salt**
- **2 teaspoons vanilla**
- **4 teaspoons baking powder**
- **½ cup milk**

Cream softened butter and sugar in large bowl. Add eggs, milk and vanilla and mix well. In separate bowl, mix flour, salt and baking powder. Add slowly to creamed mixture, mixing well after each addition. Refrigerate for at least two hours. When ready to bake, spoon out enough to roll out on pastry board leaving rest in refrigerator. Roll to ⅛-inch thickness and cut with cookie cutters. Bake at 375 degrees for 6 to 8 minutes. Cool on wire rack. Let cookie sheet cool before putting fresh dough on it.

"In the 1920's, when Girl Scout Cookies were first thought up, a general recipe was handed out to each troop (I was in the Boston area) and each girl made her own, and sold them."

Elizabeth K. Butler
GFWC—Woman's Club of St. Mary's County
Leonardtown, Maryland

Christmas Sugar Cookies

- **1½ cups confectioners' sugar**
- **1 cup butter**
- **1 egg**
- **1 teaspoon vanilla flavoring**
- **½ teaspoon almond flavoring, optional**
- **2½ cups flour**
- **1 teaspoon baking soda**
- **1 teaspoon cream of tartar**

Mix sugar and butter. Add egg and flavoring. Sift the dry ingredients and blend together. Refrigerate. Roll and cut. Bake 375 degrees for 7–8 minutes.

Becky Rugland
GFWC—Bethel Woman's Club
Bethel, Connecticut

Fruit Cookies

3 cups sugar
2 cups butter or oleo
1 cup molasses
6 eggs
8 cups flour
2 teaspoons soda dissolved in a little hot water
2 cups raisins
1 cup currants
1 cup nuts
1 teaspoon salt
1 teaspoon cloves
2 teaspoons cinnamon
Powdered sugar
Orange juice

Beat eggs separately, cream sugar and butter; add molasses. If raisins and currants have been in refrigerator, I usually warm them in microwave a little and sift some flour over them before adding all to dough. Let the dough rest in refrigerator a couple of hours before rolling out. Bake at 350 degrees for 12–15 minutes. Ice the bottom side with a mixture of powdered sugar and orange juice.

"Recipe over 50 years old."

Lucille Fruendt
GFWC—Clintonville Woman's Club
Clintonville, Wisconsin

Ice Box Molasses Cookies

1 cup butter or margarine
2 cups sugar
2 eggs
½ cup molasses
3 scant teaspoons ginger
1 teaspoon salt
1 teaspoon soda
4 cups flour

Mix ingredients together thoroughly. Form into two rolls. Cover with waxed paper and chill in refrigerator until firm. Slice and bake at 350 degrees for 10 minutes.

"My Aunt Rose gave me this recipe 25 years ago. It stores in the refrigerator a week or two."

Corrine Hieb
GFWC—Kirkland Woman's Club
Kirkland, Washington

Aunt Sadie's Skillet Cookies

- **1 egg**
- **½ cup milk**
- **1¼ cups raisins**
- **3½ cups flour, sifted**
- **1 cup sugar**
- **2 teaspoons nutmeg**
- **1½ teaspoons baking powder**
- **1¼ teaspoons salt**
- **½ teaspoon soda**
- **1 cup shortening**

Beat the egg with the milk. Add raisins (may use yellow if you like). Put aside. Sift together all the remaining ingredients, blend the shortening into sifted ingredients. May mix with hands until mealy; pour milk and raisins over flour all at once and mix well with hands. Wrap in waxed paper to chill, at least 1 hour or overnight. Make into 2 rolls with hands. Cut ⅜-inch cookies. Put on oiled pan over low flame. As the bottom browns, the top gets shiny and puffy. Watch as they will burn easily. Turn when bottom is brown. The dough may be kept in refrigerator for several days.

Charlotte D. Connor
GFWC—San Dimas Woman's Club
San Dimas, California

Holiday Ribbons

- **2½ cups sifted flour**
- **⅛ teaspoon salt**
- **½ teaspoon baking powder**
- **1 cup butter or margarine**
- **¾ cup sugar**
- **1 egg, unbeaten**
- **1 teaspoon vanilla extract**
- **¼ cup candied cherries, chopped**
- **1 1 ounce block chocolate, melted**
- **¼ cup walnuts**
- **Red food coloring**

Sift flour, salt and baking powder. Work butter and sugar in bowl until creamy. Stir in egg and vanilla. Gradually add flour mixture. Divide into 3 equal parts: to first add vanilla, to second add cherries and food coloring to tint light pink. Blend chocolate and nuts into the third. Chill until it can be handled. Shape each into 12 × 2 × ½-inch lengths. Put together with pink layer in the center. Chill until firm. Slice in ⅛-inch slices. Bake on ungreased sheets in moderate oven, 350 degrees, for 10 minutes. Cool 5 minutes and remove to rack.

Marian J. Westling
GFWC—Ladies Tourist Club
Henderson, Minnesota

Cherry Nut Slices

- **1 cup softened butter**
- **1 egg**
- **2 tablespoons milk**
- **1 teaspoon vanilla**
- **1 cup confectioners' sugar**
- **2¼ cups flour**
- **2 cups candied cherries, soft**
- **1 cup pecan halves**

Combine all ingredients except cherries and nuts in large bowl. Mix at low speed until dough forms, 1 to 2 minutes. Stir in cherries and nuts. If necessary chill 1 hour. Form dough into 2 10-inch rolls. Wrap and chill 1 to 2 hours. Cut into ¼-inch slices. Place on ungreased cookie sheet. Bake at 400 degrees for 7 to 10 minutes.

Wanda W. Slater
GFWC—Shining Stars
Fairview Park, Ohio

Frosted Cherry Cookies

- **½ cup butter**
- **1 cup sugar**
- **1 egg**
- **1½ cups flour**
- **1½ teaspoons vanilla**
- **½ cup cocoa**
- **¼ teaspoon salt**
- **¼ teaspoon baking soda**
- **¼ teaspoon baking powder**
- **Jar of cherries, drained**
- **1 6 ounce package chocolate chips**
- **2 tablespoons cherry juice**
- **½ cup sweetened, condensed milk**

Mix all except cherries. Shape dough into balls, 1 heaping teaspoon for each. Put onto ungreased cookie sheet two inches apart. Push a cherry into each cookie ball halfway into it. Do not bake.

Frosting

- **1 6 ounce package chocolate bits**
- **2 tablespoons cherry juice**
- **½ cup sweetened condensed milk**

Heat and stir until chocolate is melted. Frost all cookies and then bake at 350 degrees for 8 minutes.

Timmy Milkawski
GFWC—Palm Beach Gardens Woman's Club
Palm Beach Gardens, Florida

Saint-Emilion's Demise

- **4 cups flour**
- **1 cup sugar**
- **½ teaspoon baking soda**
- **2 teaspoons baking powder**
- **2 teaspoons cloves**
- **½ cup margarine**
- **1 cup milk**
- **3 shots cognac**

Sift all dry ingredients together in a large mixing bowl. In another bowl, combine melted margarine, milk and cognac. Add liquid to sifted ingredients and mix. Roll dough into bite-size balls and place on a cookie sheet. Bake at 350 degrees for 15–20 minutes. Cool.

Frosting

- **4 tablespoons cognac**
- **1 package powdered sugar**
- **5 tablespoons margarine**
- **1 teaspoon vanilla**
- **½ cup cocoa**
- **Cold black coffee**

To make frosting, mix all ingredients except the coffee. Add coffee to arrive at desired consistency. Add cognac to taste. Frost one at a time; cookies can be swirled if frosting is made to glaze consistency. When frosting hardens, store in airtight container.

Michele T. Yackopcic
GFWC—Country Shore Woman's Club
Marmora-Upper Township, New Jersey

Melting Moments

½ cup cornstarch
½ cup confectioners' sugar
1 cup sifted flour
¾ cup margarine
1 6 ounce package semi-sweet morsels
½ cup finely chopped walnuts

Sift together cornstarch, sugar and flour. Stir in margarine until a soft dough forms. Chill if necessary. Roll into 1-inch balls. Place on ungreased cookie sheet. Flatten each with a lightly floured fork. Bake 20 minutes at 300 degrees until light brown. Cool. Melt chocolate. Dip into chocolate, then in nuts. Cool on waxed paper.

Annette Castiglione-Degan
GFWC—Haddon Heights Junior Woman's Club
Haddon Heights, New Jersey

Danish Coconut Cookies (Fedtebrod)

2⅔ cups sifted flour
½ pound butter or margarine
1 cup granulated sugar
½ pound shredded coconut

Work all ingredients into a dough. Divide dough into six equal parts and form into long rolls. Place three rolls on each cookie sheet and flatten to about ½ inch thick. Bake in moderate oven, 375 degrees, until slightly browned on the edges. Reverse the two cookie sheets about halfway through baking period. Frost with powdered sugar icing that has been flavored with vanilla or almond flavoring and a bit of water to thin. Cookies should be frosted immediately upon removal from oven and cut into 1-inch strips before cooling.

"This is a very old, traditional Danish cookie recipe."

Esther Jorgensen
GFWC—Hill and Valley Club
Hayward, California

Honey-Pecan Butterballs

1 cup butter
¼ cup honey
2 cups flour
½ teaspoon salt
2 teaspoons vanilla extract
2 cups pecans, finely chopped
Confectioners' sugar

Cream butter. Gradually add honey and beat well. Stir in flour, salt and vanilla. Mix well. Stir in pecans. Form into very small balls, using about 1 rounded teaspoon of dough for each, and place on a lightly greased baking sheet. Bake at 300 degrees for 30 minutes. Roll cookies in confectioners' sugar while still hot, then cool on waxed paper. When cool, roll in confectioners' sugar a second time.

Janet S. Thieme
GFWC—Kalamazoo Junior Woman's Club
Kalamazoo, Michigan

Mint Snowballs

1 cup butter or margarine
½ cup sifted confectioners' sugar
½ teaspoon salt
1 tablespoon water
1 teaspoon vanilla
2 cups sifted flour
1 cup rolled oats
54 red or green candied cherries
2 cups shredded coconut

Combine butter, sugar, salt, water and vanilla extract. Add flour; blend with creamed mixture. Stir in oats. Shape dough around cherries, into balls about 1 inch in diameter. Place on ungreased baking sheet. Bake at 325 degrees for 18–20 minutes. Cool. Dip cooled cookies into frosting, then roll in coconut.

Frosting

2 cups sifted confectioners' sugar
¼ cup milk
Few drops green food coloring
Few drops mint extract

Combine sugar, milk, coloring and extract; beat until smooth. Frosting will be thin.

"At least 40 years old."

Ann Gorthy Maring
GFWC—Nautilus
Bird City, Kansas

Angel Cookies

½ cup butter
½ cup shortening
½ cup brown sugar
½ cup white sugar
1 egg, beaten
2 cups flour
1 teaspoon soda
½ teaspoon cream of tartar
½ teaspoon salt
½ cup nut meats

Cream butter, shortening and sugar. Add ingredients in order given. Use a teaspoon to dip out dough. Roll in ball, dip top half in cold water and then dip in white sugar. Place on greased cookie sheet, sugar side up. Pat flat with fork. Leave space between cookies. Bake at 375 degrees for 8–9 minutes.

"This recipe was submitted to the church cookbook in 1951 by my aunt Josie Robbe."

Jean Ness
GFWC—Woman's Club of Falls Church
Falls Church, Virginia

Sugar Cookies

- **2 cups sugar**
- **1 cup shortening**
- **1 cup sour cream**
- **3 eggs**
- **1 tablespoon buttermilk or sour milk**
- **1 teaspoon baking soda**
- **1 teaspoon baking powder**
- **½ teaspoon salt**
- **2 teaspoons vanilla**
- **About 4 cups flour, enough to stiffen**

Mix above ingredients in order. Add flour last, 1 cup at a time. Add flour until dough begins to get stiff. Place 1 rounded teaspoon of dough on greased cookie sheet. Flatten dough with floured spoon.

Topping

- **¼ cup sugar**
- **1 teaspoon cinnamon**

Sprinkle each cookie with cinnamon and sugar. For a variety—add nuts, mini chocolate chips or coconut to dough.

Patti L. Vincent
GFWC—Junior Woman's Club of Milton
Milton, Pennsylvania

Mom's Peanut Butter Cookies

- **¼ cup margarine**
- **½ cup butter-flavored shortening**
- **1 cup granulated sugar**
- **1 cup brown sugar**
- **2 eggs**
- **1 teaspoon vanilla**
- **¾ cup peanut butter**
- **3 cups flour, spoon lightly into cup**
- **1 teaspoon soda**
- **½ teaspoon salt**
- **1 tablespoon hot water**

Cream shortening, margarine, both sugars and eggs. Add peanut butter, vanilla and hot water and mix altogether. Sift together dry ingredients, add to creamed mixture and mix thoroughly. Chill for 1 to 1½ hours. Form into balls the size of a walnut. Flatten with a fork crosswise and bake on ungreased cookie sheet at 350–375 degrees for about 10 minutes or until golden brown.

Dee Totah
GFWC—Decora Study Club
Victoria, Texas

Ginger Snaps

3 cups flour
2 teaspoons ginger
1 teaspoon baking soda
1 teaspoon cinnamon
½ teaspoon nutmeg
¼ teaspoon cloves
¼ teaspoon salt
¾ cup shortening
¾ cup packed brown sugar
½ cup molasses
1 egg

In medium bowl, combine flour, ginger, soda, cinnamon, nutmeg, cloves and salt. In mixer bowl, cream shortening and brown sugar until light and fluffy. Beat in molasses and egg. Beat in dry ingredients just until combined. Cover and refrigerate at least 2 hours or overnight. Roll chilled dough into 1-inch balls. Roll balls in ⅓ cup granulated sugar. Place on prepared cookie sheet, greased, 1½ inches apart; flatten slightly. Bake at 350 degrees for 10–12 minutes. Makes 6 dozen. 60 calories each.

Margaret Faulkingham
GFWC—Acadian Community Woman's Club
Winter Harbor, Maine

Chocolate Date Ball Cookies

1 cup peanut butter
1 cup powdered sugar
1 cup chopped dates
½ teaspoon vanilla
1 tablespoon butter, softened
1 cup chopped nuts
1 6 ounce package chocolate bits, melted

Mix peanut butter, powdered sugar, dates, butter, nuts and melted chocolate bits; add vanilla. Roll into small balls (size of walnut) and dip into dipping chocolate.

Dipping Chocolate

2 squares semi-sweet chocolate
1 inch square paraffin

Melt squares of semi-sweet chocolate and paraffin in top of double-boiler. Using a fork, dip the cookies into the chocolate and place on waxed paper to harden.

June Dean
GFWC—Pittsfield Woman's Club
Pittsfield, Illinois

Raisin Nut Drops

- **2 cups sugar**
- **1 cup evaporated milk**
- **½ cup butter or margarine**
- **1 cup or 6 ounce package semi-sweet chocolate pieces**
- **1 cup crushed graham cracker crumbs**
- **1 cup raisins**
- **1 cup chopped nuts**
- **¾ cup all-purpose flour**
- **1 teaspoon vanilla**

Combine sugar, evaporated milk and butter in saucepan. Bring to full boil, stirring constantly. Boil 10 minutes, stirring occasionally. Remove from heat. Add remaining ingredients; beat well. Drop by teaspoons onto greased cookie sheet. Cool. Makes about 40 cookies.

Barbara J. Peiper
GFWC—Murray Woman's Club
Murray, Kentucky

Christmas Fruit Cookies

- **1 cup brown sugar**
- **¼ cup butter**
- **2 eggs, beaten**
- **1½ cups flour**
- **1 teaspoon cinnamon**
- **¼ teaspoon nutmeg**
- **¼ teaspoon cloves**
- **1½ teaspoons soda**
- **1½ tablespoons milk**
- **⅓ cup apricot brandy**
- **1 pound white raisins**
- **8 ounces glazed pineapple**
- **4 ounces green cherries**
- **4 ounces red cherries**
- **4 ounces orange peel**
- **½ cup pecans**

Cream together brown sugar and butter. Add 2 eggs, beaten. Sift together the flour, cinnamon, nutmeg, cloves and soda. Add to egg mixture. Add the milk and apricot brandy. Plump the 1 pound raisins in hot water. Chop pineapple, cherries, orange peel and pecans in fine pieces. Do not use already mixed fruit. Add fruit, nuts and raisins to first mixture. Drop by small teaspoonfuls onto greased cookie sheet. Place ½ of a red cherry and a tiny piece of a green cherry on each cookie. Bake in 325 degrees oven about 15 minutes. Store in tight container.

Anne Willcox
GFWC—Arlington Heights Woman's Club
Arlington Heights, Illinois

Pineapple-Coconut Cookies

- **1 cup shortening**
- **1 teaspoon salt**
- **1½ teaspoons soda**
- **1 cup brown sugar**
- **2 eggs, well beaten**
- **2 cups rolled oats**
- **1 cup raisins**
- **½ cup coconut**
- **½ cup nut meats**
- **1 cup bran cereal**
- **3 cups sifted flour**
- **1 cup crushed pineapple, undrained**

Cream shortening and sugar; add well-beaten eggs and mix thoroughly. Add bran and let absorb all moisture. Cut raisins and nut meats up fine; add rolled oats, sifted flour, salt, soda and coconut. Rub together thoroughly. Add to first mixture alternating with the pineapple. Drop from teaspoons on greased baking sheets. Bake in moderate oven, 350 degrees for 10–15 minutes.

"My mother's recipe given 38 years ago to me."

Joann Evans
GFWC—Mary Hinton Morris Club
Hannibal, Missouri

Cream Coconut Cookies

- **2½ cups coconut, flaked**
- **⅓ cup flour**
- **⅛ teaspoon salt**
- **⅔ cup sweetened condensed milk**
- **1 tablespoon vanilla**

Mix and drop by teaspoon on well-greased pan. Bake at 350 degrees and remove in 10 minutes or when lightly brown. Can be dipped in melted chocolate when cool. Keep tightly wrapped in plastic bag or covered container for freshness. Makes 18 large cookies.

"The larger the cookie the chewier."

Aida Ortolani
GFWC—Woman's Club of Oakland
Oakland, New Jersey

Pecan Snow Drop Cookies

- **1 cup pecans, chopped**
- **½ cup oleo**
- **½ cup plus 2 tablespoons oil**
- **1⅔ cups confectioners' sugar**
- **2½ cups sifted flour**
- **2 teaspoons vanilla**

Preheat oven to 325 degrees. Cream oleo and oil together. Gradually beat in confectioners' sugar. Stir in flour, mix thoroughly; add vanilla and pecans. Drop by teaspoonfuls onto ungreased cookie sheet. Bake until just barely delicate brown, about 15–20 minutes.

"An old family recipe."

Laurie Cramer
GFWC—Charlotte Junior Woman's Club
Charlotte, North Carolina

Stuffed Date Drops

70–75 dates
Pecan or walnut halves
1/4 cup shortening
3/4 cup brown sugar
1 egg
1 1/4 cups flour
1/2 teaspoon baking powder
1/2 teaspoon soda
1/2 teaspoon salt
1/2 cup dairy sour cream

Stuff dates with nuts. Cream shortening and sugar; add egg. Sift dry ingredients together and add to sugar mixture with sour cream. Carefully fold in stuffed dates until all areas are coated. Chill well. Drop onto greased cookie sheet one date to a cookie. Bake 8–10 minutes at 375 degrees. Cool and frost.

Frosting

1 cup brown sugar
6 tablespoons thick cream
4 tablespoons butter
Powdered sugar
3/4 cup chocolate chips
1/4 cup evaporated milk
1 tablespoon butter
1 teaspoon vanilla
Pecans

Mix brown sugar, cream, and butter together. Bring to a boil. Add powdered sugar until the mixture is of a topping consistency. Drop onto cookies. Melt chocolate chips with evaporated milk over low heat. Stir in butter, vanilla and enough powdered sugar to form topping consistency. Put chocolate topping over brown sugar topping with pecans on top.

Charlene Bristol
GFWC—Fairmont Federated Woman's Club
Fairmont, Nebraska

WW II Chocolate Honey Cookies

1 1/4 cups honey
1 cup shortening
2 eggs, beaten
2 squares chocolate
1 1/2 cups oatmeal
1 teaspoon baking powder
1/2 teaspoon salt
1 teaspoon cinnamon
1/4 teaspoon baking soda
2 1/2 cups flour
1 teaspoon vanilla
1 cup chopped walnuts

Cream shortening and honey. Melt chocolate in double boiler. Add eggs and oatmeal. Sift together dry ingredients and add vanilla and walnuts. Drop by teaspoonfuls on greased cookie sheets. Bake at 325 degrees for 15 minutes.

"This recipe dates from World War II when honey was commonly used instead of sugar."

Anne Gower
GFWC—Maple River Study Club
Good Thunder, Minnesota

German Butter Cookies

1 cup butter, may use half butter, half margarine
1 teaspoon vanilla
1¼ cups sifted confectioners' sugar
1¼ cups sifted flour
¼ teaspoon salt
1 6 ounce package German sweet chocolate, ground
1 cup walnuts, ground

Cream butter. Add vanilla and sugar; cream together until light and fluffy. Add remaining ingredients and stir until well blended. Push from teaspoon onto ungreased cookie sheets. Bake in 300 degree oven 20–25 minutes. Allow to cool slightly before removing. Makes about 5 dozen.

"Recipe given to me by a German woman about 25 years ago."

Ethel Barrow
GFWC—Glenwood Woman's Club
Glenwood, Illinois

Russinkakor (Swedish Raisin Cookie)

1 cup chopped raisins
¼ cup brandy or rum
2 tablespoons water
1 cup butter, softened
1 cup granulated sugar
4 eggs
2 cups all-purpose flour

Soak raisins in brandy (or rum) and water overnight in covered bowl. Cream butter and sugar. Add eggs one at a time beating well after each egg. Add flour and raisin mixture; mix well. Drop by rounded teaspoonful 2 inches apart (they spread) on greased cookie sheet. Bake at 375 degrees for 7–10 minutes. Remove to cooling rack; store in covered tin. A soft, brown edged cookie.

"An old Swedish family recipe; it probably came with my grandmother around 1890."

Marilyn W. Benton
GFWC—Thursday Morning Club
Madison, New Jersey

"White Christmas" Cookies

2¼ cups flour
1 teaspoon baking soda
1 teaspoon salt
1 cup unsalted butter, softened
¾ cup light brown sugar
3 eggs
1 teaspoon vanilla
12 ounces white chocolate, coarsely chopped
¾ cup chopped macadamia nuts
1¼ cups golden raisins

Combine flour, baking soda and salt. Cream together butter and sugar until fluffy. Add eggs, one at a time, beating well after each. Beat in vanilla. Gradually beat in dry ingredients. Drop by teaspoonfuls onto greased cookie sheets. Bake 8–10 minutes, until golden in 350 degree oven. Cool on wire racks.

Kathy Hunt
GFWC—Junior Woman's Club of Asbury Park
Ocean Township, New Jersey

Soft Molasses Cakes

- **2½ cups sifted flour**
- **2 teaspoons baking soda**
- **½ teaspoon ginger**
- **1 teaspoon salt**
- **1 teaspoon cinnamon**
- **½ cup butter**
- **1 cup sugar**
- **½ cup molasses**
- **1 egg**
- **¼ cup cold water**
- **1 cup golden raisins**

Sift flour, baking soda, ginger, salt and cinnamon. Beat sugar, softened butter, molasses and egg until light and fluffy. Add sifted ingredients alternately with cold water and beat until blended. Stir in raisins. Drop by rounded tablespoonful, 3 inches apart onto greased cookie sheet. Bake 10–12 minutes in preheated 350 degree oven. Size should be about 4 inches across.

"This recipe was an original made by the early settlers of the 13 colonies. It was taken from the Thirteen Colonies Cook Book."

Helen Wells
GFWC—Woman's Club of Medford
Medford, New Jersey

Orange Slice Cookies

- **2 cups brown sugar**
- **¾ cup margarine**
- **2 eggs**
- **2 tablespoons hot water**
- **2 tablespoons orange juice**
- **1½ teaspoons soda**
- **4 cups flour**
- **1½ teaspoons cream of tartar**
- **½ teaspoon salt**
- **1 pound orange slices, sliced fine**
- **½ cup nuts**

Using mixer blend sugar, shortening and eggs. Combine hot water, orange juice and soda. Add alternately with dry sifted ingredients. Reserve ¼ cup flour to sprinkle over orange slices and nuts before adding to mixture. Drop on cookie sheet with spoon. Bake at 350 degrees until golden brown, 10–12 minutes.

"Taken from Rice Lake Chronotye in the 1940's and used since."

Marjorie Kucko
GFWC—Tomorrow's
Elma, Iowa

Cinnamon-Almond Mounds

- **4 egg whites**
- **¼ teaspoon cream of tartar**
- **1 teaspoon ground cinnamon**
- **⅛ teaspoon salt**
- **1½ cups sugar**
- **1 teaspoon vanilla**
- **2½ ounce package slivered almonds**

Beat egg whites until stiff peaks form. Gradually beat in the cream of tartar. Blend in cinnamon and salt. Gradually beat in the sugar. Add vanilla. Drop mixture by teaspoonfuls onto ungreased, brown paper-lined cookie sheets. Place 5 or 6 slivered almonds into top and sides of each cookie allowing about half of the almond sliver to show. Bake in 300 degree oven 50 minutes or until mounds are toasted and cookies are slightly browned or dry. Remove to wire rack to cool. Makes about 3½ dozen.

Anne Willcox
GFWC—Arlington Heights Woman's Club
Arlington Heights, Illinois

Ricotta Cookies

- ½ pound butter
- 2 cups sugar
- 2 eggs
- 1 pound ricotta
- 1 teaspoon almond extract
- 1 teaspoon vanilla
- 4 cups flour
- 1 teaspoon baking powder
- 1 teaspoon baking soda

Cream butter, add sugar gradually, add eggs one at a time. Blend ricotta and flavorings. Blend in dry ingredients. Drop by teaspoons, bake at 350 degrees for 10–20 minutes. You can leave them plain or frost them.

Gertrude G. Cerasale
GFWC—The Southington Woman's Club, Inc.
Southington, Connecticut

Meringue (Overnight) Cookies

- 3 egg whites
- ¾ cup sugar
- 1 teaspoon vanilla
- 6 ounces mini semi-sweet chocolate chips
- ½ or ¾ cup nuts, chopped fine English walnuts or pecans*

Read directions carefully before starting. Before mixing cookies, turn oven to 400 degrees. Then beat egg whites and sugar into stiff peaks. Fold in carefully the mini-chips, nuts and vanilla. Drop cookies by teaspoons onto cookie sheet covered with aluminum foil, shiny side up. Turn oven off when you put cookies in oven and leave overnight, or at least several hours. Do not open oven. Remove with a spatula. *Black walnuts are special with chopped mints.

Mary Alice Dernberger
GFWC—Mutual and Civic Improvement Club
Hebron, Ohio

Oslo Kringle

- ½ cup shortening
- 1 cup flour
- 1 tablespoon cold water
- ⅔ cup margarine
- ⅓ cup hot water
- 1⅓ cups flour
- 1 teaspoon almond flavoring
- 4 eggs

Mix first 3 ingredients as for pie crust. Press into 11 × 17-inch cookie sheet. Leave hole in middle. Melt margarine in hot water to near boiling point. Stir in flour. Remove from heat and add flavoring. Cool slightly. Add eggs, one at a time, beating after each. Drop by teaspoonfuls in chunks on bottom crust. Bake at 400 degrees for 10 minutes. Turn down the oven to 375 degrees and bake for 35 minutes. Frost with powdered sugar frosting.

Erma Thompson
GFWC—Hinton Wednesday Club
Hinton, West Virginia

Christmas Butterscotch Cookies

- **4 tablespoons melted butter**
- **2¼ cups dark brown sugar**
- **2 cups molasses**
- **4 cups flour**
- **½ teaspoon soda**
- **5 cups freshly grated coconut**

Mix ingredients in order listed. Drop small teaspoonfuls onto well-buttered cookie sheet and bake in a 375 degree oven for 5–6 minutes. Remove cookies quickly. Makes 6 dozen cookies.

"This is a family Pennsylvania Dutch recipe. My mother and her sisters used it first about 1905."

Florence Earp
GFWC—Woman's Club of Westminster
Westminster, Maryland

Carrot Cookies

- **1 cup shortening**
- **¾ cup sugar**
- **1 egg**
- **1 teaspoon vanilla**
- **½ teaspoon salt**
- **1 cup cooked, mashed carrots**
- **½ teaspoon coconut flavoring**
- **2 cups flour**
- **2 teaspoons baking powder**

Cook enough carrots to equal 1 cup, approximately 4–5. Mash carrots with fork and set aside. Cream shortening and sugar. Mix in egg, vanilla, salt and then carrots. Add coconut flavoring and dry ingredients. Spoon onto baking sheets and bake at 350 degrees for 12 minutes.

Optional: Frost with a glaze of orange juice and powdered sugar.

Mary Shoemaker
GFWC—Questers
Hutchinson, Kansas

Raisin Nut Delights

- **3 egg whites**
- **½ cup pecans, broken**
- **½ cup sugar**
- **½ cup seedless raisins**

Beat egg whites until stiff enough to keep their shape; gradually beat in sugar. Fold in nuts and raisins. Drop from spoon on baking sheet. Bake in moderate oven, 350 degrees, until browned.

"This recipe was taken from a Greenwood Woman's Club cookbook circa 1900."

Patsey Bowers
GFWC—LeBonté Woman's Club
Greenwood, Mississippi

Truly-Fruity Cookies

- ½ cup raisins
- 1 cup apricots
- 1 cup pitted dates
- 1 cup chopped walnuts
- 1 cup whole wheat flour
- ¼ cup oil
- 1 tablespoon vanilla
- ¼ teaspoon salt
- 2 eggs, slightly beaten
- 1 16 ounce can crushed pineapple, drained

Combine dried fruits, nuts and flour in a big bowl; set aside. Combine all remaining ingredients. Mix well; add to the flour and fruit mixture. Mix thoroughly, and drop by teaspoonful on greased cookie sheet. Bake at 350 degrees for 8–10 minutes. Do not overbake.

"Makes a nice fruit cake. Bake in loaf pan for 1 hour; leave in pan until room temperature."

Mrs. J. Stuart Mill
GFWC—Covington Art Club
Covington, Kentucky

Pumpkin Face Cookies

Pumpkin Filling

- ½ cup canned pumpkin
- ½ cup sugar
- ½ teaspoon cinnamon
- ½ teaspoon ginger
- ¼ teaspoon nutmeg

Stir and cook on top of stove until bubbly. Set aside to cool. You will be filling the cookies with a teaspoon of this mixture.

Cookie Dough

- ¾ cup shortening
- ½ cup packed brown sugar
- 1 egg
- ¼ cup dark molasses
- 1 teaspoon salt
- 1 cup quick-cooking, rolled oats, blended
- 2 cups all-purpose flour
- ½ teaspoon soda

Cream together the shortening and sugar. Beat in the egg and molasses. Place the oats in a blender; cover and blend until finely chopped. Mix oats, flour, soda and salt. Stir into creamed mixture, cover and chill, about 30 minutes or more. On a floured surface, roll dough to about ⅛ inch thick. Cut into 36, 3-inch circles or smaller. Place a teaspoon of pumpkin filling on top of half of these circles. Place these on an ungreased cookie sheet. Cut faces into the remaining circles. Place these cut pieces on top of the circles with the filling. Seal the edges with a little milk or water, and press all around. Press on stems cut from dough scraps. Bake at 375 degrees for 12 minutes. Makes about 18 cookies.

Pat Whalen-Shaw
GFWC—Circleville Junior Woman's Club
Circleville, Ohio

Pies

Old Fashioned Caramel Pie Filling

2 cups white sugar
2 heaping tablespoons flour
2 cups milk, very rich
4 egg yolks
2 teaspoons vanilla

Burn or caramelize 1 cup sugar in heavy skillet. Stir steadily so as not to burn in bottom. Dissolve caramel with the milk, then add rest of sugar, flour and egg yolks to mixture. Cook until thick. Add vanilla. Pour into baked pie crust. Top with meringue and brown to a golden color. Enough for a 9-inch crust.

Marguerite Burklund
GFWC—Ogilvie Woman's Club
Ogilvie, Minnesota

Photo features: Strawberry Cream Pie—Page 339
Burnt Sugar Pie—Page 352

Lemon Chiffon Pie

Filling

- 4 egg yolks, well beaten
- Juice and rind of 1 lemon
- ½ cup sugar
- 1 teaspoon flour
- 2 tablespoons water
- 2 egg whites
- ¼ cup sugar
- 1 graham cracker crust or 1 baked pie shell

Using double boiler, cook first five ingredients until thick. Remove from heat. Beat egg whites to form peaks, with gradually adding ¼ cup sugar while beating. Fold yolk mixture into egg whites. Pour filling into crust. Top with meringue.

Meringue

- 2 egg whites
- ¼ teaspoon cream of tartar
- ¼ cup sugar
- Pinch salt
- 2 teaspoons cornstarch
- ½ teaspoon vanilla

Beat egg whites slowly, adding cream of tartar and then sugar, salt, cornstarch and vanilla. Beat on high until well blended. Bake in 350 degree oven for 12–15 minutes.

Myrtle Schrum
GFWC—Clark Woman's Club
Clark, South Dakota

Captain's Table Key Lime Pie

- 2 14 ounce cans sweetened condensed milk
- 2 eggs
- 2 cups lime juice
- 1 9-inch baked pastry shell

Combine condensed milk and eggs in large bowl and blend well. Add lime juice. Pour into baked pie shell. Refrigerate several hours or overnight. May use frozen whipped topping when serving or is just delicious plain.

Pauline Wilson
GFWC—Apache Junction Woman's Club
Apache Junction, Arizona

Virginia's Coconut Pie

- 2 cups scalded milk
- ¼ cup cornstarch
- ⅔ cup granulated sugar
- Pinch salt
- 3 eggs
- 1 tablespoon butter
- 1 teaspoon vanilla
- 1 cup shredded coconut
- ¼ cup sugar for meringue
- 1 baked 9-inch pie crust

In double boiler, place the cornstarch, sugar, salt and milk and cook over medium heat until thick, stirring constantly. Remove from heat and stir in three slightly beaten egg yolks. Mix well, add butter and after melted, add vanilla and ¼ cup coconut. Pour into cooled pie crust. Beat the egg whites until stiff and on slow speed of mixer, gradually add ¼ cup sugar. Spread this on top of the filled pie, sprinkle with remaining coconut and bake at 375 degrees until brown.

Virginia Rawlings
GFWC—Middletown Woman's Club
Middletown, Indiana

Hawaiian Pie

2 baked pie shells
3 bananas, sliced
1½ cups chopped nuts
1 20 ounce can crushed pineapple
6 tablespoons flour
1½ cups sugar
1 cup coconut
Whipped cream

Place sliced bananas in bottom of pie crust and sprinkle nuts over bananas. Cook together pineapple, flour and sugar until thick. Cool before putting over bananas. Top with coconut and whipped cream.

Kay Shirley
GFWC—Sand River Woman's Club
Aiken, South Carolina

German Chocolate Pie

1 9-inch baked pie shell
⅓ cup sugar
3 tablespoons cornstarch
1½ cups milk
1 4 ounce bar German sweet cooking chocolate, cut up
1 tablespoon butter or margarine
2 beaten egg yolks
1 teaspoon vanilla
1 beaten egg
1 5⅓ ounce can evaporated milk
½ cup sugar
¼ cup butter or margarine
3½ ounces flaked coconut—1⅓ cups
½ cup chopped pecans

Combine ⅓ cup sugar and cornstarch in medium saucepan. Stir in milk, chocolate and 1 tablespoon margarine. Cook and stir until thickened and bubbly. Reduce heat, cook and stir 2 minutes more. Gradually stir about 1 cup of hot mixture into egg yolks. Return mixture to saucepan and bring this mixture to a boil. Cook and stir 2 minutes more. Stir in vanilla. Turn the hot pie filling into the baked pie shell. In another saucepan, combine the beaten egg, evaporated milk, ½ cup sugar and ¼ cup margarine. Cook and stir over medium heat just until the mixture is thickened and bubbly. Stir in the coconut and pecans. Spread the pecan mixture evenly over chocolate filling. Cool the pie on a wire rack, then refrigerate and chill thoroughly.

Dorothy M. Martzluf
GFWC—Williamsfield Home Culture Club
Williamsfield, Illinois

Custard Blender Pie

2 cups milk
½ stick margarine
1 cup sugar
4 whole eggs
1 teaspoon vanilla
½ cup buttermilk biscuit mix

Put all the ingredients in a blender. Blend on low speed for 5 minutes. Pour into a greased and floured 10-inch pie pan. Sprinkle cinnamon on top. Bake at 350 degrees for 35–40 minutes. Test as for Pumpkin Pie.

Marlene Jorgensen
GFWC—Galva Civic Club
Galva, Iowa

Maple Cream Pie

1 baked pastry shell
¾ cup dark brown sugar
5 tablespoons flour
½ teaspoon salt
2 cups milk, skim or whole
2 egg yolks, slightly beaten
2 tablespoons margarine
1 teaspoon maple flavoring
Whipped cream or topping

In top of a double boiler, combine sugar, flour and salt; stir in warmed milk slowly. Cook over boiling water until thick, stirring constantly. Cover and cook 10 minutes longer. Add eggs to mixture stirring vigorously; cook 1 minute longer. Add margarine and flavoring. Fill shell and cover with whipped cream. Chopped walnuts may be sprinkled on top. Makes one 8-inch pie.

Virginia L. Uecker
GFWC—Peterborough Woman's Club
Peterborough, New Hampshire

Black Bottom Pie

16 gingersnaps, crushed
5 tablespoons melted butter
2 cups scalded milk
½ cup sugar
4 egg yolks, well beaten
1½ tablespoons cornstarch
1½ squares dark chocolate
1 teaspoon vanilla
1 tablespoon unflavored gelatin
2 tablespoons cold water
4 egg whites, beaten stiff
½ cup sugar
¼ teaspoon cream of tartar
2 teaspoons rum
1 8 ounce carton frozen whipped topping

Mix gingersnaps and butter and press into 9-inch pie pan. Bake 375 degrees for 10 minutes. Cool. First filling: Add egg yolks slowly to hot milk. Combine sugar and cornstarch and stir into milk mixture. Cook in double boiler 20 minutes or until mixture coats spoon. Remove from heat, take out 1 cup. Add chocolate and beat until cool. Add vanilla, beat, pour into crust and chill. Second filling: Dissolve gelatin in water; add to remaining custard and cool. Beat ½ cup sugar and cream of tartar into egg whites and beat until sugar is dissolved. Add rum and fold into custard mixture. Pour over chilled chocolate filling. Top with frozen whipped topping. Shave dark chocolate for garnish.

Noma Watkins
GFWC—Warren Woman's Club
Warren, Arkansas

Chess Pie

1⅔ cups white sugar
1 stick oleo, melted
4 eggs
1 tablespoon flour
⅔ cup sweet milk
3 tablespoons cornmeal
1½ teaspoons vanilla
2 unbaked 9-inch pie shells

Melt oleo. Beat eggs well. Mix sugar, oleo and eggs. Add flour and cornmeal; mixing well. Stir in other ingredients and mix well. Pour in two unbaked, 9-inch pie shells. Bake at 325 degrees for 40–50 minutes.

Louise Steele
GFWC—Rutherford Woman's Club
Smyrna, Tennessee

Coffee Cream Pie

Nut Crust

1 egg white, stiffly beaten
¼ cup sugar
1½ cups finely chopped pecans
⅛ teaspoon salt

Add sugar and salt to stiffly beaten egg whites. Beat until satiny. Add nutmeat, mixing well. With a spoon press onto bottom and sides of a well-greased 8-inch pie plate. Bake at 400 degrees for 12 minutes. Cool.

Filling

1 tablespoon instant coffee
¼ cup water
16 marshmallows
1 egg yolk
1 cup heavy cream
¼ teaspoon almond extract

Combine coffee, water and marshmallows. Over medium heat, cook until marshmallows melt. Add slightly beaten egg yolk slowly. Cook 1 minute. Chill until it begins to set. Fold in whipped cream and almond extract. Pour into crust and chill.

Margaret Anne Smith
GFWC—Sesame Club
Hillsboro, Texas

Strawberry Cream Pie

⅔ cup sugar
3½ tablespoons cornstarch
⅛ teaspoon salt
2 cups scalded milk
2 egg yolks
½ teaspoon vanilla
1 cup hulled strawberries
1 9-inch baked pie shell

Mix dry ingredients, add scalded milk gradually. Cook 15 minutes in double boiler, stirring constantly until mixture thickens, then occasionally. Slowly pour some hot mixture onto beaten egg yolks, then return to double boiler and cook one minute. Add vanilla. Place in baked pie shell, set aside to cool. When cooled, cover with strawberries, then uncooked meringue.

Meringue

1 cup powdered sugar
2 egg whites
1 cup strawberries

Place all three ingredients in electric mixer. Beat 10 minutes until light and fluffy. Cover pie and chill ½ hour before serving.

"This recipe is 55 years old. I received it from cooking school in Lodi, California in 1933."

Evelyn Phelps
GFWC—Mesquite Club
Las Vegas, Nevada

Frozen White Chocolate Pie with Raspberries

Almond Crust

- **9 ounces blanched, slivered almonds, toasted**
- **3 tablespoons unsalted butter, melted**
- **2 tablespoons light corn syrup**

Grease 9-inch glass pie plate. Using heavy knife, chop slivered almonds into 2–3 pieces each. Transfer almonds to bowl. Stir in butter and corn syrup. Spoon into prepared plate. Press onto bottom and up sides of plate. Freeze.

Filling

- **2 alpine white chocolate with almonds bars**
- **3 tablespoons creme de cacao**
- **1 teaspoon vanilla**
- **1¾ cups whipping cream**
- **2 egg whites, room temperature**
- **2 tablespoons sugar**
- **½ pint fresh raspberries**

Melt chocolate bars in double boiler over gently simmering water, stirring until soft. These will not melt like regular chocolate, but they will soften until almost melted. Let cool until thick and paste-like, stirring occasionally. Blend in liqueur, vanilla and extract. Beat cream until stiff peaks form. Gently beat in chocolate mixture. Using clean, dry beaters, beat whites until stiff but not dry. Fold gently into chocolate cream mixture. Pour into crust, smoothing top. Freeze until frozen but not hard, about 5 hours. Remove from freezer about 20 minutes before serving, and mound raspberries in center of pie, leaving a 2-inch border. Serve.

Joan Bryk
GFWC—New Canaan Woman's Club
New Canaan, Connecticut

Frozen Lemon Pie

- **½ cup fine graham cracker crumbs**
- **½ cup sugar**
- **1 cup whipping cream**
- **¼–⅓ cup lemon juice**
- **3 egg whites**
- **3 egg yolks**
- **2–3 teaspoons grated lemon rind**

Sprinkle half of crumbs into a well-greased 9-inch pie pan. Beat egg whites until frothy. Gradually add sugar. Beat until stiff and glossy. Beat egg yolks until thick and lemon colored. Fold into egg white mixture. Mix cream, lemon rind and juice; beat until stiff. Fold into egg mixture. Pour into crumb-lined pan. Sprinkle rest of crumbs over top. Freeze to desired consistency.

Joanne Meyer
GFWC—Elgin Junior Woman's Club
Elgin, Illinois

Hays House Cranberry-Strawberry Pie

Crust

1⅓ cups graham cracker crumbs
¼ cup powdered sugar
⅓ cup melted margarine

Mix all ingredients well. Press onto bottom and up sides of 9-inch pie pan; freeze.

Filling

½ pound frozen, fresh cranberries, ground
1 cup sugar
½ pound regular size marshmallows
½ cup milk
3 ounces dry cherry gelatin
1 cup frozen strawberries
⅓ cup chopped celery
½ cup black walnuts
2 cups whipping cream

Melt marshmallows in milk in top of double boiler. As soon as lumps are gone, remove from heat and stir in gelatin. Add remainder of ingredients except whipping cream. Pour into crust and let set up firm in freezer. Whip cream and pile on top of filling. Return to freezer for at least 2 hours.

Helen E. Judd
GFWC—Talahi
Council Grove, Kansas

Pina Colada Pie

1 8 ounce package cream cheese, softened
1 cup sour cream
½ cup sugar
1 tablespoon rum or 1 teaspoon extract
1¾ cups frozen non-dairy whip, thawed
1 cup chopped ripe pineapple or 16 ounce can crushed, well drained

Combine cream cheese, sour cream, sugar and rum, beating until smooth. Blend in whipped topping. Fold in pineapple. Spoon into quick coconut crust. Chill 3 hours. Garnish with additional chopped pineapple and toasted coconut.

Crust

⅓ cup butter or margarine
2⅔ cups flaked coconut

Combine ingredients and press into an ungreased 9-inch pie pan. Bake at 400 degrees until golden brown. Cool and fill with cream cheese mixture.

Janice Franklin May
GFWC—Flint Hills Federated Club
Manhattan, Kansas

Frosty Pumpkin Pie

- 1 baked pie shell or graham cracker crust
- 1 pint vanilla ice cream
- 2–3 tablespoons chopped, crystallized ginger
- 1 teaspoon pumpkin pie spice
- ½ teaspoon salt
- 1 cup chilled whipping cream
- 1 can pumpkin
- 1 cup sugar
- ½ teaspoon ginger
- ½ cup chopped walnuts

Soften ice cream slightly; quickly fold in ginger. Spread in pie shell. Mix pumpkin, sugar, salt and walnuts. Beat whipping cream in chilled bowl until stiff; fold into pumpkin mix. Pour over ice cream in pie shell. Freeze several hours. Remove from freezer 10–15 minutes before serving.

Barbara Trombley
GFWC—The Waltham Woman's Club
Waltham, Massachusetts

Praline Pie

- 2 graham cracker crusts
- 1 can coconut
- 1½ cups pecans
- ½ stick oleo
- 12 ounce jar caramel ice cream topping
- 8 ounces frozen whipped topping
- 1 can condensed milk
- 8 ounces cream cheese

Using a black skillet, toast coconut and pecans in oleo. Mix cream cheese and condensed milk with mixer until smooth. Fold in frozen whipped topping. Sprinkle ½ of coconut mixture in crust. Pour ½ caramel topping over this. Pour all of cream cheese mixture over top. Sprinkle remainder of coconut mixture over the cream cheese mixture. Pour rest of caramel over top. Freeze.

Mary Ellen Holloway
GFWC—Civic League of Indianola
Indianola, Mississippi

Mother's Coconut Pie

- ½ cup butter or margarine
- 2 cups sugar
- Juice of 1 orange
- ½ teaspoon nutmeg
- ½ cup grape wine or juice
- 2 small coconuts, grated or 1 package frozen coconut
- 6 egg whites, well beaten

Cream butter and sugar. Add orange juice, nutmeg, wine and grated coconut. Add well-beaten egg whites. Pour into unbaked pie shell. Bake at 350 degrees for 30–40 minutes or until brown.

Joan P. White
GFWC—Amherst Woman's Club
Amherst, Virginia

Pineapple Cheese Pie

Bottom Filling

⅓ cup sugar
1 tablespoon cornstarch
8½–9 ounce can crushed pineapple

Blend all ingredients; cook, stirring constantly until mixture is thick and clear. Cool.

Crust

4 tablespoons butter
3 tablespoons sugar
1 egg
1 cup flour
½ teaspoon baking powder

Mix crust ingredients in a 9-inch pie pan and spread the dough with fingers. Spread pineapple mixture on bottom of pie shell. Pour in the cream cheese mixture; sprinkle top with cinnamon. Bake in 350 degree oven for 35 minutes or until firm and golden.

Filling

½ pound cream cheese
½ cup sugar
½ teaspoon salt
2 eggs
½ cup lite cream
½ teaspoon vanilla

Mix all ingredients and set aside.

Gloria F. Andriuolo
GFWC—Contemporary Woman's Club
Washington Township, New Jersey

Fudge Macaroon Pie

3 squares unsweetened chocolate
½ cup butter or margarine
3 eggs, slightly beaten
¾ cup sugar
½ cup all-purpose flour
1 teaspoon vanilla
⅔ cup sweetened condensed milk
2⅔ cups flaked coconut

Melt chocolate and butter in saucepan over low heat. Stir in eggs, sugar, flour and vanilla. Pour into greased 9-inch pie plate. Combine milk and coconut. Spoon over mixture leaving ½ to 1-inch border. Bake at 350 degrees for 30 minutes. Cool and serve.

Mary D. Smith
GFWC—Austell Woman's Club
Austell, Georgia

Southern Peanut Pie

- 3 eggs
- ½ cup sugar
- 1½ cups dark corn syrup
- ¼ cup butter, melted
- ¼ teaspoon salt
- ½ teaspoon vanilla
- 1½ cups chopped, roasted peanuts
- 1 9-inch unbaked pie shell

Beat eggs until foamy. Add sugar, syrup, butter, salt and vanilla. Continue to beat until thoroughly blended. Stir in peanuts. Pour into unbaked pie shell. Bake in pre-heated 375 degree oven for 45 minutes. May be served warm or cold, with whipped cream or ice cream.

Shirley Yancey
GFWC—Woman's Club of Waverly
Waverly, Virginia

Low Calorie Pecan Pie

- 3 eggs
- ¼ cup brown sugar
- ¾ cup diet brown sugar
- ½ cup diet syrup
- ½ cup dark syrup
- ½ teaspoon salt
- 1 teaspoon vanilla
- ¼ cup pecans
- 1 pie shell

Mix all ingredients together except pecans. Put pecans on top. Bake 10 minutes in a 425 degree oven; reduce to 325 degrees and bake for 40–50 minutes.

Amber Brindle
GFWC—Marshalltown Woman's Club
Marshalltown, Iowa

Prize Winning Blueberry Chess Pie

- 1½ cups sugar
- ⅛ teaspoon salt
- 2 tablespoons flour
- 1 tablespoon vinegar
- 1 pint fresh blueberries
- ½ cup butter
- 3 eggs
- 2 tablespoons cornstarch
- 1½ teaspoons vanilla
- 1 9-inch unbaked pie shell

Cream sugar, butter and salt until light and fluffy. Beat in eggs, one at a time, very well. Add flour, cornstarch, vinegar and vanilla; beat until smooth. Stir in berries and pour into pie shell. Bake at 400 degrees for 15 minutes, then reduce temperature to 300 degrees and bake 35 minutes or until firm in center. Cool well.

Bernice Fisher
GFWC—The Federated Woman's Club of Petersburg
Petersburg, Virginia

Carrot Pie (sugar free)

4 cups cooked carrots
3 cups milk
7 eggs
2 tablespoons liquid sweetener
2 teaspoons ginger
1 teaspoon cinnamon
½ teaspoon nutmeg
¼ teaspoon cloves
½ teaspoon salt

Crust

2 heaping cups flour, sifted
1 cup shortening
4–5 tablespoons cold milk or water
½ teaspoon salt

Liquefy in blender the carrots and milk. Pour out ½ mixture and add rest of ingredients to blender. Mix everything together in bowl with whisk. Put in uncooked pie shell. Bake 10 minutes at 400 degrees. Reduce oven to 350 degrees for 30–40 minutes. Pie is done when round on top and stops jiggling or knife comes out clean. Makes two pies. This recipe can be made with pumpkin, squash, or sweet potatoes. One may substitute 1 cup sugar for sweetener or eliminate crust for a carrot custard.

Cut shortening into flour and salt until mixture forms "pebbles." Add cold milk, one tablespoon at a time, while mixing with wooden spoon. Place in refrigerator. Make pie shell after dough has been chilled.

Gayle Smoot
GFWC—Gillett Woman's Club
Gillett, Wisconsin

Grandma Killion's Pumpkin Pie

2 eggs, slightly beaten
1 16 ounce can pumpkin
½ cup sugar
¼ cup dark brown sugar
½ teaspoon salt
3 teaspoons ground cinnamon
1 teaspoon ground ginger
1 teaspoon allspice
1 teaspoon pumpkin pie spice
½ teaspoon ground cloves
¼ teaspoon nutmeg
¾ cup evaporated milk
¾ cup whole milk
1 9-inch unbaked pie shell

Preheat oven to 425 degrees. Mix filling ingredients in order given. Pour into pie shell. Sprinkle mixture with some extra cinnamon. Bake 15 minutes. Reduce heat to 350 degrees and continue to bake for 45 minutes. Pie is done when knife comes out clean. Cool and cut into 8–10 slices.

Cathy M. Thomas
GFWC—Philipsburg Woman's Club
Philipsburg, Pennsylvania

Creamy Peach Pie

- **4 cups sliced fresh peaches**
- **½ cup sugar**
- **3 tablespoons flour**
- **1 tablespoon lemon juice**
- **Pastry shell**
- **2 eggs, slightly beaten**
- **1 cup heavy cream**
- **2 tablespoons butter**
- **2 tablespoons sugar**
- **½ teaspoon cinnamon**

Mix first four ingredients together and pour into unbaked pie shell. Bake at 400 degrees for 25 minutes. Then mix the rest of the ingredients and pour over baked pie and return to oven for 10 minutes until custard is set. Sprinkle top with sugar and cinnamon and bake 10 minutes more.

Jackie Vogler
GFWC—Progressive Study Club
Normangee, Texas

Hotel Hershey Derby Pie

Pie

- **1 cup sugar**
- **4 tablespoons cornstarch**
- **2 eggs, lightly beaten**
- **½ cup (1 stick) butter or margarine, melted and cooled**
- **3 tablespoons bourbon or 1 teaspoon vanilla**
- **1 6-ounce package semi-sweet chocolate pieces**
- **1 cup finely chopped pecans**
- **1 9-inch unbaked pie shell**

Combine sugar and cornstarch in a medium bowl. Beat in eggs; mix in butter, bourbon, chocolate pieces and pecans. Pour into pastry shell. Bake in moderate oven 350 degrees for 40 minutes or until puffy and golden browned. Cool completely on wire rack. Cut into slim wedges and top with derby whipped cream.

Cream Topping

- **½ cup heavy cream**
- **2 tablespoons confectioners' sugar**
- **1 teaspoon bourbon or ½ teaspoon vanilla**

Beat cream with sugar in a small bowl to soft peaks; add bourbon or vanilla and beat to stiff peaks.

"This recipe is from the Hotel Hershey's Swiss chef in Chocolate Town, U.S.A., Hershey, Pennsylvania."

Carleen M. Adler
GFWC—Westford Junior Woman's Club
Westford, Massachusetts

Fresh Pineapple Pie

9-inch double crust
1 cup sugar
⅓ cup flour
1 tablespoon lemon juice
2 eggs
2 cups fresh shredded pineapple, drained
2 tablespoons butter

Blend sugar and flour together. Beat eggs slightly. Add lemon juice and combine with sugar and flour mixture. Add shredded pineapple. Pour in unbaked crust and dot with butter; add top crust. Bake at 450 degrees for 10 minutes, then at 350 degrees for 35 minutes.

Evie Gloistein
GFWC—Monticola Club
Susanville, California

Grandmother Coe's Kentucky Blackberry Pie

½ stick butter
¾ cup granulated sugar
2 egg yolks
2 egg whites
2 tablespoons sugar
2½ cups blackberries, fresh or canned
One crust 8-inch pie shell

Cream butter, adding sugar gradually. Add egg yolks mixing well. In separate bowl, beat egg whites stiff and add 2 tablespoons sugar. Fold egg white mixture into butter mixture. Bake pie shell 5–6 minutes at 350 degrees. Remove from oven and put in berries, drained of juice if using canned. Pour egg mixture over berries. Lower oven temperature to 300 degrees. Bake 30 minutes or until topping appears set. This pie is best not refrigerated and eaten the next day.

"This recipe is over 100 years old and has been handed down for four generations."

Virginia Coe
GFWC—Athens Woman's Club
Athens, Tennessee

Cherry-Berry Pie

1 20 ounce can sour cherries
1 10 ounce package frozen strawberries
1 cup sugar
¼ teaspoon salt
2 tablespoons quick-cooking tapioca
2 tablespoons cornstarch
1 tablespoon lemon juice
Few drops red food coloring

Thaw strawberries; drain strawberries and cherries. Set fruit aside. Combine sugar, salt, tapioca and cornstarch, mixing well. Blend in juices; cook over slow heat 5–8 minutes, stirring constantly until thick and clear. Remove from heat and stir in fruits, lemon juice and food coloring. Pour into unbaked 9-inch pie shell. Top with second crust and seal edges. Barely moisten top crust and sprinkle lightly with sugar. Bake at 425 degrees for 25–30 minutes, until golden brown.

N. Carolyn Stotts
GFWC—Buckhannon Woman's Club
Buckhannon, West Virginia

Chocolate Meringue Pie

Meringue Crust

- **3 egg whites**
- **Dash salt**
- **1/3 cup chopped nuts**
- **1/4 teaspoon cream of tartar**
- **1/2 teaspoon vanilla**
- **3/4 cup sugar**

Combine egg whites, salt, cream of tartar and vanilla. Beat to stiff foam; add sugar gradually, beating until very stiff and sugar is dissolved. Spread in well-greased, 9-inch pan. Build up sides with cake decorator for frilly edge; sprinkle bottom with nut meats. Bake in slow oven 275 degrees for 1 hour. Cool and fill with chocolate filling.

Chocolate Filling

- **3/4 cup semi-sweet chocolate pieces**
- **1/4 cup hot water**
- **1 teaspoon vanilla**
- **Dash salt**
- **1 cup heavy cream, whipped**
- **1 cup frozen whipped topping**

Melt chocolate pieces in top of double boiler over boiling water; add hot water, vanilla and salt. Stir until completely smooth. Cool. Fold in frozen whipped topping. Fill shell. Chill for 4 hours or overnight. Serve with whipped cream or frozen whipped topping.

Audrey Ann McGinness
GFWC—Wa Keeney Locust Club
Wa Keeney, Kansas

Raisin Cream Spice Pie

- **3 eggs, slightly beaten**
- **1 1/4 cups sugar**
- **1/2 teaspoon salt**
- **1 teaspoon cinnamon**
- **1/4 teaspoon cloves**
- **1/2 teaspoon mace**
- **1/4 teaspoon nutmeg**
- **1/2 cup sour cream**
- **1 cup buttermilk**
- **1 1/2 cups raisins**
- **1 8-inch deep pastry shell**

Combine beaten eggs, sugar, salt, cinnamon, cloves, mace and nutmeg. Blend in sour cream, buttermilk and raisins. Pour into pie pan lined with pastry shell. Bake at 350 degrees for 25 minutes or until knife comes out clean. Use milk in pastry shell instead of water. Makes it much richer.

Marjorie Knowles
GFWC—Bement Woman's Club
Bement, Illinois

English Apple Pie

- 2 eggs
- 1½ cups sugar
- 1 cup flour
- 2 teaspoons baking powder
- ½ teaspoon salt
- ¾ cup chopped black walnut meats
- 2 cups fresh apples, pared and finely chopped

Beat eggs, add sugar and beat again. Add sifted flour, baking powder and salt into egg and sugar mixture. Add nut meats and apples to batter and beat well. Pour batter into a well-greased, 9 × 13-inch baking dish. Bake at 350 degrees for 30 minutes. Makes own crust. Cut into squares and serve with whipped cream.

Virgie Burkhamer
GFWC—Cowen Woman's Club
Cowen, West Virginia

Caramel Crunch Apple Pie

- 1 9-inch, unbaked, single pie crust
- 28 caramel candies
- 2 tablespoons water
- 6 cups tart cooking apples, peeled, cored and sliced
- ¾ cup all-purpose flour
- ⅓ cup sugar
- ½ teaspoon cinnamon
- ⅓ cup butter or margarine
- ½ cup chopped walnuts

Prepare pie crust according to recipe or package directions. Melt caramels with water, in top of double boiler over boiling water; or in medium saucepan over low heat, stirring occasionally until melted and smooth. Layer apples and caramel sauce alternately in pie shell. In a small bowl, combine flour, sugar and cinnamon mixing well. Cut in butter with a pastry blender until consistency of coarse crumbs. Stir in nuts. Sprinkle flour mixture evenly over apples. Preheat oven to 375 degrees. Bake for 40–45 minutes until done.

Vivian Atkinson
GFWC—Dalhart Woman's Club
Dalhart, Texas

Apple Pecan Upside Down Pie

- ¼ cup butter
- ½ cup pecan halves
- ⅔ cup brown sugar
- Pastry for 2 crust, 9-inch pie
- 8 apples peeled, cored and sliced
- 1 cup sugar
- 3 tablespoons flour
- 1 teaspoon ground cinnamon
- ¼ teaspoon ground nutmeg
- 2 tablespoons butter

Spread butter in 9-inch pie plate. Press pecans in butter, flat side up, in a star pattern. Cover with bottom pie crust. Mix apples, sugar, flour, cinnamon and nutmeg. Dot with butter. Cover with top crust. Bake at 350 degrees for 40 minutes. While still warm, invert on serving dish. Serve with whipped cream.

Bette J. Hesse
GFWC—Burnt Hills-Ballston Lake Woman's Club
Burnt Hills, New York

No-Meat Pear Mincemint Pie Filling

6 pounds medium chopped pears (not bartlett)
2 pounds raisins, chopped fine
3 pounds brown sugar
2 tablespoons salt
2 tablespoons cinnamon
1 teaspoon cloves
1 teaspoon nutmeg
1 cup mild vinegar

Blend all ingredients and cook gently until the pears are soft. Either can or freeze. When making the pie, add one teaspoon of butter to each pie and you can add 1 tablespoon brandy. Makes 3 9-inch pies.

Mary Lois Banks
GFWC—Canelback Woman's Club
Phoenix, Arizona

Lemon Pie with Meringue Crust

4 egg whites
1 cup plus 1 tablespoon sugar
1 teaspoon vanilla
1 teaspoon vinegar
4 egg yolks
4 tablespoons lemon juice
⅛ teaspoon salt, scant
½ cup sugar
Rind of one lemon, grated
1 cup whipping cream
1 tablespoon powdered sugar

Beat egg whites until stiff. Gradually add sugar, beating well after each addition. Add vanilla and vinegar. Beat until mixture holds stiff peaks. Pile in greased 10-inch pie pan. Smooth top having a little more near edges than middle. Bake at 300 degrees for one hour. For filling, beat egg yolks, add lemon juice, grated rind, sugar and salt. Cook over low heat, stirring constantly until thick; cool. Beat one cup whipping cream. Fold ½ of cream into cooled filling. Spread over meringue. Add 2 tablespoons powdered sugar to remaining cream. Spread on top of pile. Never try to make this pie on a day when the humidity is high. The meringue will fail. Keeps well in the refrigerator.

Mary L. Prester
GFWC—Junior Woman's Club of Rock Island
Rock Island, Illinois

Pecan Refrigerator Pie

14 crushed butter-flavored crackers
⅔ cup chopped pecans
3 egg whites
½ pint cream, whipped
1 cup sugar
½ teaspoon baking powder
1 teaspoon vanilla

Beat egg whites until very stiff. Add sugar, baking powder and vanilla. Fold in crackers and nuts. Pour into 9-inch greased pie plate. Bake in 325 degree oven for 40 minutes. Remove from oven. Cool. Top with whipped cream; refrigerate for at least 2 hours.

Joan Cummings
GFWC—Dyersville Federated Woman's Club
Dyersville, Iowa

Lemon Chiffon Pie

Pie

- **4 egg yolks, slightly beaten**
- **½ cup sugar**
- **Juice of 1 lemon**
- **Rind of 1 lemon**
- **1 tablespoon gelatin (1 package)**
- **¼ cup cold water**
- **4 egg whites**
- **½ cup sugar**
- **1 9-inch coconut crust**
- **1 cup heavy cream, whipped**

Combine first 4 ingredients and cook on the surface at 175 degrees until the consistency of thick custard. Soak gelatin in water and add to custard. Cool. Beat egg whites until stiff but not dry. Gradually beat in sugar. Fold in custard. Pour into pie shell. Chill 2–3 hours. Top with whipped cream. Serves 6.

Coconut Crust

- **1½ cups flaked coconut**
- **2 tablespoons butter, melted**
- **2 tablespoons sugar**
- **¼ cup finely crushed wafer crumbs**

Combine all ingredients, mixing well. Press firmly into bottom and sides of 8 or 9-inch pie pan. Bake at 375 degrees for 8–10 minutes. Chill. Variation: Add ¼ cup chopped nuts.

Naomi L. Harris
GFWC—Woman's Club of Glenhill
Baltimore, Maryland

Pineapple Yogurt Pie

- **1 cup butter flavored cracker crumbs**
- **1 envelope unflavored gelatin**
- **½ cup pineapple juice**
- **2 cups plain yogurt**
- **2 egg whites**
- **¼ cup melted butter**
- **1 teaspoon lemon juice**
- **3 packets powdered sweetener**
- **1½ cups frozen whipped topping**

Mix crumbs and butter. Press into 9-inch pie pan. Heat gelatin and juices until gelatin dissolves. Cool. Add sweetener, yogurt and pineapple. Chill until it begins to thicken. Beat egg whites until stiff. Fold egg whites and frozen whipped topping into pineapple mixture. Pour over crust. Sprinkle a few crumbs on top. Refrigerate.

Sandra Andrew
GFWC—Plainfield Woman's Club
Plainfield, Wisconsin

Scrumptious Velvet Chiffon Burnt Sugar Pie

Pie

- **1 cup cold milk**
- **1 envelope plain gelatin, dissolved in 1/4 cup water**
- **4 egg yolks**
- **1/4 cup sugar**
- **1 teaspoon vanilla**
- **4 teaspoons burnt sugar flavoring**
- **4 beaten egg whites**
- **1/2 cup sugar**
- **1 9-inch baked pie shell**

Beat egg yolks until thick, add 1/4 cup sugar. Add to milk and cook until custard stage. Add vanilla and burnt sugar flavoring. Let cool until thick but not stiff. Beat egg whites until foamy, gradually add 1/2 cup sugar; beat until stiff. Add gelatin to custard mixture. Fold egg whites into custard mixture; pour into 9-inch baked pie shell. Top with whipped cream that has been sweetened with powdered sugar and 1 teaspoon burnt sugar flavoring.

Topping

- **1 tablespoon butter**
- **2 tablespoons brown sugar**
- **3 tablespoons coconut**
- **4 tablespoons chopped pecans**

Mix ingredients, crumble on top of pie; toast in oven a few minutes.

Mrs. Stanley L. McCauley
GFWC—Highland Progressive Club
Highland, Kansas

Black Walnut Pie for Morrie

- **3 egg yolks**
- **1 cup whipping cream**
- **6 tablespoons sugar**
- **2 teaspoons unflavored gelatin**
- **1/4 cup cold water**
- **2 ounces maple syrup***
- **1/2 cup black walnuts, chopped**
- **10-inch graham cracker crust**

* Do not use black walnut flavoring, it will cause the mixture to separate.

Beat egg yolks gently with sugar, add syrup. Dissolve gelatin in cold water, heat to boiling; add slowly to egg mixture. Fold in whipped cream and nuts. Pour into graham cracker crust and chill until set. Top with whipped cream and garnish with chopped nuts; serve.

Barbara E. Wilkins
GFWC—Anchorage Woman's Club
Anchorage, Alaska

Champion Peanut Butter Pie

- **1 10-inch baked pie shell**
- **1 cup peanut butter**
- **1 cup sugar**
- **8 ounces cream cheese, softened**
- **1 pint whipping cream**
- **1 teaspoon vanilla**

Combine peanut butter, sugar and cream cheese. Whip whipping cream and vanilla until it forms stiff peaks. Take the two mixes and beat together for 5–8 minutes, until light and fluffy. Pour into pie shell. Refrigerate at least 3–4 hours. Sprinkle with grated chocolate.

Doris L. Doherty
GFWC—Albany Woman's Club
Albany, Oregon

Cherry-Cream Cheese Pie

- **3 tablespoons margarine**
- **¾ cup sugar**
- **1 cup non-fat dry milk powder**
- **⅓ cup boiling water**
- **12 ounce carton ½% low-fat cottage cheese**
- **8 ounces cream cheese, softened**
- **1 teaspoon vanilla**
- **⅓ cup lemon concentrate**
- **21 ounce can lite cherry pie filling**
- **Large pastry shell**

Combine first four ingredients in blender in order given. Blend. Add cottage cheese, blend until smooth. Add cream cheese and vanilla. Blend. Add lemon concentrate. Blend. Pour into pastry shell. Top with lite cherry filling. Chill. Serves 8–10.

Bernice Maynard
GFWC—Shady Spring District Woman's Club
Daniels, West Virginia

Lemon Icebox Pie

- **1 small box vanilla wafers**
- **1 can sweetened condensed milk**
- **3 lemons**
- **3 eggs, separated**
- **¼ cup sugar for meringue**

Crush 12–18 vanilla wafers and spread evenly in bottom of pie plate. Arrange whole wafers around sides. In medium bowl, pour in milk, add egg yolks and mix well. Add juice of lemons and mix. Filling will become thick. Pour into pie shell. Beat egg whites until peaks form; add sugar, beat until glossy. Bake at 400 degrees until golden brown. Cool in icebox 1 hour.

Laura Harpain
GFWC—Eloy Federated Woman's Club
Eloy, Arizona

Avocado Pie

Crust

Graham crackers
6 tablespoons butter or oleo

Mix crushed crackers and butter together and put in a pie plate. Bake in oven at 375 degrees for 6–8 minutes.

Filling

3 large avocados, mashed
½ cup fresh lemon juice
1 can sweetened condensed milk

Topping

4 ounce carton whipped topping
4 ounce carton sour cream
Walnuts

Mix avocados and lemon juice together; put in blender and blend 10 seconds. Add milk, blend another 15 seconds; pour into cooled crust, chill 1 hour.
Mix whipped topping with sour cream. Spread over filling and sprinkle with walnuts.

Helen Kelley
GFWC—El Cajon Woman's Club
El Cajon, California

White Christmas Pie

1 baked and cooled 9-inch pie shell
½ cup sugar
¼ cup flour
1 envelope unflavored gelatin
½ teaspoon salt
1¾ cups milk
¾ teaspoon vanilla
¼ teaspoon almond extract
1 package whipped topping, prepared by package directions
1 cup moist coconut
3 egg whites
½ cup sugar
¼ teaspoon cream of tartar

Mix sugar, flour, gelatin and salt. Gradually stir in milk. Cook in microwave, boiling 1 minute. Place pan in cold water. Cool until mixture mounds slightly when dropped from spoon. Blend in extracts. Make meringue of egg whites, sugar and cream of tartar. Carefully fold into first mixture. Fold in prepared whipped topping and coconut. Pile into baked pie shell; sprinkle with coconut. Chill several hours. May be frozen. Delicious topped with crushed strawberries.

Lillie Graves
GFWC—New Era
Dodge City, Kansas

Hawaiian Pie

- **1 16 ounce can crushed pineapple**
- **1 can red tart cherries, drained**
- **1 3 ounce box orange gelatin**
- **5 bananas, diced**
- **3 tablespoons flour**
- **¾ cup sugar**
- **1 cup pecans, cut**
- **1 baked 10-inch pie shell**

Mix together in saucepan pineapple, flour, sugar and bring to a boil. Remove from heat and add gelatin. Cool and as it begins to gel, fold in cherries, nuts and bananas. Pour into baked pie shell and serve with whipped cream.

Viva C. Harris
GFWC—Pekin Woman's Club
Pekin, Illinois

Grasshopper Pie

- **1½ cups chocolate wafer crumbs**
- **¼ cup butter, melted**
- **½ cup cold water**
- **1 envelope unflavored gelatin**
- **⅔ cup sugar**
- **⅛ teaspoon salt**
- **3 eggs, separated**
- **¼ cup white Creme de Cacao**
- **¼ cup green Creme de Menthc**
- **Green food coloring, as desired**
- **1 cup whipping cream**

Preheat oven to 350 degrees. Combine crumbs with butter. Form in a 9-inch pan and bake for 10 minutes. Cool. Pour the water in a saucepan and sprinkle gelatin over it. Add ⅓ cup sugar, salt and egg yolks. Stir to blend. Place over low heat and stir until gelatin dissolves and mixture thickens. Do not boil! Remove from heat. Stir the liqueurs into the mixture. Chill until mixture starts to mound slightly, about 20 minutes. Beat egg whites until stiff, then add remaining sugar and beat until peaks are firm. Fold meringue into thickened mixture. Whip the cream, then fold into mixture. Add green food coloring if desired. Turn mixture into crust. Chill several hours or overnight. Freezes well. Serves 8.

Jan Schurter
GFWC—Brookside Woman's Club
Brookside, New Jersey

Other Desserts

Banana Crunch

- 4 cups sliced bananas, (6 medium bananas)
- 1 tablespoon lemon juice
- ½ teaspoon cinnamon
- ½ cup all-purpose flour
- ½ cup packed brown sugar
- ⅓ cup chunky peanut butter
- 3 tablespoons butter or margarine

Place bananas in an 8-inch round baking dish. Add lemon juice and cinnamon, stirring lightly. In a small bowl, combine flour and brown sugar. Cut in peanut butter and butter until crumbly; sprinkle over bananas. Bake at 375 degrees for 25 minutes. Serve with whipped cream or vanilla ice cream.

Diane P. H. Williams
GFWC—Melbourne Area Junior Woman's Club
Melbourne, Florida

Photo features: Heavenly Custard—Page 372

Lemon Cake Pudding

- 3 tablespoons butter
- 1 cup sugar
- 4 egg yolks
- 1/3 cup lemon juice
- 2 teaspoons grated lemon rind
- 1/4 teaspoon salt
- 3 tablespoons flour
- 1 cup milk
- 4 egg whites

Cream butter and sugar until light. Add yolks and beat well. Add flour, juice, rind and salt. Stir well, do not beat. Stir in milk. Fold in well-beaten egg whites. Pour into 8-inch square pan. Set in pan of hot water, like custard cooking, bake at 325 degrees for 45 minutes. Cut into squares when cold.

Betsy Ruff
GFWC—North Plainfield Woman's Club
North Plainfield, New Jersey

My Egg Nog Salad Dessert

- 1 16 ounce can pears
- 1 11 ounce can mandarin oranges
- 1 teaspoon unflavored gelatin
- 1 cup sour cream
- 3/4 cup eggnog
- 1 6 ounce package lemon gelatin

Soften unflavored gelatin in 2 tablespoons of cold water. Drain and dice pears. Reserve juice. Add water to juice to make 2 cups. Bring to boil, stir in gelatin and cool. Blend sour cream and egg nog. Stir in gelatin mixture. Add lemon gelatin. Blend well and chill. When thickened, fold in mandarin oranges and diced pears. Turn into a 9½-inch flan pan or a 6-cup ring mold. Chill until firm. To serve cut into wedges.

Pauline Romero
GFWC—El Camino Woman's Club
Ventura, California

Alberta's Peach Dee-Lite

- Vanilla wafers
- 2 packages instant vanilla pudding mix
- 4 cups milk
- 1 teaspoon rum flavoring
- Strawberry Jam
- Red cherries
- Peaches, sliced and well drained
- 1 cup heavy cream, whipped
- 1/4 cup chopped walnuts

Place a layer of vanilla wafers on the bottom of a straight-sided bowl. Make pudding, add flavoring. Place a layer of jam over wafers. Continue layering ending with pudding. Top with peaches. Spoon cream around outer edge of bowl. Sprinkle with nuts. Garnish with cherries. Chill. Serve in small bowls.

Alberta Durfee
GFWC—Westborough Woman's Club
Westborough, Massachusetts

Raspberry Dessert

- **1 cup water**
- **½ cup sugar**
- **2 teaspoons lemon juice**
- **2 10 ounce packages frozen raspberries in syrup**
- **4 tablespoons cornstarch**
- **¼ cup cold water**
- **50 large marshmallows**
- **1 cup milk**
- **2 cups cream, whipped**
- **1¼ cups graham cracker crumbs**
- **¼ cup nuts, chopped**
- **¼ cup butter, melted**

Heat raspberries with ½ cup water, sugar and lemon juice. Dissolve cornstarch in ¼ cup cold water. Stir into raspberries and cook until thickened and clear. Cool. In double boiler, melt marshmallows in milk and cool. Whip cream and fold into marshmallow mixture. Mix graham cracker, nuts and butter in a 13 × 9 × 2 pan. Press firmly into bottom of pan. Spread marshmallow cream mixture over crumbs. Spread raspberry mixture over top. Refrigerate until firm.

Cindy M. Pate
GFWC—Rankin Junior Woman's Club
Rankin, Illinois

Blackberry Noodles

- **1 quart blackberries, cooked and sweetened to taste**

Noodles

- **1¼ cups sifted flour**
- **½ teaspoon salt**
- **⅜ cup shortening**
- **4 tablespoons of ice water**

Run blackberries and juice through a sieve to remove seeds. Add enough water to make a quart of liquid. Place in large pot on stove.

Prepare dough by sifting together flour and salt. Cut in shortening. Add half the ice water by sprinkling it over mixture. Mix lightly and add the remaining water, mixing gently. On a floured board, roll out dough very thin and cut it into 1-inch squares. Bring blackberry juice to a boil and drop noodles in a few at a time, keeping juice boiling. After all noodles have been added, cover pot; reduce heat and simmer 10 minutes, stirring carefully 2–3 times with a wooden spoon. Serve hot with cream.

"This is an old Cherokee Indian recipe."

Wilma Robison Fraley
GFWC—Amethyst Junior Woman's Club
Chelsea, Oklahoma

Washington Cherry Squares

Base

1½ cups rolled oats, uncooked
½ cup firmly packed brown sugar
⅓ cup margarine or butter, melted

Pre-heat oven 350 degrees.

Combine all ingredients thoroughly. Heat in shallow pan in pre-heated oven for 10 minutes. Set aside ½ cup crumb mixture. Firmly pack remaining crumb mixture into 9-inch square pan. Cool.

Filling

1 envelope unflavored gelatin
¼ cup cold water
1 13½ ounce can pineapple tidbits
¼ cup sugar
⅛ teaspoon salt
½ cup red maraschino cherry halves
½ cup coarsely chopped pecans
1 cup whipping cream

Soften gelatin in cold water. Drain pineapple, reserving juice. Add enough water to this juice to make ¾ cup. Heat pineapple juice, add softened gelatin, sugar and salt, stirring until dissolved. Remove from heat, chill until partially set. Stir in pineapple, nuts and cherries. Whip cream until stiff; pour over crumb base. Sprinkle with reserved crumb mixture. Cover and freeze for several hours until firm.

Freida M. Kelly
GFWC—Vignette
Columbiana, Alabama

Barbara's Apple Bobble

1 quart sliced apples
3 cups sifted flour
2 teaspoons salt
4 teaspoons baking powder
2 tablespoons shortening
¾ cup milk
4 cups water
2 cups sugar
1 tablespoon butter or oleo
1 cup brown sugar
1 teaspoon cinnamon

In a 9 × 13 pan, bring water, sugar, oleo and cinnamon to a boil. Combine flour, salt, baking powder, shortening and milk together. Roll out on floured board in an oblong shape about 12 × 18 inches. Spread apples over dough and then brown sugar. Roll jelly roll fashion and cut about 1 inch thick. Lay flat in boiling mixture. Bake at 375 degrees for ½ hour covered and ½ hour uncovered. Serve while warm with cream.

Frances Dickson
GFWC—Heber Springs Study Club
Heber Springs, Arkansas

Superb Pears

- **½ cup brown sugar, packed**
- **¼ cup rum**
- **¼ cup butter**
- **2 fresh, ripe pears, peeled, cored and halved**
- **½ cup raspberries, fresh or frozen**

In a 2-quart covered casserole dish, put brown sugar, rum and butter. Microwave 3–4 minutes covered. Remove from oven and place pear halves in casserole dish. Spoon sauce over pears. Cover and microwave 3–4 minutes, just until pears are tender. Put raspberries on top of pears and cover. Microwave 1–2 minutes. Serve immediately with a small amount of whipped cream or vanilla ice cream.

Joyce Johnson
GFWC—Tullahoma Woman's Club
Tullahoma, Tennessee

Macaroon-Almond Baked Pears

- **1 29 ounce can pear halves, drained**
- **¼ cup orange liqueur**
- **⅓ cup apricot preserves**
- **2 cups crumbled macaroons, heaping**
- **2 cups whipped cream**
- **¼ cup sliced almonds**

Arrange pear halves, cut side up in a 10 × 6 × 2 baking dish. Combine preserves and orange liqueur, pour over pear halves. Sprinkle macaroon crumbs and almonds on top. Bake in a 350 degree oven for 20–25 minutes. Serve warm with whipped cream.

Barbara Trombley
GFWC—The Waltham Woman's Club
Waltham, Massachusetts

Spicy Coconut Pears

- **1 29 ounce can pear halves**
- **2 tablespoons cornstarch**
- **¼ teaspoon cinnamon**
- **¼ teaspoon nutmeg**
- **⅛ teaspoon cloves**
- **½ cup sugar**
- **¼ cup lemon juice**
- **2 tablespoons butter**
- **½ cup coconut, toasted**
- **⅛ teaspoon orange rind—optional**

Drain pears, reserving 1 cup liquid. Combine ¼ cup liquid, cornstarch, cinnamon, nutmeg and cloves, stir until smooth. Set aside. Combine remaining pear liquid, sugar, lemon juice, butter and orange rind in small saucepan. Bring to a boil. Gradually stir in cornstarch mixture, cook over low heat, stirring constantly until thickened. Arrange pears in 8-inch square pan. Pour sauce over pears and sprinkle with coconut.

Nina Massey
GFWC—Huntingdon Woman's Guild
Savannah, Georgia

Apple Dumplings with Rum Sauce

Pastry

3 cups sifted all-purpose flour
1 teaspoon salt
1 cup shortening
8–9 tablespoons cold water

Sift together flour and salt. Cut in shortening until mixture resembles coarse crumbs. Gradually add water, mixing until dough just holds together. Roll out pie dough in 2 sections, each about 14 × 14 inches. Cut each into 4 squares.

Filling

8 medium baking apples
1 cup sugar
1 teaspoon cinnamon
Butter

Core apples and pare about ⅓ down. Place 1 apple on each square, fill apple centers with sugar and cinnamon mixture and top with ½ teaspoon butter. Fold pastry over apples bringing corners together; pinch edges together. Set in shallow baking pan. Bake at 425 degrees for 5 minutes. Reduce to 350 degrees and bake 45–55 minutes longer. Serve with hot rum sauce.

Rum Sauce

1 cup sugar
1 tablespoon flour
1 tablespoon cornstarch
2 cups water
1 tablespoon butter
⅓ cup rum

Sift together sugar, flour and cornstarch; stir in water. Cook until sauce thickens, stirring constantly. Reduce heat to low and cook 10 minutes. Add butter and rum. Yields about 2½ cups sauce.

Clarice Kronquist
GFWC—Newberry Woman's Club
Newberry, Michigan

Mom's Apple Dumpling

1 cup brown sugar
1 cup water
1½ cups flour
2 teaspoons baking powder
¼ teaspoon salt
4 tablespoons shortening
½ cup milk
3 apples, thinly sliced
½ teaspoon cinnamon

Make biscuit dough by sifting dry ingredients. Cut in shortening, adding milk to make soft dough. Put in oven, a 2-quart baking dish with brown sugar and water so sugar will melt. Roll dough to 8 × 12-inch rectangle. Spread with butter, cover with apples and sprinkle cinnamon on. Roll up like jelly roll, and slice into 8 pieces. Arrange on brown sugar syrup in baking dish. Bake at 425 degrees for 20 minutes. Serve with cream, warm or cold with ice cream.

Mary White
GFWC—Winchendon Woman's Club
Winchendon, Massachusetts

Apple Puff

Cake

½ pound butter or margarine
1½ cups sugar
4 eggs
4 cups flour
2 teaspoons baking soda
2 teaspoons baking powder
1 pint sour cream
White raisins

In mixing bowl, cream softened butter with sugar. Beat in eggs one at a time. Sift flour, baking soda and baking powder together; beat into egg mixture. Blend in sour cream. Spread half the mixture into a greased 10 × 15 × 1 pan.

Apple Filling

6 large apples
⅓ cup sugar
1½ teaspoons cinnamon
3 tablespoons butter

Peel, core and slice apples in saucepan; combine with all other ingredients. Cover and cook slowly until apples are soft but not mushy. Stir frequently in beginning and later occasionally to prevent sticking. Cover cake with apple filling and sprinkle with raisins to taste. Bake in pre-heated oven at 475 degrees for 45 minutes or until done in center. Cut into squares. Sprinkle with powdered sugar.

Evelyn M. Bonin
GFWC—Woman's Club of Secaucus
Secaucus, New Jersey

French Cherry Dessert

Crust

3 tablespoons confectioners' sugar
1 cup sifted flour
⅓ cup butter or margarine

Mix confectioners' sugar and 1 cup flour. Cut in butter until mixture resembles cornmeal. Press into bottom of an 8-inch square pan and bake in a 350 degree oven for 25 minutes or until light brown.

Filling

1 cup sugar
2 eggs, beaten
1 teaspoon vanilla
¼ cup flour
1 teaspoon baking powder
½ cup chopped nuts
¼ teaspoon salt
½ cup flaked coconut
½ cup drained maraschino cherries, halved or quartered

To make filling, mix together eggs, sugar and vanilla. Mix ¼ cup flour, baking powder and salt. Stir into egg mixture. Fold in nuts, cherries and coconut and spread over baked crust. Turn oven down to 325 degrees for 35–45 minutes. Cool. Serve with ice cream, sherbet or whipped cream.

Edythe R. Osborne
GFWC—Gridley Woman's Club
Gridley, California

Stuffed Oranges

- 2 oranges
- 4 eggs, separated
- 1 tablespoon cornstarch
- 2 ounces sugar
- 1 cup milk
- 2 ounces liqueur
- Whipped cream
- Maraschino cherries

Cut 2 oranges in half. Cut small slice from bottom so orange will sit evenly. Remove fruit from oranges. Beat 4 egg yolks with 2 ounces of sugar and the juice of the oranges. Add milk and cornstarch. Put the mixture in a heavy saucepan and bring to a boil over moderate heat. Keep stirring to avoid burning. Remove the pudding and cool. Beat 4 egg whites firm and fold into the pudding. Add liqueur for taste. Fill the oranges with the pudding. Top oranges with whipped cream and a red cherry just before serving. Makes 4 desserts.

"Recipe originated by chef Jack Favier of Nashville, Tennessee."

Isabel R. Edmands
GFWC—Hillsboro Woman's Club
Nashville, Tennessee

Cherry Pudding Cake

Cake

- 1½ cups sugar
- ½ teaspoon cinnamon
- 1 cup flour
- 1 teaspoon baking soda
- 1 cup nuts
- ¼ teaspoon salt
- 2 cups drained, dark cherries
- 2 tablespoons butter, melted
- 1 egg

Mix all dry ingredients; add dark cherries, well-beaten egg and butter. Add chopped nuts. Bake at 350 degrees for 45 minutes in a square 9-inch pan using cooking spray.

Sauce

- 1 cup cherry juice
- ¼ teaspoon almond flavoring
- 1 tablespoon cornstarch
- Dash salt
- ½ cup sugar

Mix all ingredients together and cook until thick. Serve with ice cream. Pour sauce over cake and ice cream.

Kay Koos
GFWC—Progressio
Harlan, Iowa

Dutch Apple Cobbler

Pastry

1 pie crust

Filling

1 cup sugar
2 tablespoons flour
1/2 teaspoon cinnamon
1/4 teaspoon nutmeg
1/8 teaspoon ginger
1/3 cup cream
6 cups peeled, sliced apples

Mix all ingredients together and put into the unbaked crust.

Topping

1 cup rolled oats
1/3 cup flour
1/2 cup brown sugar
1/2 teaspoon cinnamon
1/4 teaspoon salt
1/3 cup butter

Mix all ingredients together with fingers. Sprinkle over filling. Bake at 375 degrees about 1 hour. Serve warm with lemon sauce or warm cider sauce.

Sauce

1 cup apple cider
3/4 cup light corn syrup
1/4 cup sugar
1/4 cup butter
Juice and grated rind of one lemon
1/2 teaspoon nutmeg
Pinch ginger

Heat all ingredients together until sugar dissolves.

Martha A. Bein
GFWC—Oswego Woman's Civic Club
Oswego, Illinois

Peach Cobbler

Filling

- 4 cups fresh peaches, sliced
- 1/4 cup peach juice
- 3/4 cup sugar
- 1 1/2 teaspoons tapioca
- 1 tablespoon lemon juice
- 1 tablespoon margarine

Mix all ingredients together and set aside.

Crust

- 1 tablespoon salt
- 1 cup shortening
- 3 cups flour
- 1 egg, well beaten
- 6 tablespoons cold water
- 1 teaspoon vinegar

Mix flour, salt and shortening with fork; add egg, water and vinegar together. Add to flour mixture one tablespoon at a time. Handling lightly, on floured pastry cloth, roll out portion to fit 8 × 8 × 2-inch pan. Place in pan, then add peaches. Cover top with the rest of rolled dough, cut holes in top, press edges together and crimp as pie crust. Bake at 450 degrees for 15 minutes. Lower temperature to 375 degrees for 30 minutes. When using canned peaches, decrease sugar by 1/4 cup.

Grace E. Smith
GFWC—Woman's Club of Shadyside
Shadyside, Ohio

Three of a Kind Sherbet

- Juice of 3 oranges
- Juice of 3 lemons
- 3 bananas, mashed
- 2 cups sugar
- 2 cups water
- 1 cup cream

Bring sugar and water to gentle boil. Boil 3 minutes; then set aside to cool. Squeeze juice from oranges and lemons, and add 3 mashed bananas. When syrup is cool, stir it into the fruits and freeze. When the above is about 3/4 frozen, remove to a bowl and beat cream into it slowly. Refreeze.

Kitty Garber
GFWC—Woman's Club of Culpeper
Culpeper, Virginia

Strawberry Delight

- **1 cup all-purpose flour**
- **½ cup chopped pecans**
- **½ cup butter or margarine, melted**
- **¼ cup firmly packed brown sugar**
- **1 10 ounce package frozen strawberries, thawed**
- **1 cup sugar**
- **2 teaspoons fresh lemon juice**
- **2 egg whites**
- **1 cup whipping cream, whipped**

Combine flour, pecans, butter and brown sugar in a 8-inch square baking pan; stir well. Bake at 350 degrees for 20 minutes, stirring occasionally. Cool. Combine strawberries, sugar, lemon juice and egg whites in a large mixing bowl. Beat at high speed of electric mixer 10–12 minutes or until stiff peaks form. Fold in whipped cream. Press about ⅔ of the crumb mixture into a 9-inch springform pan; spoon in strawberry mixture. Sprinkle remaining crumbs on top; freeze until firm. Garnish with fresh strawberries, if desired.

Bette L. Brust
GFWC—Frederick Woman's Civic Club and Junior Woman's Club of Frederick
Frederick, Maryland

Debra Dunkle
GFWC—Circleville Junior Woman's Club
Circleville, Ohio

Wonderful Frozen Fruit

- **3 oranges, juice and pulp**
- **3 bananas**
- **1 20 ounce can crushed pineapple and juice**
- **3 lemons, juice and pulp**
- **1½ cups sugar**
- **⅓ cup Kirsch Liqueur**

Peel oranges and lemons. Place in food processor along with bananas, pineapple, sugar and liqueur. Mix until blended. Put in shallow pans and freeze. Allow to soften to easy spooning consistency, about 30 minutes, before serving in sherbet glasses.

Bobby Ruth Bjork
GFWC—Madison Valley Woman's Club
Ennis, Montana

Caramel Delight

- **1½ cups flour**
- **1 cup uncooked oats**
- **½ cup brown sugar, firmly packed**
- **1½ cups chopped nuts**
- **1 cup butter, melted**
- **6 ounces caramel topping**
- **½ gallon vanilla ice cream, softened**

Combine first 5 ingredients; spread in thin layer on cookie sheet and bake at 350 degrees for 20 minutes, or until brown. Cool and then crumble. Put half of crumbs in 13 × 9-inch pan. Spoon caramel topping over crumbs. Spread ice cream over topping. Top with remaining crumbs and freeze. Cut into squares to serve.

Bobby Ruth Bjork
GFWC—Madison Valley Woman's Club
Ennis, Montana

Teddy's Chocolate Dessert

- **1½ cups crushed chocolate wafers**
- **⅓ cup melted oleo**
- **1 8 ounce package cream cheese**
- **¼ cup sugar**
- **1 teaspoon vanilla**
- **2 eggs, separated**
- **1 12 ounce package of milk chocolate chips, slightly melted**
- **¼ cup sugar**
- **¾ cup chopped almonds**
- **1 cup cream, whipped**

Mix wafers and oleo. Press into a 9-inch pan and bake 10 minutes at 300 degrees. Beat cream cheese, sugar and vanilla. Add egg yolks and chocolate chips. Beat egg whites until stiff, add sugar and fold into chocolate mixture. Fold in cream and pecans. Pour into cooled shell and freeze for at least 3 hours.

Theodora Skubic
GFWC—Virginia Study Club
Virginia, Minnesota

Pink Artic Freeze

- **1 8 ounce package cream cheese, softened**
- **2 tablespoons mayonnaise**
- **2 tablespoons sugar**
- **1 20 ounce can crushed pineapple, drained**
- **1 can cranberry sauce or jelled type**
- **½ cup chopped pecans**
- **2 cups whipped cream or topping**

Soften cream cheese. Blend with sugar and mayonnaise and beat until fluffy. Add cranberry sauce and completely blend. Add pineapple and nuts by hand. Fold in the cream or topping. Pour into glass baking dish and let freeze. Slice off as needed. It keeps well.

Doris Barb
GFWC—Every Member Benefits Federated Club
El Dorado, Kansas

Yogurt-Vanilla

- **1 cup sugar**
- **2 envelopes unflavored gelatin**
- **Dash salt**
- **2 cups skim milk**
- **5 cups plain low-fat yogurt**
- **1 tablespoon vanilla**
- **2 cups frozen whipped topping**

Combine sugar, gelatin and salt in medium saucepan; add milk and let stand 1 minute. Cook over low heat, stirring constantly 5 minutes or until gelatin and sugar dissolves; let cool. Stir in yogurt, vanilla and whipped topping. Pour mixture in 1-gallon freezer can and freeze according to instructions. Serve immediately or let ripen 1 hour. Fruit may be added if desired.

Inez W. Riggs
GFWC—Camden Study Forum
Camden, Alabama

Cranberry Sherbet

- **1 quart cranberries**
- **2 cups sugar**
- **Grated rind of one orange**
- **1 pint water**
- **Juice of one orange**

Cook berries; run through a sieve and add sugar to puree. Add grated rind, heat until sugar dissolves. Add orange juice. Pour into ice cube tray and freeze. If you use a microwave to cook berries, be sure to use a dish twice the size because they expand when cooking. A blender or food processor can be used to grind the mixture, but the puree through the sieve is milder.

Sandy Iuebben
GFWC—Del Cerro Woman's Club
San Diego, California

Bridal Pudding

- **2 envelopes of gelatin**
- **½ cup cold water**
- **⅓ cup boiling water**
- **6 egg whites**
- **¼ teaspoon salt**
- **¾ cup sugar**
- **2 cups heavy cream**
- **1 teaspoon vanilla**
- **1 cup flaked coconut**

Soften the gelatin in cold water. Pour the boiling water into the gelatin and stir to dissolve. Beat the egg whites until stiff. Add salt and gradually beat in the sugar. Fold the gelatin into the whites. Beat the cream until stiff and add the vanilla. Fold the cream into the whites. Rub the bottom and sides of an 8 or 9-inch springform pan with butter. Sprinkle the bottom with ½ the coconut and pour in the cream mixture. Sprinkle the remaining coconut and chill 4 hours or overnight.

Betsy Dye
GFWC—The Woman's Evening Club of Allendale
Allendale, New Jersey

Rhubarb Pudding

- **5 cups rhubarb, sliced**
- **2 cups water**
- **1 cup sugar**
- **¼ cup cornstarch**
- **Few drops red food coloring**
- **Optional—Frozen raspberries or strawberries**

In saucepan cook rhubarb and water until mushy, about 10 minutes. Combine sugar and cornstarch, gradually stirring into rhubarb mixture. Cook, stirring constantly, until thick and transparent. Add thawed raspberries or strawberries for a different flavor while cooking the rhubarb and water.

Kristy E. Sauby
GFWC—Woman's Literary Club
Carrington, North Dakota

Rodgrod (Rote Grutze)

- **1 pound red currants or black currants, washed and stalked**
- **8 ounces raspberries, hulled**
- **4 ounces castor sugar**
- **1 ounce cornflour**
- **Few almonds, blanched and toasted**
- **¼ pint double whipped cream**

Put the fruit in a pan with sugar and a little cold water, just enough to cover. Simmer over a low heat until the currants are tender about 20 minutes. Then liquidize and sieve the fruit. In a small bowl, blend a little of the fruit juice into the cornflour, stirring to make a smooth paste. Return the remaining juice and the paste to the cleaned pan and stir over a low heat until the compote clears. Remove from the heat and allow to cool, stirring at intervals to prevent a skin forming. Pour into a glass serving dish and pipe whipped cream in swirls over the top. Decorate with toasted almonds.

Margot Carstensen
GFWC—Deutscher Hausfrauen-Bund
West Germany

Paska

- **1 pound cream cheese**
- **1 cup powdered sugar**
- **½ cup sour cream**
- **1 teaspoon vanilla**
- **1 teaspoon almond extract**
- **1 cup chopped dates**
- **½ cup chopped mixed candied fruit**

In an electric blender, blend cream cheese and sour cream until smooth. Add extracts and sugar; blend until smooth. Stir in dates and candied fruits. Refrigerate overnight. Spoon into sherbet glasses. Garnish with sliced almonds or dates.

Maxine Lane
GFWC—Clawson
Clawson, Michigan

Lil's Chocolate Luv

- **1 cup butter**
- **2 cups powdered sugar**
- **4 ounces unsweetened baking chocolate, melted**
- **4 eggs**
- **2 tablespoons vanilla**
- **1 cup chopped nuts—optional**
- **1 package plain chocolate cookies crushed—1½ cups**

Cream butter and sugar well; then beat in melted chocolate slowly. Add eggs one at a time, beating well after each addition. Add vanilla and beat until mixed thoroughly. Add nuts if desired and stir well. Place half cookie crumbs on bottom of 9 × 12 container; spoon in chocolate and top with remaining crumbs. Chill at least 8 hours; best chilled at least 24 hours and can be made two days ahead. Cut in small pieces and serve topped with whipped cream. If making ahead, cover with foil to prevent drying.

Lillian Burroughs
GFWC—Allied Gardens Woman's Club
San Diego, California

Tropic Delight

- **1½ cups vanilla wafers, crumbled fine**
- **¼ cup melted butter or margarine**
- **1½ cups shredded flaked coconut**
- **½ cup butter or margarine**
- **1½ cups sifted powdered sugar**
- **2 eggs**
- **¾ cup chopped maraschino cherries**
- **1 9 ounce can crushed pineapple**
- **1 cup broken pecans**
- **1 cup cream, whipped**

Mix melted butter and crumbs. Pat half of mixture in bottom of 9 × 9 × 2 dish or pan. Sprinkle with half the coconut. Cream butter and gradually add powdered sugar; beat with electric beater until light. Add eggs, one at a time, beating well after each. Spread mixture over coconut. Drain cherries and pineapple well; fold into whipped cream along with pecans; spread over mixture in dish. Sprinkle remaining coconut and crumbs. Chill in refrigerator 6 hours before serving.

Nita Wood
GFWC—Pen Chat
Burnet, Texas

Claudia's Chocolate Mousse Crown

- **⅔ cup cream de coco liqueur**
- **½ cup cold water**
- **2 envelopes unflavored gelatin**
- **16 ounce package semi-sweet chocolate, chopped coarse or (16, 1 ouncc squares)**
- **3 large eggs, separated, bring whites to room temperature**
- **¼ cup granulated sugar**
- **2 cups whipping cream, whipped stiff**
- **33 tubular-shaped cookies with chocolate bits**
- **Whipped cream and chocolate shavings**

Mix liqueur with water in large saucepan; sprinkle gelatin over top and let stand 1 minute. Stir over low heat until gelatin is completely dissolved, about 3 minutes. Add chocolate; stir until melted and smooth. Remove from heat; whisk in egg yolks one at a time; cool to room temperature. In large bowl beat egg whites with electric mixer until soft peaks form when beaters are lifted. Gradually add sugar; beat until stiff glossy peaks form. Stir a large dollop of whites into the chocolate mixture until blended, then fold the chocolate mixture into remaining whites. Gently fold in whipped cream. Spoon about ¼ inch mousse mixture in an 8½-inch springform pan to cover the bottom. Stand cookies in the mousse all around inside edge of pan. Gently pour in remaining mousse. Cover loosely with waxed paper. Chill at least 3 hours or overnight. Before serving, remove sides of pan; garnish mousse with whipped cream and chocolate shavings. Shave chocolate with a vegetable peeler. With sharp knife, cut into wedges 2 cookies wide. Serves 16.

Claudia D. Trommer
GFWC—Riverdale Woman's Club
Riverdale, New Jersey

Heavenly Custard

Custard

- **3 cups milk**
- **1½ cups sugar**
- **6 egg yolks, beaten**
- **1½ tablespoons unflavored gelatin**
- **6 tablespoons milk**
- **2 cups whipping cream**
- **1 teaspoon vanilla**
- **1 teaspoon almond flavoring**

Mix milk and sugar; add to egg yolks which have been beaten. Cook mixture over very low heat or in top of double boiler until mixture coats spoon. Dissolve gelatin in 6 tablespoons milk; add to the custard. Cool until custard begins to set. Whip cream and flavorings. Fold cream into the partially set custard. Pour into individual sherbet dishes; chill. Garnish with raspberry sauce.

Sauce

- **12 ounce package frozen raspberries**
- **1 tablespoon sugar**
- **1 teaspoon cornstarch**

Thaw and drain raspberries. Rub through sieve. Combine sugar with cornstarch. Add to berry juice and pulp. Cook over low heat until sauce thickens. Cool.

Juanita K. Laumets
GFWC—Coterie
Elkhart, Kansas

Orange Pudding

Sauce

- **Juice of 1 orange**
- **Rind of 1 orange**
- **1 cup sugar**
- **2 cups boiling water**
- **¼ cup butter**

Mix all ingredients together.

Dumpling

- **½ cup sugar**
- **⅛ cup butter**
- **½ cup milk**
- **1 teaspoon baking powder**
- **1 cup flour**

Mix all ingredients together and drop by teaspoonful into hot sauce. Cover. Bake at 350 degrees for 30 minutes. Serve hot.

Gertrude D. Sterrett
GFWC—Woman's Club of Brockway
Brockway, Pennsylvania

Apricot Nectar Mousse

1 12 ounce can apricot nectar
8 marshmallows, quartered or 32 miniatures
3 tablespoons granulated sugar
1 tablespoon lemon juice
1/8 teaspoon salt
1/2 pint whipping cream, whipped
2 tablespoons granulated sugar for cream

Combine 2 tablespoons nectar and marshmallows in top of double boiler; cook and stir until marshmallows are melted. Add remaining nectar, sugar, juice and salt; stir to blend. Pour into refrigerator tray, place in freezing unit and chill about 30 minutes. Fold in whipped cream to which 2 tablespoons of sugar has been added and freeze. Stir 3–4 times during the freezing process.

Thelma B. Blair
GFWC—The Woman's Club of Mt. Washington
Baltimore, Maryland

Snowflake Pudding with Crimson Raspberry Sauce

Pudding

1 cup sugar
1 envelope unflavored gelatin
1/2 teaspoon salt
1 1/4 cups milk
1 teaspoon vanilla
13 1/2 ounces flaked coconut
2 cups heavy cream for whipping

Mix first three ingredients; add milk, stir over medium heat until dissolved. Chill until partially set; add vanilla, fold in coconut. Add whipped cream and put in 1 1/2-quart mold. Chill until firm at least 4 hours. This pudding can be made and refrigerated several days before using. Serve with crimson raspberry sauce.

Sauce

10 ounce package frozen red raspberries, crushed and strained
1 1/2 teaspoons cornstarch
1/2 cup currant jelly

Thaw, crush and strain raspberries. Combine juice with cornstarch and jelly. Bring to boil; cook and stir until mixture is clear and slightly thickened. Serve warm or cold.

Alice Glaser
GFWC—Simsbury Woman's Club
Simsbury, Connecticut

Steamed Raspberry Pudding

- **1 tablespoon butter**
- **½ cup sugar**
- **1 egg**
- **½ cup sour milk**
- **1 teaspoon baking soda**
- **1 cup flour**
- **1 teaspoon vanilla**
- **1 can canned raspberries**

Combine all ingredients together except raspberries. Fill individual dishes half full with canned raspberries. Spoon enough batter on top of berries until dishes are ¾ full. Place in steaming kettle and steam ½–¾ of an hour. Serve warm with whipped cream.

Connie Entwistle
GFWC—Woman's Club of Fanwood
Fanwood, New Jersey

Hot Chocolate-Fudge Pudding Cake

- **1¼ cups sugar, divided**
- **1 cup all-purpose flour**
- **7 tablespoons cocoa, divided**
- **2 teaspoons baking powder**
- **¼ teaspoon salt**
- **½ cup milk**
- **⅓ cup butter or margarine, melted**
- **1½ teaspoons vanilla**
- **½ cup packed light brown sugar or ¼ cup packed dark brown sugar**
- **1¼ cups hot water**

In medium bowl, combine ¾ cup sugar, flour, 3 tablespoons cocoa, baking powder and salt. Blend in milk, melted butter and vanilla. Beat until smooth. Pour batter into a square pan 8 × 8 × 2 inches or 9 × 9 × 2 inches. In small bowl, combine remaining ½ cup sugar, brown sugar and remaining 4 tablespoons cocoa; sprinkle mixture evenly over batter. If nuts are used, sprinkle evenly over mixture. Pour hot water over top. Do not stir. Bake at 350 degrees for 40 minutes. Let stand 15 minutes; while spooning into dessert dishes, spoon sauce from bottom of pan over top. Good topped with whipped cream or vanilla ice cream.

Ronnye L. Sands
GFWC—Palm Beach Gardens Woman's Club
Palm Beach Gardens, Florida

Old Tyme Rice Pudding

- **4 cups whole milk**
- **6 tablespoons sugar**
- **5 heaping tablespoons long grain rice**
- **1 tablespoon butter or margarine**
- **½ teaspoon salt**
- **½ cup raisins**
- **Cinnamon**

Bring milk to boiling point, scalding; add sugar, rice, butter and salt. Transfer to buttered casserole—1½-quart size. Put in preheated oven at 350 degrees. Bake, stirring occasionally, for 60–75 minutes. When milk is practically absorbed, pudding is done. Add raisins and stir; top with little cinnamon. Serve hot or cold. May cover with additional milk or cream. Serves 4 generously. Serve in sauce dishes.

Ardyce Samp
GFWC—Athena Literary Club
Flandreau, South Dakota

Christmas Cherry Pudding

- **2 cups sugar**
- **2 cups flour**
- **1 teaspoon baking soda**
- **4 teaspoons butter**
- **2 cups canned tart cherries**
- **1 cup pecans, chopped**
- **1 teaspoon baking powder**
- **2 eggs**

Cream butter, sugar and eggs in large bowl. Add remaining ingredients and mix well. Bake in a greased pan at 375 degrees for 1 hour. Cool. Cut into large squares. Serve warm or at room temperature with whipped cream.

Patricia T. Muldoon
GFWC—Pembroke Woman's Club
Pembroke, Virginia

Yummy Yum Peach Pudding

- **4 cups raw sliced peaches**
- **¾ cup sugar**
- **3 tablespoons butter**
- **½ cup milk**
- **1 cup flour**
- **1 teaspoon baking powder**
- **¼ teaspoon salt**
- **1 cup sugar**
- **1 tablespoon cornstarch**
- **¼ teaspoon salt**
- **¾ cup boiling water**

Put raw fruit unsweetened in an 8 × 12 dish. Cream ¾ cup sugar and butter. Add milk alternately with the flour, baking powder and salt. Pour over fruit in dish. Combine 1 cup sugar, cornstarch, salt and pour over batter. Pour boiling water over all and bake at 350 degrees for 1 hour.

Ann Killinger
GFWC—Twentieth Century Federated Club
Carson, Iowa

Ris' Alamonde

- **¼ cup rice**
- **2 cups milk**
- **¼ cup chopped blanched almonds**
- **2 cups heavy cream, whipped**
- **¼ cup sherry wine**
- **1 teaspoon vanilla**
- **½ cup sugar**
- **1 envelope unflavored gelatin**

Heat milk to boiling; add rice and cook until very tender. Soften gelatin in ¼ cup water; then add to rice mixture. Mix in almonds, sherry, vanilla and sugar. Cool. Fold in whipped cream. Chill. Serve with bing cherry sauce

Sauce

- **1 can bing cherries, pitted**
- **½ cup sugar**
- **2 tablespoons cornstarch**
- **¼ cup sherry wine**

Drain cherry juice into saucepan; thicken with sugar and cornstarch; cook over low heat until thick and then cool. Add sherry wine and cherries.

Jean Ann Nelson
GFWC—Woman's Clubs of Emmaus & Macungie
Emmaus and Macungie, Pennsylvania

Orange Marmalade Pudding

- **1 cup flour**
- **½ teaspoon salt**
- **1 teaspoon baking soda**
- **1 teaspoon baking powder**
- **1 cup milk**
- **4 tablespoons sugar**
- **1 egg**
- **1 cup suet**
- **1 cup orange marmalade**
- **1½ cups bread crumbs**

Sift flour, salt, baking powder, baking soda and sugar together. Add suet and crumbs; mix well. Add slightly beaten egg, marmalade and milk. Beat well and pour into greased molds ⅔ full. Cover tightly and steam 3 hours.

Sauce

- **¾ cup melted butter**
- **1 egg**
- **1 teaspoon vanilla**

Mix butter and egg, beating until smooth; cook until thick and add vanilla. Serve over pudding warm.

Gertrude Lewis
GFWC—Federated Woman's Club of West Seattle
Seattle, Washington

Brown Pudding

- **2 cups water**
- **1½ cups dark brown sugar**
- **¼ cup butter or oleo**
- **1 cup flour**
- **1 teaspoon cinnamon**
- **2 teaspoons baking powder**
- **½ cup sugar**
- **½ cup seedless raisins**
- **½ cup nuts**
- **½ cup milk**

Boil together for 10 minutes water, brown sugar and butter. Mix together flour, cinnamon, baking powder, sugar, raisins and nuts. Stir in milk to make batter. Pour syrup mix into 9 × 13-inch pan. Drop batter by spoonfuls into syrup. Bake at 350 degrees for 30 minutes. Top with whipped cream.

Martha Melton Roberson
GFWC—Twentieth Century Library Club
Tifton, Georgia

Spicy Apple Pudding

- **½ cup butter**
- **¾ cup sugar**
- **1 egg, unbeaten**
- **¼ teaspoon salt**
- **½ teaspoon cinnamon**
- **¼ teaspoon nutmeg**
- **1 teaspoon baking soda**
- **1⅛ cups flour**
- **1½ cups chopped apples**
- **1 tablespoon cream**

Cream butter and sugar thoroughly; add egg and beat well. Sift dry ingredients and add to first mixture. Add apples and the cream. Fill 8 well-greased individual molds half full. Bake 30 minutes at 350 degrees.

Sauce

- **1 cup sugar**
- **2 tablespoons flour**
- **1 cup cider**
- **¼ cup orange juice**
- **2 tablespoons butter**
- **Maraschino cherries and juice, cut up**

Boil sugar, apple cider and flour until slightly thickened. Add rest of ingredients and bring to boil. Serve warm.

Elaine Young
GFWC—Hagerstown Woman's History Club
Hagerstown, Indiana

Steamed Pudding

Pudding

- **1 cup ground suet or ½ cup shortening**
- **1 cup bread crumbs**
- **2 cups flour**
- **1¼ cups milk**
- **1 rounded tablespoon baking soda**
- **1 cup raisins**
- **1 teaspoon cloves**
- **1 teaspoon cinnamon**
- **1 tablespoon water**

Add all ingredients and stir well. Put in top of double boiler and steam covered for 3 hours. Serve with sauce.

Sauce

- **1 cup sugar**
- **½ cup butter**
- **1 egg**
- **1 teaspoon vinegar**

Melt butter; add sugar and egg. Stir while it cooks. Add vinegar and thin with milk or cream.

Catherine E. Armitage
GFWC—Madison Valley Woman's Club
Ennis, Montana

Bread Pudding—Microwave

- **4 cups bread cubes, lightly packed into a cup, 4–5 slices**
- **½ cup brown sugar, packed**
- **½ teaspoon nutmeg**
- **¼ teaspoon salt**
- **1 teaspoon cinnamon**
- **½ cup raisins—optional**
- **2 cups milk**
- **¼ cup butter**
- **2 eggs, beaten**

Spread bread cubes evenly in an 8-inch round dish. Sprinkle evenly with brown sugar, spices, salt and then raisins. Measure milk into 1-quart measuring cup. Add butter. Microwave at high 4–5 minutes, until butter is melted and milk is warm. Rapidly stir in eggs with a fork and mix well. Pour over bread cubes; cover with waxed paper. Microwave at medium high 11–13 minutes. Rotate dish ¼ turn after 6 minutes. Center will be slightly soft but will set up as pudding cools. Serve warm or chilled.

Mary Garrison
GFWC—Woman's Club of Auburndale
Auburndale, Florida

New Orleans Bread Pudding with Whiskey Sauce

Pudding

- **1 loaf French bread**
- **1 quart milk**
- **3 eggs**
- **2 cups sugar**
- **2 tablespoons vanilla**
- **1 cup raisins**
- **3 tablespoons margarine, melted**

Soak bread in milk, crush with hands until mixed. Add eggs, sugar, vanilla and raisins. Pour melted margarine in the bottom of a thick pan and pour in batter. Bake until very firm at 350 degrees for 50–60 minutes. Cool.

Whiskey Sauce

- **1 stick butter**
- **¾ cup sugar**
- **4 tablespoons milk**
- **2 jiggers whiskey**

Cream together butter and sugar. Add milk and flavor this with whiskey. Heat. Serve over bread pudding.

Jane E. Mahoney
GFWC—Cosmopolitan Woman's Club
Mobile, Alabama

Apricot Bread Pudding

- **1 cup soft bread crumbs**
- **⅔ cup milk**
- **¾ cup cooked, drained and chopped apricots**
- **½ teaspoon grated lemon rind**
- **2 eggs, well beaten**
- **½ cup grated coconut**
- **2 tablespoons butter**
- **¾ cup sugar**
- **2 teaspoons lemon juice**
- **Dash salt**
- **6 apricot halves**

Combine crumbs, milk, butter and sugar. Heat to boiling point, stirring constantly; then cool. Add ¾ cup apricots, lemon juice, rind, salt and eggs. Turn into greased baking dish, top with apricot halves and sprinkle with coconut. Place in pan of hot water and bake at 350 degrees for 45–50 minutes or until firm.

Lenora Caswell
GFWC—Norcross Woman's Club
Norcross, Georgia

Index

Page

Appetizers

Almond Cheese Ball 11
Appetizer 30
Artichoke Chili Dip 25
Artichoke Nibbles 14
Aunt Carmella's Freselles 37
Avocado Dip 24
Baked Clams 31
Beef Rolls 34
Boursin Cheese 20
Braunschweiger Ball 12
Cauliflower Patties 13
Cheddar Curry Spread 21
Chickpea Spread 20
Chili Rellano Won Tons Appetizers 14
Chinese Chips 37
Country Ham Butter 19
Crab Meat Canape Spread 18
Cream Cheese Vegetable Dip 25
Cucumber Cream Cheese Spread 19
Curry Almond Spread 10
Curry Vegetable Dip 24
Dill Dip 23
Elegant Fruit Dip 25
Fabulous Garlic Loaf 28
Georgia Pecan Dip 26
Green Pepper Dip 21
Ham and Cheese Sandwich 29
Hot Broccoli Dip 23
Jessie's Dip 22
Joan's Cheese Ball 11
Lentil Oatburgers 29
Liptauer Spread 18
Little Smokies Appetizers 30
Low Fat-Low Cholesterol Cheese Dip 23
Macadamia Nut Cheese Ball 12
Mexican Pinwheels 14
Minnesota Wild Rice Appetizer .. 10
Missouri Pate 19
Mushroom Cheese Ball 11
Mushroom Logs 16
Mushroom Roll-Ups 15
Mushrooms Stuffed with Walnuts and Cheese 13
Olive and Curry Hors d'Oeuvres .. 16
Olive Nut Sandwich Spread 17
Omaha Crackers 36
Orange Wheat Crackers 37
Pickled Party Shrimp 32
Pineapple Cheese Ball 10
Pink Shrimp Dip 21
Polynesian Ginger Dip 22
Poor Man's Caviar 15
Roasted Pecans 35
Scotch Eggs 35
Seafood Paté 33
Seven Layer Spread 35
Shrimp 'n' Cheese Sunday Nighters 26
Shrimp Spread 17
"Small Army Stromboli" 27
So-o-o Good Cream Cheese 20
Spinach Bread 36
Stroganoff Mushrooms 16
Super Duper Taco Burger 28
Susan's Fruit Dip 24
Swedish Meatballs 32
Sweet/Hot Cracker Spread 18
Taco Tarts 31
Tangy Cheese Ring 9
Tuna Chiffon Mold 34
Tuna Paté 34
Vegetable Dip 22
Walnut Stuffed Mushrooms 12
Water Chestnut Wraps 17
Western Style Sandwich 27
Zesty Meatball Appetizers 33

Beverages

Abigail Adams' Champagne Punch 43
Amaretto Punch 44
Big Sky Slush 45
Boerenjongen's Cocktail 44
Christmas Fruit Punch 40
Christmas Punch 43
Cocoa Banana Special Drink 42
Coffee Eggnog 39
Coffee of Vienna's Empire 45
Coffee Wedding Punch 40
Frozen Fruit Punch 40
Holiday Tea 41
May Magic 41
Non-Alcoholic Punch 42
Rhubarb Punch 41
Spiced Wine Punch 43
Strawberry Iced Tea 41
Wedding Punch 42
Yolie's Old Fashioneds 44

Soups

Avocado-Cucumber Soup 50
Beaufort Cream of Crab Soup ... 50
Benson Bean Broth 50
Cauliflower Cream Soup 52
Cheese and Meatball Soup 54
Clam and Vegetable Chowder ... 53
Creamy Old Fashioned Bean Soup 47
Diet Consomme 55
Easy But Great Brunswick Stew .. 52
Egg Lemon Soup 54
Ilse's Potato Soup 57
Italian Chicken Stew (Diet) 49
Lentil Sausage Main-Dish Soup .. 56
Low-Fat Bean Soup 51
Mast-O-Khiar (Cold Yogurt Soup) 49
Mom's Old Fashioned Turkey-Vegetable Soup 53
Old Virginia Pumpkin Soup 57
Presidential Peanut Soup 52
Quick and Easy Microwave Chili . 48
Quick Bean Soup 51
Sausage Bean Chowder 49
Schnit Suppe—German Fruit Soup 55
Simple and Easy Chili 48
Swedish Fruit Soup 55
Tuna Chowder 56

Salads

A Dieter's Dream Shrimp Salad .. 74
All-You-Want-For-Lunch Salad .. 73
Apricot Salad 64
Baked Potato Dressing 91
Baked Seafood Salad 73
Beef Spinach Salad 76
Blueberry Salad 65
Bombay Salad 75
Broccoli Salad Deluxe 82
Broccoli Salad Supreme 83
Buttery Cinnamon Skillet Apples 89
Cajun Red Bean Salad 87
Carrot and Apple Casserole 89
Cauliflower Salad 60
Cherry-Cola Salad 67
Christmas Salad 68
Colonial Salad 73
Cornbread Salad 82
Creamy French Dressing 93
Crunchy Fresh Grape Salad 64
Cucumber Salad 84
Dairyland Summer Salad 78
Deluxe Pineapple/Cranberry Salad 68
Deviled Egg Salad 70
Egg White Salad 84
Emerald Salad 72
Five Minute Tomato Aspic 71
Frosted Fruit Salad 62
Frozen Cranberry Salad 64
Frozen Fruit Salad 61
Frozen Mint Salad 63
Frozen Salad 63
Fruit, Cheese and Tuna Salad ... 77
Fruit French Dressing 92
Fruit Salad Dressing 92
Fruity Ginger Ale Mold 67
Fruity-Lemon Freeze 62

Page
Garden Pasta Salad 81
Grandmother Clarke's Boiled Potato Salad Dressing 92
Honey Fruit Dressing 90
Hot Fruit Casserole 88
Hot Pineapple Casserole 89
Informal Salmon Salad Loaf 76
Jellied Beet Salad 68
Lake Arrowhead Chinese Slaw ... 86
Low-Sodium Seasoning 91
Mandarin Chicken Salad 77
Mandarin Orange Mold 66
Marinated Pork Salads 72
Mary Ann's Champagne Salad ... 63
Molded Citrus Salad 65
My Emergency Pasta Salad 79
Nadine's Pasta Salad 79
One Can Salad 85
Orange-Cream Fruit Salad 65
Oriental Pea Pod and Chicken Salad 80
Overnight Tossed Salad 59
Parmesan Potato Salad 83
Pea Salad 82
Pea Salad 83
Pennsylvania Dutch Hot Dressing 93
Pineapple-Cheese Salad 66
Pineapple Souffle 88
Popeye Salad 71
Poppy Seed Dressing 90
Red, White and Blue Salad 69
Rhubarb Salad 66
Rice and Shrimp Salad 78
Salmon Mousse 67
Salt-Free Herbed Buttermilk Dressing 91
Shoe Peg Salad 87
Shrimp Macaroni Salad 75
Shrimp Ring 74
Shrimp Spread Mold 72
Spaghetti and Pea Salad 81
Spaghetti Salad 80
Spiced Apple Rings 89
Spinach, Bacon, Apple Salad 60
Spinach Mold 71
Spinach Salad 84
Strawberry Pretzel Salad 69
Super Slender Salad 70
Sweet and Sour Macaroni Salad .. 81
Tomato/Onion Mint Salad 88
Tomato Soup Salad 75
Tortellini Vegetable Salad 86
White Peg Corn Salad 87
Wild Rice Spinach Salad 85
Zero Dressing 90
Zesty Spinach Salad with Buttermilk Dressing 61

Breads

Amish Dilly Bread 97
Apple Muffins 115
Apricot Bread 112
Athenaeum Rolls 95
Page
Baked Apple Doughnuts 107
Beer and Cheddar Muffins 114
Blueberry Pecan Bread 111
"Blue Ribbon" Pumpkin Bread .. 111
Bran Rolls 101
Bubble Wreath 97
Cheese Bread 104
Cheese Puffs 99
Cheese Strudel 98
Cinnamon Popovers 107
Cinnamon Raisin English Muffins 100
Corn Bread 117
Corn Fritters 116
Cranberry Doughnuts 108
Cranberry Orange Muffins 113
Easy Bran Muffins 115
Easy Food Processor Pizza Dough 105
Easy Potato Buns 100
E-Z Spoon Bread 116
Freezer Biscuits 118
French Bread 102
German Apple Pancake 119
German Coffeebread (Kuga) 98
German Christmas Bread 103
Grammy Hooper's Sour Milk Doughnuts 108
Grandmother's Famous Cranberry Bread 109
Harvest Bread 109
Hot Rolls (Food Processor Method) 99
Italian Bread 102
Italian Bread Sticks 107
Low Cholesterol Banana Bread .. 111
My Favorite White Bread 101
Oatmeal Bread 104
Oatmeal Dill Spoon Bread 116
Oatmeal Pancakes 119
Onion-Cheese Supper Bread 105
Orange Date and Nut Bread 109
Pancakes 119
Pineapple Nut Bread 112
Pita (Pocket Bread) 106
Pizza Crust—Whole Wheat 106
Poppy Seed Bread 110
Potato Yeast Bread 103
Prune Coffee Cake 96
Quick Apple Strudel 96
Scones 106
Soft Molasses Gingerbread 110
Sour Dough Biscuits 118
Spinach Cheese Bread 104
Sugar Plum Muffins 115
Whole Grain Muffins 113
Whole Wheat Angel Biscuits 118
Zucchini Fritters 117
Zucchini Herb Cornbread 117
Zucchini Oatmeal Muffins 114

Meats and Meat Sauces

Acorn Squash with Sausage 152
All Purpose Barbecue Sauce 164
Page
American Chop Suey 143
Apple Cider Stew 134
Baked Linguine 147
Baked Pork Chops/Rice/Green Beans 149
Barbecued Beef 135
Barbecued Ribs—Island Style 165
Bar-B-Q Pork Chops 142
Beef and Noodle Casserole 124
Beef Burgundy 132
Beef Risotto Pie 130
Beef Stroganoff 133
Beer-Braised Loin of Pork 141
Breakfast Casserole 155
Breakfast Casserole 156
Cauliflower-Ham Au Gratin 157
Cavatini 146
Chafing Dish Meatballs 131
Cheesey Beef-Stuffed Peppers ... 128
Company Casserole 141
Corned Beef 139
Corned Beef Casserole 140
Corned Beef Pot 140
Cornish Pasty 137
Cranberry-Orange Chutney 167
Creamy Chicken Livers 164
Curried Beef 'n Broccoli 127
Drunken Polish Sausages 153
Easter Pizza 148
Etta's Expandable Pork Chop Casserole 151
Family Cheese and Egg Bake 146
Fresh Sausage with Raisin Sauce .. 145
Frittata—Fresh Garden Variety .. 153
Fruited Brisket 122
German Skillet Supper 125
Gourmet Encore 125
Grandmother's Holiday Ham 145
Ham Di Parma 157
Ham Rolls, Peaches in Raisin Sauce 155
Hamburger Casserole 126
Ham-Noodle Casserole 154
Hawaiian Ham Loaves 154
Hawaiian Spareribs 159
Hecka (Oriental Dish) 142
Idaho Fresh Prune Chutney 167
Italian Beef 123
Italian Pie 138
Italian Stuffed Peppers 151
January Chili Sauce 168
Johnny Mazetti Hot Dish 159
Judy's Bar-B-Que 134
Kraut Supreme 156
Lamb Curry 161
Liver Dish (for those who think they hate liver) 163
Liver Knaefly 163
Mandarin Ham Rolls 158
Marinated Venison Roast 163
Mary's Barbecue 143
Meatball Medley 132
Meatballs with Sour Cream Sauce .. 148
Meatloaf Roll 131

Page
Miniature Ham Pies 153
Mock Ham and Cheese Souffle . . 150
Mushroom Sauce for Ham 169
Mustard Sauce 168
Old Virginia Ham 144
Ono Hawaiian Steaks 136
Oslo Pork Chops 142
Oven Stew 134
Perusky 124
Pesto Genovese (Green Sauce) . . . 169
Picante Sauce 169
Pigs in the Blanket 156
Plum Good Ribs 165
Popover Casserole 129
Pork Chops and Rice 144
Pork Dinner 149
Pork Szechwan 144
Potato Hamburger Pinwheels 127
Potato Mogsaka 126
Raisin Sauce 168
Reuben Casserole 140
Rib Eye Roast 123
Rice and Sausage 152
Rump Roast Elegance 121
Sauerbraten 122
Sausage and Peppers 145
Sausage and Rice Casserole 159
Sausage Casserole 155
Sausage Roll 152
Sausage-Lima Bean Bake 147
Schnitz and Knepp 158
Serendipity Beef 127
Short Ribs Supreme 135
Soft Tacos with Homemade Flour Tortillas 136
Spaghetti Sauce 166
Spicy Spaghetti Sauce 166
Squash Casserole 151
Steak Continental 136
Stroganoff Steak Sandwiches 133
Stuffed Cabbage (Austrian Style) . . 128
Stuffed Pork Chops with Apple Cornbread Dressing 150
Surprise Onions Italiano 147
Swedish Potato Sausage 139
Sweet and Sour Meatloaf 129
Sweet-Sour Pork Chops 143
Tenderloin Deluxe 123
Texas Hash 126
Tourtiere 138
Veal Casserole 161
Veal Parmigiana 160
Veal Scallopini 161
Veal with Green Peas 160
Venison Meatloaf 162
Venison/Wild Rice Casserole 162
Western Style Bean Casserole 137
Wild Rice and Sausage 146
Williamsburg Pork 149
Wow Meatloaf 130

Fish and Seafood

Baked Fish Au Gratin 177
Baked Stuffed Shrimp 185
Page
Bowler's Wharf Crab Cakes 183
Caviar Pie 179
Clam Sauce with Linguine 188
Codfish A La Vizcaina 176
Crab on English Muffins 182
Crab Pelau 182
Creamy Fish and Cheese Chowder 175
Deviled Crab Casserole 184
Deviled Oysters 181
Doris' Salmon Salad Pie 179
Doris' Shrimp in Garlic Sauce 187
Fantastic Fish Fillets 176
Golden Seafood Casserole 172
Lobster or Crabmeat Bisque 188
Maryland Crab Imperial 184
Mom's Deviled Clams 188
Nantucket Scallops 171
Nantucket Seafood Casserole 174
Oven Fried Fish-N-Chips 177
Oyster Pie 181
Pescatore (The Fisherman) 172
Salmon Corn Cakes 183
Salmon Crunch Casserole 178
Salmon Loaf 178
Salmon Pot Pie 179
Scallops Supreme 173
Seafood Gruyere Supreme 174
Seafood Lasagna 173
Shrimp and Artichoke Divan 187
Shrimp and Scallop Pilaf 175
Shrimp Delight 186
Shrimp Fandango 185
Shrimp Pie 186
Treadway Inn Style Individual Lobster Pie 189
Tuna Burgers 180
Tuna Florentine 180

Poultry

Apple and Herb Stuffed Chicken Breast 205
Bar-B-Q Sauce for Chicken 211
Bicentennial Chicken 195
Buttermilk Pecan Chicken 210
Celery Stuffing for Turkey 212
Chestnut Dressing for Turkey . . . 213
Chicken, Almonds, 'n Peaches . . . 203
Chicken and Noodle Cacciatore . . 197
Chicken Asparagus Casserole 191
Chicken Asparagus Rolls 203
Chicken Breast Supreme 208
Chicken Casserole 199
Chicken Dijon 208
Chicken in a Stuffing Nest 204
Chicken Kabobs 195
Chicken Lasagna 198
Chicken Supreme 204
Chicken Tetrazzini 209
Chicken (Turkey) Scallop 205
Chicken with Cashews 208
Chinese Walnut Chicken 192
Coq-Au-Vin 207
Company Chicken (Microwave) . . 199
Page
Creamy Baked Chicken Breasts . . 204
Crispy Cajun Chicken 194
Curry in a Hurry 192
Easy Baked Chicken Breasts 197
Easy Chicken 202
Enchilada Delight 200
Fantastic Chicken Breast 195
Gingered Chicken 196
Green Noodles and Chicken 198
Hawaiian Chicken 206
Honey Lemon Chicken Breasts . . 196
Italian Boneless Chicken 207
Jamaican Chicken 206
Lemon-Honey Barbecued Chicken 211
Lo-Cal Chicken Casserole 200
Old-Fashioned Fried Chicken 194
Orange Glaze Chicken 196
Oven Fried Chicken 194
Pheasant in Apricot Sauce 210
Pineapple Dressing 213
Roast Duck (with Dried Fruit Stuffing) 210
Sausage Stuffing 212
Savoury Chicken Rolls 202
Scalloped Chicken and Spaghetti 209
Stuffed Chicken Breast A La Lou Ella 201
Three Cheese Chicken 202
Turkey and Broccoli Hot Dish . . . 193
Turkey Cornbread Dressing 211
Turkey Rice Casserole 193
Turkey with Ham Dressing 212
Washington Square Special 199
Wild Rice Dressing 213

Vegetables

Ambrosia Sweet Potato Bake 229
Apple-Carrot Bake 221
Asparagus Dish 216
Aunt Elsie's Oven Green Beans . . 218
Aunt Helen's Broccoli/Corn Casserole 220
Baked Artichoke and Cheese 215
Banh Xeo 234
Best Ever Cauliflower with Cheese Sauce 222
Black-Eyed Peas Texican 226
Boston Baked Beans 219
Brandied Sweet Potatoes and Apples 229
Broccoli Casserole 220
Cabbage Crunch 221
Carrots with Herbs 221
Cauliflower Casserole 222
Chinese Vegetables 218
Colcannon 227
Company Peas 226
Corn and Tomato Casserole 223
Corn Casserole 223
Cranberry Beets 219
Different Marinated Mushrooms . . 223
Dotty's Tex-Mex Beans 216

Page
Dried Lima Beans and Tomatoes Casserole 216
Eastern Sho' Tomato Pudding . . . 233
Eggplant Parmesan 224
Four Bean Casserole 217
Grandmother's Corn Pudding . . . 223
Green Beans with White Sauce . . . 217
Hash Brown Potatoes 229
Hawaiian Vegetables 234
Honeyed Beets 219
Italian Green Beans 217
Kugeli (Potato Loaf) 228
Lemon Potatoes 227
Marinated Broccoli 220
Mushrooms Divine 224
Okra Supreme 225
Onion Pie 225
Oven Fried Sesame Eggplant 224
Peas A L'Orange 226
Potato Dumplings 227
Royal Spinach and Artichoke 230
Skillet Squash 231
Sour Cream Succotash 235
Spicy Cauliflower 222
Squash Casserole 230
Squash Puff 231
Swiss Fried Potatoes 228
Tomatoes Rockefeller 232
Tomato Surprise 232
Vegetables Chili Con Frijoles 235
Zucchini and Rice Provencal 232
Zucchini Lasagna 231
Zucchini Zest 232

Pasta
Corned Beef Egg Noodle Casserole 238
Cottage Cheese Noodle Florentine 237
Erin's Lasagna 245
Fettuccine Primavera 240
Garden Fettuccine 239
Homemade Manicotti with Cheese 242
Lasagna 245
Laurie's Spaghetti Pie 241
Macaroni Cheese Souffle 238
Manicotti Parmigiana 243
Microwave Lasagna 243
Mom's Spaghetti and Steak 244
Pierogi 239
Spaghetti-Broccoli Casserole 240
Spaghetti in a Loaf 241
Spinach Lasagna 240
Stuffed Rigatoni 244
Susan's Poppy-Onion Pasta 242

Rice and Other Grains
Aruba Sunshine Rice 250
Barley Pilaf 249
Barley-Pine Nut Casserole 253
Cheese Grits Casserole 248
Chinese Fried Rice 249
Dee's Polenta 252

Page
Festive Rice Casserole 251
Fried Rice 249
Gnocci 253
Oven Croquettes 252
Rice and Chili Pepper Casserole . . . 247
Rice Italiano 251
Santa Fe Souffle 253
Sherried Rice 250
Spicy Rice 250
Wild Rice Casserole 248
Wild Rice Hot Dish 248

Eggs and Cheese
Apple Puffed Pancake 262
Armadillo Eggs 263
Cheese Flan 256
Chicken 'n Biscuit 'n Eggs 261
Chili Egg Puff 263
Chili Rellenos Casserole 255
Confetti Egg 'n Cottage Casserole 259
Deviled Eggs Hawaiian 260
Enchiladas 257
Italian Meat Pie 257
Never Fail Omelette 260
Savoury Souffle Roll 262
Scotch Eggs 263
Scrambled Egg Casserole 259
Single's Quiche 261
Surprise Quiche 258
Swiss-Gruyere Fondue 256
Zucchini Pie 258

Cakes
Angel Food Cake 266
Applesauce Cake 289
Applesauce Honey Cake 290
Aunt Hattie's Blackberry Cake . . . 283
Banana Split Cake 285
Black Walnut Cake 280
Black Walnut Pound Cake 275
Black Walnut Sheet Cake 271
Burnt Sugar Black Walnut Cake Frosting 268
Burnt Sugar Cake 268
Chocolate Angel Food Cake 267
Chocolate Zucchini Cake 277
Coconut Cake 267
Coconut Cream Cheese Pound Cake 274
Cream Cheese Pound Cake 276
Crustless Cheesecake 281
Date Nut-Orange Slice Cake 280
Dirt Cake 272
English Tea Cake 265
Ferncrest Pound Cake 274
Filbert Cake and Frosting 270
Five Flavor Pound Cake 275
Fresh Apple Cake 279
Fresh Apple Cake 289
Fresh Cherry Cake 285
Fruit Cocktail Cake 274
Fruit Torte 277
German Jam Cake 272

Page
Grandma Jackie's Devil's Food Cake and Frosting 278
Grandma's Irish Christmas Cake . . 288
Great-Grandmother's Carrot Cake 290
Hattie's Shortcake 270
Honey Chocolate Cake and Frosting 276
Hot Milk Sponge Cake 266
Irresistible Chocolate Cheesecake . . 281
Italian Petal Torte 287
Low Sugar Banana Cake 286
Maraschino Cherry Cake 283
Mincemeat Cake 285
Molasses Zucchini Cake 291
Oatmeal Cake 269
Old Hickory Nut Cake 271
Orange Cake 284
Orange Slice Candy Fruit Cake . . 287
Paradise Cake 273
Persian Nut Torte and Frosting . . 279
Pina Colada Cake 284
Plum Cake 282
Precious Prunie 282
Punch Bowl Cake 273
Quick and Sinful Double Chocolate Cake 278
Raspberry Cheesecake 281
Rhubarb Cake 288
Rum Cake 269
Strawberry Cake 286
Ture Cake 266
Turtle Cake 280
White Chocolate Cake 277
Zucchini Cake 291

Candy
Blanch's Texas Amber 297
Butterscotch Candy Lollipops 301
Carrot Fudge 298
Cherry Drops 302
Chocolate Truffles 302
Cinnamon Candy-Firestick 301
Cracker Jack 294
Cracker Jack Squares 298
Date Loaf 296
Dream Fudge 299
Firm Ball Caramels Candy 303
Foolproof Pastel Divinity 301
Hawaiian Fudge 298
Heavenly Fudge 299
Highland Toffee 293
Homemade Granola 295
Kentucky Bourbon Pralines 304
Marie's Chocolate Fudge 300
Martha Washington Creams 302
Microwave Caramel Popcorn 295
Microwave Fudge 300
Nut Goodie Bars 300
Old English Nut Toffee 294
Peanut Brittle Candy 305
Peanut Butter Balls 303
Peanut Butter Delights 303
Pecan Cream Candy 305

Page
Pralines 304
Pulled Butter Mints 297
Rena's Peanut Butter Fudge 299
Sauerkraut Candy 306
Strawberries 297
Sugarplums 296
Swedish Nuts 295
Unbaked Coconut Drops 296
Unusual Pecan Clusters 304
Yummy Nut Brittle 306

Cookies
"Almond Joy" Bars 308
Angel Cookies 323
Aunt Sadie's Skillet Cookies 320
Carrot Cookies 332
Cherry Nut Slices 320
Chocolate Date Ball Cookies 325
Chocolate-Peanut Butter-Oatmeal Bars 313
Christmas Butterscotch Cookies . . 332
Christmas Fruit Cookies 326
Christmas Sugar Cookies 318
Cinnamon-Almond Mounds 330
Coconutty Oat Bars 311
Cottage Cheese Cookies 315
Cream Coconut Cookies 327
Danish Coconut Cookies 322
Double Chocolate Crumb Bars . . . 308
Easy Almond Bars 311
Fold Overs 317
Frosted Cherry Cookies 321
Fruit Cookies 319
German Butter Cookies 329
Ginger Snaps 325
Holiday Ribbons 320
Ho-Made Heath Bar Cookies 311
Honey-Pecan Butterballs 322
Hungarian Cookies 317
Ice Box Molasses Cookies 319
Lemon Love Notes 310
Lemon or Lime Slice Cookies 316
Melting Moments 322
Meringue Cookies 331
Mint Snowballs 323
Mom's Peanut Butter Cookies . . . 324
Nutritious Chocolate Chip Bars . . 313
Orange Slice Cookies 330
Original Girl Scout Cookies 318
Oslo Kringle 331
Overnight Macaroons 307
Peanut Butter Bars 310
Pecan Snow Drop Cookies 327
Pecan Surprise Bars 314
Peppermint Brownies 309
Pineapple Brownies 309
Pineapple-Coconut Cookies 327
Raisin Nut Delights 332
Raisin Nut Drops 326
Raspberry Marzipan 315
Ricotta Cookies 331
Rugelach 316
Russinkakor 329
Saint-Emilion's Demise 321

Page
Soft Molasses Cakes 330
Sour Cream Raisin Bars 312
Spicy Apple Bars 312
Stuffed Date Drops 328
Sugar Cookies 324
Truly-Fruity Cookies 333
Walnut Chews 314
"White Christmas" Cookies 329
WW II Chocolate Honey Cookies 328

Pies
Apple Pecan Upside Down Pie . . . 349
Avocado Pie 354
Black Bottom Pie 338
Black Walnut Pie for Morrie 352
Captain's Table Key Lime Pie 336
Caramel Crunch Apple Pie 349
Carrot Pie (Sugar Free) 345
Champion Peanut Butter Pie 353
Cherry-Berry Pie 347
Cherry-Cream Cheese Pie 353
Chess Pie 338
Chocolate Meringue Pie 348
Coffee Cream Pie 339
Creamy Peach Pie 346
Custard Blender Pie 337
English Apple Pie 349
Fresh Pineapple Pie 347
Frosty Pumpkin Pie 342
Frozen Lemon Pie 340
Frozen White Chocolate Pie with Raspberries 340
Fudge Macaroon Pie 343
German Chocolate Pie 337
Grandma Killion's Pumpkin Pie . . 345
Grandmother Coe's Kentucky Blackberry Pie 347
Grasshopper Pie 355
Hawaiian Pie 337
Hawaiian Pie 355
Hays House Cranberry-Strawberry Pie 341
Hotel Hershey Derby Pie 346
Lemon Chiffon Pie 336
Lemon Chiffon Pie 351
Lemon Icebox Pie 353
Lemon Pie with Meringue Crust . . 350
Low Calorie Pecan Pie 344
Maple Cream Pie 338
Mother's Coconut Pie 342
No-Meat Pear Mincemint Pie Filling 350
Old Fashioned Caramel Pie Filling 335
Pecan Refrigerator Pie 350
Pina Colada Pie 341
Pineapple Cheese Pie 343
Pineapple Yogurt Pie 351
Praline Pie 342
Prize Winning Blueberry Chess Pie 344
Raisin Cream Spice Pie 348

Page
Scrumptious Velvet Chiffon Burnt Sugar Pie 352
Southern Peanut Pie 344
Strawberry Cream Pie 339
Virginia's Coconut Pie 336
White Christmas Pie 354

Other Desserts
Alberta's Peach Dee-Lite 358
Apple Dumplings with Rum Sauce 362
Apple Puff 363
Apricot Bread Pudding 379
Apricot Nectar Mousse 373
Banana Crunch 357
Barbara's Apple Bobble 360
Blackberry Noodles 359
Bread Pudding—Microwave 378
Bridal Pudding 369
Brown Pudding 377
Caramel Delight 367
Cherry Pudding Cake 364
Christmas Cherry Pudding 375
Claudia's Chocolate Mousse Crown 371
Cranberry Sherbet 369
Dutch Apple Cobbler 365
French Cherry Dessert 363
Heavenly Custard 372
Hot Chocolate-Fudge Pudding Cake 374
Lemon Cake Pudding 358
Lil's Chocolate Luv 370
Macaroon-Almond Baked Pears . . 361
Mom's Apple Dumpling 362
My Egg Nog Salad Dessert 358
New Orleans Bread Pudding with Whiskey Sauce 379
Old Tyme Rice Pudding 375
Orange Marmalade Pudding 376
Orange Pudding 372
Paska 370
Peach Cobbler 366
Pink Artic Freeze 368
Raspberry Dessert 359
Rhubarb Pudding 369
Ris' Alamonde 376
Rodgrod (Rote Grutze) 370
Snowflake Pudding with Crimson Raspberry Sauce 373
Spicy Apple Pudding 377
Spicy Coconut Pears 361
Steamed Pudding 378
Steamed Raspberry Pudding 374
Strawberry Delight 367
Stuffed Oranges 364
Superb Pears 361
Teddy's Chocolate Dessert 368
Three of a Kind Sherbet 366
Tropic Delight 371
Washington Cherry Squares 360
Wonderful Frozen Fruit 367
Yogurt—Vanilla 368
Yummy Yum Peach Pudding 375